'The performance of supply chain management determines the performance of the corporation itself. In retail and wholesale industries, the effectiveness of supply chain and logistics management holds the key to provide competitive advantage. This book addresses the core issues and helps the students and practitioners to take an integrated view of supply chain management areas of making decisions in a business. The book deals with global supply chain and performance management for developing a sustainable and competitive supply chain in a highly dynamic and unpredictable business environment, and discusses the subject taking many practical examples and cases to provide the key insights. I am happy to see that Dr Rajat K Baisya, who has helped us in setting up our Indian operation, has written a book on this important subject which is expected to be extremely useful for the students, researchers and professionals. I am happy to recommend this book'.

Charles Wilson, *Former Chief Executive Officer, Booker – Tesco PLC, UK*

'It is refreshing to see an interesting book on supply chain and logistics management by Professor Baisya, who has established himself as a management educator, corporate consultant and wonderful trainer, besides a writer of substance. In this book, Professor Baisya has innovatively combined his field research and corporate experience in giving a unique perspective to SCM and logistics. Pedagogically rich, the book includes many short real-life cases, sections on benchmarking supply chain, sustainable SCM and decision criteria to resolve key issues in managing complexity in distribution management. The book also highlights performance management issues in the supply chain. Looking at the emerging global scenario, there is a chapter on "Global Logistics Value Chain Management", which is highly contemporary and relevant to the theme of the book. I am sure the book will provide a good companion to those who are in search of innovative and real-life practices, to improve the bottom line'.

Dr S. G. Deshmukh, *Former Director, Atal Bihari Vajpayee Indian Institute of Information Technology and Management, Gwalior, India;*
Professor of SCM, Department of Mechanical Engineering,
IIT Delhi, Delhi, India

'Supply chain management is one of the most important functions that offers the opportunities for cost competitiveness in businesses to be efficient and effective in delivering organizational performance. But that requires engaging every member in the chain to collaborate to deliver the end objective and constantly improving upon it using technology to be globally competitive. Professor Rajat K Baisya with his excellent academic as well as very rich industrial background as a practitioner has beautifully combined SCM and logistics and discussed in this new book with cases and illustrations to drive the latest concepts on the subject. The book will be a rich resource for the practitioners, researchers and students of SCM'.

Bojan Rosi, *Professor of Supply Chain Management, Faculty of Logistics, University of Maribor, Maribor, Slovenia*

Supply Chain and Logistics Management

This textbook discusses supply chain management and provides a comprehensive overview of all the key activities and issues of supply chain and logistics functions as an integrated discipline.

Taking a comprehensive approach, it reviews end-to-end supply chain management from procurement to production to warehousing, distribution and customer service. It explores how each interface can be managed with the ultimate objective of providing superior customer experience to ensure satisfaction at the least cost while delivering incremental value in a competitive environment.

This volume:

- Guides on designing effective development and management of the supply chain network, which is an invaluable source of sustainable, competitive advantage in today's turbulent global marketplace;
- Examines the complexities and challenges of catering to the flexible and fluctuating customer demand, warehousing, channel distribution and transportation, global logistics value chain management, and performance management;
- Discusses short practical cases to explain the decision-making process with respect to manufacturing decisions and inventory for efficient working capital management, both of which are critical for supply chain performance;
- Explores performance management matrix, maturity models and so on.

This book will be useful to students, researchers and faculty from the fields of business management, supply chain and logistics management, and mechanical and civil engineering. It will also be an invaluable companion to consultants and business executives working in the field of supply chain and logistics.

Rajat K Baisya, Professor and Head (Retired), Department of Management Studies, Indian Institute of Technology Delhi, is an internationally acclaimed management consultant and academician. Prior to this, he was President and CEO of Emami Group of Companies and Vice President-Business Development of Reckitt Benckiser. He served as Director on the board of Public Sector Undertakings and MNCs. He brings in unique experience from academics, industry and entrepreneurs. Professor Baisya is Chairman and Managing Director of Strategic Consulting Group Pvt Ltd, President of Project & Technology Management Foundation, a Fellow of the World Academy of Productivity Sciences (Canada) and an Academic Fellow of the International Council of Management Consulting Institutes (ICMCI).

Supply Chain and Logistics Management
An Integrated Approach

Rajat K Baisya

LONDON AND NEW YORK

First published 2024
by Routledge
4 Park Square, Milton Park, Abingdon, Oxon OX14 4RN

and by Routledge
605 Third Avenue, New York, NY 10158

Routledge is an imprint of the Taylor & Francis Group, an informa business

© 2024 Rajat K Baisya

The right of Rajat K Baisya to be identified as author of this work has been asserted in accordance with sections 77 and 78 of the Copyright, Designs and Patents Act 1988.

All rights reserved. No part of this book may be reprinted or reproduced or utilised in any form or by any electronic, mechanical, or other means, now known or hereafter invented, including photocopying and recording, or in any information storage or retrieval system, without permission in writing from the publishers

Trademark notice: Product or corporate names may be trademarks or registered trademarks, and are used only for identification and explanation without intent to infringe.

British Library Cataloguing-in-Publication Data
A catalogue record for this book is available from the British Library

Library of Congress Cataloging-in-Publication Data
Names: Baisya, Rajat K., author.
Title: Supply chain and logistics management : an integrated approach / Rajat K. Baisya.
Description: Abingdon, Oxon ; New York, NY : Routledge, 2024. | Includes bibliographical references and index. | Summary: — Provided by publisher.
Identifiers: LCCN 2023051224 (print) | LCCN 2023051225 (ebook) |
  ISBN 9781032603599 (hardback) | ISBN 9781032744018 (paperback) |
  ISBN 9781003469063 (ebook)
Subjects: LCSH: Business logistics–Management.
Classification: LCC HD38.5 .B346 2024 (print) | LCC HD38.5 (ebook) |
  DDC658.7—dc23/eng/20240125
LC record available at https://lccn.loc.gov/2023051224
LC ebook record available at https://lccn.loc.gov/2023051225

ISBN: 978-1-032-60359-9 (hbk)
ISBN: 978-1-032-74401-8 (pbk)
ISBN: 978-1-003-46906-3 (ebk)

DOI: 10.4324/9781003469063

Typeset in Times New Roman
by Apex CoVantage, LLC

This book is dedicated to the warm and sacred memory of my parents, Rabindra Kumar Baishya and Vidyut Prava Baishya, who have been a constant source of inspiration all through my life.

Contents

Lists of Figures	*xxv*
List of Tables	*xxvi*
Foreword	*xxvii*
Preface	*xxix*
Acknowledgements	*xxxi*
List of Abbreviations	*xxxii*
About the Author	*xxxv*

1	Understanding the Supply Chain: The Core Concepts	1
2	Evolution of Integrated Supply Chain and Logistics Management	8
3	Demand Estimation in a Supply Chain	44
4	Warehousing and Distribution Management: Complexity and Challenges	73
5	Managing Inventory for Satisfying Customer Demand	113
6	Transportation	152
7	Total Logistics Cost Management for Competitive Advantage	202
8	Sustainable Transport Logistics and Supply Chain	221
9	Global Logistics Value Chain Management	233
10	Sourcing Decision in Global Supply Chain Management	262
11	Supply Chain Performance Management	279
12	Benchmarking Supply Chain Performance	302

Index	*316*

Detail Contents

Lists of Figures	*xxv*
List of Tables	*xxvi*
Foreword	*xxvii*
Preface	*xxix*
Acknowledgements	*xxxi*
List of Abbreviations	*xxxii*
About the Author	*xxxv*

1 Understanding the Supply Chain: The Core Concepts   1

Introduction 1
SCM and Business Performance 3
Key Challenges 5
Chapter Summary 6

2 Evolution of Integrated Supply Chain and Logistics Management   8

Introduction 8
Scope of SCM 8
    Evolution of SCM: The Historical Perspective 10
    Key Objectives and Challenges of Supply Chain Integration 12
    Objectives and Challenges of SCM 13
    Role of SCM 14
    Why Is SCM So Important? 15
    Logistics: A Neglected Area – Now an Integral Part of SCM 17
    Why Is Logistics Important? 17
    Core Concept, Definition and Scope of Logistics 18
    Basic Elements of Logistics 19
    Logistics as a Discipline 19
    Types of Logistics 19
    Logistics Activities and Goals 20
    Evolution of Logistics – The Historical Perspective 21
    Procurement and Outsourcing Key Focus for Cost Competitiveness in Past Decade 23
    Incremental Value Delivery through Effective Logistics Management 23

xii *Detail Contents*

Strategic Triangle of 3Cs (Kenichi Ohmae, 1982) 24
  Theoretical Foundations of International Logistics 24
  Importance of Logistics in Economy 25
  World Competitiveness 26
Growing Indian Logistics Industry to Support Country's Economic Growth 27
  Air Cargo Sector Witnessed Significant Growth 27
  Hurdles Still to Overcome 27
  Government Initiatives 28
  Some Mega Trends Paving the Way for Logistics Sector Growth 28
  E-Commerce Logistics: Driving the Change 29
  Inland Waterways 29
  Ocean Shipping 29
  India Road Trasport: Adapting Digitisation 30
  The Future 30
  Cochin Shipyard Chalks Out Biggest Expansion with INR 17.99 Billion
    Dry Dock 30
  Technology Applications in Indian Logistics Industry 31
  Logistics Infrastructure Helping Economic Growth 32
  Physical Infrastructure and SCM Performance 32
  Cold Chain Facilities 33
  Field Heat Removal Facilities 33
  Warehousing Facilities 34
  Innovations in Supply Chain 36
  Dell's Direct Business Model of Virtual Integration 40
Chapter Summary 41

3 Demand Estimation in a Supply Chain   44

Introduction 44
Unrealistic Demand Can Make Supply Chain Management Inefficient 45
Forecasting in Supply Chain 46
Characteristics of the Forecasts 47
Factors Influencing Forecast 48
Why Forecast 49
Market Potential 49
Types of Forecasts 49
Levels of Forecasting 51
Seasonal Variations 51
Demand Forecasting 52
  Consumer User Survey Method 53
  Panel of Expert Opinion 53
  Sales Force Composite 54
  Delphi Method 54
  Bayesian Decision Theory 54
  Quantitative Forecasting Techniques 55

Detail Contents   xiii

Naive Forecasting 56
MAPE Method 57
  Moving Average Method 57
  Exponential Smoothing 58
  Linear Regression 59
How P&G Forecasted Its Detergent Sales in Italy 60
  Multiple Regression 61
  Trend and Seasonality Corrected Holt – Winter Exponential Smoothing 61
When to Use Quantitative Forecasting Methods 63
Changing Business Environment 63
Forecasting in Practice 63
What Industry Practises 64
Demand Management 64
Efficient Demand Management 65
Estimating the Total Market Demand 66
  Define the Market 66
  Divide the Industry Demand into Its Principal or Main Components 66
  Forecast the Key Drivers of Demand in Each Segment and Project How
    They Are Likely to Change 67
  Conduct Sensitivity Analyses to Understand the Most Critical
    Assumptions and to Gauge Risks to Base Line Forecast 67
Case Study 67
Case Study: Apollo Pharmacy 67
  Forecasting Methods 68
  Results 69
  For Stamlo Beta (Non-seasonal Demand) 69
  Sales Data 69
Appendix 3.1 70
  Sales Data of Apollo Pharmacy 70
Chapter Summary 71

4   Warehousing and Distribution Management: Complexity and Challenges   73

Introduction 73
Warehousing Purpose and Scope 74
Primary Functions of Warehouse 74
Efficient Warehouse Management 74
Types of Warehouses 75
Warehouse Layout Design Criteria 76
Warehousing Cost 76
Warehouse Activities 76
Factors Influencing Effectiveness of Warehouse 79
WMS as an Enabler 81
Why and When It Is Necessary 82
Advantages of Implementing WMS 82

xiv *Detail Contents*

Implementation and Setting Up WMS 83
When WMS Can Be Advantageous 83
Developing a Responsive WMS 84
New Trends in WMS 85
Productivity Improvement Tools of WMS 85
  Barcode 85
Distribution Management 86
Distribution Task 86
Definition and Scope 87
Distribution Channels 87
Distribution Methods 87
Distribution Channel Strategy 89
Customer Service Level 89
Distribution Objectives 89
Distribution Organisation 90
Activities in Distribution 90
Distribution Policy 90
Key Performance Indicator 91
Critical Success Factors 91
Sales Target 91
Geographical Area to Be Covered 91
Typical Channel Partners 92
  C&F Agents and Carrying and Selling (C&S) Agents 92
Distributors, Dealers, Stockists, Value-added Re-sellers 92
Super-stockists 92
Agents and Brokers 92
Franchisees 93
Electronic Channels 93
Wholesalers 93
Retailers 93
Distribution Cost 94
Efficiency of Distribution 94
Factors Impacting Distribution Network Design 94
Distribution Management – Key Challenges 95
Complexity in Logistics Management in India – A Case of FMCG Industry 97
India as a Country Adds to Complexity 98
Entry of Organised Retailers and E-Retailers 98
Distribution Challenge for the Base of the Pyramid Population 99
  Drivers of Distribution Complexity 100
Current Scenario – A Mixed System 101
Developing Efficient Sales and Distribution Structure 103
Measuring Sales Force and Distribution Effectiveness 103

Detail Contents xv

Impact of the Corona Pandemic on the Operations and Supply Chain of the
  Agriculture and Food Processing Sectors With Reference to MSME in India
  and the Expected Recovery Prospects 104
  Acute Shortage of Trained Temporary Workforce and Impact of Other
    Factors on Cost of Goods 105
  Impact on the Food and Beverage Industry 106
  Post-Lockdown Scenario 106
  Industry Learnt New Lessons from the Pandemic 107
  New Food Safety Standards Post-Pandemic and Compliance With
    New Standards 107
  Agriculture Sector Delivered Higher GVA 108
  Way to Recovery Needs New Strategic Direction26 110
Chapter Summary 110

5   Managing Inventory for Satisfying Customer Demand   113

Introduction 113
Inventory Management 114
Inventory Management Goal 115
Why Do We Need Inventory? 116
Inventory Impacts Business Performance 117
Types of Inventories 117
Alternative Approach for Classification of Inventories 118
Components of Inventory Decisions 120
  Cycle Inventory 120
  Safety Inventory 121
  Seasonal Inventory 121
  Level of Product Availability 121
Inventory Cost Management 122
Inventory Control 122
Effective Inventory Management 123
Order Fill Rate and Pack Fill Rate 123
Inventory Transaction 124
Stock-keeping Unit 124
Bullwhip Effect 125
Causes That Lead to the Bullwhip Effect 127
  The Effect on Supply Chain Performance 127
Reducing Impact of Bullwhip Effect 128
Business Response to Stock-out 128
Replenishment of Inventory 129
Inventory Position 130
Average Inventory 130
Order Cycle Time 131
  Interval between Orders 131
Implications of Economic Ordering Quantity 131

xvi *Detail Contents*

Materials Requirements Planning (MRP) 132
What MRP Indicates 133
Components of MRP II 133
 Master Production Schedule 133
 Bill of Materials 133
 Inventory Status File 133
Output of MRP 133
MIN–MAX Replenishment System 134
How Much Should Be Ordered? 135
Total Cost of Inventory 135
Out-of-Stock Costs 135
Inventory-carrying Cost 135
Total Cost Approach 136
Structure of Inventory-carrying Cost 136
Demand Estimation 137
 Reorder Point (ROP) 137
 Exercise 1: When Demand and Lead Time Are Constant or Fixed 137
Case Study: Vendor-managed Inventory at Tata Steel 137
 ABC Classification 139
Managing Uncertainty in Supply Chain 141
Measuring Product Availability 142
Estimating Safety Stock 142
 Example 5.1: Estimating Safety Stock from Replenishment Policy 142
 Example 2: Estimating Safety Stock from Desired Cycle Service
  Level (CSL) 143
Reorder Point (ROP) 144
 Example 1: When the Demand Is Variable but Lead Time Constant 144
 Service Level 145
 Example 2 146
 Solution 146
 Example 3 146
 Solution 146
 Example 4 147
 Solution 147
Single-period Model 147
Continuous Stocking Levels 148
 Example 5 148
Impact of Uncertainties 149
Walmart Outperforms Its Competitors 149
Chapter Summary 149

6 Transportation 152

Section I: Transportation in Integrated Supply Chain 152
Introduction 152

Detail Contents xvii

Role of Transportation 153
Functions of Transport 154
Mode of Transportation and Criteria of Decision 155
  Road Transport 155
  Water Transport 156
  Ocean Transport 156
  Air Transport 157
Package Carriers 158
Pipeline 158
Intermodal 158
Major Mode of Transportation 159
Transportation Infrastructure 159
Key Considerations on Decision on Type of Transport to Be Used 159
Factors Impacting Road Transport Cost 160
Mode of Transportation – India 160
  Domestic Cargo 160
International Transportation 160
Hazards in Transportation 161
Hazards and Risks 161
What Is Risk? 161
State of Ocean Transport 162
Highly Fluctuating Business 162
Large Shipping Lines and Global Alliance 163
  P3 Network-Global Politics 164
  The G6 Alliance 164
  The CKYH Alliance 165
New Global Alliances in Ocean Transport 165
  New Ocean Alliance 165
Shipping Route and Competition 165
The Future of the Canals 166
Suez and Panama Canals 166
Other Important Ship Canals 166
Current Issues 167
  Shake Out Ahead 167
  The Next Few Years 167
Global Trends in Transportation and Logistics 167
  Bringing Production Location Closer to the End Customers 168
Investments in Larger Vessels Created Overcapacity in Container Shipping 168
Sustainability and Compliance Becoming Important Issues in the Global
  Transport Industry 168
Major Acquisitions in the Global Logistics Industry 169
How Acquisition Helps Global Logistics Company 169
Green Transport Solutions Preferred Over Air Freight 169
Major Shift to Surface Transport 170

xviii   *Detail Contents*

Impact of Growing E-commerce on the Supply Chain 170
Increased Internet Shopping Changes the Supply Chain 171
Increased Demand on Containerisation 171
Reasons for Containerisation 171
Global Shift in Trade Pattern 171
Custom Bonded Warehouse 172
Customs-bonded Warehousing Solutions to Shorten Lead Times 172
Buyer's Consolidation Service and E-solutions to Keep Track of the Goods 172
Future of Green Carrier and the Logistics and Transport Market in China 172
The Global Shipping Industry Will Face New Sulphur Regulations 172
Ocean Freight 173
Air Freight 174
Hazards of Air Freight Transport 174
Road Transport 174
Rail Transport 174
Case Study: Maersk Line 175
Maersk's Business Strategy 175
Reliability 175
Simplicity 176
Environment Sustainable Strategy 176
Financial Performance 177
Making Loss in a Decade 178
Performance in 2017 178
Market Share Price Movement 179
Financial results for the last 5 years 179
Maersk's Commitment to Environment and Sustainability 181
Maersk Is Sponsoring Corals' Plantation and Preservation 183
Decarbonising Logistics 183
Customer Engagement 183
Partnership 184
Visibility 184
Cost Management 184
India's 'One Country, One Price' Fulfilment Solution Launched 184
One Country, One Price and One Billing India Initiative 184
Business Development Strategy 185
Denmark's Maersk Changes Ownership Structure to Boost Finances 186
Maersk Acquires Hamburg Süd 186
Crippling Overcapacity 187
Section II: Packaging Issues in Transportation 188
Introduction 188
Importance of Packaging in Transportation 189
International Packaging Issues 189
Functions of Packaging 190
Packaging Protects Goods 190

Detail Contents xix

Packaging Provides Information about the Product 190
Facilitating Storage and Warehousing 191
Packaging Is Indicative of Quality of the Product Packed 191
Ensure the Right Transport Packaging Solution 191
Packaging and Safety Regulations for Hazardous Goods 191
Packaging Regulations 193
Case Study: Container Corporation of India Ltd (CONCOR) 193
Main Functions of CONCOR 194
Case Discussion Questions 199
Chapter Summary 199

7 Total Logistics Cost Management for Competitive Advantage 202

Introduction 202
Organisations Are Huge Cost Centres 202
The Law of Lowest Total Cost 203
Logistics Cost – Brief History 203
Elements of Logistics Cost 203
Financial Accounting 204
Management Accounting 204
Logistics Cost Management Models 205
Logistics Is Omnipresent 205
Logistics Improves Business Performance 205
Difficulty in Estimating Logistics Cost 206
Analysis of Logistics Cost 206
Activity-Based Costing 207
When ABC Method IS More Useful 207
Total Logistics Cost 207
Total Cost Approach in Logistics 208
Holistic View of Total Logistic Cost 209
Inventory Cost 209
Warehousing Cost 209
Production and Supply Cost 210
Channel Distribution Costs 210
Total Distribution Cost 210
Supply Chain and Logistics Cost 211
Cost Associated with Assets and Return on Investment 211
Information Processing Cost 211
Communication and Data Processing Costs 212
Administrative Costs 212
Transportation Costs 212
Material-handling Costs 212
Packaging Costs 213
Customer Service Costs 213
Examples of Customer Service 214

xx   *Detail Contents*

Levels of Customer Service 214
Elements of Customer Service 215
Cost Audit 215
Benchmarking Logistics Cost and Performance 215
Case Study 216
Outsourcing Logistics Services 216
Reason Why Logistics Cost Management Programme Is Not Always
 Effective 216
Key Task to Improve Logistics Cost 217
Case Study 218
Maruti Suzuki – How They Reduced Their Logistics Cost 218
Chapter Summary 219

8   Sustainable Transport Logistics and Supply Chain 221

Introduction 221
Defining Sustainability 222
Transportation Impacts on Sustainability 222
Simple Sustainability Indicators 223
Sustainable Transport in Global Trade 223
Economic Benefits of Sustainable Transportation 223
Key Issues in Sustainable Transportation 224
Sustainability Helps Business 224
Case Study: Volvo's Strategy for Sustainability 225
Corporate Overview 225
Sustainability as a Central Strategic Issue 227
Key Drivers of Sustainability Strategies 228
Legislative Pressures 228
Life-cycle Perspective 229
Genuine Caring 229
New Business 229
Volvo's Curitiba Story 230
Chapter Summary 231

9   Global Logistics Value Chain Management 233

Introduction 233
International Logistics 234
Key Drivers for Evolution of International Logistics 234
First: Global Sourcing of Components 234
Second: New Product Development – Global Expertise 234
Third: Mining Companies Driving the Process 234
Fourth: High Level of Customer Satisfaction 235
Fifth: High Degree of Process Orientation 235
Sixth: Driven by Cost Quality Considerations 235
Seventh: Channel Linked to Expertise in the Areas 235

Detail Contents xxi

Methods and Tools Facilitating International Logistics 235
Storage Facility 236
Logistics Centres (Nodal Points) 236
Decentralised Logistics System 237
Outsourcing Logistics Services 237
Logistics and Environment 237
Firm's Value Chain 237
Transforming the Value Chain 238
Linkages within Value Chain 239
International Business 239
Features of International Trade 240
International Logistics Challenges 241
Barriers to Global Logistics 242
Impact of Globalisation on International Logistics 242
Role of Global Logistics 243
Supply Chain and the Internet 243
Global Logistics Capabilities 243
Global Operating Levels of Logistics Companies 243
Arm's Length 243
Internal Export 243
Internal Operations 244
Insider Business Practices 244
Denationalised Operations 244
Global Operations Level 244
Stages of Regional Integration 245
Free Trade Agreement 245
Customs Union 245
Common Market 245
Economic Union 245
Complexity of Logistics Management 246
Entry of Global Retailers in Indian Market 246
Logistics – A Source of Competitive Advantage 247
Value Chain in Sales 247
Integrated Supply Chain and Logistics Value Chain 248
Management Challenges for Integrated Supply Chain 248
Optimising the End-to-end Value Chain through an Integrated Solution 248
Multifaceted Analytical Functions 249
Integrated Logistics System 249
Integration of Logistics with the Organisation 249
Stages of Integration 250
Benefits of Integration 250
Logistics and Security 251
Logistics Security Issue 251
Supply Chain Security Initiatives in USA 251
Technology to Tackle Security 252

xxii   *Detail Contents*

Logistics Industry in India 252
Case Study: Anand Milk Producers Union Limited (AMUL) 254
Logistics Challenge of AMUL 255
  Procurement Logistics 255
  Logistics/Coordination 255
Coordination between Participating Entities 255
  Main Function of VDCS 257
  State Cooperative Milk Federation – Main Function 257
  Upstream Procurement 257
  Cold Storage Network 257
  Distribution Downstream 258
  Complexity of Distribution Operation 258
  Technology to the Rescue 258
  Automatic Milk Collection System 258
  Transformation 258
Chapter Summary 259

10   Sourcing Decision in Global Supply Chain Management　　　　　　262

Introduction 262
Sourcing Challenges and Strategies 263
Future Factories 263
Four Levels of Global Sourcing 264
Global Sourcing Challenge and Sustainability of Supply Chain 264
Models and Frameworks for Sourcing 265
Characteristics for Successful Global Sourcing 266
Global Sourcing and Logistics 266
  Methodologies for Measuring Savings 266
Global Sourcing Trends 266
Global Sourcing and Business Performance 268
Degree of Outsourcing and Performance 270
Key Issues in Global Sourcing 271
Technological Performance and Sourcing Decisions 271
Factors Influencing Outsourcing 271
Case Study A: Industry Sector: Retail 273
  Global Sourcing Strategy: (Perspective of Global Sourcing Director) 273
  Positive Factors 273
  Negative Factors 273
  Main Mode of Transport 273
  Key Priorities of Global Sourcing Strategy 273
  Supply Chain Risk Management Tools and Techniques 273
  Major Risk Identified in Global Sourcing Decisions 274
  Environment and Infrastructure Considerations 274
Case Study B: Industry Sector: FMCG Food and Drink 274
  Global Sourcing Strategy: (Perspective of Global Head of
    Procurement) 274

Detail Contents xxiii

Positive Factors of Global Sourcing Strategy 274
Negative Factors of Global Sourcing Strategy 274
Main Mode of Transport 274
Key Priorities of Global Sourcing Strategy 274
Supply Chain Risk Management Tools and Techniques 275
Major Risk Identified in Global Sourcing Decisions 275
Environment and Infrastructure Considerations 275
Chapter Summary 275

11 Supply Chain Performance Management 279

Introduction 279
11.1 Supply Chain Management Performance Criteria 280
11.2 The Key Elements of Supply Chain Management 281
11.3 Supply Chain Performance Management as a Basis for Industry 4.0 281
11.4 Digitalisation of Supply Chain Changing Today's Performance Management 282
11.5 Current State of Supply Chain Performance Management 282
11.6 Implementing Robust Performance Management System 283
Key Differentiators in Implementation 284
    1. Supply Chain Strategy Sets the Direction and Defines the Steering Focus 284
    2. Supply Chain Management Processes Must Be Linked with Transparency of Inventories and Supply Chain Cost 284
Trends in Management Reporting on Supply Chain Performance 286
11.7 Performance Measurements and Metrics in SCM 286
Order Entry Method 287
Order Lead Time 287
The Customer Order Path 287
Evaluation of Supply Link 287
Evaluation of Suppliers 287
Performance Measures and Metrics at Production Level 288
Evaluation of Delivery Link 289
Measures for Delivery Performance Evaluation 289
Number of Faultless Notes Invoiced 289
Flexibility of Delivery Systems to Meet Particular Customer Needs 289
Measuring Customer Service and Satisfaction 289
Customer Query Time 290
Post-transaction Measures of Customer Service 290
Starting Performance Management Programme in the Organisation 290
Planning Performance Evaluation Metrics 292
Sourcing Performance Evaluation Metrics 293
Production Performance Evaluation Metrics 293
Delivery Performance Evaluation Metrics 294
A Framework for Performance Measurement in a Supply Chain 295
Maturity Models to Measure Supply Chain Performance 296

xxiv   *Detail Contents*

Overview of SCM Maturity Models 297
SCM Process Maturity Model 297
Chapter Summary 299

12   Benchmarking Supply Chain Performance   302

Introduction 302
What Is Benchmarking? 302
Benchmarking Supply Chain Performance 303
How to Start 304
Scope of Supply Chain Benchmarking 304
Supply Chain Performance Metrics for Benchmarking 305
Supply Chain Benchmarks of Standard Processes 305
Importance of Identifying Right Companies to Be Benchmarked 306
Improving Performance 306
Some Common Misconception in Benchmarking 307
Case Study 307
Supply Chain Performance Measurement of an Automotive
Industry: Applicability of SCOR Model 307
Introduction 307
The Supply Chain Operations Reference (SCOR) Model 308
Basic Approach to Determine Performance 308
Brief Description of the Company 309
Supply and Production Control 309
Administration of the Sales 309
Establishing Performance Metrics 310
Best Practices Proposed by the SCOR Model 312
Conclusion 312
Chapter Summary 313

Index   *316*

Figures

1.1	Supply Chain Linkages and Stages	4
2.1	Scope of Supply Chain Management	9
2.2	Complexity in Supply Chain in Li & Fung Business Model	15
2.3	Corporation and Competition Differentiate Only on Cost	24
2.4	Dependence of World Competitiveness on Logistics	26
2.5	Cost Build-up and Trade Margins for Agro Commodities in India	33
3.1	Decision Tree for Three Expected Events	56
3.2	Fitment of Trend Regression to Seasonality-adjusted Sales Data	60
4.1	Warehouse Layout Design and Activities Performed	77
4.2	Cube Space Utilisation and Accessibility	79
4.3	Distribution Challenges of BOP Market	99
4.4	Degree of Sophistication in Distribution	102
4.5	Logistics Complexity of FMCG Category	102
5.1	Wholesaler/Distributors' Orders to the Manufacturers	126
5.2	Consumer Offtake at Retail Sales Point	126
5.3	Manufacturers' Order to the Suppliers/Vendors	126
5.4	Reorder Point for Inventory	129
5.5	Economic Ordering Quantity	131
5.6	Reorder Point with Variable Demand	144
5.7	Reorder Point with Safety Stock	144
5.8	Service Level Determines the Safety Stock	145
6.1	Business Strategy Initiatives of Maersk Line	177
6.2	Share Price Movement of Maersk Lines	179
6.3	Sustainability Initiatives of Maersk Shipping Lines	181
6.4	Sustainability Initiatives by Maersk	182
6.5	Decarbonisation Plan of Maersk Shipping Lines	183
7.1	Logistics Is Omnipresent and Encompasses All Functions in Business	205
7.2	How Logistics Cost Impacts ROI	206
9.1	Firm's Value Chain	238
9.2	Global Logistics Strategy Drivers	240
9.3	India against Global Indicators of Logistics Infrastructure	254
9.4	AMUL Value Chain	255
9.5	Supply Chain Network of AMUL	256
9.6	Decentralised Organisation Structure of AMUL at Different Levels	256

Tables

3.1	Determining a Seasonal Index from Historical Sales Data	51
3.2	Different Methods for Forecasting	52
3.3	Expected Profit in Three Scenarios	55
3.4	Impact of Probability Factors on Expected Profit	55
3.5	Naïve Forecast from the Earlier Period Actual Sales	56
3.6	Applicability of the Methods	62
3.7	Comparison of Measurement Errors Obtained for Okacet and Stamlo Beta Using Time-Series Forecast Models	68
4.1	Warehouse Performance Metrics	85
4.2	Sectoral GVA for Quarter 1 (April–June) of FY 2019–20 and 2020–21 at 2011–12 Prices	109
5.1	Order Point System versus MRP System	134
5.2	Principle of Min–Max Replenishment System	134
5.3	Class of Inventory at Tata Steel	140
5.4	Refractories Purchase Records for 2009–2010	140
5.5	Comparison of Walmart and Its Competitors	149
6.1	Top Ten Container Carriers	162
6.2	Top Ten North American Ports	163
6.3	Top Ten Container Ports	163
6.4	Financial Performance of Maersk Lines	179
6.5	Classification of Dangerous Goods	192
6.6	Packing Groups for Hazardous Items	193
7.1	Logistics Cost Break-up	208
8.1	Transportation Impacts on Sustainability	222
9.1	Comparison on Key Parameters: India versus Global	253
9.2	Logistics Performance Index of India, China and Germany on Select Parameters	254
10.1	Recent Waves in Global Sourcing	268
10.2	Advantages and Disadvantages of Global Sourcing	269
10.3	Perspectives on Global Outsourcing	272
11.1	Framework of Supply Chain Performance Matrix	295
11.2	Maturity Levels of the Supply Chain Maturity Model	298
12.1	The Best Practices Proposed by SCOR Model	313
12.2	The Scorecard Containing Performance Metrics Measured for the Company	314

Foreword

Supply chain management (SCM) has evolved over the years from an initial concept of moving goods and services from a point of origin to a point of consumption to a highly interlinked and interdependent discipline to be managed for better performance. What was originally started in the early 1980s in the USA when global sourcing was the key imperative to respond to a highly competitive business environment has now evolved as a fully developed integrated discipline supported by technology.

Logistics is a very important function in business and offers considerable scope for improvement. One of the important areas in SCM is logistics issues within the supply chain itself, and, therefore, it is better to manage logistics as an integrated function. In the current context, SCM covers everything from procurement to delivering the product to customers. Managing supply chain for performance, thus, also needs effective and efficient management of logistics functions.

This book has been designed to cover important issues of both SCM and logistics management to enable the readers and students of SCM and logistics management to take an integrated view. Starting with the issue of why SCM is so important for businesses for their survival and global SCM issues, the book brings in many short real-life cases and helps in cost management in supply chain for competitive advantage. It has sections on benchmarking supply chain, sustainable SCM, decision criteria for manufacturing in-house versus out-house, key issues and managing complexity in distribution management. The book also deals with performance management issues in supply chain, as well as transportation and global logistics value chain management.

The book helps you to design an effective development and management of a supply chain network, which is an invaluable source of sustainable advantage in today's turbulent global marketplace, where demand is difficult to predict and supply chains need to be more flexible and customer-focused.

The book will be a valuable addition to the existing literature available for students and practitioners in SCM and operations. Some examples have been taken and discussed from global business operations and will be useful for students abroad. The book covers a wide range of subjects and topics with real-life cases to help students and practising managers get key insights into SCM as we understand it now.

I know Professor Rajat K Baisya very well. He has served as a visiting professor at our institute, teaching international students both supply chain and logistics management. He has served for three decades working with leading industries and also as an academician and a researcher with global exposure and association. He is also a corporate trainer and consultant of global repute. He, thus, brings with him a unique mix of industry experience to provide practitioners' perspectives as well as academic rigour and discipline.

xxviii *Foreword*

I am happy to recommend this book to students and faculty of supply chain and logistics management as well as of production and operations management. The book will also serve as a good reference book for practitioners in consulting and industry.

– **Professor Bojan Rosi**
Former Dean, Faculty of Logistics,
University of Maribor
Slovenia

Preface

Supply chain management (SCM) has evolved as a full-grown discipline and a subject of specialisation in education and research as well as an important function in business to be managed during the past two decades. Business consultants are talking about the importance of effective and efficient management of supply chain function as an essential prerequisite for delivering company's bottom-line performance objective. To be cost-effective and competitive in the marketplace, managing the procurement, production and distribution function as a closely coordinated function is the key imperative. Businesses now compete through better SCM practices. Supply chain, therefore, has to be market-driven and is synonymous with value chain.

Around the late 1980s and early 1990s, the process of globalisation was witnessed in businesses all over the world and in response to that environment, most of the global players opted to source the products and services from places where these were the cheapest and best. Forces of globalisation in subsequent years forced companies to improve SCM functions, and we have seen the era of global manufacturing and sourcing.

In today's highly competitive global marketplace, organisations are looking for avenues to create higher value for their customers and in that context, there is an increasing recognition that through efficient logistics and effective SCM, both cost reduction and enhancement of service delivery can be achieved. Through supply chain, firms thus aim to achieve both cost-effectiveness and improved customer satisfaction. Technology plays a vital role in managing supply chain and making it efficient and effective in all its operations, and, as such, decisions in supply chain are now mostly based on information.

The book has been designed to cover both SCM and logistics functions to enable students and practitioners to take an integrated view for logical decision-making. Logistics companies around the world are offering value-added extended service and becoming strategic partners for manufacturers, marketers and organised retailers. Corporations with global presence have to bring in incremental benefits to their business, forging these key alliances, and this is most important for the global retailers and wholesalers, where profit comes only from better SCM and logistics management practices.

The book has nine chapters and deals with all key activities and issues of the supply chain and logistics functions of the business, including demand forecasting and inventory management, and then dealing with the complexities and challenges of warehousing and distribution as well as transportation. The book covers global logistics value chain management as well as performance management in supply chain and deals with topics such as performance management matrix and maturity models. The book also covers the benchmarking and sustainability issues in supply chain to remain relevant and competitive in business with case studies to drive key insights into sustainability issues in supply chain and how those can help in terms of increased xxx *Preface*

value delivery. There are short cases and real-life issues that are discussed to provide key insights into the decision-making criteria.

Integration of areas such as procurement, processing and distribution is possible through proper management and control of supply chain operations. In developing countries like India, distribution is highly complex and it takes years for businesses to develop an efficient distribution function, which is vital for business performance. Global companies are even seen acquiring companies in India only to get access to and familiarise themselves with the complex and difficult tasks of setting up distribution functions as their key entry strategy into the Indian market. The book discusses these complexities and challenges.

The book is targeted towards both academics and practitioners of SCM. In academics, the book should be appropriate for MBA students as well as engineering students interested or specialising in SCM and logistics management.

Rajat K Baisya
Professor and Head (Retired)
Department of Management Studies,
Indian Institute of Technology Delhi

Acknowledgements

This book has referenced a few cases which are based on some practical data collected and reported by researchers. These case studies have been suitably adopted to explain and discuss certain theories and/or methods which I duly acknowledge.

I also gratefully acknowledge the support from Professor S. G. Deshmukh, Former Director, ABV IIITM, Gwalior, and Professor of SCM, Department of Mechanical Engineering, IIT Delhi, for his critical review of the contents of my book and also for writing the endorsement for the book.

Distinguished Professor, friend and contemporary Professor Bojan Rosi kindly wrote the foreword for the book, and I am very thankful to him for his support.

Often, when you work on a book, it takes up a lot of your time, which sometimes inconveniences your family; the same happened with mine too. However, they are also the happiest at the completion of this book, and I gratefully acknowledge the overwhelming support from all of them. I thank my wife Susmita for standing by me all through the way and sometimes taking more responsibilities towards the family than due. I express my affection towards my son Rishabh and daughter Deepshikha and son-in-law Olav and appreciate their patience and help through this journey. Both my children are successful professionals in their own right and have often offered suggestions and constructive feedback, especially my son, who has a keen interest in this subject.

Finally, my publisher Taylor & Francis has done a great job in terms of providing all the support to release the book on time. I gratefully acknowledge the help, cooperation and support and also the valuable suggestions from Mr Amit Kumar, Senior Commissioning Editor, and Ms Diksha Bhugra, Editorial Assistant of Routledge, while working on this project. I thank them for their constant help.

There are many people who have helped in small and big ways, and it is not possible to mention all of them; however, I would like to say that I recognise and appreciate their help at every step and humbly acknowledge that this book would not have been possible without all their support.

Abbreviations

ABC	Activity-Based Costing
AFACT	Asia Pacific Council for Trade Facilitation & Electronic Business
AGV	Automated Guided Vehicle
AI	Artificial Intelligence
AMCS	automatic milk collection system
APL	American President Lines
ASEAN	Association of Southeast Asian Nations
ASNs	advanced shipment notifications
B2B	business-to-business
B2C	business-to-consumer
BOD	Board of Director
BOP	bottom of the pyramid
BPCS	Business Planning Control System
BPR	Business Process Re-engineering
C&F	carrying and forwarding
C&S	carrying and selling
C+D	Connect+Develop
CAFE	Coffee and Farmer Equity Initiative
CAGR	compound annual growth rate
CCTs	commodity competence teams
CEO	chief executive officer
CFO	chief financial officer
CLM	Council of Logistics Management
CMI	co-managed inventory
CMM	Capability Maturity Model
CMM-I	Integrated CMM
CONCOR	Container Corporation of India Ltd
CPFR	collaborative planning, forecasting and replenishment
CSFs	critical success factors
CSL	cycle service level
CTO	chief technology officer
C-TPAT	Customs Trade Partnership against Terrorism
DCS	Dairy Cooperative Society
DSE	Delhi School of Economics
DTMS	Domestic Terminal Management System
EDI	electronic data interchange

EDLP	everyday low pricing
ELV	End-of-Life Vehicle
EOQ	economic order quantity
ERAP	emergency response assistance plan
ERP	enterprise resource planning
ETMS	Export/Import Terminal Management System
EU	European Union
EXIM	export–import
FCI	Food Corporation of India
FCPA	Foreign Corrupt Practices Act
FIFO	first-in, first-out
FMC	Federal Maritime Commission
FMCG	fast-moving consumer goods
FPY	first-pass yield
FTA	free trade agreement
FTEs	full-time equivalents
GCMMF	Gujarat Cooperative Milk Marketing Federation
GDSN	Global Data Synchronisation Network
GIS	Geographic Information Systems
GRN	goods receipt note
GST	Goods and Services Tax
HRM	human resource management
HUL	Hindustan Unilever Limited
IATA	International Air Transport Association
ICDs	inland container depots
IDSN	integrated demand – supply network
IMDG	International Maritime Dangerous Goods
IMI	International Maritime Institute
IMO	International Maritime Organization
IPD-CMM	CMM for Integrated Product and Process Development
IS	information system
ISMS	information security management system
IT	information technology
JIT	just-in-time
KPIs	key performance indicators
LCL	less than container load
LPI	Logistics Performance Index
LYC	last year consumption
MAD	mean absolute deviation
MAPE	mean absolute percentage error
MLM	multi-level marketing
MMT	million metric tonnes
MNCs	multinational corporations
MRP	material requirements planning
MSC	Mediterranean Shipping Company
MSE	mean squared error
NCPDM	National Council of Physical Distribution Management
NIIF	National Investment and Infrastructure Fund

xxxiv *Abbreviations*

OOCL	Orient Overseas Container Line
OSEM	Office of Safety and Emergency Management
OTC	over-the-counter
P&G	Procter & Gamble
PCs	personal computers
PDS	public distribution system
POP	point of purchase
POS	point of sale
QMMG	Quality Management Maturity Grid
R&D	research and development
ROCI	research on capital invested
ROI	return on investment
ROPs	reorder points
RORO	roll-on/roll-off
S&OP	sales and operations planning
SBU	strategic business unit
SCC	Supply Chain Council
SCM	supply chain management
SCOR	Supply Chain Operation Reference
SCPM	supply chain performance management
SE-CMM	CMM for Systems Engineering
SKU	stock-keeping unit
SOX	Sarbanes–Oxley Act of 2002
TDGR	Transportation of Dangerous Goods Act & Regulations
TLC	total logistics cost
TLEs	transaction learning experiments
TPL	third-party logistics
TPOP	time-phased order point
TQM	total quality management
TRU	Thompson Rivers University
VMI	vendor-managed inventory
VMS	Volvo Mobility Systems
VPPs	value payable parcels
WACC	Weighted Average Capital Cost
WCO	World Customs Organization
WES	Winters' exponential smoothing
WIP	work in progress/process
WMSs	warehouse management systems
WTO	World Trade Organization

About the Author

Rajat K. Baisya
PhD, FIMC, FIIChE, FIE, FWAPS, ICMCI-Academic Fellow
Professor and Head (Retired), Department of Management Studies,
Indian Institute of Technology Delhi
Chairman – Strategic Consulting Group Pvt Ltd
President- Project & Technology Management Foundation

OTHER BOOKS PUBLISHED BY THE AUTHOR

1. Aesthetics in Marketing published by SAGE in 2008
2. Changing Face of Processed Food Industry in India – by Ane Books in 2009
3. Winning Strategies for Business by SAGE in 2010
4. Globalization and Innovative Business Models by Ane Books in 2012
5. Branding in a Competitive Marketplace by SAGE in 2013
6. Managing Start-Ups for Success - Entrepreneurship- in Difficult Times by Taylor & Francis, UK 2021
7. Makers of Jadavpur- A Technological Perspective by Jadavpur University Press, Kolkata, 2021
8. Inside Innovation- Looking from Inside Out (Edited jointly with Alex Bennet)- MQI Press, USA 2023

1 Understanding the Supply Chain

The Core Concepts

Learning Objective

- Understand the core concept of supply chain in terms of its definition and what it covers
- Identify the impacts and implications of supply chain management on business performance
- Understand key challenges of supply chain management to overcome for delivering results
- Appreciate the role of an efficient and effective supply chain in creating a competitive advantage for the business

Introduction

Supply chain management (SCM) as a discipline has developed during the past two decades, although business consultants have been discussing the importance of managing supply chain efficiently as a prerequisite for delivering the expected level of performance of any business since the late 1980s. But it was only during the post-liberalisation and globalisation era that the importance of supply chain management was recognised by business leaders all over the world. Supply chain management as a function has gone through significant changes during the past two decades. In course of the time, the scope and limits of SCM got extended to become end-to-end supply chain management. Today, it covers a wide range of functions in business starting from procurement to production and operation, and warehousing to distribution. Earlier, the focus of business was on marketing and finance, which were considered the key functions responsible for the delivery of business performance, and then came an era that businesses were focusing on people from the thought that it is the people who deliver the result and, therefore, employee engagement and retention and talent development had taken all the attention of the business leaders. This may be uniformly true for all functions, and under the Industry 4.0 environment which we are now passing through talent has always been seen by business leaders all over the world as the top-most driver for global manufacturing competitiveness (Global Manufacturing Competitiveness Index Report, 2018, by Deloitte). A supply chain in today's business covers almost all line functions and, therefore, attracts the attention of the business. If the supply chain function is not efficient and effective, businesses will not remain competitive in the marketplace, and even the survival of the business itself will be threatened.

Since the concept of the supply chain was initially developed as an integrated function, a lot of development has taken place since then. Today, it is highly technology driven. Procurement was once upon a time considered as a very mundane function, and very little attention was given by businesses, which subsequently was found to be a very important function offering considerable scope for cost reduction and competitive advantage.

DOI: 10.4324/9781003469063-1

2 Understanding the Supply Chain

The purchase function was initially managed by some low-key executives by inviting quotations and going through negotiations to get the best possible price for the item(s) to be procured. Purchase managers were trying to focus on getting the best possible price for key items required for manufacturing. It is much later that businesses realised that over 75% of the cost of the product is constituted by procured items or bought-out items and, therefore, if a company has to be cost competitive, greater opportunity lies in managing procurement function better, and, thereafter, the procurement function is improved, adding a lot of incremental value to the business. Today, the procurement function is highly developed, and a lot of technology including e-auction, vendor-managed inventory (VMI) and so on are used in addition to the concept of just-in-time (JIT) inventory as well as focused and preferred supplier zeroed on after carrying out vendor development and vendor rating based on predetermined criteria. Businesses even use third-party funding and bill discounting to reduce the procurement cost.

After making significant improvements in procurement functions, businesses start focusing on core activities. And we have seen that companies started shifting manufacturing facilities to places that cost the least and satisfy all quality criteria and also from the perspective of better customer service. We have seen that companies started focusing on what they know better and thus manufacturing operations were shifting to outside the business. During the early 1990s, almost 100% production was carried out in the company's own manufacturing plants, but by the end of that decade almost 100% manufacturing was contracted out and businesses were only focusing on marketing, research and development (R & D) and business development activities. Today, most of the manufacturing operations are outsourced to smaller companies to benefit from the lower logistics and inventory holding cost, and thus manufacturing operations were also spread over many locations and coming closer to customers' locations. Globally, manufacturing operations shifted to China, it being a low-cost mass-production country. China emerged as a global supply source.

India lost out on the race to become the global manufacturing hub, and a large part of that reason is in terms of key global manufacturing competitiveness drivers. India lacks in many of those parameters, including infrastructure and legal and regulatory framework. These issues are discussed in detail in the book. Many businesses follow many innovative processes to improve supply chain efficiency. For example, Benneton produces all T-shirts in white and prints them closer to the season when they can get a more accurate estimate of demand for the colour of the garments required in a particular year, thereby reducing the inventory. Otherwise, excess and unsold stock may have to be rejected or disposed of as a discounted stock losing out on profitability. Dell manufactures laptops on getting confirmed orders to reduce the inventory.

It has now been observed that manufacturing in a global location in say China and selling the end product globally have other ramifications and complexity. In this scenario, many a time input material has to come from many countries all over the world wherever those are best and cheapest, say China, and then re-transported to the countries where it has to be sold, and that increases cost and complexity. Because of the distance between selling countries and production countries, inventory holding gets larger blocking costly working capital. The transportation cost also becomes higher, and global corporations are carefully analysing those parameters to decide the best ways to manage the global supply chain with a clear objective of the least cost and best service to the customers. These issues are now changing the supply chain management processes, from the earlier established practices. Many items and product categories are now standardised and delivered to customers based on orders received in knocked-down conditions and it is assembled at the customer's premises. IKEA is a Swedish-founded multinational group that designs and sells ready-to-assemble furniture, kitchen appliances and home accessories, among other useful goods and occasionally home services. The IKEA model of furniture business is

Understanding the Supply Chain 3

now practised and replicated by even domestic furniture manufacturers. International furniture manufacturers also enter countries with franchise routes to be cost competitive. They supply in bulk only the panels which are cut to size as per customers' orders and fabricated at customers' locations or wherever they want. The business model is changing only from competitiveness point of view. As competition is increasing, businesses are trying to become more and more innovative to improve upon value delivery and therefore, on both benefits in terms of quality and functionality as well as on cost, businesses are constantly improving. And SCM offers the greatest opportunity for incremental value delivery.

The logistics which covers warehousing and transportation is increasingly becoming costlier and can form a significant part of the cost of the entire supply chain. In the USA, logistics cost is about 8% of the GDP whereas in India it is about 15%. There are significant opportunities for improving the logistics cost, as well as managing warehousing better through the use of technology. Logistics cost is the new area that businesses are now concentrating after taking care of procurement and production or manufacturing. There are inbound and outbound logistics to be tackled and non-value-adding activities to be eliminated. Logistics therefore is an integral part of the supply chain now and needs special attention. From considerations of logistics cost, we can see that some East European countries are also now emerging as preferred locations for cost-effective manufacturing for global players. Companies in East European countries are producing auto components and accessories for all leading brands of automobiles. For this reason, logistics management has been emerging as an independent discipline to focus on R&D in this area, and in many institutions abroad logistics is offered as a separate area for specialisation.

In this book, we have taken an integrated view of SCM and logistics; therefore, chapters have been designed accordingly, which offers greater scope to take an integrated view and derive the advantage of cost efficiency. Today's supply chain involves all parties, directly or indirectly working together in fulfilling the customer expectations. SCM, thus, requires ability to work together with people and organisation, both within the business and outside the business.

SCM and Business Performance

The length of the supply chain in manufacturing and marketing of products will depend on the type of products and also on the processes followed, which determines the number of intermediaries and partners as well as associates involved in the entire value chain. A typical fast-moving consumer products like food and household goods will involve the following stages:

- Customers
- Retailers
- Wholesalers and distributors
- Manufacturers
- Raw material, packaging material and other input material suppliers

Under each stage, as mentioned earlier, the supply chain is connected by the flow of products, funds and information, which happens in both directions and will be managed by one of the stages or even by an intermediary. Accordingly, the design of the supply chain depends on customer needs and roles played by the stages involved. The supply chain complexity increases with the number of intermediaries in each stage. For example, if a company has both in-house and out-house manufacturing facilities, then the input material suppliers are also required to supply materials and components to the contract manufacturers, which in turn also will supply to both company and its distributors and wholesalers as per the model, and if they are located at

4 Understanding the Supply Chain

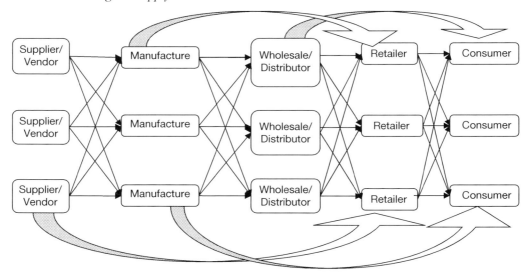

Figure 1.1 Supply Chain Linkages and Stages

different geographical locations then the complexity takes a much bigger dimension to be managed. The complexity increases further if the suppliers are also located overseas and customers are located in other countries outside the parent company's location. It can, thus, take an enormous proportion of challenges which we have discussed in other chapters. A simplified supply chain stage can be shown as given in Figure 1.1.

The discipline of supply chain management has evolved over several decades of managing industrial production and distribution. A considerable amount of academic research leading to innovations as well as practitioners' experience and experimentation have gone into the development of the SCM discipline and subject of study as we know it today (Chen and Paulraj, 2004). These disciplines are operations management, industrial engineering as well as physical distribution. As can be understood that supply chain management involves multiple management functions and therefore it is an inter-disciplinary subject requiring knowledge of many other functions. Earlier each of those functions was managed independently in silos but now those have been integrated into one, as integrated SCM. Each of the components of an integrated supply chain can be considered as a separate stream, which can be broadly classified as:

- Sourcing and procurement and supply chain
- Materials management
- Logistics and distribution management

Procurement occupies a predominant position in the supply chain for the reason that it impacts both cash flow and profitability of the business and requires to be managed efficiently. If a company decides to manufacture all its products through third parties and also distributes the products to its independent distributors, then the whole supply chain will be a function of sourcing and procurement and delivery. Online retailers such as Amazon and Flipkart are actually operations like that.

The materials management function includes demand forecasting, inventory management, warehousing, stock keeping and scheduling as well as production planning and control. As over

Understanding the Supply Chain 5

60% of the manufactured cost is constituted by the bought-out items, materials management offers considerable scope for improvement in terms of route to cost reduction and, therefore, is considered very important. However, in relation to SCM, materials management can be regarded as the flow of material into, through and out of the enterprise.

Logistics function is actually derived from the military or defence logistics for managing military supply lines. Council of Logistics management defines that it is that part of the supply chain management process that plans, implements and controls efficient and effective forward and backward flow and storage of goods and services as well as information from the point of origin to the point of consumption to meet the customers' requirement. The distribution function in businesses in that sense comes under logistics and is very important to be managed effectively to deliver the overall performance of the SCM functions. Logistics comes for both bringing the input materials inside the manufacturing premises and for taking finished products out for sales and distribution, and as such we call that inbound and outbound logistics. Transportation has significant costs due to rise in fuel prices and energy costs. Appropriate strategies need to be developed to contain the cost of transportation and logistics. These issues have been discussed in greater detail in the chapter on transportation (Chapter 6).

Businesses are required to deliver incremental value on a sustainable basis to ensure survival and growth, and, therefore, unlocking the hidden value in the entire supply chain is of primary focus. Also because of the very dynamic nature of the business, demand fluctuates and SCM has to gear up to meet the fluctuating demand. Manufacturing operations need to be flexible and agile. That has influenced the development of a flexible and an agile supply chain to reduce the response time. To manage today's supply chain thus requires an integrated view supported by competitive operational strategies. Sustainability is another key area that requires attention and focus including environmental concerns which will require judicious selection of technology and processes ensuring green logistics and so on, which are the key concerns of the global supply chain and logistics operators. These issues have been adequately covered in the book. This book has been designed to get an integrated view of the supply chain for providing a holistic approach to SCM.

Key Challenges

With increased awareness and concerns about the protection of environment, supply chain has added complexity and challenges. The regulations regarding environmental protection are forcing businesses to view the whole task of organising the supply of products and making available what customers want. The recent challenges of the government asking FMCG companies such as Hindustan Unilever Limited (HUL) and Procter & Gamble (P&G) to be responsible for taking care of their own waste coming from the use of packaging material-particularly non-biodegradable packaging material used for production of items that the company sell is a pointer in that direction. Environment-friendly countries like Ireland have decided to do away with the inner box that is normally used for packing toothpaste tubes. In Ireland now toothpaste tubes are sold without the box. Food regulatory authorities have now banned the use of recycled plastic for packing food products. Virgin polyester (PET) is non-biodegradable and also costly packing material for packing food products like sauces, ketchups, beverages and mineral water. PET is a product from petroleum refinery. Processes now have been developed to completely decompose used and recycled PET by pyrolysis and then reconstruct the virgin PET material again from the components to recycle the used food-grade polyesters. New technologies are developed to overcome and address these challenges.

6 *Understanding the Supply Chain*

There are also new security concerns with respect to the movement of stocks in global trade. Terrorism, cross-border tension, trade rivalry, political conflict, piracy etc. pose increased threats to the movement of cargo in global trade. The increased security concerns and related regulatory issues pose additional challenges for logistics and SCM in terms of securing the cargo and conforming to country-specific regulations. In addition to all these, there are issues related to piracy, theft and pilferage and tempering of cargo as a challenge to global logistics operators.

As transportation is an integral part of logistics operation, with rising fuel cost, transportation cost is also increasing, which is the key challenge to logistics operators. Sulphur content of the bunker fuel and new regulations for that is coming as a big challenge. With the rising cost of transportation, global logistics players are trying many alternative strategies to contain those to be competitive. As a result, many acquisitions and strategic alliances are now being seen to be happening. Sustainable transportation is another challenge to logistics operators.

Handling of hazardous and inflammable cargo requires additional safety measures, and there are regulations with respect to those to be complied with. SCM covers wide areas and functions in a business. A large part of the capital investment also is made in these areas to be effective. Supply chain represents key components of costs in business; managing supply chain effectively and efficiently is therefore the key imperative to derive competitive advantage in business. Businesses are seen to be experimenting with new ideas and strategies to create competitive advantage in the business. This book has discussed many such practical cases to drive the point. Managing supply chain better also improves the success rate of new businesses, new products and start-ups.

The book is an attempt to see SCM and logistics management as an integrated discipline in terms of managing the new challenges in the supply chain, which is so vital for succeeding in the marketplace.

Chapter Summary

This chapter discusses the new concepts of SCM as we know today, covering a wide range of business functions which were earlier managed in silos but now being managed as an integrated holistic function. The chapter also addresses the importance of SCM in terms of delivering improved business performance and remaining competitive to ensure survival and growth. The increased complexity and management challenges of supply chain have been elaborately discussed highlighting the inter-relationship of various functions now included and considered as part of the supply chain. The new regulatory, safety as well as packaging and environmental issues are also discussed, which are posing new challenges to be effectively managed. Lastly, this chapter addresses the newfound importance of logistics management in supply chain and key issues that make a very valid case of managing supply chain and logistics as an integrated function.

Discussion Questions

1 What are the key functions that SCM encompasses in the current context?
2 Why SCM is so important in business in terms of delivering a competitive advantage?
3 How logistics management has emerged as key discipline and is part of the supply chain now?
4 What are the key considerations to manage SCM as an integrated discipline?
5 Discuss the key complexities and challenges of supply chain management function

References

Chen, I. J., & Paulraj, A. (2004) "Understanding Supply Chain Management: Critical Research & Theoretical Framework", *International Journal of Production Research*, 42(1), 131–163. Published online in February 2007.
Deloitte. (2018) *Global Manufacturing Competitiveness Index (Report)*. New York: Deloitte.

Bibliography

Fisher, M. L. (1997, March–April) "What Is the Right Supply Chain for Your Product?", *Harvard Business Review*, pp. 83–93.
Kopczak, L. R., & Johnson, M. E. (2003, Spring) "The Supply Chain Management Effect", *Sloan Management Review*, pp. 27–34.
Robensen, J. F., & Copacino, W. C., eds. (1994) *The Logistics Handbook*. New York: The Free Press.
Slone, R. E. (2004, October) "Leading a Supply Chain Turnaround", *Harvard Business Review*, pp. 114–121.

2 Evolution of Integrated Supply Chain and Logistics Management

Learning Objective

- Understand how SCM has evolved over the years as a discipline
- Get exposure to scope and key components of supply chain and their implications
- The historical perspective of integrated supply chain and logistics management
- The role and functions of integrated supply chain and key deliverables

Introduction

SCM in the current context covers a very wide area of business functions. What had started in the early 1980s as a new concept initiated and introduced by consultants in the USA to improve business performance is now a full-grown integrated end-to-end supply chain from procurement to production to distribution and customer order processing and customer service. Even some of the erstwhile sales and distribution functions including debtors' management and channel partners management are now covered under integrated SCM. SCM as we understand now covers a very wide range of activities including procurement, warehousing, transport and logistics, inventory management, production, demand management, distribution and customer services. It, thus, assumes great importance in managing the business in terms of cross-functional expertise, efficiency and effectiveness. We can say that organisations are very large cost centres, and everything we do inside the organisation are only costs which have to be transacted with the prospective customers with a margin of profit. In an ever-increasing competitive environment, margins are getting squeezed and to retain the desirable level of margin, businesses have to drastically improve the efficiency of SCM including logistics. And as end-to-end SCM represents the major part of the cost in the business, an efficient and effective integrated SCM largely determines the overall business performance and profitability in the current context and new business environment.

Scope of SCM

By the way we understand SCM now, we can define it as the integration of key business processes across the end-to-end supply chain for the purpose of creating value for customers and other stakeholders. SCM revolves around an efficient integration of suppliers, manufacturers, warehouses, stores, wholesalers, retailers and customers. It also optimises the organisational resources to ensure an ideal level of servicing as per the customer demand or requirement at all times.

This would mean that supply chain management is the management of a network of interconnected businesses involved in the ultimate provision of product and service packages required by end customers (Harland, 1996). To compete in the global market and networked economy,

DOI: 10.4324/9781003469063-2

interorganisational supply network can be acknowledged as a new form of organisation itself. An Ideal level of SCM performance needs synchronisation of various other direct and indirect business functions starting from demand forecasting, procurement, production, warehousing, distribution, logistics etc. SCM now covers a wide variety of functions and, therefore, we look at these interconnected functions in business and try to manage as an integrated activity because of their functional interdependencies. And, as such, inefficiency in one function will impact the performance of other associated and interlinked functions. In the context of current global business environment and complexity, SCM, therefore, has to be viewed as a unified integrated function. This function is so important that businesses have to derive their competitive advantage through significant innovation in the entire SCM functions. What started initially in the early 1980s as global procurement challenges has now evolved as an integrated as well as very critical discipline in business.

The three main streams of integrated SCM are as follows:

- Sourcing, procurement and supply management
- Materials management and demand management
- Logistics and distribution management

A customer will be buying the product from the end selling point, which could be a retail store in the neighbourhood. But to make the product available in time for the customer to buy, there are numerous interconnected activities and associates, vendors and suppliers are involved in a networked environment, all working in harmony to make that happen in an integrated and effective chain of activities as has been shown in Figure 2.1.

The supply chain is thus dynamic and essentially involves the constant flow of information, products and funds among various interconnected partners. In e-commerce trade, a customer places an order online on say Amazon or Flipkart on their website and transfer the fund to buy a particular product after going through the information available on the website about the product, price and availability. An e-retailer like Amazon may decide to supply it from

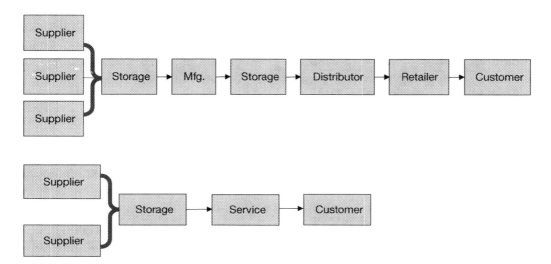

Figure 2.1 Scope of Supply Chain Management

10 *Evolution of Integrated Supply Chain and Logistics Management*

their warehouse or even from their registered suppliers' network stock points, involving either courier services or delivery service vendors, to ensure that the product is delivered within the agreed delivery terms of the order of the customer which needs to be processed immediately. Upon receiving the product, if the customer finds it defective or not as per the expectation, he/ she can either return the product or get it replaced within a prescribed time, giving reasons thereof. The e-retailer then has to take back the product, credit the customer, debit the supplier or vendor and also adjust the inventory record immediately, which is in fact a reverse logistics task to be managed. The operation as described, in fact, comes under the SCM and as can be seen, it is highly complex.

Sourcing and procurement are important areas of SCM. Earlier, procurement was considered a very mundane function, but soon businesses realised its importance in terms of cost reduction possibilities, which has drawn the attention of top management. The materials management function, in fact, includes multiple functions such as forecasting, inventory management, store management, warehousing and stock keeping as well as scheduling. Logistics and distribution were initially derived from military parlance that dealt with movement and maintenance of armies, but when its application came to be recognised in business, it was intended to cover physical movement of goods and services across a supply chain till it reached the end consumer for better service and satisfaction.

Evolution of SCM: The Historical Perspective

The integrated SCM has evolved over the years as a result of several business development challenges in the global supply chain.

There are five major movements or major industry-led initiatives that we can observe as the evolution of the SCM as we now understand. These are as follows (Magretta, 1998).

1 **Creation era**
   SCM was first coined by a US industry consultant in the early 1980s. At that stage, SCM included the need for large-scale changes, re-engineering and downsizing, driven by cost-reduction programmes to remain competitive in the marketplace in the global business environment. Cost was always considered a major competitive advantage for business. Offering the same or more benefits at a lower cost is always a winning strategy, and in the creation era, SCM was focused on many cost-reduction programmes. We have seen since then that there are initiatives on business process re-engineering (BPR), total quality management (TQM), continuous improvement, kaizen etc. The primary objective of all these initiatives was to eliminate the non-value-adding activities in the business to make the business more cost competitive, proactive, flexible and responsive to the ever-changing and competitive business environment. The competitive forces of businesses during those years have made these changes a logical imperative.

2 **Integration era**
   After the initial phase came the integration era to cash on the various initiatives the businesses have been seen to be undertaking in order to absorb the benefits of those initiatives in the business as a whole or the organisation itself. This was triggered by the development of electronic data interchange (EDI) systems in the 1960s and developed through the 1990s by the introduction of enterprise resource planning (ERP) systems. In this phase, the industry was concentrating on productivity improvement as well as on resource optimisation, and ERP was making inroads into business. Organisations were seen to be implementing ERP at a huge cost in the 1990s, which is now available at 10% of the original cost of the package in

Evolution of Integrated Supply Chain and Logistics Management 11

those days. Even relatively smaller businesses have also now implemented a customised ERP package in their business for optimising the resource allocation and uses that is linked with the sales order processing. It was always debated by the businesses whether that huge investment in implementing ERP packages like SAP, BAAN and BPCS etc has really delivered the commensurate result or benefits to the business. But large industries thought that their existence would be threatened if they do not go ahead with such large investment programmes in ERP. In the 1990s, all large global businesses implemented SAP or other costly ERP packages at a huge cost and time, and those large investments coupled with the engagement of trained IT professionals to help run the system and churn out various kinds of management reporting systems to understand the efficiency and effectiveness of the management functions. ERP did not help reduce manpower in the organisation, which was originally thought of, but definitely brought in a new view of the business performance and helped businesses to take an integrated view of many interconnected functions which were earlier viewed and managed in silos.

3 Globalisation era

During the third phase, which was in the 1990s, globalisation, regionalisation and so on had started impacting businesses. There were global realignments of businesses. Large acquisitions and mergers happened during that time. Manufacturing was shifting to the countries where it was most economical to produce. The third phase of the movement of SCM development was triggered by the globalisation era and can be characterised by the attention given to global systems of supplier relationships and the expansion of supply chains over national boundaries and into other continents. During this phase, we have seen that manufacturing locations were moving to places where it was costing the least to produce and global sourcing as well as outsourcing in a major way, increasing the complexity in business. In this era, raw materials and input materials were sourced from the countries where best quality and reliability were ensured at least cost, and final production was carried out in yet another country where cost of production was the least to be shipped to the world market as per customer requirements. During this phase, China emerged as a global manufacturing hub for most of the global brands and as such it was able to attract global investors to set up global factories to satisfy their customer requirements around the world. This complexity of the movement of raw materials and finished products has thrown many challenges in terms of logistics as well as regulatory to be effectively managed to run a global factory.

4 Specialisation Era I: Outsourced Manufacturing and Distribution

The specialisation era was experienced in two phases during which SCM was realised to be a service function like many other functions in business such as finance and marketing, and that has enlarged its scope to include customer services and distribution as well. During this era, everything in business was seen as a way to provide better service to the customer, and organisations have been seen to be totally focused on customer retention by providing better service and satisfaction in relation to their own competition. Service quality, customer retention, flexibility and mass customisation gained importance, and these were the additional challenges for an SCM team in any business to be addressed as an added complexity. Many changes were noticed during the two phases of the specialisation era of SCM.

In the 1990s, industries began to focus on 'core competencies' and adopted a specialisation model. Companies abandoned vertical integration, sold off non-core operations and outsourced those functions to other companies which could perform these better at a lower cost. Most of the organisations are now focusing on their core competence which they can do

12 *Evolution of Integrated Supply Chain and Logistics Management*

better than others, and the rest of the activities and business functions are outsourced. In the early 1990s, outsourcing of manufacturing and production operations was seen to be the beginning of this era, but today most of the large and global enterprises have divested their own production and manufacturing facilities and started sourcing from third parties whom they have developed over the years, and that has also increased the complexity in the management of business processes. Domestic companies have also been seen shifting manufacturing operations to areas where tax holidays and other investment-related incentives were available. They were flexible to shift manufacturing locations only to reduce the cost of production, taking into account the tax incentives that were made available to attract investors in areas which were less industrialised.

5 Specialisation Era II: Supply Chain Management as a Means of providing Service
During this phase, the logistics function gained tremendous importance, as it was realised that logistics is the next largest cost after procurement that businesses are incurring, and the performance of logistics greatly influences the SCM performance. During this phase, third-party logistics (TPL) and so on were greatly studied and investigated. Logistics which was earlier synonymous with transportation was now being addressed as a holistic function and a fully grown discipline.

Specialisation within the supply chain began in the 1980s with the inception of transportation brokerages, warehouse management and non-asset-based carriers, and has matured beyond transportation and logistics into aspects of supply planning, collaboration, execution and performance management. During this phase, which is clearly visible in the current business context, we were witnessing the importance of logistics as a key function with a lot of opportunities for improvements and cost reduction and also a focus on integrated end-to-end SCM. Logistics has now evolved as one of the key drivers of providing competitive advantage to the business, and it also has to be seen as an integral part of the extended SCM.

As logistics is an integral function of end-to-end SCM, we will be discussing SCM and logistics functions together as an integrated function

Key Objectives and Challenges of Supply Chain Integration

For integrated supply chain management, a great degree of internal as well as external factors of the business needs to be aligned to improve the overall performance of SCM. This also results in networking as well as technology selection and implementation. For efficient SCM integration, one has to consider the various components, put together appropriate structure and framework in place in order to produce the desired result. For efficient management of an integrated SCM, businesses need to have an elaborate planning and control mechanism and work process structure, management methods and practices as well as organisation structure to ensure smooth flow of materials and facilities supported by appropriate information flow and system. This is possible with competent and capable leadership with well-defined organisation structure and design and favourable organisation culture and attitude with adequate risk mitigation strategies wherever required, including reward structure. This aspect will get more clarity when we take up case studies in this chapter itself.

The primary objective of all supply chains has to be to maximise the overall value generated in the chain, which would also mean to generate supply chain surplus which can be defined as follows:

Supply Chain Value = Customer Value – Supply Chain Cost

Evolution of Integrated Supply Chain and Logistics Management 13

The customer value is in fact the price a potential customer is willing to pay for the product offering, which depends not only on the product type, quality and benefits that it offers to the target customers but also on how the product has been positioned in the customers mind and how it is promoted and marketed. The customer value, therefore, has got to do with the effectiveness of the marketing function in the business. However, marketers need support and cooperation to succeed in the marketplace in a competitive environment. The distribution which was earlier a sales function is now integrated into the supply chain function. Supply chain thus now play a more integrated role. Without the cooperation, involvement and effectiveness of the supply chain, it would be difficult for the marketers to create a steady and growing demand for the product. Supply chain, therefore, plays a complimentary role for the marketing function and if supply chain fails, marketing also will fail.

Objectives and Challenges of SCM

The key objectives that reflect the performance of SCM in the business world would ultimately depend on achieving the cost reduction objective and to achieve that we have many challenges. We need to coordinate activities across the SCM to improve performance by:

1 Reducing total cost
2 Increasing customer service level
3 Reducing the impact of the bullwhip effect
4 Better utilisation of organisational resources
5 Effectively and proactively respond to changes in the marketplace

To achieve the objectives listed businesses have to have well-defined and actionable strategies to manage the SCM functions across the entire value chain. As the entire supply chain has to be managed with the sole objective to meet the customers' real-time demand, estimating the demand accurately will hold the key to managing the supply chain effectively. The performance of supply chain is also led by a few critical or key drivers including inventory control and management, transportation, facilities planning and information flow and accuracy. Unless these key strategic drivers are managed well, the integration benefits will not emerge. These strategic drivers illustrate the opportunities and challenges associated with SCM integration which will include the following:

1 Supply chain strategies: push, pull and push-pull systems
2 Demand-driven strategies
3 Effective distribution strategies

Pull strategies are always better in the sense that in pull strategy the demand is managed from the point of view of the real-term demand of the customers, and it is the task of the marketers to create the customer demand by effectively executing demand pull marketing strategies and promotion including advertisement. Push strategy, which is manufacturers and marketers driven, often leads to artificial demand, raising the level of the trade stock, which in turn can cause other problems like an increase in expiry stock and stock return and high debtors. The aim of the efficient supply chain is to optimise the two apparently opposing objectives so that real-term demand is satisfied and we don't lose out on sales, and at the same time we also don't overstock the trade by over-trading, raising the working capital locked up in the system leading to underperformance.

14 *Evolution of Integrated Supply Chain and Logistics Management*

Role of SCM

SCM really works by bringing positive impact by servicing the customers better and thereby helping businesses to grow faster in terms of increased sales, growth and profits. The primary role of supply chain management is to optimise the organisational resources to maximise sales and profits by servicing real-term customer demand. In this task, SCM primarily performs the following activities:

- Communicator of customer demand from point of sale to supplier (POS to the supplier)
- Physical flow process that engineers the movement of goods
- Optimises the organisational resources to satisfy the customer's demand

The key benefits that can accrue from the efficient SCM are, therefore, many and will include the following:

- Reduction of product losses in transportation and storage by making the processes and functions more efficient and effective.
- Providing competitive advantage to the business by unlocking a lot of hidden value in the entire supply chain
- Increase of sales resulting from better customer service ensuring customer satisfaction
- Dissemination of technology, advanced techniques, capital and knowledge among the chain partners, thereby helping the channel partners to also be more competitive and efficient in their own businesses.

It is a common practice for large businesses to help contract manufacturers and contract packers to become more cost-effective by infusion of technology and knowledge and even sometimes investment in vendor's facilities and then share the added value so created for the benefit of both. This is a win–win situation for both principal and vendors. Sometimes it is much easier to either experiment or practice on vendor's premises rather than in their own facilities and premises of large global players because of rigidity and inflexible policies and practices, which require time to change. We have discussed P&G case to bring in more clarity in this regard. P&G is generally recognised as more proactive and innovative in relation to their own competitive sets, and they are constantly experimenting to find better solutions to the newer challenges of the global market. The case will, therefore, reveal some of their key strategic drivers to find innovative solutions which can significantly improve business performance and reduce risk of failures.

Supply Chain in Competitive World: A Case of Li & Fung

Victor Fung of Li & Fung gave an interview which was published in HBR, Sept-Oct 1998. He said,

Say we get an order from an European retailer to produce 10,000 garments. For this customer we might decide to buy yarn from a Korean producer but have it woven and dyed in Taiwan. So we pick the yarn and ship it to Taiwan. The Japanese have the best zippers . . . so we go to YKK, a big Japanese zipper manufacturer, and we order the right zippers from their Chinese plants . . . the best place to make the garments is Thailand. So we ship everything there . . . the customer needs quick delivery, we may divide the order across five factories in Thailand. Effectively, we are customizing the value chain to best meet the customer's needs.

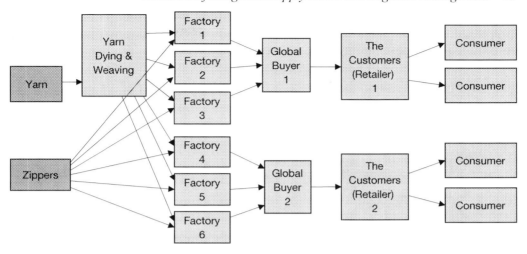

Figure 2.2 Complexity in Supply Chain in Li & Fung Business Model

The complexity as explained in the case of Li & Fung is explained diagrammatically in Figure 2.2, which will show the complexity of the whole process of executing the European order of garments by Li & Fung in order to deliver the best value to the ultimate customer to ensure the sustainability of the whole business process, which is hinging on the ultimate customer satisfaction with quality, time as well as price. Li & Fung is Hong Kong's largest export trading company. It has also been innovative in supply chain management. In the interview example, it can be seen that Li & Fung created a supply chain for the purpose of meeting a customer's needs. In general, this case is more the exception than the rule but serves to illustrate some of the pieces of a global supply chain which not only is complex but also requires management knowledge and expertise.

A value chain is another name for a supply chain. The concept of value chain was introduced by Michael Porter (1985) and what we understand today by value chain is in fact another name for extended end-to-end supply chain. A supply chain is a sequence of organisations – their facilities, functions and activities – involved in producing and delivering a product or service.

In supply chain, the members linked in the chain serves both as customers and as suppliers as they receive input materials from someone else and converts that to the finished product to sell to their own customer and as such each partner performs both roles. In the case of Li & Fung, as discussed earlier, the Korean yarn producer and Japanese Zipper producer are probably suppliers and also the customer's customer. Supply chain management therefore links the organisations within the supply chain to meet the demand across the entire chain efficiently. In typical non-brokered supply chains, one or more of the organisations in the chain can also provide the management function.

Why Is SCM So Important?

In today's business, sourcing is done from places and factories where cost is least and which are most efficient in terms of quality and delivery. As mentioned by Fung of Li & Fung worldwide, there are various products now being produced in China or in East European countries by

16 *Evolution of Integrated Supply Chain and Logistics Management*

sourcing components and raw materials from various parts of the world and that makes SCM so vital and important for the performance of the business by impacting numerous criteria of performance such as cost, quality, time, customer service, reduction of wastage, environment-friendly processes, productivity, skill level of people, innovation, sustainability etc. Efficient management of SCM is thus essential and critical to the performance of business and that is why it is so important. SCM is managed to produce multiple benefits to the business, which will thus include the following.

- For improved efficiencies in procurement, distribution and logistics
- For making outsourcing activities more efficient
- For reduction of cost of transportation of inventories
- For managing the inventories required across the supply chain
- For making the businesses more cost-effective and globally competitive
- For managing the complexities of the supply chain
- For managing the new challenges from e-commerce
- For absorbing competitive pressures from shorter development cycle time, more new products and demand for more customisation
- For meeting the challenges of globalisation and longer supply chains

However, managing supply chain to achieve the desired outcome is not an easy task simply because different organisations in the supply chain may have different, conflicting objectives and other internal constraints including resource constraints and business objectives. For example, the partners in the supply chain can have typically conflicting interests and objectives as mentioned earlier and those need to be optimised for overall performance.

- **Manufacturers:** long-run production, high quality, high productivity, low production cost
- **Distributors:** low inventory, reduced transportation costs, quick replenishment capability
- **Customers**: shorter order lead time, high in-stock inventory, large variety of products, low prices
- **Consumers:** availability, affordable cost, value for money, after-sales service, product performance

Supply chains are in fact dynamic in nature in any organisation, and they evolve over time and also change with the change in business environment. Supply chain thus needs to be managed as a vertically integrated function. For any organisation, vertical integration will involve either taking one or more suppliers backwards and one or more of the distribution activities forward. For example, a backward vertical integration for say a peanut butter manufacturer would be deciding to start growing peanuts instead of buying peanuts from the supplier for processing and a forward vertical for the same manufacturer would entail that peanut butter manufacturer decides to market their peanut butter directly to the grocery stores and retailers instead of going through the existing channel partners. In a supply chain, some functions related to suppliers as well as distribution might be performed by the manufacturers directly if that provides cost competitiveness to the business. Such decisions are normally taken when businesses realise that some of those functions can be better managed by themselves instead of getting it done by third parties over whom manufacturer marketers have no control and as such decisions taken when those functions are better managed with lesser costs by manufacturers themselves.

Evolution of Integrated Supply Chain and Logistics Management

Logistics: A Neglected Area – Now an Integral Part of SCM

Peter Drucker (1962) has said that 'logistics is the economy's dark continent. It is the most neglected but very promising business area'. Global sourcing has posed serious challenges and opportunities for logistics companies. Businesses are still learning how to use logistics effectively and logistics thus has become a key source of competitive advantage.

Efficient logistics function management is the key driver to deliver competitive advantage to businesses. Businesses, therefore, need to develop a strategic plan for effective logistics function to unlock the value in the logistic management chain, and logistics thus has emerged as one of the key functions in business.

Logistics is an integral part of supply chain management encompassing the planning and management of all activities involved in sourcing and procurement, conversion, and all logistics management activities. In addition, it also includes coordination and collaboration with channel partners, which can be suppliers, intermediaries, third-party service providers and customers. In essence, supply chain management integrates supply and demand management within and across companies. And logistics is the integral part of all interfaces. Logistics, in fact, takes care of the way a company acquires materials such as raw materials, packaging materials or parts, spares and components and intermediates, how a company handle them once they arrive at the company's manufacturing premises, and how they are shipped out. Logistics, therefore, is the intervening facilitator from the time material input is sourced and brought inside the company's manufacturing locations till it reaches the end customer as the final product to be consumed. On the basis of this, very broadly logistics can be divided into inbound logistics and outbound logistics. While Inbound logistics deals with the input material, outbound logistics deals with physical distribution and marketing logistics.

Physical distribution means the way a company delivers its product to the market, which could be intermediaries, customers or retailers and end users and marketing logistics which are basically the physical distribution of goods. Marketing logistics involves planning, delivering and controlling the flow of physical goods to a market as well as the material and information necessary to meet customer demands. Marketing logistics even cover market returns which need to be either disposed of or reprocessed, as required and that is a part of reverse logistics. The demands of the customer must be met at a profit that increases revenue for the organisation.

Why Is Logistics Important?

Logistics can help improve value delivery to customers, and, therefore, it can also improve customer satisfaction and help businesses become more competitive in the marketplace. And that is the key to success. In order to succeed in the marketplace businesses have to consistently deliver superior value to their target customers and consumers in relation to their own competitive set. All businesses have their identified competitors with whom they compete and it is essential that you deliver superior value in comparison to your identified competitors to succeed. In this regard, it also should be mentioned that all players in the same business are not necessarily competitors and as same strategy will not address the challenges of all competitors. Therefore, it is essential that businesses identify their competitors judiciously. And in that task effective and efficient logistics management holds the key.

Things began changing with the advancement in transportation systems. Population began moving from rural to urban areas and to business centres. No longer did people live near

18 *Evolution of Integrated Supply Chain and Logistics Management*

production centres, nor did production take place near residential centres where goods and services are mostly consumed. The geographical distance between the production point and consumption point thus increased. And logistics also thus gained importance.

Logistics is one of the most important functions in business today. No marketing, manufacturing or project execution can succeed without logistics support. For companies, 10–35% of gross sales are logistics costs, depending on the types of business, geography and weight/value ratio of the product.

Other factors also have come into play recently. Since the early 1990s, the business scene has changed. Globalisation, the free market and competition require that the customer gets the right material, at the right time, at the right point, in the right condition and at the lowest cost, which has implications in a global competitive environment where players out trying to outsmart their competitive counterpart in order to thrive in the business.

> Business spent a huge sum on managing logistics activities within the supply chain. For example, in USA 25–35% of product's sale value is attributed to logistics cost for international logistics and 8–10% for domestic logistics. In 1993 USA has spent 10.7% of GDP which goes to cover the cost of logistics, twice of the spent on national defence. In 2000 USA has spent 10% of the price of all goods which was attributed to the cost of logistics.[1] Costs of logistics in any organization and in businesses depends on three major factors, namely level of economic activity, efficiency, the transition of managing SCM from the perspective of goods to orientation towards providing better services to customers.

Core Concept, Definition and Scope of Logistics

Logistics is the function that enables the flow of materials from suppliers into an organisation through operations within the organisation out to the customers. It is derived from the Greek word 'logistikos', which means 'to reason logically'. It basically consists of all operations required for goods (both tangible and intangible) to be made available in markets or at specific destinations.

According to the Council of Logistic Management (USA), 'Logistics is the process of planning, implementing and controlling the efficient, effective flow and storage of goods, services and related information from the point of origin to the point of consumption for the purpose of conforming the customer requirements'.[2]

The Council of Supply Chain Management Professionals (CSCMP), the largest professional organisation in logistics, has provided the most useful definition of logistics, and according to that 'Logistics management is that part of the supply chain management that plans, implements and also controls the efficient and effective forward and reverse flows as well as storage of goods, services and other related information between the point of origin and the point of consumption in order to meet the customers' requirements'.

> Logistics management activities will typically include both inbound and outbound transportation management, fleet management, warehousing, materials handling, logistics network design, inventory management, order fulfilment, planning of supply and demand as well as management of third party service providers.
>
> To varying degrees, the logistics function also includes sourcing and procurement, production planning and scheduling, packaging and assembly, and customer service. It is involved in all levels of planning and execution – strategic, operational and tactical.

Based on this, it can be said that logistics management is an integral function which coordinates and optimises all logistics activities with the other functions in the business, including sales and marketing, productions, operations and manufacturing, finance and information technology.[3]

The early years of the twenty-first century were characterised by a slow evolution from logistics to supply chain management in both academic and business circles.

Small and medium-sized companies have been seen to be slower in terms of accepting the emerging concept of supply chain management. However, large professional organisations continued to be active in assisting academicians and practitioners in the logistics and supply chain discipline.

The logistics side is well represented by the CSCMP. The CSCMP defines supply chain management as follows: 'Supply chain management encompasses the planning and management of all activities involved in sourcing and procurement, conversion, and all logistics management activities' (CSCMP, 2013). The handbook *Transportation and Logistics Basics* states: 'The supply chain includes all partners in the logistics process. The idea is to have integrated information sharing among all trading partners (vendors, manufacturers, and customers)' (Southern, 1997, 248).

In business terms, logistics means the physical movement of goods from the supplier point to the receiver point. Based on practical need, integrated organically the variety of the basic functional activities including transportation, storage, loading and unloading, handling, package, distribution and information management, etc., are originally integrated based on the practical needs of the business.

Basic Elements of Logistics

Whereas the term 'logistics' covers a very wide area of activities and functions as discussed earlier, the basic elements of logistics include the following functions:

1 Transportation
2 Warehousing
3 Inventory management
4 Packaging and utilisation and
5 Information and communication

Logistics as a Discipline

Logistics, over the years, has evolved as a discipline or management science, and it covers strategic planning, forecasting, material handling, warehousing, transportation, distribution and operation research. Logistics now is a multidisciplinary function. The scope of study of logistics as a discipline depends also on the type of logistics, including logistics costs and financing and third-party logistics (TPL).

Types of Logistics

We can see that logistics is involved in every human endeavour and activity. Some of the activities where logistics is the key to meeting the objectives such as war logistics and disaster logistics have become independent areas or disciplines for study now. There are activities and services where logistics will determine the performance and success, which include tourism

20 *Evolution of Integrated Supply Chain and Logistics Management*

logistics and medical logistics. Broadly, we can have the following types of logistics, which is only indicative but not exhaustive.

- Business logistics: moving cargo
- General logistics: moving cargo and moving people

The activities involved in managing logistics function for moving cargo which we consider as business logistics will be different from when it has to be for moving people. Although transportation is common function in both, their objective and criteria of performance would be different.

We normally refer to moving cargo or business logistics in this book. Although airlines or travel services are part of the logistics functions, we will refer to only business logistics in the sense that it relates to moving cargo or goods. Other types of logistics will include the following.

- Inbound logistics or procurement logistics
- Production logistics or internal logistics
- Outbound logistics or distribution logistics or marketing logistics
- Reverse logistics
- Green logistics
- Defence logistics
- Medical logistics
- Disaster logistics
- War logistics
- Agricultural logistics
- Tourism logistics

As the name indicates, the types of logistics have their own performance criteria and objectives as well as their own challenges to be managed, and each type of logistics now needs to be discussed in specialised training and academic programmes. A great deal of research activities is undertaken to make these logistics more cost-effective and efficient.

Logistics Activities and Goals

Logistics is about getting things to where they need to be and is much broader than transportation of goods from one location to another location. The overall goal of logistics thus would be to achieve a targeted level of customer service at the lowest possible cost. Logistics activities cover a wide range of tasks including the following:

- Network design
- Information processing
- Transportation
- Inventory management
- Warehousing, material handling and packaging

The operational objectives of a logistics system can have several objectives including:

- Rapid response
- Minimum variance

Evolution of Integrated Supply Chain and Logistics Management   21

- Minimum inventory
- Movement consolidation
- Quality
- Life cycle support

Logistics thus is a support function to operations. Also integrated logistics emphasises the need to coordinate with suppliers and customers.

Evolution of Logistics – The Historical Perspective

In the initial years, logistics was synonymous with transportation, but today transportation is only one of the subfunctions but a very important function of logistics. Logistics as a discipline has developed into a very important function and part of the end-to-end supply chain management. Today, logistics covers a wide range of activities and serves as a key integrator of SCM. It has developed during the past five decades although in the beginning it was relevant to military operations and the focus was on transportation.

However, during the past few decades, it has developed from narrowly defined distribution management to integrated management and linked to the global supply chains. The mission of logistics management is to plan and coordinate all activities to achieve desired levels of delivered service and quality at the lowest possible cost. In order to succeed in today's global marketplace, companies must be ever cognizant of these trends and develop a logistics management strategy that capitalises on the best-of-breed technology solution available today, so that they can meet the demands of their customers today and be well prepared for the future. Logistics function has evolved through five distinct phases as narrated later from transportation to physical distribution to business logistics.

1. 1950s Transportation Era

During the 1950s, the emphasis was on transportation, and at that time several university offered programmes with transportation as major, which did not include topics like logistics, physical distribution, physical supply and supply chain management. Computers or even calculators were not available to calculate or quantify the data, nor was there much discussion on the systems or total cost approach as we take today. Also, the idea of collaboration with vendors and suppliers or customers were not the priority or concern of the businesses in those days and the terminology logistics was used in military or defence context only whose primary focus and key imperative was getting the right supplies to the right place at the right time during wartime conditions.

James A. Houston (1996) surveyed the significance of logistics in the military and said, 'This work is a general historical survey of logistics in the American Military experience'.

Although initial work on logistics was focused on military logistics, today logistics covers a vast range of subjects.

2. The 1960s Physical Distribution Era

During the 1960s, all studies related to transportation were related to physical distribution and to a lesser degree on logistics. The National Council of Physical Distribution (NCPDM) USA representing professional physical distribution managers was formed in 1963, which changed into the Council of Logistics Management (CLM) in 1985 and again changed its name to the

22   Evolution of Integrated Supply Chain and Logistics Management

Council of Supply Chain Management Professionals (CSCMP) in 2004. Today, CSCMP has more than 14,000 members. And physical distribution (outbound logistics) and physical supply (inbound logistics) were considered as two distinct functions.

During this decade, physical distribution had received a lot of attention in the literature. And one of the first textbooks that focused on physical distribution and logistics was published. (One of the earlier textbooks that dealt with physical distribution and logistics during that decade was titled *Physical Distribution Management Logistics Problems of the Firm* written by Smykay et al. (1961), which focused on physical distribution and logistics was published during this decade.) And this subject got a great deal of attention from researchers during the 1960s. The first issue of the *Transportation* journal was published in 1961 by the American Society of Traffic and Transportation and in 1966. US President Lyndon B. Johnson signed Public Law 89–670 establishing the Department of Transportation, and Alan S. Boyd was selected as the National Secretary of Transportation.

> During this decade, a great deal of emphasis was laid on the importance of logistics in economy and business, and as a consequence a lot of academic activities were seen to have been initiated.

3.   The 1970s Physical Supply and Physical Distribution

During the early 1970s, physical supply or materials management, which is basically inbound logistics, received considerable attention. Later in the decade, there was a move to combine physical distribution with physical supply to emphasise the much broader concept of logistics management. During that time, there was advancement of basic concepts of logistics, and thus we found that universities and academic journals and textbooks as well as professional organisations all contributed to make this a productive decade for the development of logistics as a discipline that we know today.

Rail and roads are the most important modes of transport of goods within many countries as well as in international logistics operation, and their cost, performance criteria, service quality, effectiveness and efficiency etc. received attention.

4.   The 1980s Transportation Deregulation, Physical Distribution

By the 1980s, the term 'physical distribution' was phased out and the term 'logistics' was emphasised. To cite an example, the authors James C. Johnson and Donald F. Wood had even changed the title of their textbook *Contemporary Physical Distribution* to *Contemporary Physical Distribution and Logistics* in 1982.

5.   The 1990s Business Logistics

During the 1990s, business logistics continued to be an important discipline, and most of the cost-focused businesses became aware of the opportunities for savings in cost through better negotiations with their freight carriers and implementation of the system approach and total cost concept to management.

During that time, many transport companies also picked up the concept of logistics function and were trying to promote the idea that they were not simply transport companies or truck operators and tried to position themselves in the market that they provide total logistics solutions. During the same time, the major factors affecting logistics were developments in electronics and communication technology such as the Internet and Electronic Data Interchange (EDI). Also, there was growth with regard to third-party logistics organisations, and strategic alliances and partnerships and businesses started to view the logistics function as an integral component of their overall business strategy.

Logistics management as a discipline got so important that a leading *Journal of Supply Chain Management* published a lead article titled 'Thirty Five Years of the Journal of Supply Chain Management: Where Have We Been and Where Are We Going?' (Carter and Ellram, 2003) This article provided a much greater understanding of the evolution of purchasing and supply research during the journal's existence from 1965 to 1999. The authors concluded that the legal and regulatory issues were the major focus during the earlier years from the 1960s through the 1970s. Procurement function was considered important during the later 1970s. The areas of importance during the 1990s included procurement strategy, strategic impact on business through purchasing as well as the role of procurement in new product development, involvement of purchasing function in supplier or vendor development and strategic supplier alliances. And only after 1994, the emphasis was on the broader areas of supply chain issues.

Procurement and Outsourcing Key Focus for Cost Competitiveness in Past Decade

As we understand now, logistics is part of total supply chain management. In the era of globalisation, businesses were facing stiff competition from players around the world and in order to compete in that global environment businesses were constantly struggling to improve on competitiveness. One of the key criteria of competitiveness was delivering goods and services at lower cost than competition. In the past decade, businesses focused on procurement functions to reduce the procurement cost and a significant result was achieved. In the past decade itself, we have seen a shift in manufacturing operations where it is costing the least, and you know that China has emerged as the choice destination for global manufacturing. Businesses also have resorted to outsourcing the manufacturing or production function. Most of the large multinational corporations have now stopped manufacturing themselves and are sourcing from cheaper and smaller contract packers to reduce the cost of goods and services. And that too – contract packers were identified close to the customers' cluster to further reduce the distribution, redistribution and customer servicing costs. Material procurement functions also have now been done through e-auctions to get the most competitive rates. There are numerous developments taking place using technology to reduce \product cost, and this area seems to be totally exploited. In procurement functions, bill discounting and competitive discounting are now being practised to make the entire process of procurement more cost-effective and competitive.

Incremental Value Delivery through Effective Logistics Management

Currently, the entire focus of the business community is on logistics, which acts as a critical chain in the entire end-to-end supply chain management. We will gradually understand the role of international logistics in terms of its capability to deliver superior value.

And, therefore, let us clarify the core concept of value. Value is defined as benefits divided by cost. The benefits include both tangible and intangible benefits. Intangible benefits are associated with the brand. And cost would mean the cost of acquiring the product. You can, therefore, see that value can be improved either by increasing the benefits or by decreasing the cost or even both. And effective and efficient logistics management can impact both numerators and denominators positively and thereby can improve the value delivered very significantly.

24 *Evolution of Integrated Supply Chain and Logistics Management*

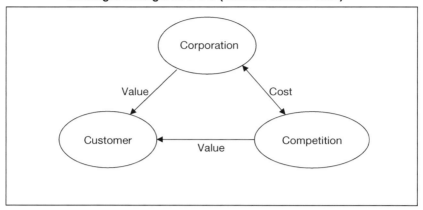

Figure 2.3 Corporation and Competition Differentiate Only on Cost

While effective and efficient logistics management can create incremental value in the business, creating value alone is not enough, it is also essential that you capture that value so created and deliver that for the customers' benefit. Only then business results will be forthcoming. In this connection, Kenichi's strategic 3Cs model (Ohmae, 1982) makes abundant sense that the corporation and competitor are both trying to deliver value to the customers but they themselves only differentiate by costs (Figure 2.3).

Strategic Triangle of 3Cs (Kenichi Ohmae, 1982)

The practical significance of Strategic Triangle 3Cs is that your 'corporation' has to perform against your 'competition' by delivering better and higher value to 'customer' based on the differential cost between your product against that of your competitor.

Peter Drucker (1962) long ago had said that logistics is the most neglected area till now. Businesses are trying to learn to improve that function. A lot of work has been done in the recent past in this area, and today we understand logistics in a much broader sense of the term.

Theoretical Foundations of International Logistics

Let us now discuss how international logistics has evolved over the years and the theoretical foundations of international logistics, which would mean as to understand how several factors that have led to internationalisation of logistics management.

Four key management functions of logistics management within the company like any other businesses are operational, financial, marketing and informational. When such systems of inter-linked companies are located all over the world and when one such function is shared, it will be called international logistics.

Operational cooperation at an international scale often has similar objectives like lean management or agile management. Using shared service like IT services or HR services at much lower cost and shared risks with consequential benefits. In such an environment, businesses often apply similar concepts of inventory management such as co-managed inventory (CMI), vendor management inventory (VMI), collaborative planning, forecasting and replenishment

Evolution of Integrated Supply Chain and Logistics Management   25

(CPFR). The environmental concern and regulatory issues in many countries encourage the concept of green logistics and reverse logistics.

The other triggering factors for international logistics are using similar methods of goods flow management like JIT and Kanban. The other factors include the implementation of the latest transportation technologies and tracking system, implementation of latest warehouse management systems and technologies, automated control and monitoring system, use of robots and artificial intelligence and so on. Other factors responsible may include uniform measures and standardisation of methods and processes and construction of vast computer networks, implementation of modern communication system, video conferencing, internet etc. with an overall objective to improve the functional efficiency of the entire interlinked organisation itself.

The global forces have also compelled businesses to collectively improve things and operations such as joint cost reduction programmes and joint financial control and management, including cost control. Marketing cooperation such as making a common face and image and making a common bid to make it more competitive using collective strengths. Also using integrated IT system that supports and facilitates in pricing and policy areas and also use Global Data Synchronisation Network (GDSN) and exchange of information via EDI.

Importance of Logistics in Economy

Why logistics is so important for the economy of a country? Globally logistics is about 10% of the GDP. In the USA it is about 8%; in India, 15%; in China, 12%; in Slovenia, 11%; and in Germany it is 9%. What is important is that logistics cost has a relationship with the economic health of a nation. The logistics cost also has a direct relationship with the status of the infrastructure in a country. Poor infrastructure and complex tax structure cost of logistics in India is still quite high when compared to other developed countries of the world.

It has been established that Logistics Performance Index (LPI) is correlated with the country's international trade performance. Country's with stronger logistics performance generally tend to see a higher percentage of their overall services export although it flattens after achieving a peak level performance. In India logistics infrastructure are now developing and it is still poor resulting into high logistics cost in the business. Because of poor logistics infrastructure, many large public projects get delayed resulting into time and cost overrun. In fact, most of our large projects, as per planning commission's report incurred huge overrun up to three times of original budgeted cost of the project and main reason could be logistics failure. Many hydel power projects get delayed just because it was found that the road leading to the project site is not suitable to take the load of large turbine to be carried to the site for generation of power which was not originally visualised when project was planned and constructing yet another road can come under the purview of many agencies including state government including other local bodies which is time consuming to overcome due to complexity and other associated issues and problems including legal issues that need to be resolved. The result is delay and huge cost overrun.

There are many firm-level data which prove the point. For example, Shepherd (2011) has reported that poorer trade facilitation data as measured by longer lead times of export and import are always associated with a higher level of trade-related corruption, as poor performance always acts as an incentive to flout the rules by paying money.

26 Evolution of Integrated Supply Chain and Logistics Management

World Competitiveness

Competitiveness has a direct relationship with the level and state of logistics infrastructure.

It has been also reported that a variety of trade business environment constraints affect trade performance and logistics costs as well as competitiveness measurement in the international market. Similarly, Li and Wilson (2009) also demonstrated that time to export is an important determinant of firm-level trade behaviour and competitiveness.

Competitiveness is normally measured at three levels: country level, industry category level and firm level. Country-level competitiveness impacts all players similarly, whereas industry-category-level competitiveness impacts all players in the same category (e.g. steel or cement) similarly. But companies compete with each other at the firm level and, therefore, managing firm-level competitiveness effectively demands that logistics parameters are managed better than others.

Logistics cost has a direct bearing on a country's competitiveness and an organisation's profitability. For a country, an improved infrastructure results in an efficient logistics sector, which encourages investment from domestic as well as international investors fuelling production and consumption and, therefore, the economic growth. India's logistics infrastructure has developed over the years, which has attracted new investment resulting in faster economic growth and development. A case on India's logistics industry covering current status and future growth has been discussed in this chapter to indicate that improved logistics infrastructure in India has helped the country to attract more inflow of capital in the form of foreign direct investment (FDI).

For an organisation, efficient logistics management reduces the cost of delivering products, increases trade, opens new markets and improves sales, revenue and profit margins.

World Competitiveness report defines competitiveness as the ability to increase market share, profit and growth in value added service and to stay competitive for a longer duration. Reducing logistics costs and ensuring faster delivery to customer premises, therefore, can increase enterprise competitiveness. Logistics, therefore, has a distinct role in enterprise competitiveness (Figure 2.4).

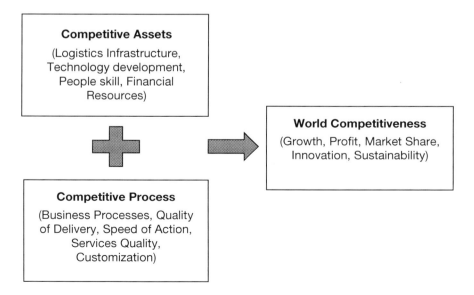

Figure 2.4 Dependence of World Competitiveness on Logistics

Competitive assets and competitive processes can only help you to get the benefits of world competitiveness. Competitive assets can include logistics, infrastructure, technology development, people skill and financial resources; competitive processes can include business processes, quality of delivery, speed of action, service quality and level, and customisation; and world competitiveness would ensure market share, growth, profit and sustainability. This has been demonstrated in Figure 2.4.

Growing Indian Logistics Industry to Support Country's Economic Growth

A decade ago, Indian logistics and infrastructure were poor in comparison to those in developed countries, and Indian goods were not globally competitive. Our logistics cost in relation to the sales revenue was much higher. But during the past decade or so significant investment was made in this sector, and many large infrastructure projects were implemented in public–private partnership mode. Many new projects are also under implementation. That has helped the country in terms of faster economic growth.

The Indian logistics industry is on a growth path. According to the rating agency ICRA, the Indian logistics industry is expected to grow at the rate of 8–10% over the medium term, which is a significant growth over the earlier five years' CAGR of 7.8%. The logistics industry in India was estimated to be around USD 160 billion, and post-GST implementation, this estimate was revised to about USD 215 billion in the next two years, according to the Economic Survey 2017–2018. According to the Global Ranking of the World Bank's 2016 LPI, India jumped to the 35th rank in 2016 from the 54th rank in 2014 in terms of overall logistics performance index. The World Bank Survey, in fact, revealed that India's logistics sector has improved its performance in all six parameters: efficiency of the clearance process by border control agencies, including customs; quality of trade- and transport-related infrastructure covering ports, railroads, roads and IT; ease of arranging competitively priced shipments; competence and quality of logistics services (transport operators and customs brokers); ability to track and trace consignments; and timeliness of shipments in reaching destination within the scheduled or expected delivery time.

Air Cargo Sector Witnessed Significant Growth

Indian air cargo sector has witnessed unprecedented growth in the past few years. As per the latest report of CRISIL, India's air cargo segment grew 14–15% in the fiscal year 2018, up from 12% growth in the previous year. With the support of enhanced connectivity, improved infrastructure and regulatory environment, this sector is expected to grow even further in the next five years. The government policy is also supportive, which can be seen from the initiatives taken to boost growth in the sector including the recent National Civil Aviation Policy, which has given a major thrust to boost air cargo business in view of rising e-commerce activities and exports. Besides, Civil Aviation Ministry, Government of India, has set up Air Cargo Logistics Promotion Board with the objective to ensure efficiency, reduce cost and improve inter-ministerial coordination for growth. In addition, significant investment in infrastructure and technology by the government authorities has also supported the growth trajectory.

Hurdles Still to Overcome

Although there are improvements on various parameters, in a competitive scenario India has to further improve related to infrastructure and logistics costs and availability of skilled manpower to emerge as a global air cargo hub. The other obstacles include the lack of common policies across

28   *Evolution of Integrated Supply Chain and Logistics Management*

all sectors of transportation and logistics within India. Also, border control processes in India are still tedious and time-consuming, adding to delays and costs. The cost of logistics to GDP should be about 8%, but in India it is still over 14%. This increases with more regulatory intervention and more touch points in the movement of cargo within the country, although some argue that the cost could be lowered by increasing the business scale. However, with the enabling policies, entrepreneurs get enthusiastic to invest more in business activities, which in turn can make the business scale bigger.

Many initiatives from the private sector also help in terms of catalysing the growth. For example, all systems must be process-driven without human intervention. Indian logistics players can collaborate with their counterparts in developed countries to develop cost-effective logistics models with the infusion of technology to benefit from the projected growth environment in India. The flexible solution in warehousing, based on the concept that you pay only when you make use of the facilities as well as leased warehouse avoiding huge investment to start with and implementing effective WMS and automation, will help in accelerating the growth process.

Government Initiatives

The Indian logistics industry has really grown during the past five years, and GST implementation has also created a positive impact; as a result, more and more corporations are consolidating their operation by moving closer to the consumption centres, thereby driving the demand for the larger warehouse. Leasing activity was primarily driven by the expansion and consolidation of businesses such as e-commerce, TPL, retail, engineering and manufacturing, which together accounted for more than 75% of the leasing reported in recent surveys. The grant of infrastructure status to the logistics and warehousing sector has in fact increased investors' interest, as it has helped developers to gain access to infrastructure lending at easier terms and with enhanced limits. Further, the government has also set up the National Investment and Infrastructure Fund (NIIF) in partnership with certain domestic and international investors as a quasi-sovereign wealth fund with a corpus of INR 0.4 trillion. Relaxation of FDI norms has further created a positive impact on the investment climate in the country's logistics sector. Also, the government has proposed to develop 35 multimodal logistics parks, which will ease the movement of freight and reduce transportation costs to spur further growth in the sector. Another initiative is to increase the load capacity of heavy vehicles by 20–25% and bring it to par with global standards, which will reduce the logistics cost. The government's plan to develop a National Logistics Information Portal which will be a single online window to link seven ministries including railways and highways under one portal will also be helpful for various stakeholders in the logistics industry.

These initiatives have led to the addition of over 20 million sq. ft new supply (both A and B grades) to enter the market by the end of 2019. The entry of various private equity firms and foreign players in the Indian logistics market would boost quality supply, propelling the demand. Cities such as Mumbai, Pune and Chennai have attracted major investments including Delhi-NCR and Bengaluru.

Some Mega Trends Paving the Way for Logistics Sector Growth

The new trends which will have significant growth in logistics sectors are seen to be the following:

- Demand-driven supply chain
- Robotics increasingly seen to be helping to reduce cost and improve efficiency

- Omni-channel logistics solutions
- Autonomous trucks to take logistics forward
- Blending of logistics and technology services
- Internet of things strengthening the SCM
- Hyper-local supply chains
- Blockchain technology

E-Commerce Logistics: Driving the Change

With the robust growth in consumer demand for online purchases, the Indian e-commerce industry has emerged as one of the most dynamic and fast-paced growth industries and is at its inflection point. The rapid growth of smartphones and internet connectivity across the country, especially in tier-II and tier-III cities, has led to the growth of online retailers, and thus direct beneficiary of this is the logistics industry. Whereas many retailers are still losing money, the logistics industry including the courier industry has shown a significant positive impact. Developments such as digital payments, analytics-driven customer engagement by the use of artificial intelligence (AI) and machine learning tools, and government-led initiatives have supported the growth of this sector. The biggest challenge, however, in this cycle of the supply chain depends on last-mile delivery. Connect India is committed to designing the largest and most robust last-mile distribution e-ecosystem by creating a model through 100,000 bricks-and-mortar store entrepreneurs, covering up to panchayat-level distribution, which will create proximity to the customers in rural India, which is the future of India. However, the challenge here is skilled manpower, higher fuel costs impacting margin due to increased cost and lack of volumes in many rural areas.

Inland Waterways

The Ministry of Shipping aims to double the share of transportation of cargo through coastal shipping lines and inland water navigation by 2025 under Sagarmala programme. The estimated volume of the total cargo transported by coastal shipping in 2017–2018 is 110 million tonnes. Coastal shipping has also experienced a growth of 9% CAGR over the past three years as against 4.5% CAGR over the preceding three years. The National Waterways Act, 2016, has declared 106 new national waterways in addition to 111 national waterways across 24 states with a total navigable network of over 20,000 km of waterways as it exists now (Cargo Connect, Vol IX, Nov 2018).

Ocean Shipping

Shipping lines have experienced consolidation over the past few years. Supply is still high with most services having a higher capacity than demand. The higher capacity and lower demand lead to price competition and rate cutting. Most carriers are expecting larger vessels to be delivered during the next one to two years, and some are even placing new orders. The pressure on rates will continue unless demand moves up significantly. The industry is working on digitising the entire shipping value chain to positively impact the shipper, the consigner and the consignee, and provide much greater control of their shipments by offering instant price quotes and bookings, transparency and tracking, simplified paperwork and proactive customer care.

30 Evolution of Integrated Supply Chain and Logistics Management

India Road Trasport: Adapting Digitisation

The Indian transportation industry is continually growing at a CAGR of 15%. Over 7 million goods vehicles are moving around the country, and the freight volume has reached 1325 billion tonne-km, which is expected to double by 2025. India spends about 14% of its GDP on transportation in comparison to 6–8% in developed countries. The industry is still very fragmented, traditional and unorganised. However, the Indian trucking industry has already started accepting digitisation in its business, and online truck booking is now common. In the trucking industry, the spot market plays a pivotal role in India. Both big and small players have to reach out to the spot market to fulfil their daily transport requirements. Technology-enabled players have taken a substantial chunk of the market in the past three to four years. Companies are now seen using machine learning (ML) and AI to predict the kind of volume which would happen at routes and lanes.

The Future

Some of the researchers suggest that the logistics industry of India, which was at INR 6.4 trillion in FY 2017, would grow at a CAGR of 13% over the next three years to get to INR 9.2 trillion by FY 2020. The government is also extending a lot of support. The Ministry of Commerce and Industry has decided to give a one-time funding of INR 8 million to the sector for building up initial infrastructure and also phase-wise support of INR 33.9 million in four years to bring down the logistics cost from its current level to 10% in four years' time. This is a significant move to boost the competitiveness of the sector to provide greater impetus for its further growth.

Projects Worth INR 2.35 Trillion Under Sagarmala in Maharashtra Alone

The Ministry of Shipping is planning to undertake work worth INR 2.35 trillion under the Sagarmala project in Maharashtra alone. Eight projects entailing an investment of INR 53.84 billion have already been completed, while 45 other projects involving an investment of INR 270 billion are in various stages of implementation. This investment includes INR 1 trillion for waterways development. At least five rivers in the state are included for exploiting potential of water transport in India. An Indian company has forged a joint venture with the Russian firm United Shipbuilding for ethanol-powered 'watercrafts' in the Ganga River.

Port Blair Airport to Get a New Terminal Building

Port Blair airport, which is now known as Veer Savarkar Airport, will have a new terminal building soon. A world-class terminal building is coming up at the airport at an estimated cost of INR 4.17 billion by 2020. The built-up area of the new terminal will be 40,000 sq. m and will be able to handle 1200 (600 domestic and 600 international) passengers at a time during the peak hours. The new building will have 3 floors, 10 elevators, 6 escalators, 28 check-in counters and an in-line scan system for handling baggage with 3 conveyor belts at the arrival section (2 for domestic and 1 for international). The entire terminal will have 100% natural lighting, which will be achieved by skylight along the roof.

Cochin Shipyard Chalks Out Biggest Expansion with INR 17.99 Billion Dry Dock

Cochin Shipyard Ltd is India's biggest state-owned shipbuilder by dock capacity and will start work on a new dry dock at a cost of INR 17.99 billion. The dry dock will generate employment opportunities for 2000 people, directly or indirectly, in core shipbuilding and ancillary

Evolution of Integrated Supply Chain and Logistics Management   31

industries. It will also help Cochin in diversifying its product portfolio to build large, complex and technology-intensive vessels such as LNG vessels, jack-up rigs, drill ships, dredgers and a second indigenous aircraft carrier of much higher capacity than the one it is building for the Indian Navy. The dry dock can accommodate aircraft carriers of 70,000 tonnes docking displacement and tankers and merchant vessels of 55,000 tonnes docking displacement. Larsen & Toubro was awarded the turnkey contract for the new dry dock for INR 12.99 billion.

Technology Applications in Indian Logistics Industry

The Indian logistics industry is approximately USD 215 billion. After implementation of GST supported by the favourable policy of the government, the progress seems to be faster and racing ahead of its global counterpart. Logistics companies across the globe have been investing in product innovations, business expansions and new facilities to keep up with growing demand and strengthening their foothold in the industry. Investment in technology is one of the major drivers leading the growth story. This includes investment in automation, robotics, wearable technology, drones, self-driving vehicles, blockchain and IoT. Industry experts have been appreciating and understanding the way technology is transforming the industry. It is quite evident that those who are not embracing the technology will be facing obsolescence. A report by Cisco has estimated a Trillion $ opportunity for the logistics industry in 2022. The logistics industry is now keeping the customers informed at every stage and leg where their products are, which helps them manage their inventory better, thereby reducing the cost towards carrying inventory in the system. Blockchain technology has a huge potential in the Indian logistics industry in terms of cutting costs and creating transparency.

Blockchain is highly secure and safe, and it allows all stakeholders of a supply chain including carriers, shippers, custom authorities and transporters to communicate effectively, safely and most cost-effectively. While blockchain was invented way back in 2008, its usage has gained prominence now. Considering the current dynamic nature of the Indian logistics industry, technology is being widely adopted and used throughout the supply chain, and blockchain would be a game changer as it is enabling smart contracts between players, automating the processes of purchase, and cutting time and cost. Storing all transaction information in one single ledger dramatically improves transparency, cutting inefficiencies and risk of tempering, which the supply chain industry always had to deal with. Every piece of every consignment as it moves in the Hub and Spoke network at every touch point both in and out is tracked. Every vehicle in the network is also tracked through a centralised network monitoring system using GPS. Artificial intelligence and machine learning are used for tracking high-risk consignments and data is used proactively to control the performance of the network across the 27,000 origin-destinations pairs, confirms the MD of Spotcom Logistics Pvt Ltd.

Technology also has metamorphically changed the way warehouses function these days. Warehouses are more agile, dynamic and smart. The warehouses are guided by algorithms which are influenced by AI and ML. The industry is on the cusp of a new era of automation that will bring rapid changes from the warehouse and loading dock to the road.

Forklifts have been a vital component of warehouses for decades, and we are now going to see a shift towards programming this share of the supply chain. Amazon is a leading example in this space, thanks to the acquisition of Kiva Systems, now known as Amazon Robotics. As Amazon and other companies have shown, implementing robotics and autonomous machinery in the folder can reduce delivery time to just 24 to 48 hours. Autonomous forklifts and robots can pick up products much faster than humans, which means companies need not have to keep forklift operators. Material-handling systems providers are providing customised solutions for the logistics sector,

32 *Evolution of Integrated Supply Chain and Logistics Management*

automatic storage and retrieval systems, automated guided vehicles, augmented reality tools and warehouse management systems that are integrated with automation tools, data capture tools, data generation and others. Augmented reality will be utilised to render warehouses paperless. AR tools will assist warehouse employees in locating shipments and fastening the overall process of storage and retrieval, without depending on hard copies of shipment location information. Other technologies that are going to change the warehousing sector include cloud computing for warehouse management systems, distributed order management systems, big data and analytics for inventory and demand forecasting etc.

The potential to utilise artificial intelligence to improve decision-making transform business models and networks and modify customer experiences. A recent industry survey indicated that 59% of the establishments are still assembling data to shape their AI tactics, while the rest have already made advancements in directing or implementing AI solutions; using AI appropriately will result in big digital dividends.

As technologies continue to carve out their role in the global logistics industry, we are likely to see unimagined levels of optimisation throughout the supply chain – from manufacturing to warehousing to delivery. The Indian logistics industry is embracing new generation technologies to integrate with the requirement of faster movement of goods and merchandise of global trade.

Logistics Infrastructure Helping Economic Growth

India is now considered to be a promising emerging market and the fifth-largest global economy. It grew at an average annual rate of 6.6% in the past decade till 2019–2020. In 2022–2023 expected growth rate is 7.2%.

The cumulative amount of FDI received by India during 2015–2016 to 2019–2020 was around USD 312 billion, which was about 59% more than the total FDI of about USD 197 billion received during 2010–2011 to 2014–2015. FDI Equity inflow in manufacturing sectors has increased by 76% in FY 2021–2022 (USD 21.34 billion) compared to the previous FY 2020–2021 (USD 12.09 billion). This was possible because India has been identified as a major growth market. The logistics industry in India also attracted significant investment during this period and played an important role in the country's growth.

Over 7 million goods vehicles are moving around the country, and the freight volume has reached 1325 billion tonne-km, which is expected to double by the year 2025. India spends about 14% of its GDP on transportation in comparison to 6–8% by developed countries. We still have to improve the logistics efficiency in comparison to developed countries to be globally competitive.

Physical Infrastructure and SCM Performance

In some areas, the performance of a supply chain largely depends on the physical infrastructure in place. A supply chain becomes inefficient if the infrastructure is not up to the mark or is deficient. For example, for an agricultural or horticultural supply chain, cold chain storage facilities and infrastructure are the key determinants of the performance of the agricultural supply chain. Industries which use agricultural or horticultural products as raw materials incur higher costs resulting from poor infrastructure for managing the inventories from the stage of post-harvesting of the crops. These infrastructures are normally developed either by publicly funded organisations, by the government or even by private companies, and the efficiency and effectiveness of these infrastructures determine the cost of the input and also the performance of the agro-based

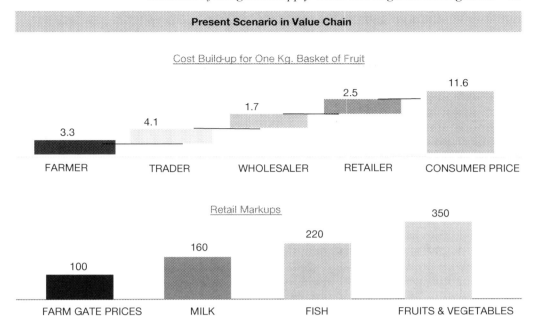

Figure 2.5 Cost Build-up and Trade Margins for Agro Commodities in India

industries, including food-processing industries. In India, an agricultural supply chain is still in its infancy, resulting in very high farm-level wastage. We have a scenario where the farm gate price, as well as the cost of farm labour, is one of the lowest in the world, but the market price or price at which these agricultural items are delivered to customers is almost 3.5–4 times the farm gate price (Baisya, 2012), as shown in Figure 2.5.

The agricultural supply chain needs the support of necessary infrastructure for reducing wastage. The poor infrastructure results in high logistics costs, pushing the price of agricultural commodities and making them globally uncompetitive. The agricultural logistics effectiveness is thus a key to the growth of agro-based industries in India. These are as discussed further.

Cold Chain Facilities

For managing an integrated supply chain in the agriculture sector, cold chain facilities are essential to control the quality, shelf life and wastage of the primary agricultural produce. For this purpose, we need the following:

- Industrial cold stores in the production zones
- Refrigerated vehicles for long-distance transport
- Refrigerated room in wholesale markets

Field Heat Removal Facilities

Upon harvesting, the temperature of the crops should be brought down as soon as possible before storage in cold chain facilities, which normally will help in extending the shelf life of the

34 *Evolution of Integrated Supply Chain and Logistics Management*

crop. These facilities are normally not available at the field site. However, as soon as possible the harvest should be brought to the storage centres or warehouses, where temperature control facilities can help in extending the storage life of the product. There are various low-cost technologies available for the storage of agricultural crops to extend the life and quality of the crop. The key concern of storage of grains is to bring down the product temperature upon harvesting by immediately transferring the crop to a controlled temperature warehouse as the major fraction of the heat load need to be removed that influences the rate of reactions during storage.

These facilities do not exist in India as required or have very limited availability, resulting in high post-harvest losses and also higher costs of the agricultural and horticultural crops, which in turn make the agro-based industry non-competitive in the global market.

Warehousing Facilities

To store the grains and other agricultural crops, we also need adequate warehousing facilities which should provide ideal storage conditions to maintain the quality of the grain and also temperature and humidity conditions as well as proper pest control and other infestation control facilities to ensure that crops are not damaged during storage.

Criticality of Supply Chain Efficiency in Agriculture Sector – A Case of Food Corporation of India: (TOI Report)[4]

In the past three years, the Food Corporation of India (FCI) has allowed 46,658 tonnes of food grains to rot in 1889 warehouses across the country. Again, 143.74 tonnes were reported stolen. *Times of India* reported stolen. The *Times of India* reported[5] that this much of food grains could have fed 800,000 people from priority families under the National Food Security Act for an entire year. It could have fed 10% of Bengaluru's population or 6% of Mumbai's citizens if each person received 5 kg of food grains per month.

Such problems have been plaguing the FCI for decades, and it is trying to reduce the buffer storage. A study by the London-based Institution of Mechanical Engineers (IME) on global food wastage found that about 21 million tonnes of wheat go wasted in India. The Indian government buys food grains from the farmers but does not have the space to store them. The Food Corporation has an insufficient number of grain silos (modern storage facilities), so grains are stored in outdoor depots across the country. This makes grains prone to rodents, moisture, birds and pests. Unexpected rainstorms and bad weather make matters even worse.

FCI has an excess of 15.65 million tonnes (MMT) of food grains of the prescribed buffer norms as of April 1, 2016. But according to the norm, which was reviewed in January 2015, FCI should have stocked only 21.04 MMT of food grains as of April 1, but had 36.65 MMT. The problem of storing additional grains plagued FCI in later years also.

One of the reasons for the wastage of food is that grains are not moved out of the warehouses in time and distributed. Due to this inefficiency in transporting grains out of the warehouses and to the ration shops, massive quantities of grains pertaining to the years 2008–2009 were found in the FCI warehouses even in March 2012.

In June 2012, the grain stock with the state agencies had crossed 75 million tonnes for the first time in the country's history. However, the covered storage area available was only for 50 million tonnes, which would mean that 25 million tonnes of food grain would have to be kept in open storage with either kachcha or pucca plinths and thus would be exposed to large-scale damage and

Evolution of Integrated Supply Chain and Logistics Management   35

pilferage. How much would get damaged and lost is anyone's guess. The quality of the covered storage in many places was also questionable. While the record production would give satisfaction to many, when they see that a sizeable chunk of this stock is likely to get wasted as they would get soaked and damaged in rain it will be definitely a disappointment for everyone. However, if some measures are taken on war footing some quantity of that surplus could possibly be saved. This quantity is estimated to be about 9 to 10 million tonnes out of the surplus of 25 million tonnes. Still, the wastage to the extent of about 15 million tonnes is a distinct possibility and that itself is a huge loss. The initiative that the government could take was to provide incentives to state governments to transport the stock to various public distribution system (PDS) stock points so that those can be sold to the public through PDS.

A question normally that arises is, how did we get into this situation? Good monsoon in the earlier four years has resulted in increase in crop production from 231 million tonnes in 2007–2008 to 252 million tonnes in 2011–2012. But consumption of cereals has not been going up. The demand for cereals, in fact, has not gone up and on the contrary people are consuming more of protein and fruits and vegetables and less of cereal. Dietary habits have changed significantly over the years, thanks to the sustained campaign of food marketers. The export of wheat was banned in February 2007, and it was opened again only in September 2011 coupled with good harvest, which has led to the accumulation of stocks whereas the storage capacity has not increased commensurately. Some state governments, notable amongst those is Madhya Pradesh, which has given a bonus of INR 100 per quintal in wheat, which has thrown private operators out of the market, and government procurement has increased significantly from less than 2 million tonnes in 2009–2010 to more than 6 million tonnes in the year 2012. Rajasthan also followed the same example in 2012, and its procurement had increased by almost 194% in 2012–2013, compared to 2010–2011. Also states like Punjab and Haryana have levied much higher statutory levies on wheat and rice at 14.5% in Punjab and 12.5% in Haryana, which again pushed private traders out of the market and significantly pushed the state procurement upwards. It is like the state takeover of grain trade in these states, which had created an unprecedented problem and scarcity of storage space.

Rice could have been exported if we had encouraged export, possibly excess rice stock could have been taken care of. In 2011–2012, India was expected to export about 6.5 to 7 million tonnes of rice and the same performance could have been repeated in the year 2012–2013, making India the second-largest rice exporter in the world. But wheat export was not possible as Russian and Ukrainian wheat really reduced the price of wheat in global trade. As such real challenge was to store the wheat stock. The cost of carrying the stock, which includes storage and interest costs would be about 20%, and this amount could possibly be given as incentives to state governments to lift the stock and send that to PDS. The payment of bonuses by certain states as well as the demand of statutory levied by certain states have added to the problem by keeping private players out of the grain trade. FCI, therefore, is a source of loss of precious food grains for not having adequate storage facilities for storing grains. The scenario is the same even for fruits and vegetables and, as a result, India, as a country, loses a huge amount for not having the logistics infrastructure, which is so vital to the economy.

Inadequate storage facilities can result in huge losses to the exchequers. In a country where there are people who still don't have two square meals a day, losing such magnitude of grain due to shortage of storage space and resulting wastage is criminal. Such a thing can only happen because of not having the right procurement policies and also not having the required supply chain infrastructure. This is the state of affairs with respect

36　*Evolution of Integrated Supply Chain and Logistics Management*

to grain storage which can be stored at ambient storage conditions. The situation is still worse with respect to perishables where refrigerated storage conditions or cool chambers are required to store the surplus. This situation of food grains rotting at Food Corporation's warehouses which are ill-equipped for proper storage is not something new. A few years ago, it was reported that the government had approached the Delhi School of Economics for suggestions to manage the bumper crop for which FCI did not have even facilities to store and large-scale wastage and damage was inevitable. Economists from DSE suggested that surplus grains may be distributed free to the poor. Obviously, the government did not act on their advice but that would have been a good thing to do to give food free to people who are starving instead of allowing the food grains to rot for want of storage facilities.

The government is granting many incentives for setting up storage facilities including cold chains. I know a couple of entrepreneurs who have set up cold storage in northeastern regions. But they are not very happy with the utilisation of space as those cold storages are running less than 50% of their capacities. I asked them why they had gone for such projects without making any detailed study of the surplus stock to be stocked in the region. The reply was very simple. They said the government was giving a 50% subsidy on the cost of the project. Giving a blanket subsidy for locating the storage warehouse at any place has led to a very peculiar situation. On the one hand, we have inadequate infrastructure and, on the other hand we have unutilised space. This can happen only when the facilities created are not well planned following an appropriate strategy.

What we need is a comprehensive plan and actions. Sporadic decisions are not going to be yielding the expected result. The whole infrastructure will have a consequential impact on the price of the commodities as well as of fruits and vegetables, which in turn will influence the product prices in the market. And price is a key influencer on demand and thus the growth of the entire industry. A holistic view is thus necessary to be taken to build the supply chain infrastructure for the food industry. Only talking about the need for supply chain infrastructure is not enough, It needs to be comprehensively planned and implemented. The criticality of the infrastructural needs to be understood in view of what the industry needs and how it can be provided. The efficient supply chain is actually the backbone of the industry. The industry clearly understands the fact that over 70% of the cost of product is contributed by the material cost and, therefore, efficient supply chain management is the key to providing the competitive edge. And a large part of the infrastructure has to be provided, by design, by the government and that is the country's role to make the industry category competitive in global trade.

Innovations in Supply Chain

To make the supply chain efficient and competitive, there has to be constant innovations in every facet and interface of SCM starting from product development, procurement, production and distribution in order to have sustainable growth in revenue and profits. These innovation approaches need a company-wide programme and not isolated affairs of sporadic development taking a quick-fix approach. Not many companies have been able to achieve that objective although businesses are pursuing their own innovation agenda. In this connection, Proctor & Gamble seems to be ahead of others in the competition, which has helped them to triple the innovation success rate in a highly competitive market. Let us examine the model that P&G has been following to have key learning from their experiment and success stories.

How P&G Tripled Its Innovation Success Rate

Proctor & Gamble has a very elaborate innovation management and new product development practices, and the company takes direct feedback from its over three million customers with whom they interface to understand the customer expectations, which they take into consideration in its development and innovation efforts.

Tide is the biggest brand in the company's fabric and household care category. The laundry detergent is an almost 60-year-old detergent brand and still dominates its core markets but of late it is not growing fast enough as expected. But P&G pursued its systematic innovation-led strategic growth, which resulted in almost doubling its revenue from USD 12 billion to USD 24 billion. How could this be achieved through P&G creativity, speed and reliability? Their leaders devised a 'new growth factory' that is still ramping up. Already it has helped the company strengthen its core businesses and its ability to capture new-growth opportunities. P&G spends almost USD 2 billion on R&D, which is almost double the amount of what its nearest competitors spend. In spite of big investment in R&D, in the early 2000s, only 15% of its innovations were meeting their revenue and profit targets, and to address this, the company set about building organisational structures to systematise innovation to drive new growth targets. In 2004, Gil Cloyd, then chief technology officer, and A. G. Lafley, then CEO, tasked two P&G veterans John Leikhim and David Goulait, with designing a new growth factory whose intellectual underpinning would derive from the Harvard Business School Professor Clayton Christensen's disruption – innovation theory. They formed a group of new growth business guides to help teams working on disruptive projects. For example, this small group augmented an existing entity to create new brands and new business models and dedicated teams within the groups conducted market research, developed technology, created business plans and tested project-specific assumptions to produce a process manual containing step-by-step guidelines for creating new growth business. This manual describes opportunities and identifies requirements for success as well as monitors progress and makes go/no-go decisions for running demonstration projects for show casing the merging factory work. One of these was a line of pocket-size products called Swash, which can quickly refresh clothes. For example, someone in a hurry can give a not-quite-clean shirt a spray rather than putting it through the normal wash.

P&G's four types of innovation are sustaining, commercial, transformational-sustaining and disruptive. Sustaining innovations bring only incremental improvements in existing products and processes. Commercial innovations use creating marketing and promotional approaches to grow existing offering. Transformational-sustaining innovations reframe existing categories. They normally bring some fundamental changes to a business that can lead to some breakthroughs in the market. In 2009 P&G introduced a wrinkle reduction cream Olay Pro-X launching at USD 40, a bottle which was possibly a questionable strategy, but P&G went ahead as it was a clinically tested product and the first year's revenue was USD 250 million from food retailers and drug stores alone. The disruptive innovations represent new to the world business opportunities. A company enters entirely new businesses with radically new offerings as P&G did with Swiffer and Fabreze.

By 2008, P&G had a working prototype factory which was able to dramatically increase the innovation output by focusing the factory on fewer but bigger initiatives and in that direction. McDonald and Brown's team drove three critical improvements. First, it increased emphasis on transformational-sustaining innovations, which deliver major new benefits in the existing business

38   *Evolution of Integrated Supply Chain and Logistics Management*

category. Second, P&G strengthened organisational support for the formation of transformational – sustaining and disruptive – businesses. It established several new-business-creation groups, larger in size and scope than any previous growth-factory team, whose resources and management are kept carefully separate from the core business. These groups – dedicated teams led by a general manager – develop ideas that cut across multiple businesses and also pursue entirely new business opportunities. Third, P&G revamped its strategy development and review process. Innovation and strategy assessments had historically been handled separately. Now CEO, CTO and CFO explicitly link company, business and innovation strategies. This integration, coupled with new analyses of such issues as competitive factors that could threaten a given business, has provided more opportunities for innovation. The process has also prompted examinations of each unit's 'production schedule', or pipeline of growth opportunities, to ensure that it's robust enough to deliver against growth goals for the next seven to ten years.

P&G has also customised formulations for emerging markets. Ethnographic research showed that about 80% of consumers in India wash their clothes by hand. They had to choose between detergents that were relatively gentle on the skin but not that good at cleaning clothes, and more potent but harsher agents. With the problem clearly identified, in 2009 a team came up with Tide Naturals, which cleaned well without causing skin irritation. Mindful of the need in emerging markets to provide greater benefits at lower cost-'more or less' – P&G priced Tide Naturals 30% below comparatively effective but harsher products and that made Tide brand accessible to 70% of Indian consumers and has helped to significantly increase Tide's market share in India. Now Tide Dry Cleaners represents an entirely new business model. It started when a team began exploring ways to disrupt the dry-cleaning markets, using proprietary technologies and a unique store design grounded in insights about consumers' frustration with the existing options. Many cleaning establishments are dingy, unfriendly places. Customers have to park, walk and wait, and often the cleaners' hours are inconvenient. P&G alternative was bright, boldly coloured cleaners featuring specialised treatments, drive – through windows, and 24-hour storage lockers to facilitate after-hours drop-off and pick up. Tide's innovation efforts have been closely coordinated through regular dialogues among several leaders – CEO McDonald, CTO Brown, the vice Chair of the household business unit and the president of fabric care division (Brown and Anthony, 2011).

Lessons for Leaders:

Efforts to build a new growth factory in any company will fail unless senior managers create the right organisational structures, provide the proper resources, allow sufficient time for experimentation and learning, and personally engage themselves. That journey for P&G suggests six lessons for leaders looking to create new growth factories.

1 **Closely coordinate the factory and the core business:** Leaders sometimes see efforts to foster new growth as completely distinct from efforts to bolster the core. A healthy core produces a cash flow that can be invested in new growth. A core business is rich with capabilities that can support new-growth efforts. P&G has excellent relationships with major retailers. Those relationships are a powerful, hard-to-replicate asset that helps the factory expedite new growth opportunities. Some of the tools for managing core efforts, particularly those that track a project's progress, are also useful for managing new growth efforts and finally the factory's rapid learning approach often yields insights that can strengthen existing product lines. The critical

Evolution of Integrated Supply Chain and Logistics Management 39

discovery that babies who wore disposable diapers fell asleep 30% faster and slept 30 minutes longer than babies wearing cloth diapers was an obvious benefit for infants and their parents – this campaign helped make Pampers the number one brand in several emerging markets.

2 **Promote a portfolio mindset:** P&G communicates to both internal and external stakeholders that it is building a varied portfolio of innovation approaches ranging from sustaining to disruptive ones. It uses a set of master planning tools to match the pace of innovation to the overall needs of the business. It also deploys portfolio-optimisation tools that help managers identify and kill the least promising programs and nurture the best bets. Portfolio approach helps to set up the expectation that different projects will be managed, resourced and measured in different ways just as an investor would use different criteria to evaluate an investment opportunity.

3 **Start small and grow carefully**: Remember how the new growth factory began: with a simple two-day workshop, which is then followed by small-scale pilots in several business units before becoming a company-wide initiative. It also provides targeted experimentation. A staged approach also helps in avoiding any quick-fix solution, which will not be a lasting solution.

4 **Create new tools for gauging new businesses:** Anticipated and nascent markets are notoriously hard to analyse. P&G now conducts 'transaction learning experiments' or TLEs, in which a team 'makes a little and sells a little' thus letting consumers vote with their wallets. New sales organisations or new selling methods and processes can be experimented with before it is implemented company-wide.

5 **Make sure you have the right people doing the right work**: Building the factory forced P&G to change the way it staffed certain teams. At any given time, the company has hundreds of teams working on various innovation efforts. In the past, most teams consisted mainly of part-time members – employees who had other responsibilities pulling at them. But the disruptive and transformational-sustaining efforts require undivided attention as the old saying goes that nine women cannot make one baby in a month. There need to be people who wake up each day and go to sleep each night obsessed about the new business and new business models of growth but the team has to be small.

6 **Encourage intersections:** Successful innovation requires rich cross-pollination, both inside and outside the organisation. P&G's Connect + Develop program is part of a larger effort to intersect with other disciplines and gain new perspectives. P&G has shared people with noncompeting companies. In 2008 P&G and Google swapped two dozen employees for a few weeks. P&G wanted greater exposure to online models of business, and Google was interested in learning how to build power brands.

P&G also has engaged even more outside innovators. In 2010, P&G refreshed its Connect and Develop (C+D) goals. It has expanded the program to forge additional connections with government labs, universities, small- and medium-sized entrepreneurs, consortia and venture capital firms. It has also brought in outside talents. P&G traditionally promoted from within, but it recognised that total reliance on this approach could stunt its ability to create new growth business. So, it began bringing in high-level people to address needs beyond its core capabilities, as when it hired an outsider to run Agile Pursuits Franchising to acquire expertise in franchise-based business models, which would have otherwise taken years to build organically.

40   Evolution of Integrated Supply Chain and Logistics Management

P&G's efforts appear to be working well. Today 50% of its innovation efforts are meeting the profit and revenue targets as against only 15% earlier. Their experience tells us that although individual creativity can be unpredictable and uncontrollable, collective creativity can be managed. This innovation process can create a sustainable source of revenue growth – no matter how big a company becomes.

Dell's Direct Business Model of Virtual Integration

Dell has a very successful and well-performing global supply chain model of virtual integration – advantages of a tightly coordinated supply chain traditionally facilitated by vertical integration combined with focus and specialisation. Dell also has leveraged the investments others have made and focused on delivering solutions and systems to customers. They have been able to greatly take partner support to their advantage which has led them to manage fewer things, which would mean that only fewer things can go wrong. Suppliers' engineers are part of Dell's design team, and Dell also has a few partners who were selected to work in association with Dell to co-create significant value.

Dell is an example that enjoyed tremendous success based on its supply chain design, planning and operation by adapting its supply chain in response to shifts in technology and customer expectations.

With channel partners, Dell shares information on a real-time basis and stitches together a business with partners who are treated as if they are inside the company. The focus changes from how much inventory there is to how fast it is moving, which is in fact model of asset collecting risks around them one way or the other. Their product also requires limited or no testing for using Sony monitors.

Dell has only three manufacturing centres in Austin, Ireland and Malaysia. The information flow is on real-time and inventory levels, and replenishment needs sometimes are conveyed to vendors on an hourly basis. It also substitute information for inventory and ship only when the company has real demand from real end customers. It has clever segmentation and focuses on institutional markets – 70% to very large customers with annual purchases exceeding USD 1 million. From 1993 to 2006, Dell experienced unprecedented growth in both revenue and profits by structuring a supply chain that provided customers with customised PCs very quickly and at a very reasonable cost.

Dell had exited from retail business after making a wrong entry in 1989. Customer segmentation is managed by remaining close to customers and having access to valuable information. Demand forecasting is done with the involvement of partners and they developed a critical tool in demand forecasting. It helps global customers manage their total purchase of PCs by selling them a standard product globally. And Dell server loads software on customers' computers and meets customers' needs faster and more efficiently than any other model. This innovative virtual integration model worked well for them. By 2006, Dell had a net income of more than USD 3.5 billion on revenues of just over USD 56 billion. This success was based on two key supply chain features that supported rapid and low-cost customisation. First, Dell decided to sell directly to end customers, bypassing distributors and retailers, making it more cost-effective and responsive to customer demand. The second key aspect of Dell's supply chain was the centralisation of manufacturing and inventories in a few locations where final assembly was postponed until receipt of the confirmed order from the customer. Dell was also able to supply a large variety of PC configurations as required by the customers while keeping a very low level of component inventories.

Dell also responded to changing market environment when it was seen that customers were going for very low level of customisation and buying standard products and were seen to be satisfied with few standard models when they adjusted to the changing market structure by adjusting their supply chain with regard to both direct selling and building to order when they also started selling their PCs through retail chain like Walmart in the USA and GOME in China.

Chapter Summary

This chapter discussed the evolution of supply chain management and logistics management through the past few decades from their early stage of development as a discipline to what we understand today and also the core concept of integrated supply chain management in terms of its definition, scope, objectives and challenges. The key components of the SCM are discussed in detail with examples and short cases. The chapter also discussed why supply chain and logistics functions are so important for sustaining a business in the current context of a global competitive environment and how managing effectively these functions can help provide competitive advantage to the business. It also discussed why and how logistics management performance contributes to the country's economic growth. India's logistics industry and development have been discussed as a case study to show how investment and development of logistics infrastructure help the country's faster progress and economic development.

Key components and basic elements of SCM and logistics function were explained as well and various types of logistics were discussed. The complexity of integrated supply chain management has been demonstrated taking the case of Li & Fung. The chapter has covered in detail the evolution of logistics as a full-grown discipline and also outlined the importance of international logistics and its implications in business. Logistics which started initially as transportation gradually emerged as product distribution and finally as business logistics covering the scientific research and development work including the technology development and interface of various information technology and ERP in running modern businesses now. A brief mention was made of how robots as artificial intelligence are now being used for managing the logistics and warehouse functions, as well as material-handling functions in modern factories. Two case studies – one of Food Corporation of India to discuss how poor logistics infrastructure resulted in huge losses and wastage of food grain in FCI warehouses and, two, a case of Procter and Gamble to discuss how innovations in SCM and related areas – helped them to gain competitive advantage following disruptive innovation for radical improvement in business performance. Also, a case on Dell has been discussed showing how Dell decided to change their supply chain network to improve both cost and response time to significantly improve the performance of the business.

Discussion Questions

1 Discuss the core concept of SCM as it is known today and its scope and coverage. Why is SCM so important?
2 How have the SCM functions evolved over the years? What are the basic elements of logistics, and how it is now an integral part of SCM?
3 How can efficient SCM practices provide the key competitive advantage to the business? Discuss taking a case.

42 *Evolution of Integrated Supply Chain and Logistics Management*

4 How important is the logistics function in business as well as the overall economy? What are the different types of logistics?
5 Discuss the key role of SCM in delivering business performance. Discuss the criticality of supply chain efficiency in India's agriculture sector.
6 Discuss the key success criteria which has helped P&G to triple its innovation success rate. What are the key lessons learnt from their innovation management and new product development practices?
7 Discuss briefly how Dell manages its supply chain and operations to deliver significantly improved performance?

Notes

1 Council of Supply Chain Management Professionals (CSCMP), https://ftp.turbomachinery. The National Council of Physical Distribution Management (NCPDM) was established in 1963 to represent professional logistics managers. This organisation was renamed the Council of Logistics Management (CLM) in 1985 and the Council of Supply Chain Management Professionals (CSCMP) in 2004.
2 Council of Supply Chain Management Professionals (CSCCMP).2013. http://ww17.cscmp.com/org/about-us/supply-chain-managmemnt (accessed on 19 August 2019)
3 IT; Council of SCM professionals [CSCMP] 2013, https://csmp.org/CSCMP/Educate/SCM_Definations_ and_ Glossary_ of_terms_/CSCMP/Educate/SCM__Definations_and_Glossary_of_terms.aspx? hkey =60879588-f65f-465f-4ab5–8c4b-6878815ef921 (accessed on 3 September 2019)
4 See: https://timesofindia.indiatimes.com/india/grains-rotting-with FCI-could -have-fed-8L-for a year/ articleshow/52068428.cms (accessed on 24 march 2019)
5 See: https://times of india.indiatimes.com/India/India-waste- 21-million-tonnes-of-wheat-every-year-Report/articleshow/17969340.cms

References

Baisya, R. K. (2012, June) "Criticality of Supply Chain Efficiency in Agriculture", *Processed Food Industry*, 15(9), 18–20.
Brown, B., & Anthony, S. D. (2011, June) "How P&G Tripled Its Innovation Success Rate", *Harvard Business Review*, 65–72.
Carter, C., & Ellram, L. (2003) "Thirty-Five Years of the Journal of Supply Chain Management: Where Have We Been and Where Are We Going?", *Journal of Supply Chain Management*, 39(1), 27–39.
Council of Supply Chain Management Professionals (CSCCMP) (2013) http://cscmp/org/about-us/supply-chain-managmemnt-deficition (accessed on 19 August 2019).
Drucker, P. F. (1962, April) "The Economy's Dark Continent", *Fortune*, p. 103, 265, 268 and 270.
Harland, C. M. (1996) "Supply Chain Management: Relationships, Chains and Networks", *British Journal of Management*, 7, S63–S80.
Houston, J. A. (1996) *The Sinews of War: Army Logistics, 1775–1953*. Washington, DC: Government Printing Office.
Li, Y., & Wilson, J. (2009) "Time as a Determinant of Comparative Advantage". *Policy Research Working Paper 5218*. Washington, DC: World Bank.
Magretta, J. (1998, September–October) "Fast Global and Entrepreneurial: Supply Chain Management, Hong Kong Style", *Harvard Business Review*.
Ohmae, K. (1982) *The Mind of Strategist, The Art of Japanese Business*. New York: McGraw-Hill.
Porter, M. E. (1985) *Competitive Advantage: Creating Sustaining Superior Performance*. New York: The Free Press, Ch. 1, pp. 11–15.
Shepherd, B. (2011) "Logistics Costs and Competitiveness: Measurement and Trade Policy Applications", *MPRA Paper 38254*. University Library of Munich, Germany.
Smykay, E. W., Bowersox, D. J., & Mossman, F. H. (1961) *Physical Distribution Management: Logistics Problems of the Firm*. New York: Macmillan Publishers.
Southern, R. N. (1997) *Transport and Logistics Basic*. Continental Traffic Publishing Company.

Bibliography

Cavinato, J. L. (2002, May–June) "What's Your Supply Chain Type?", *Supply Chain Management Review*, pp. 60–66.

Fuller, J. B., O'Conner, J., & Rawlinson, R. (1993, May–June) "Tailored Logistics: The Next Advantage", *Harvard Business Review*, pp. 87–98.

Lambert, D. M. (2004, September) "The Eight Essential Supply Chain Management Processes", *Supply Chain Management Review*, pp. 18–26.

Lee, H. L. (2002, Spring) "Aligning Supply Chain Strategies with Product Uncertainties", *California Management Review*, pp. 105–119.

Marien, E. J. (2000, March–April) "The Four Supply Chain Enablers", *Supply Chain Management Review*, pp. 60–68.

Movahedi, B., Lavassani, K., & Kumar, V. (2009) "Transition to B2B e-Marketplace Enabled Supply Chain: Readiness Assessment and Success Factors", *The International Journal of Technology, Knowledge and Society*, 5(3), 75–88.

Robeson, J. F., & Copacino, W. C., eds. (1994) *The Logistics Handbook*. New York: Free Press.

Slone, R. E. (2004, October) "Leading Supply Chain Turnaround", *Harvard Business Review*, pp. 114–121.

3 Demand Estimation in a Supply Chain

Learning Objective

- Understand role and importance of forecasting in managing business as well as supply chain
- Identify characteristic of forecasts and factors influencing forecast
- Identify types and levels of forecasts
- Get acquainted with the various qualitative and quantitative methods of forecasting
- Analyse demand forecasts and estimate forecasting errors
- Seasonal variations and fluctuations in demands

Introduction

Businesses are created to serve and satisfy customer demand. Only through satisfying customer demand and expectations organisations generate revenue from sales and make profit for the shareholders, and that is the sole purpose of the existence of the corporation. Supply chain management functions and processes are designed to effectively service the demand. However, the task of creating demand rests with the sales and marketing team of the business, whereas meeting and satisfying that projected demand is the job of the supply chain management (SCM) team. Marketers are relentlessly trying and working hard to increase the demand and delivering the projected growth of the business, and marketers are always under pressure to deliver growth often more than realistically possible and often they try to push stocks in the market. SCM team has to meet that ever-changing demand in a dynamic market and ensure customer satisfaction. Management gives higher targets to sales marketing team of the business. However, growth can come only from increased customer demand, and as the same customer is unlikely to consume more, new customers need to be created. New customers can come from either deeper penetration into the existing market of the business or through geographical expansion. Sales team will try to exploit both avenues. Either way, the task of supply chain management changes in terms of complexity of demand management. These two very important functions of the business, therefore, have to work in close harmony in tandem and support each other, which makes a valid case for discussing integrated supply chain management.

The market is highly dynamic as well as competitive; satisfying a customer, therefore, in this complex and challenging environment is all the more difficult. But satisfying the customer requirement is always a sacrosanct task of the business. Customers have many choices and businesses are dependent on the customers. Hence, pressure on the SCM team in that environment is, therefore, immense. We will separately discuss in this chapter how a corporation's sales team can make SCM teams' lives all the more difficult. To deliver business performance to be effective is more important, but to be effective one needs also to be efficient. The efficiency and effectiveness of the SCM function are, therefore, of paramount importance to ensure the delivery of

DOI: 10.4324/9781003469063-3

Demand Estimation in a Supply Chain 45

budgeted cost and profit of the business. Although customer demand has been created by the marketers, demand has to be managed effectively by managing the inventory optimally. A large part of the profit of the business is linked with the efficiency of the supply chain, which is again a function of developing a realistic demand forecast in its totality, considering the seasonal fluctuation in demand, if any, as well as due to dynamic nature of the business environment beyond the control of the business and also considering the fact that stock-out situation has to be avoided for the reason that in a fiercely competitive marketplace customer has many choices and alternatives to choose from. Losing loyal customers will have a negative impact on business. As inventory has to be optimised to effectively manage the demand, the two very important aspects of the business are also being discussed together in this chapter.

Unrealistic Demand Can Make Supply Chain Management Inefficient

The business planning exercise in any organisation starts with the sales numbers projected in a given year by the company involving its sales, marketing and planning team following the view and goal and objective of the top management. While top management expresses a desire to achieve a certain goal and market share, the sales management team has to deliver that. Involving these three teams to prepare the corporation's annual budget is therefore a very vital and important task of the business every year. Once sales numbers are finalised and approved, the planning function works with the supply chain management team to ensure that the production planning is robust enough to produce and deliver those quantities as per the sales requirement. Supply chain management in fact has to be dependent on the accuracy of the demand forecast emanating from the sales department approved by the top management who in turn will approve other resources, including financial and manpower resources for the business. Achieving the sales target including in terms of its periodicity at the SKU level is a key imperative to the business. But it is not an easy task to project demand to that level of accuracy, and there will always be a mismatch between actual demand of the market and budgeted sales forecast. Thus, a constant adjustment in terms of production planning and procurement planning would be necessary to align the supply chain with the change in demand resulting from a changed business environment. This often results in a conflict between the sales and SCM teams. The sales team is also responsible for achieving top-line value performance month-wise and in order to do they often demand more quantity of items to be sold, which the company may not have the capacity to produce to pass the blame to SCM for lack of supply for their underperformance. The sales team at times even do it deliberately knowing well that the SCM team cannot deliver the incremental demand over and above the budgeted numbers. We have therefore observed that in business there is a constant rift between the sales and supply chain management teams. This conflict is mostly unavoidable but the more accurate the demand forecast will be, the less the conflict and friction between two departments will be, which are so vital for organisational performance. Sales is the most difficult function in the business, but everything else and all other functions in business depends on the sales. Everything else becomes meaningless if the sales function does not perform. The sales team therefore is always under pressure to perform, often demand is there to outperform, and sometimes top management even pushes the sales team to deliver something unrealistic, creating additional pressure in the system, which can even escalate the conflict.

It makes good sense that SCM is geared to deliver realistic customer demand and not pseudo demand and to achieve that demand forecast must consider that opportunities for growth are fully captured so that there is no loss of sales for non-supply and at the same time demand should not be over projected resulting into stock built-up blocking working capital and high debtors. Demand forecast is therefore a very important task, and annual exercise is reviewed periodically for any

46 *Demand Estimation in a Supply Chain*

correction for the business to be undertaken with all seriousness and rigours to ensure minimal forecasting error. A great deal of past experience in the business helps in this task.

Forecasting in Supply Chain

For effective SCM, businesses need a reasonably reliable forecast to start with as demand forecast is the basis of all supply chain planning exercises. Businesses which have product lines which have a regular pattern of established demand are much easier to manage in terms of designing, planning and implementing their end-to-end supply chain. For this business, there is a pull of the brands and product lines that already exist. But when products need to be pushed into the market to achieve targeted sales volume forecasts may not be that much accurate. The pull process is triggered by customer demand, whereas the push process is triggered by the managers of the company based on what they want to achieve which may not have any real-term relationship with customer demand or requirement. Businesses which have multiple locations have to generate forecasts from each location and then collate the same for company-wide forecasts. Also, those businesses that operate franchise models need to generate collaborative forecasts based on an established process.

For large multinational companies forecasts has to be globally aggregated collecting local country-specific forecast. The accuracy of the forecasts is a key concern for both the supply chain management performance as well as overall business performance. Even resource allocation also has a bearing on the quality and accuracy of the forecasts. Forecasting, therefore, is a very important function of the business done annually although, in reality, many or even large numbers of businesses do it just as a ritual. This category of businesses just keeps a growth factor in mind every year and builds on the actual sales performance of the previous year. In general and broadly these two approaches are followed for demand forecasting which can be classified as Bottom-Up Approach or Top-Down Approach. In the bottom approach corporation attempts to generate the sales forecast taking the projections from the front-line salespersons who really know what can be realistically delivered given a certain support and competitive scenario. To help the front-line salespersons generate the primary numbers of the forecast for the coming financial year, corporations normally prepare and share documents where business portfolio analysis, competition analysis, business environment analysis as well as company's focus on certain categories of products including any plan for new products to be introduced during the year as well marketing and promotional support that will be available provided businesses can deliver the expected level of performance. This document normally outlines the expectations of the shareholders of the company. The bottom-up approach generates some sales numbers which invariably will fall short of meeting management's expectations. A process then starts which is in fact an iterative process of discussion to find out ways and means to come closer to the management expectations and, finally, democratically agreed figures are canned as the year's sales budget product group wise, broken down into individual brands as well as SKUs and then calendarisation is done taking into account any seasonal fluctuations and then progressed to get sales projection for even salesman-wise in details.

Reckitt Benckiser an Anglo-Dutch multinational corporation in the FMCG sector used to start the annual budgetary exercise in late August for the next financial year. There will be a global business review document covering company's own business performance review and futuristic perspective and forecasts including competitive analysis globally as well as for regions. This document becomes the basis of country-specific initiatives for generating the sales projection in each country, which creates yet another document discussing similar parameters for the country itself and gives indications of future growth avenues where the company intends to focus which includes the existing business and brands giving reasons why. This document is discussed in the country's management committee and approved for sharing with the sales and marketing team and then percolates down to front-line salesman. The bottom-up figures are generated and collated from all regions and then checked if those figures match or come closer to top management perspective to translate shareholders' expectations locally as well as if it also integrates and delivers expectations of the global headquarters in London. Once this is approved that becomes the final canned budget which is a sacrosanct document for the business unit to deliver. This entire process is spearheaded by the corporate planning and business development department both at the headquarter level and at local country level. The final budget document gets the approval of the topmost authority like the board of directors in their meeting. This entire process normally takes about three months to complete. And this approved document finally becomes the starting or basis of supply chain management planning and implementation. The large companies invariably will have their Enterprise Resource Planning software like SAP which is supporting the monthly production and procurement and despatch planning. It is needless to say that in spite of following such elaborate and rigorous system of budgeting with a milestone and involvement of everyone in the organisation occasional trouble related to short supply, out of stock or even excess stock, over-trading leading to higher debtors could not be avoided. It can therefore be understood that SCM is a very complex and dynamic document requiring frequent review and course correction. And the reasons are many which we will discuss in this chapter. Some of the MNCs even prepare what they call the 'Goal Book', which contains the budget document for five years. The first year is firm and the next four years are tentative, and this is in fact a rolling forecast and every year is reviewed and revised and updated. No business accepts a growth rate lower than the industry category growth rate because if the growth rate of a product category is projected or forecasted lower than this it would mean that the business is losing market share in that product category itself which consciously no businesses can accept as it will trigger the downward journey for that brand and product category. The growth forecast is thus normally higher than the category growth rate but how much is determined by all the factors influencing the performance of the product in the marketplace including competitive actions. Businesses also give more emphasis while doing budgetary exercises on volume forecast and not value forecast and value is normally derived and also impacted by any inflationary factors resulting in price increase. The real measure of growth is thus volume growth.

Characteristics of the Forecasts

In spite of best intentions, forecasts can be in general inaccurate and only a degree of inaccuracy might defer from company to company or even product to product in the same company. An established product forecast will be more accurate, but a new product forecast will be inaccurate and to manage that supply chain constant adjustments and flexibility will be required. Forecasts can also be inaccurate for unrealistic growth ambition of the business. For this reason, any forecast must have both the expected value of demand and a measure of the forecast error or demand uncertainty. Businesses don't normally keep any record for discrepancies of real-term demand against the projected or forecasted demand nor do they normally try to analyse the reasons for such errors simply for the fact that reasons for error at different times would be different and also the focus for the business is always to deliver budgeted profit, and that focus many a times forces businesses to either overtrade on certain brands and SKUs or create artificial demand on item(s) to get to the desired profit figures. These actions from the sales and marketing side of the business are always supported by the management obviously at the cost of disorientation of all plans of the SCM team. But this is the reality of uncertain and dynamic nature of the business

48 *Demand Estimation in a Supply Chain*

environment and competitive actions which makes all forecasts very difficult to implement by the SCM team. In spite of all efforts to make sales and SCM teams work in tandem and harmony, the problems and conflicts still surface. Take the case of two businesses in similar product categories, both expecting a healthy growth rate and delivering similar numbers in terms of sales volume but forecast error can make the SCM plans different for these two companies. The lesser the forecast error, the better it is to manage.

Demand forecasts are normally made for short term, medium term and long term. Short-term forecast, say for the month, will be more realistic and deliverable than medium term, say for quarterly, or say longer term, say for the year. As such long-term forecasts are less reliable and hence have greater errors than short-term forecasts. Long-term forecasts have larger standard deviation of error in relation to mean than short-term forecasts.

> A couple of years ago, Proctor & Gamble (P&G) implemented a project called 'Project Golden Eye' applying the Pareto principle of 20% distributors, generating 80% of the sales volume. They decided to focus and deal with this 20% distributors, and the remaining 80% distributors were put under the 20%, which had reduced the complexity of the business hugely, and P&G was able to get rid of large numbers of sales force and create a lean organisation which was more efficient. By reducing the number of direct distributors to be serviced, huge costs savings was made possible. And by implementing an ERP software package like SAP, P&G was able to directly link the small numbers of distributors and replenish the stock sold in the earlier period. The frequency of servicing the distributors and stockists also improved, resulting in lower stock holding in the trade and hence lower working capital and higher profit. Customer service levels also increased significantly.

However, aggregate forecasts are normally more accurate than disaggregate forecasts for the reason that they have smaller standard deviation of error in relation to the mean. It is not difficult to forecast the gross domestic product (GDP) for a country with less than 2–3% error. But it is really difficult to forecast the sales revenue of a company in the same country with that much accuracy. It is in fact even more difficult to forecast the sales volume of a product with the same level of accuracy which arises due to the degree of aggregation. The greater the aggregation greater, will be the level of accuracy of the forecasts.

Factors Influencing Forecast

The forecast for the company's product lines depends on many internal as well as external factors. Internal factors largely include the company's advertisement and promotional plan, product's past demand in the same market, introduction of any new product variants in different price segment, competitive action in the same market, economic growth, product category growth rate etc. If the product has a long performance history and has a dominant position in the marketplace, having strong brand projection or forecasting becomes easier and that is more reliable also. The problem starts when the forecast has to be made for other products including new products. Depending on the amount of valid information and data available in a given situation, forecast methodology is decided. When heavy promotion is resorted to for an established and strong brand to raise short-term demand, then customers might even decide to stock the product when such promotional or price discounting is announced and then buy less in subsequent months when the price is brought back to normal. Such a situation happens when there is a steady demand for the product and artificial demand created by price discount and or promotion has resulted in excess stocking but not consumption by the customers. But for a lesser-known brand or a product, such schemes are directed to generate trials and create new sets of customers. Forecast in such scenarios will impact supply chain plan as well as performance.

Demand Estimation in a Supply Chain 49

Why Forecast

The entire enterprise resource planning commences when sales forecasting exercise is completed and approved. The forecast of annual budgetary revenue is therefore very important for all businesses irrespective of their types, nature and character. The bigger the company more complex the forecast processes would be. Many decisions including recruitment or staffing, organisation structure and design are linked with the business forecast as well as brand marketing plan to achieve the forecasted volume.

Inaccurate demand predictions can have disastrous consequences on business performance and profitability.

> For example, Hewlett–Packard was unable to predict the proper product mix for their customers for two quarters in a row many years ago (Hograth, 1975). Demand for low-end printers and workstations was high, and demand for commercial printers was low. As a result, earnings were 14% less than the prediction or forecast given by the analysts. The stock market also reacted sharply by knocking the company's stock price down by 5% in one day. This demonstrates the importance of being able to measure the size of the market opportunities as well as the kind of opportunities following a reliable forecasting method that suits better for a company's product category in a given market.

Market Potential

Market potential is actually the maximum demand over a given period of time based on the number of potential users and their purchase rate. In fact, actual industry sales are normally less than the market potential. Some potential always remains unexploited for various reasons. However, businesses must know about the total potential to identify as well as understand the gap in the market. A company's sales projection can only be a part or a portion of the total industry demand for a particular product category. It is the maximum the company can sell at a given period of time, which again will depend on many other factors, including the state of the product life cycle the product currently is and also on the competitive actions and the company's own sales marketing plans and promotions.

Types of Forecasts

The entire end-to-end supply chain planning actually stems from the sales forecast, and the main purpose of planning is to allocate company resources in such a manner as to achieve these targeted and budgeted sales figures. A company can forecast the sales either by forecasting market sales which we can call market forecasting and then making a prudent assumption of what percentage of that market company can expect to get in a given environment and that share of the total market can become the company's sales forecast. However, this estimate will be at an aggregated level when business planners will be interested in forecasts at product level and even product SKU level. There are numerous techniques that can be used for preparing sales forecasts, which will be discussed in this chapter. Let us look at the three basic levels of short-, medium-and long-term forecasts and their practical utility.

1 **Short-term Forecasts:** These short-term forecasts are usually for periods of up to three months. The general sales trend is not important here, and these forecasts are normally used for tactical purposes such as production planning to take into consideration any fluctuation in sales.
2 **Medium-term Forecasts:** Medium-term forecasts are usually for a period of one year. This is thus the annual budget of the business and has significance for the planners. This is in fact

50   *Demand Estimation in a Supply Chain*

the starting point of sales forecast and if sales forecast is incorrect entire budget is incorrect. If the forecast is over optimistic, then the company will have unsold stock in inventory which has to be funded from working capital. Or it will be lying as unsold stock at the channel partner's warehouses resulting in higher debtors or even expiry of the stock resulting in write-offs, reprocessing etc., impacting the bottom-line performance of the company. Whereas if the forecast is pessimistic and is lower than the market opportunity for the company, there will be loss of opportunity resulting in underperformance and loss of market share to competition, which will have longer-term implications for the business. Establishing the required process and rigours within the business to develop an annual sales budget realistically is the key to delivering the business for realising its potential.

3 **Long-term Forecasts:** These are usually for periods of three years and upwards but not more than five years as beyond five years it is not realistically possible to forecast, considering the expected changes in the business environment, including technology. In industries, three years is generally considered long term, but in the steel industry or even the energy sector, a ten-year horizon will be generally considered as long term. They are worked out from the macroeconomic and environmental factors, such as government policy and economic trends. Long-term forecasts are normally referred to and discussed by corporate finance and the board of directors for long-term capital investment or for allocation of other resources as such decisions might even involve the construction of new factories or new technology and or upgradation of existing facilities.

In addition, other functions in business can be directly and indirectly affected in their planning considerations as a result of the sales forecast, and such functions will include the following:

- Production and operations department needs to know the sales forecasts so that they can arrange production planning. There needs to be close coordination and liaison between production and sales to determine customer priorities in the short term. Production also needs to know long-term forecasts so that capital plant decisions can be made in order to meet anticipated sales in future.
- Purchase department normally gets its cues to purchase from production via purchase requisitions or bills of materials. For long delivery items or for strategic sourcing of key inputs, it is useful that the purchase department gets some advance intimation or even warning for such a situation might arise so that they can better plan their purchases in terms of pricing and delivery schedule requirements.
- Human resource management is also interested to know the sales forecast from the manpower planning point of view.
- Finance and costing department needs to know the medium-term sales forecast for their budgeting purpose. Longer-term forecasts will be required by financial accountants and top management for critical decisions related to capacity building and resource planning.
- Research & Development department also needs to know the forecasts although their requirement is more from a technological point of view. They would be particularly interested to know the expected life of the existing products and how technology is impacting their costs and performance etc. in relation to competition to plan and direct their R&D activities. They will also use the market research reports to design and develop future products for the company suited to the changing marketplace. Such a view reflects a marketing-oriented approach to customer requirements.
- All sales promotion and marketing activities are aligned with the sales forecast to ensure the budgeted numbers are achieved and therefore sales forecast forms the critical input for the business to align all activities to happen in an integrated manner.

Demand Estimation in a Supply Chain   51

Levels of Forecasting

Forecasts can be prepared at different levels of aggregation starting from global to national level ulti-mately to SKUs month-wise as well as weekly salesperson territory-wise taking into account the sea-sonal impact on sales performance and consumer demand, which can really help the corporation in designing and planning supply chain to satisfy the projected demand of the customers. For example, an organised retail store buyer can take an easy approach by asking the store manager of each store to give a forecast for his store and then the buyer adds up the individual store-level forecasts to get the total ordering quantity for the company. It is based on the local market intelligence that the store has but store managers are forecasting well ahead of actual demand and therefore might even go wrong and forecasts might be inaccurate. In this case, it is better to forecast the demand at the aggregate level for ordering with the supplier, particularly for long delivery or long lead time items. And then the buyer can ask the store managers to forecast when the store wants the stock to be delivered to stores nearing the season – when local market intelligence of the store management team will be closer to the reality and hence more accurate.

Seasonal Variations

In large companies, forecast is always an annual exercise when annual sales budget is approved and canned for planning purposes from which monthly budgets are also derived and supply chain function is planned to meet and service those targets. As the environment is dynamic, constant or at least periodic review is generally done. The seasonal impact is normally taken into consideration when monthly budgetary figures are drawn up for production planning and control taking more realistic views of numerous issues including seasonality. If the seasonality is not considered a good forecast, it might ultimately turn out to be poor because of the failure to consider seasonal factors. When historical sales figures are taken to forecast, the accuracy of the forecast will improve if suitable adjustments are made to eliminate the seasonal effects. It should be noted that seasonal adjustments are widely used in business and seasonal adjustments to reduce forecasting errors.

Some of the businesses are highly seasonal. For example, carbonated soft beverages like Pepsi and Coke are dependent on the impact and duration of the summer season, and in India and more par-ticularly in northern territories, sales can be highly skewed in summer months to the extent that about 45–50% of the year's sales will happen in a few summer months. The impact of the summer season will

Table 3.1 Determining a Seasonal Index from Historical Sales Data

Quarter	Year				Four-year Quarterly Average	Seasonal Index
	1	*2*	*3*	*4*		
1	45	52	53	71	55.25	0.74*
2	72	92	85	95	86.00	1.13
3	86	85	90	96	89.25	1.17
4	77	58	87	76	74.50	0.98
Four-year Sales = 1250/16 = 76.25 (average quarterly sales)						

Note: Seasonal Index = Average sales for four quarter/Average quarterly sales= 55.25/76.25= 0.72

52   *Demand Estimation in a Supply Chain*

be there in every region but may not be as skewed as in north India. For Mumbai or western India, impact could be around 30–35% and in eastern India it could be about 35–40%. Similarly, for a product like ice cream, sales in winter months in northern regions come down drastically. Seasonal factors therefore have to be invariably considered for certain categories of products for determining the sales forecast. Besides, in a country like India, festival season of October–November and Western countries' Christmas and holiday season, when all brands and businesses offer heavy discounts to clear the inventory, automatically put pressure on supply chain management function to meet the unrealistic demand. For many businesses, last three months of sales could be as high as 35–40% of the sales of the year. During this festival period, there will be over-trading for artificial demand when consumers get their annual bonus, which will invariably make the beginning of the new year start with a low volume of business. All these types of fluctuation have to be managed optimally by effective SCM practices.

Demand Forecasting

Broadly we can divide the methods of forecasting into the following:

- Qualitative or subjective or judgemental
- Extrapolation
- Quantitative

Table 3.2 summarises the possible methods that can be applied under each broad classification of forecasting methods. We will be discussing some of these methods with case studies and examples in this chapter for better clarity. Industry uses these methods to various degrees. Sales force composite which is in fact a bottom-up approach is quite commonly used by industry and more particularly in fast-moving consumer goods (FMCG) industry for their reliability and confidence.

A major component of demand management is forecasting the amount of product that will be purchased by consumers or end users. In the integrated supply chain, all other demand will be derived from the primary demand. The key objective is to anticipate and respond to primary demand as it occurs in the marketplace. Primary, secondary and tertiary sales (consumer offtake)

Table 3.2 Different Methods for Forecasting

Type of Methods	*Actual Methods*
Qualitative/Subjective/ Judgemental	• Sales force composite • Jury of executive opinion • Intention to buy survey • Industry survey
Extrapolation	• Moving average • Per cent rate of change • Leading indicators • Unit rate of change • Exponential smoothening • Line extension
Quantitative	• Simple regression • Multiple regression • Econometric models

need to be balanced with excess stock at each level linked to service frequency of the business to avoid disharmony of having excess stock resulting in over-trading. As integrated supply chain decisions are normally derived from primary sales numbers, primary sales projection must have some good correlation with real-term consumer offtake for which marketers must have a sense of reading the pulse of the ultimate consumers.

In a typical channel distribution of fast-moving consumer goods, actual consumer demand needs to be managed through managing channel partners. The manufacturers need to satisfy the demand reflected by consumer offtake by ensuring adequate stock levels at wholesalers', distributors' as well retailers' end, which calls for managing adequate inventory levels at all points. Businesses normally subscribe to the retail survey (audit) data that are routinely done by market research organisations like A.C. Nielsen. Referring to these databases will provide insight into trade stocks as well as consumer offtake in different customer segments as well as geographical territories to understand the reality of product movement in each customer segment even at the SKU level. Subscribing to these databases helps in forecasting and planning and also in taking corrective action wherever required and therefore serves as a useful tool in terms of managing the demand and inventory in the system.

There are three basic types of forecasting models, namely, 1. judgemental, 2. time-series analysis and 3. cause and effect relationship. Qualitative forecasting also sometimes referred to as judgemental forecasting involves using judgement and intuition and is preferred in situations where there is limited or no historical data available such as with a new product introduction. Judgemental forecasting techniques include surveys and analogue techniques, among others. Judgemental techniques are subjective as they are dependent on opinion and less on mathematics in their formulation and as such they are often used in conjunction with other quantitative techniques.

Consumer User Survey Method

The method essentially involves asking customers about their likely purchase intention during the forecasting period. For an industrial product where the number of customers is not too many, such research is often carried out by involving the salesperson responsible for servicing those customers. But if there is competition in the product category that your business represents, then it may not be easy to ascertain what percentage of that incremental demand of that customer will really be sourced or purchased from you. Yet another problem is that the salesperson as well as the customers tend to become optimistic when forecasting future requirements, and that might lead to a higher degree of inaccuracy in the resulting forecast. Clearly, this way only a small sample size can be covered and, therefore, has limited utility for forecasting for fast-moving consumer products, where customers are wide and large in numbers and spread all over.

Panel of Expert Opinion

This is also sometimes referred to as the Jury method, where specialists or experts on the product categories who have knowledge of the product and industry are asked to forecast. Most often, these experts will come from outside the company and can also include management consultants who operate within the particular industry, and sometimes external experts may also include the customers who are in a position to advise from the point of view of the buying company and as such the panel of experts may finally consist of both internal and external experts. These experts will come up with a prepared forecast and will defend their projection in committee in the presence of other members on which the discussion will follow. The individual

54 Demand Estimation in a Supply Chain

projections may subsequently be altered based on the opinion and discussion that will follow in the committee and in the end, if disagreement still follows a mathematical aggregation may even be necessary to arrive at a compromised forecast. This is in fact a 'top down' exercise for an industry category from which a company can derive their own share from the overall growth of the industry in that category. This method has also its limitation in the sense that even if the company is in a position to estimate a demand from the total projected industry demand volume, getting into individual product and their variants levels in different sales territories will still not be easy and will involve some elements of guess from the past experience. This method will thus be again subjective and inaccurate (Kahn, 1998).

Sales Force Composite

This method involves salesperson making a product-by-product forecast for their particular sales territory. The sum total of all salespersons' forecasts covering the entire sales territory would normally be equal to company's sales forecast taking a bottom-up approach and sometimes it is also considered a 'grassroots' approach. This approach sometimes can be realistic as salespersons involved in the generation or forecasting of the numbers in their own territory will be eventually responsible for delivering these forecasted numbers and hence company can rely on this forecast. However, an inherent problem or shortcoming in this approach is that as salesperson's own remuneration and incentive will depend on realising the forecasted numbers, they themselves projected, there will be a natural tendency to underreport the projected forecast volume. Hence, a better approach could be the fusion of both bottom-up and top-down figures.

Delphi Method

This method bears resemblance to the 'expert opinion' method, and forecasting team is chosen using similar criteria. The main difference doesn't meet in committee. The project administers a structured questionnaire to each member of the team. The questionnaire can be administered in different stages to ultimately bring out a forecast for the company covering the product categories that the company sells. The questions addressed normally are of behavioural nature. For example: Do you envisage new technology products would replace some of our product lines in the next three to five years? If so by what percentage market share? This question can then proceed to ask more pointed questions about specific individual companies with the ultimate objective of translating opinion into some form of forecast. After each round of questionnaires, the aggregate response from each is circulated to members of the panel before they complete a questionnaire for the next round so that members of the panel are not completing their questionnaire in a void but can moderate their response in the light of the aggregate results.

Because of the fact that the members have not met in committee, their response is not going to be influenced by majority opinion, and, therefore, a more objective forecast might result from Delphi. However, it has a greater value in terms of generating industry trends and as a technological forecasting tool in addition to providing useful information regarding new products and processes to direct company efforts in the development of new products. For developing forecast sales territory-wise and product line-wise its usefulness is still limited.

Bayesian Decision Theory

This theory has been placed under qualitative techniques of forecasting although it is in reality a mix of both subjective and objective techniques. The technique is similar to the critical path

Demand Estimation in a Supply Chain   55

Table 3.3 Expected Profit in Three Scenarios

Events (E)	Export Now (£)	Delay 1 Year (£)	Delay 2 years (£)
Economic conditions remain good	800,000	600,000	500,000
Moderate downturn in economy	500,000	390,000	250,000
Economic recession	– 350,000	60,000	100,000

Table 3.4 Impact of Probability Factors on Expected Profit

Event	Profit for optimal act	Probability	Expected value (£)
A	800,000	0.5	400,000
B	500,000	0.4	200,000
C	100,000	0.3	30,000
			£630,000

analysis in that it uses a network diagram, and probabilities must be estimated for each event over the network. Bayesian decision theory is a relatively new and somewhat controversial method for dealing with future uncertainties. The technique, however, incorporates the firm's own parameters as data inputs into the calculation of a sales forecast.

Let us assume that the management feels that the country's economy in the next 12 months can go either of the following ways, namely, continue to be buoyant (Event A), a moderate downturn (Event B) and a serious recession (Event C). Each of these can be considered as an external event on which management has no control. If, however, management wishes to make a decision to max-imise the profit, they will assign subjective prior probabilities to each of the possible events. These expected external events will impact the sales performance of the company, but they are actually not within the control of the company. Management has taken three possible scenarios for expected profit, which is shown in Table 3.3.

The management wishes to make the decision that can maximise the firm's expected profit after assigning the probability factor on each expected event's happening, the impact of that is shown in Table 3.4.

These prior probabilities are now incorporated into a decision tree which is made up of a series of nodes and branches as shown in Figure 3.1.

If more information is available based on a survey conducted by the company to further improve upon the forecast, then those survey indicators should influence the probability factors to be considered, which in turn can change the decision tree.

Quantitative Forecasting Techniques

This is also sometimes referred to as objective or mathematical techniques. Quantitative tech-niques are based on the manipulations of historical data.

The underlying assumption of time-series forecasting is that future demand is solely depend-ent on past demand. For example, this year's demand is 10% more than the last year's actual sales. Time-series analysis takes into account the historical sales over a longer period of years to arrive at a realistic level of the projected sales. Cause and effect (also referred to as associative forecasting) assumes that one or more factors are related to demand and that the relationship

Demand Estimation in a Supply Chain

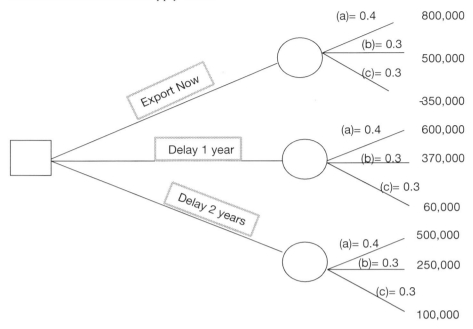

Figure 3.1 Decision Tree for Three Expected Events

between cause and effect can be used to estimate future demand. This uses simple as well as multiple regression techniques. In simple regression, demand is dependent on only one variable, whereas for multiple regression demand is dependent on two or more variables. For example, financing options can increase the demand and high interest rate can decrease the demand for a particular commodity or product.

Table 3.5 Naïve Forecast from the Earlier Period Actual Sales

	Quarter			
	1	2	3	4
Actual Sales in units	59	65	85	92
Naïve Forecasts in units		59	65	85

Naive Forecasting

The naïve forecast is the simplest forecasting technique and is often used as the standard of comparison with the forecasts derived from other methods. A large number of companies (over 30%) used this method of forecasting on a regular basis. This method actually assumes that nothing is going to change and therefore next quarter's forecast will be actually the current level of sales performance. Table 3.5 can be used to predict the sales for the next quarter taking actual sales of the earlier quarter.

Demand Estimation in a Supply Chain   57

The error in the naïve forecast for quarter 2 is the difference 59 and 65 and the percentage error would be:

$$\text{Percentage Forecasting error} = \frac{\text{Forecast} - \text{Actual}}{\text{Actual}}$$

$$= 59 - 65/65 = 9.23\%$$

If the data are adjusted for seasonality forecasting error for quarter 2 will come down to a much lower value (6.6%), which is an acceptable figure.

MAPE Method

When you would like to compare the forecasting accuracy over several time periods, the mean absolute percentage error (MAPE) is the method used by most businesses (Lancaster and Wright, 1983). The MAPE can be calculated from:

$$\text{MAPE} = \frac{(\text{Forecast-Actual})/\text{Actual}}{N} \times 100\%$$

$$\text{MAPE} = \frac{\sum_{i=1}^{n}(\text{Forecast} - \text{Actual})/\text{Actual}}{N} \times 100\%$$

where N is the number of forecasts to be made. The main advantage of MAPE is that it allows easy comparison of forecasting errors across product categories and companies.

Business normally prepares their annual budget containing projected sales numbers, which is also calendarised month-wise for production planning. The budget numbers are very broad, and the same undergoes many iterations during the budget year as several things change including unforeseen activities in the market, changing the demand which SCM has to consider in a continuous manner. The budget document includes in detail the market analysis report to decide at what rate possibly business can grow under the given market environment and in a given resource scenario. The broad figures for sales contained in the budget can be generated following several methods and the easiest of those is applying projected growth factor over last year's actual sales achievement. The projected growth factor has to be equal to or more than the industry category growth rate to retain the market share of the business. Higher growth rate can be taken if any special activities and resource allocation are planned by the business to gain incremental market share. Usually, projecting the next year's sales forecast from the last year's actual sales by applying the growth factor is normally practised by the industry. This, however, is the most simplistic approach or method of estimating or forecasting demand. The more elaborate sales forecast can however be generated by the Delphi technique involving experts, time-series analysis etc. Whatever may be the method, generating demand forecast with about 10% accuracy is a reasonable figure to plan production, procurement and inventory. Resorting to correction factor in every production and inventory cycle based on actual achievement is likely to lead to an effective SCM management plan for implementation.

Moving Average Method

Moving average method actually predicts future sales on the average sales performance for the same product categories in the recent past. As such average sales revenue actually achieved for

58   *Demand Estimation in a Supply Chain*

several periods in the recent past is used to predict or forecast the sales for the next period using the formula:

$$F_{t+1} = \frac{S_t + S_{t-1} + S_{t-2} + \ldots \ldots S_{t-n+1}}{N}$$

where
F_{t+1} = forecast for the next period
S_t = sales in the current period
N = number of periods in the moving average

Moving average method assumes that the future will be the average of the past achievement. And therefore when there is a strong trend in a time series, a moving average forecast without the trend adjustments lags behind. However, this lag could even be an advantage when there is sudden increase and decrease in sales volume because in that case moving average forecast will be more accurate. It should be pointed out here that the limitation of moving average is that it does not consider the dynamic nature of the business environment where each period could behave differently. However, it must be remembered that moving average really does move. For example, sales data from Table 3.1 can be used to make a two-period moving average as follows:

	Quarter			
	1	2	3	4
Actual Sales	45	72	86	77
Two period moving average			58.5	79

Exponential Smoothing

An important feature of exponential smoothing is its ability to emphasise the recent information and data and systematically discount old information. A simple exponentially smoothed forecast can be derived from the following equation:

$$\overline{S}_t = \alpha S_t + (1-\alpha)\overline{S}_{t-1}$$

where
S_t = smoothed sales for period t+1
α = smoothing constant
$\overline{S}_t$ = actual sales in period t
$\overline{S}_{t-1}$ = Smoothed forecast for the period t−1

This equation in fact combines a portion (α) of current sales with the discounted value of the smoothed average calculated for the previous period to give a forecast for the next period.

	Quarter			
	1	2	3	4
Actual Sales	45	72	86	77
Smoothed Forecast			57.8	77.6

Using the data given in Table 3.5, we can work out taking smoothing constant of 0.4 as shown next.

The forecast for period 3 can be obtained by multiplying the smoothing constant 0.4 of the current sales for period 2 plus 0.6 times of current sales of the period. 1 which will work out to 57.8 and similarly for the period 4 smoothed forecast will be 77.6. The critical decision with respect to exponential smoothing is selecting an appropriate value for the smoothing constant (a), which actually ranges from 0 and 1, with low value indicative of stability and high value allowing a rapid response to sales changes. And as such using the smoothing constant as 1.0 will give smoothing forecast same as that are obtained by the naïve method. Forecasts produced with a low smoothing constant, for example 0.2, lag behind and forecasts generated with high values of smoothing constant such as 0.8 will likely overestimate sales at turning points. If a business has historical data, it must try to find out optimum smoothing constant by trying out different values of 'a' to see which one fits the best. Regression techniques have advantages in situations in which managers wish to incorporate other variables which can influence the sales volume in their forecasting programme.

Linear Regression

In a simple linear equation, the relationship between sales (X) and some variable (Y) can be assumed as linear and therefore can be represented by a straight line. The equation then would be $X = a + bY$, where a is the intercept and b is the impact of the independent variable. The main steps for deriving a linear regression equation are to find the values for coefficients a and b that gives the line that best fits the data and that can be obtained by employing a least squares procedure as illustrated in Figure 3.2, where sales (X) have been plotted against time (Y). The equation $X = 63.9 + 3.5Y$. Two-variable regression equations can thus be easily calculated. However, a limitation in this is the assumption that sales follow a linear pattern, which is not correct. And there are cyclical sales patterns as well for many parameters impacting the sales which a linear equation cannot capture. In that case, the sales analyst can base the forecasting equation on the logarithm of the time-series data to generate an improved version of forecasting equations. Another problem is to decide how much of the past data to include in the calculation to forecast. Although all past data points can provide greater stability, sometimes shorter period regression can do a better job of tracking changes.

The simple regression equations that have been described use time as an independent variable, which is very common in sales forecasting and with time as the independent variable, a regression approach also becomes a trend forecast. However, other variables which are closely related to sales forecast such as income growth of the targeted consumers, frequency of use etc. can also be used. But when sales seem to be associated with several independent variables, multiple regression procedures can be used to build the forecasting model.

60 *Demand Estimation in a Supply Chain*

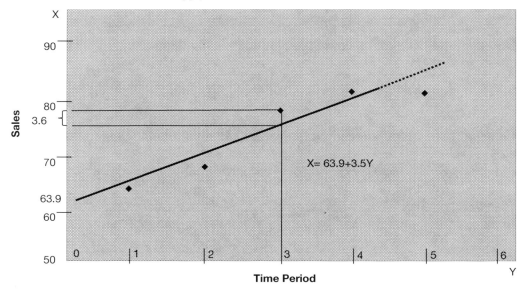

Figure 3.2 Fitment of Trend Regression to Seasonality-adjusted Sales Data

How P&G Forecasted Its Detergent Sales in Italy

Proctor & Gamble is a global leader in detergent. P&G is considered as most innovative company in the FMCG sector, and to keep its supremacy P&G invariably will bring in some new features in tangible and if not at least on intangible platform to differentiate P&G products from others and most importantly differentiating from its immediate competitor Unilever. P&G's Italian subsidiary produces both liquid and powder detergents and the Italian company has a staff strength of 400. Their annual sales volume used to be about USD 385 million per year. They regularly prepare sales forecasts for two variants of powder detergents and one variant of liquid detergent for use in washing machines. In addition, P&G Italy also prepares sales forecasts for one more brand of powder and liquid detergent, which are used in hand- and bucket-washed clothes. For established brands like Ariel, P&G Italy uses their historical sales data and adjust those for incremental advertisement and promotional plan for the brands during the year and then uses a computer program to prepare sales forecasts. Under normal circumstances, they use previous three years' sales data to prepare the forecast for the current year. Forecasts of sales volume for P&G Italy are prepared for medium term to long term, and their most detailed forecasts are for three years. For new products, the forecasts were normally prepared from targeted market share to be built up to the targeted level over a given period of time. As liquid detergents are a new category, there is no historical sales figure available to go by. As forecasting error in P&G is normally a few percentage points only, they are fully satisfied with their forecasting process and efforts of preparing a sales forecast to be supported by an elaborate supply chain planning to meet the projected demand.

It can be pointed out here that sales forecasting in most of the FMCG companies are done through projection from historical data of say three years to see the trend taking into consideration the impact of marketing and advertisement plan for the year in addition to the market environment,

Demand Estimation in a Supply Chain   61

economy and competitive activities. This plan is in addition to taking a bottom-up approach for generating product category-wise sales forecast involving front-line sales staff. It is also important to note that sales forecast is generated product category-wise and brand-wise taking into account the brand marketing plan to achieve the projected numbers and in that respect the entire plan is integrated as a common objective and goal for the year.

Multiple Regression

When projected sales volume is dependent on multiple variables, we need to use multiple regression and if the number of variables is many a computer is used to build forecasting based on historical relationships between sales and several independent variables. These independent variables need to be selected judiciously based on past trends and experience to identify those which have a significant impact on sales. The multiple regression equation must capture some of the best indicators of sales performance. The suggestive factors could be economic growth rate, marketing and promotional budget for the category, industry category growth rate, interest rates, growth in target population etc. However, these factors need to be predicted for future time periods before loading them into the forecasting equation. There are other variables which would be product specific, such as growth of infrastructure and real estate in a given geographical area, new investment in certain projects can also impact the sales volume and those impact on sales will not be very difficult to predict. The decision whether to use simple or multiple regression forecasting model often depends on the values of three statistics that are calculated by the computer forecasting program. For example, if the R2 value is 0.70, your equation explained 70% of the variation observed in your data. Forecasting equations with high R2 are generally preferable to equations that explain only 5–10% of the variation. The standard error of the estimate tells you the range within which you can expect to find the true value of the variable that you are predicting. Also, errors in the coefficients for the variables in your equation should be smaller than the coefficients. If, however, the errors are larger than the coefficients, there is good reason to drop that variable from the forecasting equation. With regression forecasting, you need five observations for every independent variable in your equation. Thus, an equation with one predictor variable would need five observations and an equation with three variables would need 15 observations. If your data set does not meet these requirements, then another forecasting method should be selected. Despite complexities of multiple regression forecasting, this technique is the most popular of all the quantitative methods mentioned in Table 3.1 and has been reported to be used regularly almost 13–15% of the firms. A real data set that you can use to build a multiple regression forecasting equation is discussed under problem 3 in this chapter for better clarity and understanding.

Trend and Seasonality Corrected Holt – Winter Exponential Smoothing

The trend corrected exponential smoothing as per Holt's model is appropriate when demand is assumed to have a level and a trend in the systematic component, but no seasonality which would mean that:

Systematic Component of Demand = Level + Trend.

Whereas both trend and seasonality corrected exponential smoothing as per Winter's model is appropriate when the systematic component of demand has a level, a trend also a seasonality factor which thus would mean that:

Systematic Component of Demand = (Level +Trend) X Seasonal factor

62   *Demand Estimation in a Supply Chain*

Once data have been captured for the time series to be forecasted, the analyst's next step is to select a model for forecasting. Various statistical and graphic techniques may be useful to the analyst in the selection process. The best place to start with any time-series forecasting analysis is to graph sequence plots of the time series to be forecasted. A sequence plot is a graph of the data series values, usually on the vertical axis, against time usually on the horizontal axis. The purpose of the sequence plot is to give the analyst a visual impression of the nature of the time series. The presence/absence of such components can help the analyst in selecting the model with the potential to produce the best forecasts. After selecting a model, the next step is its specification. The process of specifying a forecasting model involves selecting the variables to be included, selecting the form of the equation of relationship, and estimating the values of the parameters in that equation. The model can be selected based on the trend analysis, historical data and data quality available.

The forecasting methods we have discussed in this chapter can be used in different situations as given in Table 3.6.

We normally obtain an initial estimate of level and trend by running a linear simple regression between demand D_t and time period t of the form

$$D_t = at + b$$

Running a linear regression between demand and time periods is appropriate because in Holt's model assumption is that demand has a trend but no seasonality and therefore their relationship is linear. The constant b measures the estimate of demand at period $t = 0$, which can be taken as the initial estimate L_0. The slope a measures the rate of change in demand per period and initial estimate of the trend T_0. In period t from the given estimates level Lt and trend Tt, the forecast for the future period will be as:

$$F_{t+1} = L_t + T_t \text{ and } F_{t+n} = L_t + nT_t \qquad 3.1$$

And on observing the demand for the period t, the estimates of Level L_t and trend T_t the forecast for future periods is expressed as:

$$L_{t+1} = \alpha D_{t+1} + (1 - \alpha)(L_t + T_t) \qquad 3.2$$

$$T_{t+1} = \beta(L_{t+1} - L_t) + (1 - \beta) T_t \qquad 3.3$$

where α is smoothing constant for the level and β is the smoothing constant for the trend having a value between 0 and 1. You should observe that for two updates of level and trend and a weighted average of the observed value and the old estimates.

Table 3.6 Applicability of the Methods

Forecasting Methods	*Where applicable*
Moving Average method	No trend or seasonality
Simple Exponential Smoothing	No trend or seasonality
Holt's Model	Trend but no seasonality
Winter Model	Trend and Seasonality

Demand Estimation in a Supply Chain 63

For the Winter model, assume periodicity of demand to be p. We need the initial estimates of the level L_0, trend T_0 and seasonal factors S_1 to S_p. In period t the estimates level L_t, trend T_t and seasonal factors $S_t, \ldots S_{t+p-1}$ the forecast for the future period can be obtained from:

$$F_{t+1} = (L_t + T_t) \, S_{t+1} \text{ and } F_{t+l} = (L_t + lT_t) \, S_{t+1} \qquad\qquad 3.4$$

After observing the demand for the period $t+1$, we can revise the estimates for level, trend and seasonality factors as:

$$L_{t+1} = \alpha \, (D_{t+1}/S_{t+1}) + (1-\alpha) \, (L_t + T_t) \qquad\qquad 3.5$$

$$T_{t+1} = \beta \, (L_{t+1} - L_t) + (1-\beta) \, T_t \qquad\qquad 3.6$$

$$S_{t+p+1} = \gamma \, (D_{t+1}/L_{t+1}) + (1-\gamma) \, S_{t+1} \qquad\qquad 3.7$$

where α is the smoothing constant for the level, β is the smoothing constant for the trend and γ is the smoothing constant for the seasonal factor being between 0 and 1. We can observe each of these impacts, and the revised estimate is a weighted average of the observed value and the old estimate.

When to Use Quantitative Forecasting Methods

Quantitative forecasting techniques are best employed in situations where we have access to historical data, and it is also helpful if the time series we are trying to forecast are stable and do not often change direction. Quantitative methods have distinctive advantage in situations where frequent forecasts are to be made for very large numbers of product and product categories which also may need the use of computers and forecasting software because of a large number of calculations. Forecasters also need to be conversant and familiar with the various statistical tools and procedures used by these techniques. Additionally, quantitative techniques are most useful in situations where management understands and also endorses their application to sales forecasting problems. However, it should be remembered that simple procedures such as naïve, moving averages and exponential smoothing often have lower forecasting errors than other complex methods (Dalrymple et al., 2003)

Changing Business Environment

The numerical methods for forecasting sales normally attempt to make projections from historical data, and often it does not take into consideration the impact of any significant development in the business environment on sales numbers. Percentage rate of change, unit rate of change and two-variable regression are in fact poor predictors of series under significant turning points in business. Naïve, moving average and exponential smoothing are somewhat better because they tend to lag and then adapt to new realities. If the identification of such a turning point is important for business, the use of qualitative procedures is often the better approach. These methods can pick up environmental cues that signal the turning points which are missed quite frequently by numerical methods. Leading indicators can be included in multiple regression equations to help predict those unexpected turning points.

Forecasting in Practice

For deriving realistic forecasts, close coordination between sales and supply chain management teams and also the channel partners including the IT team of the company is very much desirable.

64 *Demand Estimation in a Supply Chain*

Share only those data which are valuable for the specific business function. The value of the data depends on where one is located in the entire chain. For example, a retailer finds point-of-sale data very valuable in terms of measuring the performance of the store. However, a manufacturer selling to a distributor or wholesaler who in turn sells to the retailer does not find point of sales data that useful and instead manufacturers find the aggregate demand data to be very useful. Historical sales data should not be confused with historical demand because there can be occasions of loss of sales due to stock shortages and also there can be occasions when businesses have resorted to over-trading creating artificial stock pressure in the system which has resulted in high debtors but the volume so traded appears in their official sales figures. Those situations of over-trading and under-trading needs to be corrected to get to the exact demand forecast.

What Industry Practises

Industry tends to use simplistic methods to forecast sales as has been explained earlier. The only concern is of the degree of errors in their method. If the degree of error is very low or and does not put the supply chain management tasks in difficulty in terms of handling possible stock-out situations resulting in loss of sales or sudden spurt in demand offering short-term opportunities to capture and grow, then the methods that are being employed are for all practical purposes working well for the company.

However, quantitative methods are also used under certain circumstances and situations. For example, quantitative forecasting techniques are best employed in situations where you have access to historical numerical data and also when the time series that you intend to forecast are stable and do not often change direction. Quantitative methods have distinct advantages where forecasts need to be generated frequently and that too for hundreds or thousands of products. Because of the large number of calculations required by quantitative forecasting methods, it often requires the use of computers and forecasting software and in addition one has to be well versed in statistical procedures used by these techniques. Most importantly, quantitative techniques are most useful where management understands and endorses their application to sales forecasting problems.

Demand Management

Demand management is one of the key areas which will impact the supply chain performance. Ideal performance of a supply chain will, however, be when the end-to-end chain and link in the entire value chain are led by the real-term customers' demand. If businesses can achieve that status of seamlessly meeting customer demand by coordinating and managing the production operations as well as inventory without any excess stock at any stage, that would be the ideal situation. Demand management thus is a very critical area of influence that determines the performance of the business.

Demand management can be defined as focused integrated efforts to realistically estimate and manage customer demand with the intention of using this information to shape the operating decision related to production and operations strategies and plan of the business. The essence of demand management is to continuously improve the ability of the firm's SCM practices on flow of product, services, information and capital through a collaborative approach involving customers or, in other words, demand has to be managed as customer demand led supply chain management. The desired end result should be to create greater value for the end user or consumer, for whom all supply chain activities should be undertaken. Estimating the demand as accurately as possible will result in better supply chain

Demand Estimation in a Supply Chain 65

decisions and will likely result in benefits flowing through the supply chain. The demand can be generated either through push or pull methods. Demand pull creates better and ideal SCM practices, whereas creating demand by push strategy can often lead to unnecessary stock hold up in trade channel if such demand is not corroborated by real-term customer demand and that can negatively impact supply chain performance and also corporation's business performance.

Demand management is a complex subject in the sense that accurate forecasting in terms of what items we need, where we need and when we need are not easily determined. Besides, in a dynamic business environment, it always changes and fluctuates. Oversupply will add to the build-up of trade stock resulting in higher working capital. Over stocking the trade can also lead to wastage and write off and bad debts resulting in significant negative impact on the business. On the other hand, restricted supply may lead to loss of sales and in some cases and for some categories of products like perishables and food products etc. it may be a permanent loss of sales which also has the risk of customers shifting to competitors' products and that would mean a possibility of losing the customer permanently as well and not simply short-term loss of sales. Demand management has to be seen from these perspectives. Effective demand management will help to unify channel members with the common goal of satisfying customers and solving customer problems. However, for effective demand management, accuracy of demand estimate is an essential prerequisite. The accuracy of demand depends on many factors which can include the following:

- Customer data relating to the demographics, consumption patterns, their buying habits
- Seasonality of demands, if any
- Break-up of demands by customer segments including institutional customers and bulk customers
- Information regarding how, when and where the expected demand has to be met. Also information regarding channel intermediaries
- Common trade practices and trade terms
- Developing and executing the best practices for logistics, transportation and distribution methods to deliver products and services to consumers in the desired format.

Gathering this information and analysing knowledge about customers, their problems and their unmet needs would help. Another way is the designing the supply and distribution chain and identifying partners to perform the functions needed in the demand chain. And also helping the channel members to perform effectively and efficiently and effectively is important. Sharing the knowledge about consumers and customers, available technology, and logistics challenges and opportunities with all members of the channel will improve channel effectiveness.

Efficient Demand Management

Efficient demand management would mean servicing the customer requirement on real-time basis at least cost or at affordable cost, which would entail delivering the customer order wherever required and whenever required at minimal cost of servicing. Some companies have developed systems and processes to deliver customer orders most efficiently. Their service level and frequency are much higher than their competitors. For example, Kao Corporation of Japan competes with MNCs like Unilever, Colgate Palmolive and Proctor & Gamble and can service its two hundred thousand retailers in Japan within 24 hours of receiving orders irrespective of the location of the customer. Efficient demand management requires efficient communication management. Sales order processing is the primary information for implementation of Enterprise

66   *Demand Estimation in a Supply Chain*

Resource Planning (ERP), which most of the companies now have to bring in cost economy and service efficiency in the business.

Communication between various departments within the business results in little or no coordinated response to demand information. Sometimes too much emphasis is placed on forecasts of demand with little attention paid to collaborative efforts and strategic and operational plans that need to be developed from the forecasts. Demand information is often used more for tactical and operations purposes than for strategic purposes. Primary emphasis should be on using demand information to create likely scenarios of the future as they relate to product supply alternatives. Resulting business successes will be an outcome of the better match of demand to product availability.

As end-user demand begins to decline, the situation clearly has shifted to one of oversupply. This is largely due to the industry's planning processes and systems, which are primarily designed to use previous period demand as a gauge. The net result of these behaviours in aligning supply and demand is that a large majority of product is sold during the declining period of profit opportunity, thereby diminishing substantial value creation opportunities for industry participants.

Estimating the Total Market Demand

Industry always tries to follow the method that suits them best and that will be industry category specific as well as individual business itself. For this purpose, businesses must get a good fix on the overall market demand for an industry category in order to forecast the demand for the product(s) for the individual business itself, which again will be a factor of the company's existing and past real-term demand and market share data as well as the projected market share which will have a direct bearing on category growth rate, past growth rate and marketing and promotional plan for the current year. To arrive at a reasonably reliable estimate of the total demand, following steps will be useful (Barnett, 1988).

Define the Market

While defining the market, it is necessary to consider the potential and existing substitute of your product. There are several ways that you can make sure that you include all important current and potential substitute products. Market research can lead to insights about consumer products and speaking with experts in the relevant technologies can help you identify potential developments that could threaten your industry. The demand curves will have a relationship between price and volume. With appropriate definition, the total industry demand curves will often be steeper than the demand curves for individual products in the industry. For example, consumers are more likely to switch from Nescafe to Brook Bond's coffee if Nescafe's prices increase. But if prices of both brands increase there could be a fall in demand for coffee as a category itself.

Divide the Industry Demand into Its Principal or Main Components

The second step in forecasting is to divide total demand into its main components or segments for separate analysis. There are two criteria to keep in mind when choosing segments: make each category small and homogeneous enough so that the drivers of demand will apply consistently across its various elements; make each category large enough so that the analysis will be worth the effort. In thinking about market divisions, managers need to

68 *Demand Estimation in a Supply Chain*

management policy. Trade channel partners and distributors mostly decide on stock ordering and inventory levels based on their past experience.

While non-availability of prescription items in one pharmacy are not usually life-threatening for any patient, the inconvenience caused due to delay may result in loss of customer loyalty. Hence product should be available at retail outlets when customer demands. Apollo Pharmacy Retail Chain does not follow any established demand forecasting technique. However, such forecasting can help the distributor to better manage the inventory of critical drugs as well as fast-moving drugs including OTC drugs.

Forecasting aims at reducing uncertainty that confounds future decisions. However, difficulties arise while fulfilling the assumptions of Economic Order Quantity (EOQ) model, which includes a continuous, constant and known rate of demand (Hill, 1988). Prescription items can be substituted for one another (generic substitution and me-too drugs with similar active molecules), which obviates EOQ assumptions.

For products where demand history is available, future demand can be predicted better using quantitative models from sales in the previous cycle (Tersine, 1994). Time-series analysis predicts future attributes from the historical past and prior experience. This method uses time as the independent variable to predict demand. The causal relationship is applicable under the assumption that there exists a cause-and-effect relationship between an input variable and its corresponding output (Wheelwright and Makridakis, 1985).

The sales data of Apollo Pharmacy belonging to the Alwal region of Hyderabad, Andhra Pradesh, is given in Table 3.7 specifically adopted for the study. Apollo Pharmacy belongs to a large umbrella group organisation that follows consistent marketing/sales policies across all its retail outlets.

The case study attempts to identify a suitable forecasting model for use by the Apollo Retail group from the various methods discussed in order to recommend one based on the best fit from the values of Mean Absolute Deviation (MAD), Mean Squared Error (MSE) and Mean Absolute Percentage Error (MAPE).

Forecasting Methods

The Simple Moving Average technique is chosen for its simplicity of use. It is easy to understand and implement. The Simple Exponential Smoothing technique takes into account the weighting factor/smoothing factor and thus helps in adjusting better to recent changes in demand. The Winter's

Table 3.7 Comparison of Measurement Errors Obtained for Okacet and Stamlo Beta Using Time-Series Forecast Models

	Okacet			*Stamlo Beta*		
Technique Error	*6-month Moving Average*	*Simple Exponential Smoothing*	*Winter's Exponential Smoothing*	*6-month Moving Average*	*Simple Exponential Smoothing*	*Winter's Exponential Smoothing*
MAD	117.35	420.01	92.28	47.19	615.74	83.21
MSE	21,048.03	198,950.33	14,635.74	3158.69	394,719.07	10,305.11
MAPE	42.43	157.39	27.50	45.62	550.30	61.86

Exponential Smoothing uses a seasonal component in addition to the trend component making it the most appropriate technique for the forecast of the study. The chosen forecasting models were applied to Microsoft Excel spreadsheets, and simple excel functions were used following equations given in the literature. These simple models formed the basis of the study with an objective to delineate/identify the most suitable forecast model for the chosen product, by comparing actual sales value and predicted sales value.

The forecasting techniques are evaluated based on their accuracy in forecasting actual demand data. Thus, Mean Absolute Deviation, Mean Squared Error and Mean Absolute Percentage Error are used to measure the error of forecast obtained by using various techniques. Because MAPE is a percentage, it is a relative measure and is thus sometimes preferred to the MAD. The MSE, which is a squared measure, is selected as it helps in penalising errors more heavily.

Results

The actual demand data obtained from the Apollo retail pharmacy are recorded in Table 3.7 of supporting data. Table 3.8 depicts the measurement errors, obtained by using each of the three forecasting techniques for the two prescription drugs.

The following observations were made from Table 3.8 for Okacet (seasonal demand).

Winter's Exponential Smoothing captures the seasonality in sales of Okacet. Seasonality is evident in the sales volume of Okacet, which peaks in early December compared to reduced sales in the month of April (774 units versus 118 units). Winter's Exponential Smoothing (WES) provides sales forecast most accurately compared to the other three models (MAD = 92.28, MAPE = 27.50, MSE = 14635.74).

For Stamlo Beta (Non-seasonal Demand)

Six-month Moving Average best predicts the demand for Stamlo Beta, which has a relatively stable demand during an entire year or the time period in question. It accurately provides sales forecast (MAD = 47.19, MSE = 394719.07, MAPE = 45.62) compared to the other models. Although Winters' model forecasts the demand equally well.

In summary, comparative values indicate that Winter's Exponential Smoothing (WES) is a superior forecast model to predict sales of pharmaceuticals when demand fluctuates and or varies seasonally. And Six-month Moving Average is a better forecast model to predict the sales of pharmaceuticals whose demand remains fairly constant. Average works reliably for non-seasonal pharmaceuticals for the chosen Apollo Pharmacy retail.

Sales Data

Daily sales data for the two products mentioned were collected for the period starting from December 2010 and ending in November 2013. Data were obtained by contacting the selected retail outlet manager. As observed, Apollo Pharmacy maintains electronic data of its daily product sales using an ERP solution. Data such as number of units sold, product code and number of items remaining in inventory were of particular importance for this study.

70   *Demand Estimation in a Supply Chain*

Appendix 3.1

Sales Data of Apollo Pharmacy

Actual Demand Data for 36 Months – Okacet and Stamlo Beta – Apollo Pharmacy, Hyderabad

Period	Mon-Year	No. of Okacet Issued	No. of Stamlo Beta Issued
1	Dec-2010	413	233
2	Jan-2011	399	171
3	Feb-2011	307	258
4	Mar-2011	350	96
5	Apr-2011	277	169
6	May-2011	341	82
7	Jun-2011	536	133
8	Jul-2011	383	142
9	Aug-2011	486	167
10	Sep-2011	503	97
11	Oct-2011	485	86
12	Nov-2011	482	167
13	Dec-2011	744	66
14	Jan-2012	371	174
15	Feb-2012	376	81
16	Mar-2012	216	168
17	Apr-2012	118	32
18	May-2012	208	84
19	Jun-2012	202	135
20	Jul-2012	288	165
21	Aug-2012	415	180
22	Sep-2012	434	145
23	Oct-2012	301	236
24	Nov-2012	269	91
25	Dec-2012	359	174
26	Jan-2013	267	156
27	Feb-2013	281	190
28	Mar-2013	193	141
29	Apr-2013	216	171
30	May-2013	143	120
31	Jun-2013	255	293
32	Jul-2013	228	122
33	Aug-2013	419	118
34	Sep-2013	405	96
35	Oct-2013	286	63
36	Nov-2013	480	145

Source: Anusha et al. (2014)

Demand Estimation in a Supply Chain — 71

Case Questions:

1 Which of the forecasting models, among Simple Moving Average, Exponential Smoothing and Winter's Exponential Smoothing, yields the least error? The quantitative indicators used to be used to assess forecast error are MAD, MSE and MAPE.
2 Which of the forecasting models, among Simple Moving Average, Exponential Smoothing and Winter's Exponential Smoothing, most accurately predicts demand for a seasonal pharmaceutical item, Okacet 10 mg tablet?
3 Which of the forecasting models, among Simple Moving Average, Exponential Smoothing and Winter's Exponential Smoothing, most accurately predicts demand for a random pharmaceutical item, Stamlo Beta tablet?

Source: The case is based on the data reported by S. Lakshmi Anusha et al, "Demand Forecasting for the Indian Pharmaceutical Retail: A Case Study", *Journal of Supply Chain Management Systems*, Volume 3, Issue 2 (2014).

Chapter Summary

The chapter starts with explaining the critical role of forecasting in the supply chain. Realistic demand forecast actually forms the basis of all supply chain planning, management and control. Basic approaches to demand forecasting were explained and the various types of forecasts and their implication in terms of efficient supply chain management were then discussed. Various methods of forecasting including Time-Series Analysis, Moving Average method and exponential smoothing were elaborately discussed with examples to explain where these methods can be used and will be useful. How historical data regarding actual performance of companies help generate forecasts in the business and the forecasting methods used in real-life business with case studies were discussed in this chapter. Lastly, the role of information technology in demand forecasting as well as forecasting practices was discussed. Sales forecast many a time is higher than the real-term demand from the customer and it is important to manage the supply chain to cater to the realistic demand which necessitates that companies learn to distinguish between sales target and real-term demand. Chasing unrealistic sales target can create distortion in trade and also business in terms of their performance in real term which is not desirable, whereas meeting the real-term customer demand really serves the purpose of managing the supply chain effectively. The unusual demand due to introduction of new product, fluctuating demand during seasons for seasonal products.

Discussion Questions

1 What are the various approaches to demand estimation, and what are the types of forecasts businesses make and for what purpose?
2 Why do we need forecast, and what internal and external factors influence the forecast and how?
3 What criteria decides the level of forecasting? Discuss how seasonality influenced the forecast taking examples.
4 Discuss different methods of demand forecasting. Discuss the advantages and disadvantages of sales force composite and industry survey methods.
5 When you should use the quantitative methods of forecasting. Discuss multiple regression technique with example.
6 Why is MAPE method useful? Discuss Moving Average Method and Exponential Smoothing methods of forecasting.

72 *Demand Estimation in a Supply Chain*

7 How P&G forecasts its detergent sales in Italy, and why they are satisfied with their method and approach?
8 What is the normal industry practice for forecasting demand while doing their annual budgetary exercise?
9 Discuss the criteria which influences the accuracy of demand, and what you would understand by efficient demand management?

References

Anusha, S. L., et al. (2014) "Demand Forecasting for the Indian Pharmaceutical Retail: A Case Study", *Journal of Supply Chain Management Systems*, 3(2).

Barnett, William P. 1988. 'Fore Steps to Forecast Total Market Demand'. *Harvard Business Review* (July): 1–9.

Dalrymple, D. J., Cron, W. L., & Decarlo, T. E. (2003) *Sales Management-Concepts and Cases* (7th ed.). Singapore: John Wiley & Sons (Asia) Pte Ltd, 228–246.

Hill, W. J. (1988) *Alternative Inventory Control Methods for Use in Managing Medical Supply Inventory*. MS thesis, AFIT/GLM/LSM/88S-35. School of Systems and Logistics, Air Force Institute of Technology (AU), Wright-Patterson AFBOH.

Hograth, R. (1975) "Cognitive Processes and the Assessment of Subjective Probability Distributions", *Journal of American Statistical Association*, 70(350), 271–289.

Kahn, K. B. (1998, Summer) "Revisiting Top-Down Versus Bottom Up Forecasting", *Journal of Business Forecasting Methods & Systems*, 17(2), 20.

Kahn, K. B. (1998/99, Winter) "Benchmarking Sales Forecasting Performance Measures", *Journal of Business Forecasting Methods & Systems*, 17(4), 20.

Lancaster, G. A., & Wright, G. (1983) "Forecasting the Future of Video Using a Diffusion Model", *European Journal of Marketing*, 17, 2.

Tersine, R. J. (1994) *Principles of Inventory and Materials Management* (4th ed.). Englewood Cliffs, NJ: Prentice Hall.

Wheelwright, S. C., & Makridakis, S. (1985) *Forecasting Methods for Management* (4th ed.). New York: John Wiley and Sons.

Zachary, G. P. (1989, August 15) "Hewlett to Post About Flat Net for 3rd Period", *Wall Street Journal*, p. 10.

Bibliography

Brown, R. G. (1959) *Statistical Forecasting for Inventory Control*. New York: McGraw Hill.

Georgoff, D. M., & Robert, G. M. (1986, January–February) "Manager's Guide to Forecasting", *Harvard Business Review*, pp. 2–9.

Gilliland, M. (2002, July–August) "Is Forecasting a Waste of Time?", *Supply Chain Management Review*, pp. 16–23.

Gilloth, V. R., & others. (1979) *An Evaluation of Seasonality in the United States Air Force Medical Material Management System*. MS thesis, LSSR 13–79B. School of Systems and Logistics, Air Force Institute of Technology (AU), Wright-Patterson AFB OH.

Hanke, J. E., & Reitsch, A. G. (1992) *Business Forecasting* (4th ed.). Boston: Allyn and Bacon.

Jobber, D., & Lancaster, G. (2005) *Selling and Sales Management* (6th ed.). Singapore: Pearson Education Pte Ltd, pp. 411–442.

Makridakis, S., & Wheelwright, S. (1989) *Forecasting Methods for Management*. New York: Wiley.

Pilinkienė, V. (2008a) "Selection of Market Demand Forecast Methods: Criteria and Application", *Engineering Economics*, 3(58), 19–25.

Rachmania, I. N. (2013) "Pharmaceutical Inventory Management Issues in Hospital Supply Chains", *Management*, 3(1), 1–5.

Saffo, P. (2007, July–August) "Six Rules of Effective Forecasting", *Harvard Business Review*, pp. 122–131.

Sarang, D. N., & Laxmidhar, M. (2006) *Exploratory Investigation of Sales Forecasting Process and Sales Forecasting System*. Masters in management thesis. Jönköping International Business School, Sweden.

Sarker, S. (2010) "Increasing Forecasting Accuracy of Trend Demand by Non-Linear Optimization of the Smoothing Constant", *Journal of Mechanical Engineering*, 41(1), 58–64.

4 Warehousing and Distribution Management
Complexity and Challenges

Learning Objective

- Understand purpose, scope and functions and types of warehouses
- Design criteria and designing the layout of a warehouse for efficient warehousing activities
- Calculate warehousing cost and criteria impacting warehousing performance
- Understand warehousing management system and performance metrics
- Understand distribution management: objectives, tasks, methods, channels, strategies, policies and challenges
- Recognise key performance indicators of distribution and designing a distribution network
- Create distribution organisation and channel structure for specific product categories

Introduction

Finished goods warehouses are located in strategic locations from where ultimate customers as well as trade channel partners are serviced. Objective of locating a warehouse is to respond to the customer demand in quickest possible time and at least cost. Companies do a lot of surveys as well as mathematical modelling to decide on the location for finding out optimum solution for transportation and distribution of products, which is a subject matter of operations research. Dynamic programming and simulations such as Monte Carlo Simulation etc. are carried out to take appropriate and logical decisions for such crucial activities in business. Warehousing has a significant cost in terms of total logistics cost. Besides, effective and efficient warehousing is critical to distribution efficiency. Location and type of warehousing and its management is thus a critical decision to business. Complexity of warehouse operation depends on the number of SKUs to be handled and the number of orders received and filled. Order filling rate as well as stock filling rate have to meet customer requirements as per the order conditions in addition to meeting the delivery time and schedule to ensure high level of customer satisfaction. Most activity in a warehouse is material handling which improves the warehouse operational efficiency as well as help reduce wastages and damage. But material handling also adds significant cost in terms of both capital and operational cost and as such warehouse has to be designed to minimise the need of material handling. Distribution efficiency is also linked with warehouse management efficiency in addition to the location of the warehouse. A specific warehouse can only service that many customers around its location. The management perspective has to consider managing both warehouse and distribution function as an integrated function. And, as such, in this chapter, two interrelated subjects such as warehousing and distribution are discussed together.

DOI: 10.4324/9781003469063-4

74 *Warehousing and Distribution Management*

Warehousing Purpose and Scope

Warehousing is actually a large intermediate storage space for holding stocks of finished goods till such time these stocks are sold to be delivered to the customer as per the customer ordering quantity and input materials such as raw and packaging material and spares and components to be transferred to production and manufacturing departments as and when required. Depending on type of inventory kept at warehouse, the customer could be internal or external. For example, raw material and packaging material kept in warehouse will be used internally by the production department, whereas finished goods kept in warehouse will be for the external customers or buyers. For distribution, warehouses are located in strategic locations identified in relation to customers concentration. Distribution warehouse, therefore, normally holds finished goods for sales. Whereas warehouse located in the vicinity of the manufacturing or production locations contains both finished goods and input materials and for finished goods, it normally serves as the feeder warehouse to distribution warehouses. Businesses incur storage cost in warehouse as well as handling cost. Warehouse needs to be designed to improve the movement of stock for dispatch unhindered with minimal or nil handling to reduce the cost. Efficient warehouse management will help the business to improve profitability. From this point of view, warehouse can be defined as part of logistics management system that stores the products for subsequent distribution to meet customer demands. Warehousing provides time and space utility for raw and packaging materials and other inputs including spares and consumables, industrial goods and finished products to help customers as a dynamic value-adding tool, which can ultimately provide competitive advantage to business. Warehouses if located in a strategic location can significantly increase value to the customers by reducing delivery time and cost as well as helping the customers to lower their inventory level, which helps customers to improve their profitability, and in that sense warehousing can play a strategic role in business.

Primary Functions of Warehouse

A warehouse, in fact, has multiple functions and those include the following:

- **Consolidation for Transportation:** Depending on the customer order, the lot size is consolidated collecting stocks in various SKUs as per order from various storage locations within the warehouse before transportation.
- **Mixing of Products:** Products are grouped under various product mix configurations, which can facilitate their identification and also consolidation to execute customer orders expeditiously.
- **Docking:** Products of various groups as identified are kept and stored at designated docking stations for loading and dispatch immediately on demand without holding the stock. In docking stations product comes and is unloaded and reloaded to another destination.
- **Customer Service:** Meeting the customer requirement in terms of ordering quantity, product mix configuration as well as SKUs and service frequency. Both internal and external customers are serviced by the designated warehouse itself.
- **Buffer against contingencies:** It helps in meeting fluctuating customer demand, including seasonal demand and other variable demand situation during unusual situations in the marketplace.

Efficient Warehouse Management

The designated warehouse performs its primary function to deliver the objective as listed earlier but the functional efficiency of the warehouse will be determined by many performance criteria which are the primary objectives of efficient functioning of the warehouse. These performance criteria are listed next.

- **Providing timely service to the customer:** Customer orders have to be executed as fast as it can be to ensure that customer never goes out of stock and also for customer satisfaction. These days customers demand more frequent deliveries in small quantities rather than large deliveries to reduce the cost of stock holding that needs higher service frequency, which could add to the cost to marketers. In competitive environment, cost has to be contained by bringing in savings in production and operations
- **Keeping track of items to find them readily and correctly when needed:** This helps in faster execution of customer orders and also in terms of managing the warehouse better. This is essential for computerisation of warehouse management and is part of the design and implementation of efficient warehouse management system.
- **Minimise the physical effort and material handling to save cost:** Design of the warehouse and stock storage plan should be such that movements inside the warehouse are managed most efficiently at least cost. The layout design should be such that material handling is minimal which is a non-value-adding activity and is kept at minimal level to save cost incurred on moving goods into and out of the warehouse. Material handling can be minimised by properly designing the layout following industrial engineering principles and ensuring linear movement of stocks and using material-handling equipment to improve efficiency by reducing cost and wastage.
- **Providing communication links with customers:** Warehouse has to be an important link for sales system of the company and the customers and for that purpose warehouse records will have to be accurate and up to date. Real-time information often needs to be provided to sales force as well as to customers so that they also can plan their activities more efficiently.

Types of Warehouses

As warehousing is a significant cost in business and, therefore, several alternative methods and models were experimented and followed in real-life practices. Businesses are constantly exploring possibilities of reducing the cost of warehousing, and we can see the various types of warehouses that are in use including the following:

Public Warehousing: Public properties are available for businesses to be used as warehouse on rent or lease. For example, port trust authority which owns the warehouse space in the port areas is normally given on long- or short-term lease to private business through a public tendering process. These warehouses are operated by warehouse operators and are given on fixed or variable commercial terms to manufacturers and marketers for use. Businesses having international operations prefer stock holding facilities in the port areas from the considerations of cost and convenience.

Private Warehousing: Privately built or constructed warehouse available on rent or lease at convenient locations to service the customers. For example, before entering large cities like Mumbai most of the companies have their warehouse located at Bhiwandi at a lower cost instead of bringing the stock to Mumbai city where cost of warehouse will be many times higher. The same is true for other large and smaller cities around the country. Locating warehouse on the outskirts of large, costly cities will also save the entry tax to be paid for entering and other constraints like longer waiting time incurring cost before transport vehicles are allowed to enter the city limits and hence will work out more economically.

76 *Warehousing and Distribution Management*

Third-party Warehousing or Contract Warehousing: In this type of warehousing, the goods are given to a third party on contract basis under some agreed commercial terms to be stored on behalf of the company. The traditional C&F agents also serve similar purpose. Post-implementation of GST (Goods & Service Tax) the role of C&F (Carrying and Forwarding) has become irrelevant in the traditional sense, but they also serve the purpose of warehousing for their principal as well as for redistribution of stocks as C&F agent actually functions as an extended arm of the marketers from where company can bill to distributors, wholesalers as well as other categories of customers, including institutional customers and large retailers like organised retailers and e-tailers in e-commerce.

Multi-client Warehousing: Here one warehouse is being used by many clients, and this helps in terms of sharing the space as per requirement of the individual companies and also sharing the common area including utilities and security services and cost thereof. This often becomes economical. In this model, warehousing can even be directly linked dynamically with the space utilised for keeping the stock instead of paying for a fixed storage space to make it as used payment basis and that will be very economical.

Warehouse Layout Design Criteria

The internal layout of the warehouse has to be designed keeping the following design criteria in mind with the object of efficient operations at the least cost. The warehouse should be located in a single-storey building having maximum height and least number of columns inside to ensure large space availability. A square building is preferred as space utilisation is maximum in square building and wastage of space is minimum. This will help in making an effective storage plan. The layout design must ensure maximum utilisation of the height and available space of the storage area. Also, ensure maximising aisle space for efficient movement of material-handling equipment like forklifts etc. The material-handling equipment that will be used in warehousing must be efficient, the movement of the goods should be always in straight line and the entire layout design must follow the principles of industrial engineering. Any forward and backward movement should be avoided or eliminated. A typical layout design of a warehouse and activities performed in different sections are shown in Figure 4.1.

Warehousing Cost

There are two broad elements of cost, namely, capital cost and operating cost. Capital costs include the costs of space and material-handling equipment and also warehouse management system software which, of course, are incurred by those who have implemented computerised warehouse management system. A large part of the cost of warehouse is the material-handling systems and equipment. The operating costs, however, will include the cost of direct labour, utilities as well administrative cost and communication and documentation costs.

Warehouse Activities

As mentioned earlier, there are numerous activities a typical warehouse has to perform which are as follows:

Receive Goods: This would entail accepting goods from suppliers and vendors as well as outside transporters and other factories; checking the quantities received against orders and the bill of loading; inspecting goods as per order specifications and reporting discrepancies, if

Warehousing and Distribution Management 77

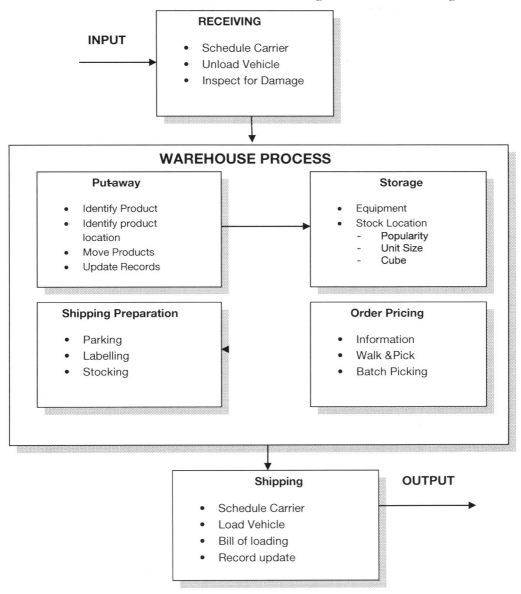

Figure 4.1 Warehouse Layout Design and Activities Performed

any, and also checking for damages and report as necessary for replacement or adjustment in record. Goods are normally received at receiving dock for inspection and issued Goods Receipt No (GRN) for tracking the goods against each order subsequently, which is also required for making supplier payment. Goods are also returned for damaged or otherwise unsellable stock from the customers and market.

Identify Goods: Items are identified with the appropriate stock-keeping unit (SKU) number and or part number as the case may be and the quantity received has to be recorded.

78 *Warehousing and Distribution Management*

Transfer Goods to Storage Area: Goods are sorted and put away at their designated storage locations for the reason that as and when required it is easy to trace and retrieve to ensure that there is no loss of time while we need to retrieve for making use and or further dispatching.

Hold Goods: Goods are kept in storage in their designated storage location well protected to avoid any damage and to facilitate subsequent utilisation when needed.

Pick Goods: Items required from stock must be selected from storage and brought to a marshalling area from where actual dispatch and or shipping can be executed. Picking should be done on first-in first-out basis (FIFO) for efficient stock movement from the warehouse.

Pick Goods: Items required from stock must be selected from storage and brought to a marshalling area from where actual dispatch and/or shipping can be executed. Picking should be done on first-in, first-out (FIFO) basis for efficient stock movement from the warehouse.

Marshalling Shipment: In this area goods making up a single order are brought together and checked for omissions or any errors or any other discrepancy. And then order records are updated.

Dispatching Shipment: Orders are packaged, shipping documents are prepared and goods are loaded on the vehicle.

Provide Information: Record must be maintained for each item in stock showing the quantity on hand, quantity received, quantity issued and their location in the warehouse. Appropriate information system should be used to ensure accuracy of the information.

Record Keeping and Documentation: Records of the warehouse stock, locations, dispatches, age of the stock, near-expiry stock, order deliveries and customer-wise service records should be kept for ready reference at any time for sales system and customers to access through the warehouse and inventory management system.

For maximising the warehouse productivity and minimising the cost of operation, we need to maximise the use of space which forms the largest part of the capital cost. The other significant capital cost is the investment made in the material-handling equipment, which will depend on the degree of automation and computerisation. As such, for minimising the operating cost, businesses have to ensure effective and efficient use of labour and equipment. Labour being the largest component of the operating cost, automation and computerised controlled modern warehouse can operate without any labour or with drastically lesser numbers of workers. Many large corporations have completely automated warehouse operations running without involvement of any labour using automation and artificial intelligence.

For example, an international pharmaceuticals company KRKA (pronounced as Karka) factory in Europe has completely automated warehouse management system. Their factory in Slovenia is completely automatic and computerised controlled; most of the functions are either automatic or run by a few robots starting from batch weighing, mixing, tableting, packaging, warehousing and dispatch. There is no manpower involved in certain functions. The entire warehouse function for finished goods, raw materials and packaging materials is being managed through a pre-programmed computer-controlled trolley and forklifts moving on guided rails. The goods are automatically picked from the designated storage areas and loaded in transport vehicles for dispatch against a particular order of a client or sales invoice which is entered in the system and the rest is automatic. Another auto seat manufacturer TVP, producer of automobile seats for all brands of cars and supplies worldwide, is completely managed by robots and controlled through artificial intelligence.

Factors Influencing Effectiveness of Warehouse

There are many factors impacting effectiveness of warehouse such as cube utilisation and accessibility, stock location, order picking and assembly, physical control and security of stocks.

Cube Utilisation and Accessibility: Goods are stored not just on the floor but in the cubic space of the warehouse; warehouse capacity depends on how high goods can be stored. The available height of the warehouse and volume of space should therefore be fully utilised. For forklift operation, a minimum of 18 to 20 ft high warehouse is selected. Those who use telescopic forklifts in automatic operation even go for still higher in height. Utilising the complete volumetric space reduces the cost significantly. Accessibility means being able to get at the goods wanted with a minimum amount of work. The warehouse design and storage patterns and identification and location codes should facilitate minimum time to access the items stored whenever required. Utilising both horizontal and vertical space to the extent possible will determine the cost of holding the stock (Figure 4.2).

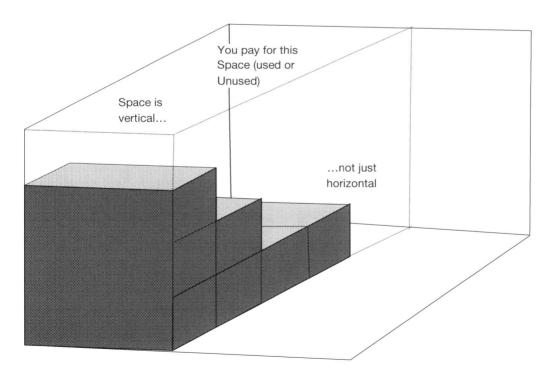

Figure 4.2 Cube Space Utilisation and Accessibility

80 *Warehousing and Distribution Management*

Stock Location: Objectives of designating specific stock location are to provide the required customer service and also to keep track of where items are stored to minimise effort to receive, put away and retrieve items.

Locating the various kinds of stocks within the warehouse to facilitate identification and shipment when needed can follow different types of stock locating system as mentioned next:

1 **Basic Stock Locating Systems**: Classify the goods stored in the warehouse in some order based on their functions or use to facilitate easy identification in a large warehouse. Several such systems with respect to grouping of stocks are in use such as:

   - Functionally related items together
   - Fast-moving items together
   - Physically similar items together
   - Locate working stock and reserve stock separately

2 **Fixed Location:** In this system, an SKU is assigned a permanent location, and no other items are stored there. But fixed-location systems usually have poor and less efficient cube utilisation and, therefore, are usually used in small warehouses, where throughput is small, and there are few SKUs to be handled and managed. Fixed location, however, helps in terms of easy identification and audit of the stock. When stocks are scattered conducting an audit becomes difficult.

3 **Floating or Random Location:** Goods are stored wherever there is appropriate or suitable space available, and the advantage of this system is that cube utilisation is significantly improved. It also requires accurate and up-to-date information about the stock location and quantity SKU-wise. Warehouses using floating-location systems are usually computer-based. In industry, this practice is widely prevalent for the reason that no businesses would like to keep space un-utilised as space is money. Whenever a delivery van comes to deliver stocks, there will be urgency to unload the stock to make space for next van to arrive and park. Under that kind of situation, goods are kept after unloading wherever space is available.

4 **Point-of-use storage:** Inventory stored close to where it will be needed and normally used in repetitive manufacturing and JIT systems. Keeping the stock close to where it is required for use has several advantages, including lesser cost and time of handling and movement. A key advantage is that materials are readily accessible to users and material handling is reduced or eliminated altogether.

5 **Central storage:** This contains all inventory in one central location, which helps in reduction of cost, and materials are accessible all the time. Safety stock level is reduced as users do not need to carry their own safety stock. Central storage is much easier to control and inventory record accuracy is easier to maintain. Central storage also facilitates specialised storage, if required. Large corporations normally follow this practice for better control and accurate information in a central location. For large businesses, central warehouse is normally located in strategic locations and serves as a feeder warehouse to feed stock to other local warehouse located closer to customer locations to facilitate better service and flexibility.

Order Picking and Assembly: When an order is received, items must be obtained from the warehouse, grouped and prepared for shipment, and to manage that function efficiently, industries follow various types of methods or systems as described next:

1 **Area system:** Order picker circulates throughout warehouse selecting items on an order, and an order is ready to ship when order picker finishes picking the stocks as per an order

Warehousing and Distribution Management   81

requirement. This requires a little longer time to assemble one order for delivery. This is practical for a small warehouse dealing in limited numbers of products and SKUs.

2 **Zone system:** Warehouse is divided into several zones, and each picker works only in an assigned zone. Order is normally divided by zone, and the items from each zone are sent to the marshalling area for executing the order. When product groups are large and each one is managed as a separate profit centre and or SBU, zone system is better. For example, a company deals with fast-moving consumer products, industrial products as well as pharma products. Zone system also will avoid intermixing of stocks and ensure better control.

3 **Multi-order system:** This is the same as the zone system, except that each picker collects items for a number of orders at the same time. In reality, this multi-order system is practised. In large retail stores, orders are picked up throughout the day, and in the evening all orders are executed to facilitate deliveries indicated in the order.

Physical Control and Security Elements: The goods stored inside the warehouse have to be secured and safe at all times and should be in control of the warehouse management team. Some standard practices must be followed to ensure security and safety of the stock. These are as follows:

1 Goods parts numbering system should be simple but has to be unique to facilitate easy identification. It also should have simple and well-documented transaction system involving identifying the item, verifying the quantity, recording the transaction and physically executing the transaction.

2 Inventory must be kept in a safe and secured (locked) place with limited general access or access through identity checks by those who are authorised. It should be accessible only to authorised people. Well-trained workforce should be engaged to manage the warehouse to eliminate damages, wastages, and pilferages as well as thefts. Adequate surveillance systems such as CCTV monitoring etc. will help. But in spite of all these precautions, pilferage still happens and businesses have to absorb that cost. Needless to say, ultimately, end customer has to bear all those costs. To be competitive, businesses have to control all such possible pilferage.

3 Modern warehouses are fully automated and computerised, and customer orders are processed by picking up stock from the designated locations and managed through central data processing and inventory control stations. Most of the large ports these days have warehouse including bonded warehouse, where stocks are kept and taken as per need paying the custom duties. This type of operation has brought in significant improvement in operational efficiency in the business. Some of these warehouses are used by multi-clients on space-sharing basis providing space utilisation efficiency.

Warehouse Management System

WMS as an Enabler

Warehouse management system is a proven, advanced WMS software solution for manufacturing, distribution, and retail enterprises and third-party logistics providers (3PLs) that can be used by enterprising organisations of all sizes. It helps companies maximise product placement strategies, prioritise tasks, implement fair productivity standards and increase logistics efficiency.

The evolution of WMSs is very similar to that of many other software solutions such as ERP and material requirements planning (MRP). There is an overlap in functionality among planning, transportation management systems, supply chain planning, advanced planning and scheduling, and manufacturing execution systems will only increase the level of confusion

82   *Warehousing and Distribution Management*

among companies looking for software solutions for their operations. Businesses have to decide on an appropriate software system out of many such options available and that task is not easy. Only those businesses which are very clear about their requirement can find an ideal solution for them. An efficient ERP like SAP can serve as a useful tool and control software system for managing the warehouse for a business. But still many businesses opt for WMS software. The effectiveness of a WMS depends on how efficiently information processing and organisation and handling of stock and type of automated environment as well as material-handling equipment are installed and managed. A WMS, therefore, also involves significant investment in capital expenditure to derive commensurate benefits.

Why and When It Is Necessary

WMS is not always useful and has to be implemented when it is necessary, and there are valid reasons for taking such decisions.

- Not every warehouse needs a WMS. Certainly, any warehouse could benefit from some of the functionality, but businesses need to assess the benefits that can be derived to justify the initial and ongoing costs associated with WMS. Warehouse management systems are big, complex, data-intensive applications. Large, automated operations can definitely benefit.
- You need to manage your warehouse management system (WMS) efficiently to derive the full advantage. Otherwise, WMS could end up as an additional complexity and cost in your business. Many times, large operations will end up creating a new information system (IS) or IT department with the sole responsibility of managing the WMS. And that cost and complexity can offset the benefits of WMS. This is therefore a tricky decision that businesses need to take with utmost care. Otherwise, WMS can only add to complexity and cost with no commensurate benefit forthcoming.

Advantages of Implementing WMS

WMS if properly implemented and supported by the necessary inventory data can lead to several benefits such as:

- Reduction in inventory
- Reduction in labour costs
- Increase in storage capacity
- Better customer service
- Increase in inventory accuracy
- Better management of complex warehouse structure
- Optimise warehouse activity
- Increase in trace and trackability of materials in warehouse
- Facilitate mobile data entry
- Increase in efficiency
- Reduce customer complaints

The implementation of a WMS along with automated data collection will likely to give the business better inventory data accuracy, reduction in labour costs and a greater ability to service the customer by reducing cycle times. The predominant factors that control inventory levels are lot sizing, lead times and demand variability. However, WMS is unlikely to impact these factors.

Warehousing and Distribution Management   83

Beyond labour efficiencies, the determining factors in deciding to implement a WMS tend to be more often associated with the need to do something to service the customers that the current system does not support (or does not support well) such as first-in-first-out, cross-docking, automated pick-replenishment, wave picking, lot tracking, yard management, automated data collection and automated material-handling equipment.

Implementation and Setting Up WMS

There are various requirements for implementing and setting up WMS, which are listed next.

- The set-up requirements of WMS can be extensive and also expensive. The characteristics of each item and location must be maintained either at the detail level or by grouping similar items and locations into categories, as discussed earlier. And these details would include exact dimensions and weight of each item in each unit of measure the item is stocked (such as inches, cases, pallets) as well as information such as whether it can be mixed with other items in a location, whether it is rack-able, max stack height, max quantity per location, hazard classifications, finished goods or raw material, fast versus slow-moving items etc.
- Although some operations will need to set up each item this way, most operations will benefit by creating groups of similar products. In reality most operations have a much more diverse product mix and will require much more system set-up. Setting up the physical characteristics of the product and locations is only part of the picture. The real-term requirement is very extensive in terms of organising the layout, data regarding inventory type and group and logic of taking decisions based on which WMS will operate.

When WMS Can Be Advantageous

WMS can lead to many other operational benefits in addition to those listed earlier as functional benefits that can accrue to the business if it is implemented properly. It should be pointed out here that only very large and complex business organisations with very diversified product portfolio and very large and well-dispersed customer base to service can really benefit from the implementation of WMS. Some of those other benefits are listed next:

- **Wave Picking/Batch Picking/Zone Picking:** Support for various picking methods varies from one system to another. In high-volume fulfilment operations, picking logic can be a critical factor in WMS selection. Appropriate picking logic is therefore a key criterion for efficient WMS operations.
- **Task Interleaving:** Task interleaving describes functionality that mixes dissimilar tasks such as picking and putting away to obtain maximum productivity. It is used primarily in full-pallet-load operations, task interleaving will direct a lift truck operator to put away a pallet on his/her way to the next pick. This requires standard operating system to be implemented in warehouse operations.
- **Integration with Automated Material-handling Equipment:** If you are planning on using automated material-handling equipment such as carousels, ASRS units, AGVs, pick-to-light systems, or sortation systems, you'll want to consider this during the software selection process. Since these types of automation are very expensive and are usually a core component of your warehouse, you may find that the equipment will drive the selection of the WMS. If the WMS is integrated with automatic material-handling system, efficiency improves significantly.

84 *Warehousing and Distribution Management*

- **Advanced Shipment Notifications (ASNs):** If your vendors are capable of sending advanced shipment notifications (preferably electronically) and attaching compliance labels to the shipments, you will want to make sure that the WMS can use this to automate your receiving process.
- **Cycle Counting:** Most WMS will have some cycle counting functionality. Modifications to cycle counting systems, as required are common to meet specific operational needs. WMS needs to support the cycle counting practices prevailing.
- **Cross-docking:** In its purest form cross-docking is the action of unloading materials from an incoming trailer or rail car and immediately loading these materials in outbound trailers or rail cars, thus eliminating the need for warehousing (storage) altogether. This requires synchronised operations and planning as well as coordination.
- **Pick-to-Carton:** For parcel shippers pick-to-carton logic uses item dimensions/weights to select the shipping carton prior to the order-picking process. Items are then picked directly into the shipping carton. Shipping cartons are normally standardised to ensure ideal usage and items to be shipped are normally picked directly into the shipping cartons.
- **Slotting:** Slotting describes the activities associated with optimising product placement in pick locations in a warehouse. There are software packages designed just for slotting, and many WMS packages will also have slotting functionality and needs to be selected to match the requirement.
- **Yard management:** Yard management describes the function of managing the inventory of trailers parked outside the warehouse, or the empty trailers themselves. Yard management is generally associated with cross-docking operations and may include the management of both inbound and outbound trailers. For efficient yard management goods truck parking, queuing needs to be programmed based on a logic.
- **Activity-based costing/billing:** This functionality is primarily designed for third-party logistics operators. Activity-based billing allows them to calculate billable fees based upon specific activities. ABC also helps in terms of improving cost criteria by eliminating non-value-adding cost from the process. Billing is linked with the activities required to be performed and therefore more logical and efficient.

Developing a Responsive WMS

If a large corporation implements a responsive and well-functional WMS, there are various other benefits and supports that will be available for improving the business performance. WMS can thus lead to other advantages including the following:

- Support goods returns processing and reverse logistics
- Use task interleaving to minimise deadheading
- Improve order consolidation, wave planning, inventory allocation and pick sequencing
- Identify consolidation opportunities to free space and reduce outside storage requirements
- Support bill of material, work order and value-added processing
- Update inventory records as events occur
- Provide accuracy that allows replacement of full physical with scheduled cycle counts
- Time stamps each transaction and identify the operator who performed it
- Provide feedback to the workforce and support performance measurement
- Measure supplier and carrier performance

Table 4.1 Warehouse Performance Metrics

Category	Measure	Definition
Order Fulfilment Performance	On-time delivery	Orders delivered on time as per customer requirement
	Order fill rate	Orders filled completely on first shipment (delivery)
	Order accuracy (pack fill rate)	Orders picked, packed and shipped perfectly according to customer order
	Line (product category) accuracy	Lines picked, packed and shipped perfectly
	Order cycle time	Time from order placement to shipment
	Perfect order completion	Orders delivered without changes, damages or invoice errors
Inventory Management measure	Inventory accuracy	Actual inventory quantity to system-reported quality
	Damaged inventory	Damage measured as a % of the value of the inventory
	Storage utilisation	Occupied space (square foot) as a % of the total storage capacity
	Dock to Stock Time	Average time from carrier arrival until product is available for picking
	Inventory visibility	Time from physical receipt of goods to customer service notice of availability
Warehouse Productivity	Orders per hour	Average number of orders picked and packed per person hour
	Lines per hour	Average number of order lines picked and packed per person hour
	Items per hour	Average number of order items picked and packed per person hour
	Cost per order	Total warehousing costs – fixed space, utilities and depreciation including operational cost
		Variable: labour/supplies and administration overheads
	Cost as a percentage of sales	Total warehousing cost as a percentage of total company sales revenue

New Trends in WMS

The recent trend in WMS is resulting into further consolidation of industry as well as in terms of alliances with ERP and other enterprise systems providers. WMS facilitates now activity-based costing, which in turn helps in cost reduction. Latest WMS embedded profiling tools are used for space use analysis to facilitate relay out and inventory slotting. Also, introduction of object-oriented tool kits for requirements of modelling and WMS development has helped in the warehouse management performance.

Productivity Improvement Tools of WMS

Barcode

A barcode is magnetic stripes against a light background normally used to identify a stock. They are usually instantaneously identified by a barcode reading system. A barcode is read through the reflectance and absorption of light. A light of a given wavelength is beamed and moved across the bar code at a consistent speed and reflected light is measured with a photo receptor.

86 *Warehousing and Distribution Management*

The pattern of the barcode creates an electrical wave which is sent to a computer chip called 'decoder'. Barcode technology is a widely used method of automatic identification. Automatic identification encompasses automatic reading of information most commonly through printing and reading of information encoded in the barcode and thus eliminates any human error.

Bar Code System Requirement:

- **Bar code label and printer**: Barcode labels are printed using barcode label printers. These printers are normally faster printers than the normal laser printer. These labels are then attached to an asset class or product for easy identification.
- **Scanning Equipment for data collection**: The scanner accurately identifies, reads and deciphers the information contained in each barcode label.
- **Capturing the data to an external database**: To be able to effectively use the codes a database is required to relay the information.
- **Put to light and pick to light**: In a 'pick to light' system lights will guide the operators to a specific SKU locations where they will pick or select the orders from. And in a 'put to light system' light modules will guide the operators to the correct location to sort or to 'put' the item into where it belongs.

If the products are bar coded, put to light system helps in faster sorting of product based on their SKUs and product category. In a large manufacturing organisation with large numbers of products and variants, this system will really help the business. As mentioned earlier, to make WMS very effective the inventories and information system needs to be organised to make the warehouse performance efficient and effective.

With 'put to light' the operator simply grabs an item and scans the label with a RF unit. Lights illuminate at locations where the particular item resides as well the quantities required to fill a customer order. The process is thus repeated till the customer order is fulfilled. This is extremely fast and accurate and error free. 'Pick to light' and 'put to light' systems can be remarkably fast and accurate helping significant increase in warehouse productivity. It is also the most cost-effective means of providing dramatic improvement in warehouse cost reduction and in increased productivity. Pick to light is a paperless solution that increases the pick rate productivity, accuracy and cost efficiency of this otherwise labour-intensive operation by reducing the walk time, eliminating reading errors and also simplifying the task throughout the process.

Distribution Management

Distribution is an essential part of the sales function, but now it has come under the broad umbrella of integrated supply chain management. The key task of distribution is to make the goods and services available from where consumers would like to buy them. Efficient distribution is, therefore, key to ensuring consumer offtake, and the success of any product is largely influenced by the effective and efficient distribution management.

Distribution Task

It depends on the product(s) to be distributed, target consumers to be reached and serviced, geographical areas to be covered, width and depth of distribution to be achieved and also on service levels and frequency of service desired. Distribution objective is normally influenced by the customer expectations and also company's sales and distribution policy. It defines the extent of time, place and possession utility which the customer can expect out of the channel network.

Definition and Scope

The scope of distribution covers many activities to ensure timely availability of goods and services wherever required. The scope thus includes:

- The management of the efficient transfer of goods from the place of manufacture to the point of sale (POS) or consumption.
- Distribution management encompasses such activities as warehousing, materials handling, packing, stock control, order processing and transportation.
- According to   Mossman and Norton (1965), 'Distribution is the operation which creates time, place and form utility through the movement of goods and persons from one place to another'.

Distribution Channels

Distribution channels are sets of interdependent organisations involved in the process of making a product or service available for use or consumption. Seven R's of distribution are Right product in Right quantity in Right condition at the Right time and at Right place for the Right customer at Right cost.

Channel partners are intermediaries or middlemen. They help in the management of the distribution process. They also perform various roles and facilitate distribution and redistribution of stocks. The other benefits that are accrued from distribution include the following:

- They exist because producers cannot reach all their consumers directly and therefore need partners or channel associates to reach ultimate consumers.
- They multiply reach and provide efficiency to the marketing process as channel partners can help accelerate the distribution process and improve efficiency.
- Channel intermediaries can facilitate smooth flow of goods and services and create time, place and possession utilities.
- They are selected based on their core competence, infrastructure and facilities as well as reach.
- Channel intermediaries provide contact, experience, specialisation and scales of operation.

An example is provided next:

If a consumer wants to buy a tube of toothpaste (a product) from a retail outlet located close to her residence (the place) to be made available at 8 pm on a Tuesday evening when she wants it (time) from where she can pay for the toothpaste and take it away (possession)

The company's distribution function has made all this possible in most cost-effective manner. The situation would be similar if a customer wants to buy a soap, a refrigerator or medicines or even an electric motor.

Distribution Methods

Distribution methods are normally determined based on several issues and criteria as well as on company's policy to decide what is the best method of achieving the distribution objective to effectively service the target customers.

The distribution methods to be adopted will generally depend on the following:

- Product types
- Buying behaviour

88 *Warehousing and Distribution Management*

- Consumption pattern
- Buying frequency
- Buyers type and demographics
- Market characteristics
- Infrastructure, complexity and reach
- Competitive practice on distribution
- Geographical area to be covered
- Service frequency and service levels desired

Basically, management has the choice of one of the following different types of distribution systems and practices prevailing in industry:

1 **Direct:** The manufacturer does not use a middleman and sells and delivers direct to the end customer. Channel length is short but effective. Business-to-Business (B2B) model is a preferred mode of distribution.
2 **Selective:** The manufacturer sells through a limited numbers of middlemen who are chosen because of their special abilities or having facilities to enable the product to be distributed better. Company can even choose to have their own distribution outlets instead of having a channel partner.
3 **Intensive:** Maximum exposure at the point of sale is needed, and the manufacturer sells through as many outlets as possible. Servicing and after-sales service is less important, for example, FMCG products like food, cigarette and detergents. Channel length is longer in this case. For intensive distribution multiple, channel intermediaries are involved in reaching and servicing the clients covering very wide range of socio-economic strata.
4 **Exclusive:** Manufacturer sells through a restricted number of dealers normally used for high value durable items like say car, where distributor must provide desired level of stock holding and after-sales service etc. Investment from distributors in this case is also high. Exclusive distribution is also practised for very high-end products and services like say fashion stores or beauty parlours, which also can even be owned by the manufacturers-marketers. Exclusive stores provide special ambience and décor as well as specialised customer service by well-trained customer service executives who are capable of answering all questions of a prospective customer and influencing the decision of such customer visiting such distributor's premises and as such it also acts as sales promotion centre.
5 **Multi-level Marketing (MLM):** MLM is a product distribution and marketing strategy in which the sales force is compensated not only for sales they generate but also for the sales of the other sales-people that they recruit. This recruited sales force is referred to as the participant's 'downline' and can provide multiple levels of compensation. MNCs like Amway and Oriflame created successful global brands through MLM production distribution and marketing strategies. In this system sales force are really working as independent agents and not as company employees. Agents engaged in MLM are self-motivated individuals who work as commission agents taking product from the company's warehouses located in strategic locations and selling directly to the customers and developing their own line of sub-agents to drive the process at multiple levels of the operations and as the chain expands, they gain collectively. MLM has been discussed in detail later in this chapter.
6 **Online Marketing**: In e-commerce trade businesses are receiving orders online on their portal and delivering the stock directly to the end customers. The typical channel partners are non-relevant for online retailers like Amazon and Flipkart. However, many

manufacturers-marketers are also taking advantage of online trade to significantly improve their performance and growth as that helps in getting faster penetration in the market at a lower cost. Some global established brands are also now distributing online. The online sales team has helped Dell to significantly improve its performance for customised servers in terms of both responsiveness and cost. For standardised laptops, however, the online channel is significantly less attractive because its main strength which is reduction of inventory through aggregation is not as valuable for standardised configurations. Simultaneously, the weaknesses of online channels, which are poorer responsiveness and higher transportation costs, become more significant for standardised configurations.

Distribution Channel Strategy

It is derived from the corporate strategy and the marketing strategy. Primarily distribution objectives as mentioned next will have to be defined first for designing the distribution strategy:

a Defining customer service levels
b Distribution objectives and goals
c Sales target
d Set of activities
e The distribution organisation
f Geographical area to be covered
g Key performance indicators (KPIs)
h Critical success factors (CSFs)
i Distribution policy

Once clarity is there regarding the customers to be targeted, penetration to be achieved, service level and frequency of service to be achieved, distribution strategy is developed with regard to what would be the best distribution methods and strategy to achieve the desired goal. Channel strategy will have to be implemented through an efficient distribution organisation.

Customer Service Level

As a policy, a company has to decide on a competitive service level for its customers for implementation in the business based on the following criteria:

- It is defined by the nature of the industry, the products, competition and market shares.
- Affordability also decides the service level.
- It should at least match competition.

Customer expectations have no limit – the more you do the more they expect. However, distribution strategy has to satisfy the customer expectation. A desired level of customer service is a key decision of the management.

Distribution Objectives

The distribution objective depends largely on the type of product and the level and extent of reach a corporation intend to achieve over a period of time in a given geographical area. It also depends on the company's resources, competitive environment and available distribution infrastructure. The primary objective is to service the target segments effectively at least cost

90 *Warehousing and Distribution Management*

and without facing any stock-out situation so that there is no loss of sales and at the same time maintaining healthy level of stock without unnecessary stock built up of trade stock reflecting on the age of the stock as well as high debtors.

Distribution Organisation

The type and structure of the distribution organisation will depend on the distribution methods adopted, which again will depend on the type of products. Distribution is normally achieved through third party who participate as channel partners. Organisation normally maintain a lean structure to deal with the external channel partners following the company's policy and guidelines. As these channel partners are external to the organisation, they are selected on the basis of the partner's knowledge, infrastructure, experience and financial status. The company's own distribution organisation is very lean and mostly stock controllers responsible for defined geographical area. Stock controllers and distribution managers coordinate with the sales department and channel partners for servicing customer orders.

Activities in Distribution

These depends on the manner in which the company and its marketing channels go about achieving the customer service levels. Some of these steps could be as follows: sales forecasts, dispatch plans, market coverage beat plans, journey plans for service engineers and sales staff, collection of sales proceeds and carrying out promotional activities. The company also decides as to who is to perform which task. Distributors are the key link with the other channel partners like wholesalers and retailers to reach the ultimate customers and as such they need to service the market as per the defined and agreed service frequency. These days FMCG companies and more particularly multinationals like say HUL frequency of service is increased to twice or thrice a week and for achieving such level of services distributors must have required infrastructure and system in place.

Distribution Policy

All businesses have their well-defined distribution policy and implementation guidelines described in their operating manuals, and they can vary depending on companies as well as on the product category and distribution methods.

Broadly, the policy guidelines should include the following:

- Code of conduct for channel members
- Stock management including ordering and inventory levels
- Pricing and credit policy
- Pricing and stocking policies including stock level to be maintained
- Promotional scheme operational processes
- Margins, billing and customer service levels
- System for redressal of customer complaints
- Any additional subsidies, margins
- Handling institutional business policy
- Utilisation of promotional and POP (point of purchase) promotional materials
- Record keeping and documentation
- Rural market and van operation policy

Warehousing and Distribution Management 91

- Stock return and quality control policy
- An out-of-warranty and expiry stock handling and management policy

Key Performance Indicator

For measurement of effectiveness of distribution some of these indicators are as follows:

- Consistent achievement of targets by product groups, periods and territories
- Achievement of market shares
- Achievement of profitability
- Zero complaints from customers
- No stock returns
- Ability to handle emergencies and sudden spurts in demand
- Balanced sales achievement during a period – no period end skews in sales
- Market coverage with ready stocks against taking orders to be delivered later – advantages versus disadvantages
- Excellent management of accounts receivables
- Minimise losses on account of stock-outs
- Minimise damages to products
- Very low incidence of complaints and settlement of complaints

Critical Success Factors

The distribution strategy also needs the support and encouragement of top management to succeed. Some of the CSFs are as follows:

- A clear, transparent and unambiguous policy and procedure
- Settling the claims and grievances of the channel partners expeditiously
- Serious commitment of the channel partners
- Fairness in dealings
- Clearly defined customer service policy
- High level of integrity
- Equitable distribution at times of shortage
- Timely compensation of channel partners
- Transparent and fair distribution and compensation policy
- Competitive practices as per industry standards

Sales Target

Achieving sales target is the key objective of the business, and hence also of the distribution channel strategy. The channel types and number of intermediaries will change with the sales target to be achieved.

Geographical Area to Be Covered

For business growth strategy, businesses often need to extend the geographical boundaries, and thus distribution channels need to consider that in terms of formulating distribution strategy as some area(s) are covered sometimes with different channel partners depending on the potential of the area.

92 *Warehousing and Distribution Management*

Typical Channel Partners

C&F Agents and Carrying and Selling (C&S) Agents

Both C&F and C&S agents are on contract with the company and its distributors, and both are transporters who work between the company and its distributors, collect products from the company, store them in a central location, break bulk and dispatch them to distributors against indents. Goods belong to the company till such time it has not changed hands through transactions.

C&Fs also act as an extended arm of the manufacturers-marketers and represent them in the market. Sometimes companies use C&F locations and addresses to bill the company's product to avoid interstate sales taxes. Before the implementation of GST, we had both central and state taxes like CST and ST and in that environment C&F provided a very useful role in saving taxes.

Distributors, Dealers, Stockists, Value-added Re-sellers

They are the channel partners in the business performing the role of stocking the company's product(s) and then redistributing and or reselling to retailers and customers. Stockists will keep the company's stock from where customers and retailers can buy, whereas value-added re-sellers sometimes carry out some additional functions on behalf of the company and as directed by the company. Their role is thus very important in terms of delivering company's distribution objective and performance.

- Their name denotes the extent of redistribution done by them.
- Distributors invest in the products – buy products from the company.
- They are on commission, margins or mark-up.
- They may or may not get credit – but extend credit to the market.
- Distributors cover the markets as per a beat plan. All others merely finance the business.
- Distributors could be exclusive for a company.
- Sometimes same distributors are working for multiple marketers.
- Agents bring buyer and seller together.

Super-stockists

They perform multiple functions of the channel intermediaries, which are as follows:

- They perform the roles of both C&F agents and distributors.
- Small companies as well as new entrants prefer to appoint them for distribution.
- New businesses as well as new products prefer this method of appointing super-stockists to make it simple and for better control.

Agents and Brokers

They represent the company.

- Agents and brokers canvas for a company's products and solicit business.
- They have their own distribution network.
- They are often independent and work for many clients.

Franchisees

Following are the features of franchisees:

- They are given the right to represent a company's product as given to them.
- Franchisees work under given agreed terms independently.
- Their performance is periodically audited.

Electronic Channels

Following are the features of electronic channels:

- These are used by online players and in e-commerce.
- These are accessible only where internet access is there.

Wholesalers

They are required for redistribution of products for the markets which a company cannot cover directly. They are an important part of the product distribution. Their functions include the following:

- They operate out of the main markets.
- They deal with a number of company products of their choice.
- They are not on contract with any company.
- They sell to other wholesalers, retailers and institutions and even to end consumers.
- They negotiate about 15 days credit from company distributors – also provide credit to their customers. However, all companies do not extend credit. Also, some wholesalers don't extend credit and work only on cash basis with very low margin.
- They operate on high volumes and low margins.
- They cover rural distribution and areas where a company's own dealer – distributors network cannot reach.
- They are the redistributors and help in taking stocks to places covering the tertiary market.

Retailers

Retailers have the following features:

- They are the ultimate link with the customers.
- They are the final contact with consumers.
- They operate out of their shops and sell a large assortment and variety of goods.
- They sell multiple and competing brands and products.
- They are located closest to consumers.
- They buy from companies, distributors or wholesalers.
- They have highest margins in the network.
- They provide personalised services to their customers.
- They can influence customers' buying decision if higher margins are available to them. Smaller companies depend on them to push sales by influencing them with higher margins.

94 *Warehousing and Distribution Management*

Distribution Cost

Distribution costs typically include the following:

- Transportation
- Travel cost of sales force and distribution staff
- Channel sales force wages and distribution organisation
- Channel partners margin
- Handling and storage costs
- Damages, wastage and out-of-warranty costs
- Insurance and taxes
- Warehousing and inventory and stockholding costs
- Insurance and administrative costs
- Infrastructure and documentation costs

Normally, additional sales force are kept on distributors' payroll and are also included in the cost of distribution. These salespersons recruited under distributors or channel partners are also known as pilot salesmen who are normally used to canvas and collect orders from the market to be handed over to the distributors to execute.

Efficiency of Distribution

Criteria of effectiveness and efficiency include the following:

- Cost of distribution
- Level of service
- Incidence of consumer/customer complaints
- Stock turnover ratio
- Damages and stock return
- Outstanding and payment discipline
- Inventory age and level

Although the efficiency of distribution is determined by various criteria as mentioned earlier, their relative weightage on overall performance and efficiency will be different. The most important criterion, however, is the cost of distribution, which has to be within budgeted limits and level of service accomplished reflected by customer complaints. The level of service has to match at least competition and industry practice.

Factors Impacting Distribution Network Design

Distribution effectiveness is of primary concern to any business. More so if the product is a mass-consumption product then effectiveness of the distribution channel is the key and therefore it receives attention at the highest level. Top management perspective on performance of a distribution network of the company would essentially consider two broad factors:

1 Value provided to the customer
2 Cost of satisfying customer needs

Demand Estimation in a Supply Chain 67

decide whether to use existing data on segment sizes or to commission research to get an independent estimate.

Forecast the Key Drivers of Demand in Each Segment and Project How They Are Likely to Change

The third step is to understand and forecast the drivers of demand in each category. Here you can make good use of regressions and other statistical techniques to find some causes for changes in historical demand. But this is only a start. The tougher challenge is to look beyond the data on which regressions can easily be based to other factors where data are much harder to find. Then you need to develop a point of view on how those other factors may themselves change in the future.

Conduct Sensitivity Analyses to Understand the Most Critical Assumptions and to Gauge Risks to Base Line Forecast

Managers who rely on single-point demand forecasts run dangerous risks. Some of the macroeconomic variables behind the forecasts could be wrong. It is necessary to identify potential risks and discontinuities like what things could cause this forecast to change dramatically or developments in competing technologies, in customer industry competitiveness and in supplier cost structures. Then, once a baseline forecast is complete, the challenge is to determine how far it could be off target. At one level, such a sensitivity analysis can be done by simply varying assumptions and quantifying their impact on demand. However, a more targeted approach usually provides better insight.

Even when the work is sound, though, uncertainties will remain: discontinuities will still be difficult to predict, especially if they are rooted in momentous political, macroeconomic, or technological changes. But managers who push their thinking through the steps in this framework will have a better chance of finding these discontinuities than those who do not. And those who base their business strategies on a solid knowledge of demand will stand a much greater chance of making wise investments and competing effectively.

Case Study

We would like to discuss a case of demand estimation in the pharmaceutical distribution industry. Pharmaceutical like FMCG is a category where competition is intense and distribution system and structure is highly complex. Added to this India is a huge country with huge population living in rural settings which makes the task of FMCG marketers all the more difficult.

Case Study: Apollo Pharmacy

The pharmaceutical industry is a highly regulated market. Most of the pharmaceutical products are sold as prescription drugs. There are some products that are sold as OTC. Regulations restrict most of the prescription drugs marketing strategies directed to generate prescriptions following canvassing and convincing medical doctors like GPs to prescribe the company's prescription drug. Whether a particular doctor is prescribing or not can be understood from the sales performance of the chemists and pharmacies around the area. The prescription sales impact inventory

When businesses evaluate various distribution network options, they must assess the impact on customer service and cost. The revenue is generated by satisfying identified customer needs by delivering the product through the distribution network. Distribution cost thus will determine the profitability of the delivery network. Although customer value delivery depends on various factors, businesses need to focus on measures that are influenced by the structure of the distribution network which are not only measurable but also controllable and that will include the following:

1 **Response time:** Amount of time it takes for a customer to receive an order
2 **Product type:** Number of different products or variants that are offered through the distribution network
3 **Product availability:** Probability of having a product in stock when customer order arrives
4 **Customer experience:** The ease with which a customer can place and receive orders and the extent to which this experience is customised including how customer experience is positively impacted by sales staff dealings and other interfaces with the customers
5 **Time to market:** Time it takes to bring a new product to the market
6 **Order visibility:** This is the ability of the customer to track their orders from ordering to receiving the delivery
7 **Returnability:** If customer is not happy with the product or if it does not meet the specification how easy it is to return the merchandise and the ability of the network to handle such stock returns
8 Product movement in the market in the sense whether fast moving or slow moving
9 Product category and distribution methods

It is not necessary that a customer always wants a high level of performance in all these stated dimensions. The customer can even trade off with some dimension for any other tangible benefit. For example, a little longer delivery period may be acceptable to the customer against a lot of varieties or even better quality and competitive price available in a store like Amazon. To give a unique experience to the customers, businesses have to design the network for which they might be incurring a significantly higher cost. For single-day delivery commitment, a traditional store will be required to have many stores in a defined geographical area or market, which may even run into hundreds as against a relatively much lesser number of stores at say Amazon.

Changing the distribution network design can, therefore, impact various supply chain cost drivers such as inventories, transportation, facilities and handling as well as information, in addition to sourcing and pricing drivers.

Distribution Management – Key Challenges

Through effective distribution, consumer demand is serviced. Consumers would like to buy the products from the nearest available sales outlet and that could be a retailer, distributor or showroom as the case may. Adequate stock level needs to be maintained as required to avoid any eventual stock-out situation resulting in loss of sales and in some cases even permanent loss of sales. Distribution function is therefore extremely important. Effective distribution is essential to succeed in the marketplace.

Logistics management offers significant complexity for businesses in India to service the end customers particularly for the reasons of a very long distribution channel involving multiple partners. Distribution cost also, therefore, is relatively higher in relation to overall product cost. Bringing down distribution and logistics costs thus can provide the competitive advantage

96 *Warehousing and Distribution Management*

to the business. Large businesses particularly in B2C models in fast-moving consumer goods segment such as Unilever, Nestle, ITC as well as online retailers such as Amazon.com or Flipkart.com are trying innovative methods to deliver to their end customers in the most cost-effective way, which is a big challenge to the businesses in a highly complex and large market like India. This chapter attempts to trace the complexity of logistics management issues for B2C segment with particular reference to organised retailing and e-retailing. Producing in multiple locations either directly or through contract manufacturing route is common for liquid, bulky and light-weight goods of daily use. Using local channel partners and wholesale routes for redistribution of goods to reduce cost of handling and storage is very common triggered by the complex tax structure in India. Businesses here in India trying to be smart in managing the complexity. In India it is not smart logistics but smarter ways to manage the challenges of logistics issues.

Distribution is one of the essential elements for success of any product or brand. And having distribution strength is what new multinational entrants into a new market like India are lacking in comparison to their Indian or local counterparts. If brand has to be big, it has to achieve a high level of penetration amongst the target consumers by extending both depth and width of distribution. New MNCs in India, therefore, have options of gradually developing their own distribution infrastructure or acquiring a local company that is engaged in similar business. It is the latter route that is preferable because it takes long time and high cost to develop effective distribution strength. MNCs are not even aware of and experience of complexity of distribution in the Indian business environment. Marketers generally believe that if distribution is achieved for a product up to the desired level, half of the battle is already won. Getting the required distribution of the product is also indicative of the fact that the trade channel has accepted and agreed to stock the product and if desired level of stocking as per norms which is directly related to the type of outlet and type of products then it is all the more desirable and encouraging. Also simply having the distribution infrastructure may not be enough. It should also be geared to reach the right place for the target consumers. Distribution infrastructure must be developed in line with product types and target market. For example, an industry having good rural distribution will not be suitable for a product which is designed predominantly for urban higher-income group upper-class consumers and vice versa. Optimisation of distribution cost vis-à-vis desired reach is, therefore, what all marketers will look for. Worldwide several experiments for this optimisation have been tried and attempted. In India we seem to have got stuck with our traditional mode of distribution although of late, other alternative models are tried and also being tested. Traditionally, in India we have distribution through wholesale route, which is a preferred option for new entrants and small companies in the SME sector. The other option is through appointed distributors and stockists serviced from either company warehouse or through stock points and clearing and forwarding agents. The latter is also a necessity because of our federal tax structure and system of multiple tax points of state and central tax and interstate tax including entry tax. This scenario has now changed after GST (Goods and Service Tax) was implemented. In the current system distribution cost will come down as tax structure is rationalised through the implementation of unified tax regime GST.

In the current system, cost of distribution can range between 25% and 35% of product cost because of the involvement of multiple agencies depending on whether it is for an established brand or a new brand. Additionally, a high level of trade inventory gets locked up which has its own cost.

Ultimately, consumer has to pay for all these hidden costs also for system inefficiencies. But if goods and merchandise can be directly taken from company warehouse to the consumer much of these costs can be avoided. In today's context of increasing global competition, organisations will explore ways and means to optimise distribution cost to reach the end consumer in quickest possible time at least cost.

Warehousing and Distribution Management 97

Towards this, the lead is taken again by multinationals.

Oriflame, a Swiss cosmetic manufacturing company entered into the Indian market in the early nineties with a range of high-priced cosmetic products. Obviously, the product is targeted for the upper-upper income group segment and company had opted for direct home-to-home selling through appointed agents who only work on commission. The commission offered to the agents is about 25%, which is much lower than traditional cost of distribution appointing stockists, distributors, wholesalers and finally retailers to reach end customers. As the product is directly reaching the ultimate consumers, trade stocks are thus avoided. This mode of direct marketing is not only proved to be a little cheaper, but it also helps the company to remain in direct contact with the target consumers which itself is a great advantage to brand marketers. The negative side of this mode of direct distribution is that the process is slow but sure. This negative aspect of the whole system of direct-to-home distribution has also been resolved by Amway Corporation – a ten-billion-dollar American multinational and the largest home-to-home consumer goods company. Amway manufactures daily use high-quality household products. In India they entered by importing the products in the first phase but later on got their products also manufactured through contract route. They appoint individuals as distributors who will work and sell the product directly to end consumers. Directly appointed distributors don't have to invest in the business but will be earning a high commission. These first-layer distributors again appoint others known to them as agents who will also get supplies directly from the company and sell the product to homes. These second level of distributors again will appoint sub-distributors who again can extend the chain further through their own known circles and thus the link extends and as a result the whole multilevel distribution system as we call them spreads like wildfire as long as the link continues to grow. As long as the chain continues to grow each link in the whole chain benefits from each other's performance and, therefore, making an effective and enterprising individual as a distributor makes it more effective and efficient. The company will have stock points at convenient and strategic locations to service the target market. In multilevel marketing, there are advantages as well in the sense that there is no damaged stock, stock return, write-offs, outstanding, trade debtors, doubtful debts and consumer complaints to deal with as opposed to the indirect traditional system of distribution. Absolutely no hassle, company provides 100% money-back guarantee for dissatisfied customers to ensure reliability and consumer confidence by giving quality assurance and guaranteed satisfaction. Amway has in fact written a new chapter by establishing multilevel distribution in India for FMCG products from which others have learnt from their experience and experiments.

Complexity in Logistics Management in India – A Case of FMCG Industry

In the past decade, there are couple of end-to-end third-party logistics (3PL) providers offering solution to businesses, but their offering is limited to B2B model. Even multinational logistics companies such as DHL, Fed Express and local competitors such as Gati, Safex etc. are also active in India offering end-to-end solutions to the businesses. Of course, at a cost (Baisya, 2015a).

In India we have about 13 million small retail outlets which cater to the consumers. These retailers are serviced by the distributors and wholesalers, who are in turn serviced by the manufacturers from their strategically located stock points or warehouses and depending on the market penetration, businesses can have even over two hundred such stock points. 3P logistic companies deliver company stock to those stock points from company manufacturing locations. The competition has forced manufacturers to decentralise manufacturing operations and go for contract manufacturing routes. Earlier, MNCs were having their own manufacturing facilities but many of them including Unilever, Reckitt Benckiser, P&G etc. have been increasingly outsourcing their manufacturing operations primarily because it also reduces the logistics cost as

98 *Warehousing and Distribution Management*

contract manufacturing locations can be established close to distribution points. Companies like P&G is sourcing from their Thailand manufacturing plant for their Indian market requirement to optimise global logistics cost.

Bigger is the enterprise, more complex is their logistics issues. Earlier logistics used to mean transportation (freight) and warehousing but now we mean it in a more holistic sense. Logistics operators now are required to provide an integrated solution covering raw materials and packaging materials shipment to production plants to warehousing and distribution of finished goods to end consumers. In a dynamic market, demand fluctuates which results into inter-location transfers and retransfers of goods adding to the complexity.

A typical large FMCG company will have about three to four company-owned manufacturing locations, about 10–12 contract manufacturers (co-packers), about 8 to 10 warehouses, over 1000–1200 distributors and wholesalers and 13 million retail universe. Normally through direct distribution about 1 to 1.5 million retail outlets are covered, and rest is covered through redistribution route. Direct reach of companies like Unilever can be a little higher. The vendors supplying input to the manufacturing locations will be numerous, and that will include even imported raw materials and packaging materials. This will explain the complexity of the logistics management task in a country like India with population of over 1.3 billion.

Depending on the size of the operation and their geographical spread, the distribution will be either, intensive, selective or exclusive. For example, an organic food brand can have selective distribution designed to cover their target segment but for an FMCG company manufacturing daily use products like tea and biscuits will have to have intensive distribution network and in Indian context the task is very complex.

India as a Country Adds to Complexity

India is a huge country having land mass of 3,287,240 sq km (largest is Rajasthan having land mass of 342,239 sq km and smallest is Goa having land mass of 3702 sq km) and 29 states. While Rajasthan is largest in size, population is largest in Uttar Pradesh (200 million). Population of India is 1.3 billion (2.4% of world's land area but 17.5% of world's population) and over 50% of the population is under 25 years of age (a high spending segment in many markets) and about 31% of the population below the age of 14 years and about 25% of the total population falls in the age group of 20 and 35 years. India is thus a young country contrary to developed countries like Europe, which has an aging population.

The market is so diverse in the sense that demographic and psychographic profiles of the consumers in various regions vary widely. The country is so huge that in one part there could be flood when the other part is facing serious drought conditions. In addition, it also offers socio-cultural complexity.

Seventy-two per cent of the population lives in rural areas in 638,000 villages. Rural market is, therefore, very large and still untapped. MNCs and large FMCG companies derive 20–40% revenue from the rural market.

Life expectancy is 69 years, literacy rate is 64%, We are a trillion-dollar (-USD 3.176 Trillion in 2021) economy and GDP growth rate is 6.7%. In India we have 100 million internet users. You cannot, therefore, ignore India if you want to do business on a global scale.

Entry of Organised Retailers and E-Retailers

Leading global retailers like Walmart and Tesco have already entered the Indian market through joint ventures or on their own in a big way. Walmart recently acquired majority stake in Flip Kart, the largest e-commerce player in India to have their entry into e-retailing to fight Amazon outside the USA. Besides, there are a host of domestic retailers such as Big-Bazaar, Reliance and Aditya Birla Group competing with global retailers. Of late, online retailers like Amazon.com have also entered the fray competing with local online retailers like Flipkart.com, Snapdeal.com and many others. These companies have been investing heavily in their business hoping to make good sense of their investment in the long run. In wholesale trade in cash and carry mode, we have global players like Bookers and Metro (Macro) competing with our traditional distributors and wholesalers. Walmart also has 22 large-format wholesale cash and carry stores in India. The success of these ventures into retail and wholesale operations will depend on how effectively they will be able to manage the logistics cost more effectively in terms of the following parameters:

- Time to deliver the goods to the customers
- Reducing the inventory in the system without losing out on delivery commitment
- Cost of logistics

These parameters will essentially provide them competitive advantage as only other parameter that they have to control and manage is procurement efficiency, and major suppliers are large global players and organised retailers or even cash and carry operators don't have any incremental buying power with them (Baisya, 2015b).

Distribution Challenge for the Base of the Pyramid Population

According to the National Sample Survey Organisation (NSSO) definition, persons spending less than USD 75 per month on consumables fall under bottom-of-the-pyramid population and according to that definition about 114 million households or 76% of the rural population actually comes under BOP. Delivering goods and services to this section of population is really a challenge for the marketers in India. There are three major factors that explain the complexity of distribution for base of the pyramid. These can be depicted as shown in Figure 4.3 (Hammond et al., 2008; Huhmann, 2004).

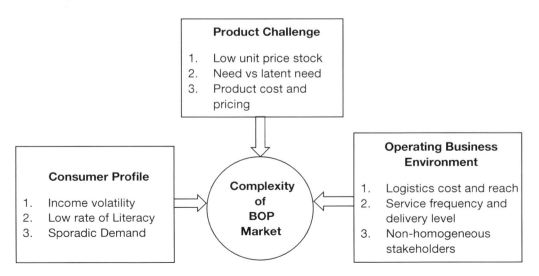

Figure 4.3 Distribution Challenges of BOP Market

Source: Adapted from IFMR – A Centre for Development Finance Publication (Shukla and Bairiganjan, 2011)

100 *Warehousing and Distribution Management*

In the rural market which constitutes the BOP segment, only way to reach is through the redistribution route involving wholesalers who have small rural redistributors to cover rural retail outlets. Very slow-moving vehicles including bullock cart, cycle rickshaw, auto rickshaw, or even boat running through waterways (as in Kerala) are used to manage the logistics issue. Salesmen using by-cycle or even on foot delivering door-to-door customers or to village retailers and tobacco shops are also common sight in rural and sometimes even in urban distribution systems for fast-moving consumer goods, such as food or even tobacco products. The unique system is being followed to cover every opportunity to deliver growth in a complex market like India particularly to face challenges of BOP opportunity. For the BOP segment of the market, marketers need special product pack and pricing keeping in mind the consumer profile in that segment and also for overcoming the distribution challenges offered by the typical environment as well as incremental cost involved in the distribution reach. To penetrate this market smart logistics is not enough but what is needed to act street smart (Shukla and Bairiganjan, 2011).

Drivers of Distribution Complexity

The overall retail market is estimated to be about USD 300 billion growing at an average of about 6%. India has been the host of many consumer products multinationals, including giants like Unilever, ITC and Nestle, operating in India for several decades. Still, for many, India is relatively a new territory with a number of interrelated factors, which make the task of distribution very challenging. These factors are follows:

1 Dispersed Population

There are 30 cities in India which have over 1 million population, but this constitutes only 15% of the total population. The rural market still constitutes 30–50% of the market. The market again is not homogeneous with many income groups and demographic and psychographic variations.

2 Retail Density

With about 13 million retail outlets, India has one of the highest retailing densities in the world. Mom and Pop stores account for about 95% of the total retail universe. Organised retailing has just begun to emerge and has about 4–5% of the total market.

3 Channel Intermediaries

As indicated in Figure 4.3, there are many channel partners or associates which are required to ensure the desired reach of the target market. There are various models of distributions starting from wholesalers' route to organised retailing to reach end consumers, and each has its own advantages and disadvantages. For example, wholesale route provides wider distribution but control is very low on both trade and market. Distributor model run through appointed distributors is better controlled, but cost is higher and too complex to manage efficiently.

4 Infrastructure Complexity

There are very few full-service distribution companies operating in India, and they are also not affordable by all businesses. Unless brands can fetch very premium price, using the services of such end-to-end distribution companies will only add to significant cost and, therefore, loss of profit. Most of the FMCG businesses, therefore, have to depend on multiple agencies who operate as channel partners in this complex logistics management task.

Warehousing and Distribution Management 101

Consider a case of typical FMCG goods like a biscuit manufactured in northern state in Utta-rakhand such as Baddi – a tax-free zone where manufacturers will prefer to make new investment in production facilities to get excise and sales tax holidays. When this biscuit has to be sold in a destination in the state like Tamil Nadu down south, first the stock will be handed over to a local transporter who will keep the stock in his warehouse in Baddi and then this trucker will take almost 15 days to reach the manufacturer's distributor in the state headquarter Chennai in Tamil Nadu passing through eight states and multiple checkpoints. From the company's distributor in state head-quarter, the stock will move to district town distributor in smaller truck or even in three wheelers. The district town distributors will also give stock to local wholesalers from whom rural retailers will buy, and these wholesalers will sell stock to rural distributors and the stock, in smaller quantity, will move either in state transport buses or even by bullock cart. The whole process can take over a month. Only very large companies have been able to reach through their distribution network to markets with say about 50,000 in population. The smaller market uses local transport to reach rural market, and efficiency will depend on the pull of the product. Company's stock moving from say state headquarter to smaller district-level distributors and rural distributors in state-owned buses, three wheelers, or bullock carts are very popular sights in India. In addition, small orders are also executed by companies through government-owned postal system in VPP (value payable parcels) and railways, which have much greater reach but are time-consuming and have no control over their operations, and therefore no commitment can be given about the time to reach customers. Still goods for public distribution system (PDS) such as wheat, rice and salt largely move in rail transport just because state-controlled railways will have to get business and not for cost or efficiency reasons.

5 Unorganised Markets

For most consumer products, market will be unorganised. Large businesses will work with about 1000 to 1200 appointed distributors. Companies like P&G have made two-tier distribution system following 80:20 principle as 20% of the distributors deliver 80% of the sales. They, thus, a decade ago implemented a project called 'Golden Eye' and directly sell the goods to company-appointed large distributors (20%) who have under them smaller distributors (80%). With this change and consolidation, P&G reduced the strength of the sales force drastically and also simplified the complexity in the system. Manufacturers have varying degrees of distribution structure designed to meet their objectives.

6 Choosing the Right Mix

Organising an efficient channel of distribution is thus an enormous task for businesses. One has to, therefore, strike a right balance between various models. The evolution of distribution is shown in the following diagram (Figure 4.4), which indicates the degree of sophistication.

In India, we have a mix of all in a typical manufacturing–marketing company of FMCG products.

The more sophisticated the market, the higher the control of the marketers in the distribution system but lower the reach as depicted in Figure 4.4 (Bhalla et al., 2007).

Current Scenario – A Mixed System

In order to reduce the transit inventory of goods, constant en-route and live monitoring of vehicles are being used by incorporating devices like RFID or similar GPS-based monitoring technology. With connectivity being available, this online and real-time monitoring is now being done by select and large 3P logistics providers. However, technology solutions are not offered by all 3P logistics

102 *Warehousing and Distribution Management*

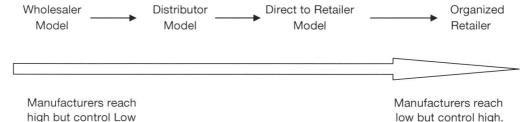

Figure 4.4 Degree of Sophistication in Distribution
Source: Adapted from a BCG analysis (Mossman and Norton, 1965)

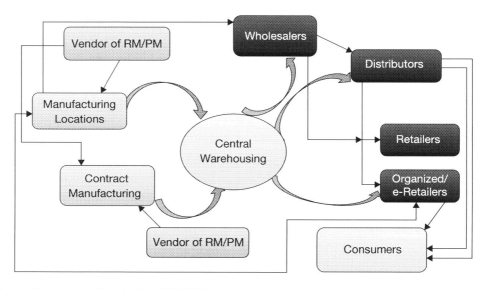

Figure 4.5 Logistics Complexity of FMCG Category

providers, and majority of freight and transport service providers in India are only geared to provide point-to-point transport service. As market is highly fragmented, the requirement of goods in certain areas is low resulting in not having full load of goods, and that adds to the problem and it goes through multiple handling causing delays in delivery and as a result consumers also get relatively older stock compared to high consumption market in metro and mini metros, where relatively fresh stock is available. For low shelf-life goods and for the goods which require refrigerated storage and transport system, cost of distribution is significantly high and efficiency low. Small towns and villages get stock through redistribution route which is not serviced directly by the manufacturers. The complexity is mounted by multiple tax regimes when goods and services are moving from one state to another which includes central sales Tax (CST), state sales tax (VAT), entry tax etc., and complexity is more if the goods are excisable such as liquor, which has to move in bonded warehouse while even on the move in transport vehicle. Typically, fast-moving consumer goods (FMCG)

Warehousing and Distribution Management 103

companies will have flow of goods as shown Figure 4.5. With introduction of GST, tax structure has broadly been rationalised but it is still not uniform and leaves aside some products like liquor etc. While introduction of GST made the movement of transport vehicle carrying goods faster resulting in reduction in transportation time to some extent complexity of the distribution function has still remained because of the huge retail universe spread over in such a diverse country with varying degrees of logistics infrastructure that businesses need to service.

Figure 4.5 will explain the complexity of the goods distribution system in a long chain intensive distribution category of products like FMCG such as processed foods and daily consumables.

The distribution complexity and cost forced businesses to go for contract manufacturing route to set up small third-party manufacturing units to cater to the smaller market in a highly dispersed and scattered market like India. And if the product is bulky and light weight or heavy or liquid, the logistics cost would even be much higher in relation to other products. As per labelling requirement, the name and address of manufacturing locations are to be mentioned statutorily on the product label. And if one takes a look at the label of a national brand of tea Label one can see the manufacturing locations which can run up to even 10–15 locations. Liquid products like bottled water or beverages are also manufactured in multiple locations to save on the distribution and logistics costs.

Developing Efficient Sales and Distribution Structure

It takes years for businesses to develop an efficient sales and distribution infrastructure. Successful companies take as much attention to keep the right distributors with appropriate infrastructure and goodwill in the trade to work for them for as long as they take in appointing senior employees. Companies that provide training programmes, coaching and sales support to their distributors to perform better in the marketplace when compared to their competitors. Sales force effectiveness is thus important for companies to derive competitive advantages.

Having an efficient and well-entrenched distribution system in India holds the key to success. Many MNCs fail on that ground, and many MNCs were seen to acquire local companies simply to get control over the distribution system. For example, Coca-Cola acquired local beverages company Parle Beverages only to get control and entry into local beverage distribution system which takes years to build, and Coca-Cola acquired it paying a huge price. Coca-Cola left India in 1977 and at that time they had 26 franchised bottler, and they were controlling over 80% of the soft beverage market in India. Second to Coke was Parle Beverages and their subsidiary Bisleri which owned the remaining 20%. When Coke decided to come back again post-liberalisation, the market structure reversed by then and Parle was controlling close to 75% market in the same product category and Coke found the acquisition of Parle brands and business as the best route to get access to local distribution when their arch-rival Pepsi was already there well entrenched. Even Pepsi also acquired Dukes from Pandoles to get entry to soda water distribution. Distribution is the most important function to be managed for a product to succeed in the market place.

Measuring Sales Force and Distribution Effectiveness

Constant monitoring of performance of sales and distribution system, therefore, is done by most FMCG companies and parameters include tracking the primary, secondary sales and consumer offtakes (tertiary sales) market segment wise with rural–urban focus in addition to sales volume, profit of the sales route and distributor ranking, order fill rate, pack fill rate, cost of distribution etc. Other measures include tracking the debtors, age analysis of debtors, cost of operations per unit of

104 *Warehousing and Distribution Management*

sales, sales growth rate, customer-wise sales volume and value, profitability by customer segment or even customer-wise, new customer creation and retention of existing customers, sustainability are some of the key performance indicators.

The magnitude of the task to manage the logistics in FMCG companies as can be seen is enormous. Only a few companies have well-entrenched mixed distribution system to get the desired reach growing faster than others. The BOP segment, which is a complex segment requiring multiple channels and partners, offers considerable growth prospect as their purchasing power is increasing. This is significantly different from the situation in the developed world, where market is saturated and in some places even shrinking and where distribution system has evolved to reach every prospects. But doing business in India requires different skills and knowledge. Learning that or acquiring that is essential for success. Only having smart logistics solution is not enough. In India, you need to act smarter. Otherwise, you will only scrape through the surface of the total market opportunity and can never be a partner to take advantage of all-inclusive growth.

The socio-political including climatic conditions in the various markets in India, including the consumer buying behaviour are so different that each market requires separate attention. The market is heterogeneous – there is thus no one uniform solution that will work in all markets. Each market needs separate attention for finding a solution as it will offer different degrees of complexity to the business depending on their products' profile, characteristics and target market requirement.

Source: Baisya (2015a)

Impact of the Corona Pandemic on the Operations and Supply Chain of the Agriculture and Food Processing Sectors With Reference to MSME in India and the Expected Recovery Prospects

The food industry is largely an unorganised sector processing seasonal surpluses to produce value-added products for the domestic and international markets. The Indian food processing industry is dominated by large numbers of small-scale and Micro, Small and Medium Enterprises (MSME) processors that have limited resources and a low level of technology adoption.

Agricultural and food processing and allied activities have been impacted by the Corona pandemic, and the meat and poultry sector, too, has been hit severely, which is the fastest-growing sector of the agricultural eco-system, where we have already created a foothold in the global market. India is the third-largest producer of eggs and the fifth-largest producer of broilers, and this sector is said to have incurred losses to the tune of INR 1.5 to 2.0 billion every day during the pandemic, which again is compounded by the social media spreading misinformation linking the Corona virus infection with the consumption of meat and poultry, resulting in demand disappearing and price crashing to INR 10–15 per kg, when production costs were around INR 70 per kg. The meat, poultry and marine processing industry has been affected by logistics restrictions. Fishing vessels were not able to go for deep-sea fishing, which was banned to avoid large gatherings.

In addition, prices of other food grains, including soybean and maize, also experienced a steady decline during the peak pandemic period (Baisya, 2020d).

The prices of fruits and vegetables also rose due to limited availability as well as restricted movement of goods. The edible oil sector in India is largely (70 per cent) dependent on imports, which also got disrupted. The perishable raw materials were not processed due to a shortage of labour. During the mango season, processors were having shortage of labour due to the large-scale migration of the temporary workforce in MSME sectors, and at the same time, processors did not get any confirmed order for mango pulp, which is almost 50 per cent of the activity of the fruit and vegetable processing units.

The year 2020 was particularly good for mango production, but processors could not benefit out of it. In the mango season, processors were desperately trying to start processing of mangoes to meet their commitment. And they have been airing several types of issues that they were facing, starting with the non-availability of labour, high labour cost, transport cost and restriction on their movement, cost of raw materials, operational issues to comply with various kinds of government stipulations and compliance related to the Corona pandemic.

During the last mango season, processors did not get a supply of raw mangoes to be processed. For those who could get, the quantity was not sufficient to run the plant even one shift a day, when in the mango season plants normally run round the clock in three shifts for three to four months. In the case of large processors, migrant workers stay within the factory premise or in close vicinity. But this year, there were no workers available (Baisya, 2020b).

The sales of various categories of processed food, like fruit juices and pulps and ready-to-eat food products, drastically dropped, resulting in the closure of small retail and grocery outlets in the neighbourhood.

The supply chain was disrupted during lockdown, which hampered the movement of stock during the pandemic, and large stocks of processed food were spoiled and became unfit for human consumption due to the expiry of the stock, adding to already mounting losses. The non-availability of workers became a major cause of disruption at different stages of the value chain. Even large processors have faced a decrease in demand in both domestic and international markets.

When lockdown was abruptly declared without any plan, cash inflow suddenly stopped for all industries – big, small, and tiny included. A large part of them had to down their shutters. The government earlier gave two shocks to industries with the introduction of GST and demonetisation, which were man-made, and now COVID-19, which is said to be not man-made, although controversy still persists (Baisya, 2021).

Production and distribution halted almost instantly without any possibility for industry to plan it out, and that created a shock in the processors' planned schedule and commitment. A pre-warning by a couple of days would possibly have reduced the suffering of millions of migrant workers and consequently the impact on industries.

Acute Shortage of Trained Temporary Workforce and Impact of Other Factors on Cost of Goods

Through a contract route that primarily employs migrant workers, the food industry engages a seasonal temporary workforce. After years of working in the same industry, these workers have been trained to deliver the expected productivity level of the industry. Now that trained migrant workers are gone and will not return in the near future, the industry has to manage with an untrained workforce, and their availability and numbers are also uncertain. Thus, wages and cost of processed food will also increase. The industry will not have adequate time to plan for the processing and packaging of seasonal fruits, which are largely exported in bulk as either fresh produce or in the form of pulp and juice – both canned and in concentrated form in aseptic bags. Furthermore, exporters have not been able to contact their buyers to determine their requirement during this uncertain situation, as buyers don't have a fix on their requirement, as they themselves are also impacted by the Corona pandemic, and processors have no clue about the cost of the product under the new situation as the cost of the product is likely to go up due to higher labour wages, input material cost, utility cost as well as transport cost. And on top of all these, there will be incremental costs

106 *Warehousing and Distribution Management*

for providing protection for the safety and health of the employees and customers. The situation, therefore, is totally fluid, and it is difficult to conclude the deal in international trade, where risk is much higher for non-performance of the contract. Our manufacturer exporters are, therefore, going through uncertain phases. The impact has been so severe that such things have never been experienced by industries ever before.

The majority of processors have been facing severe cash flow issues and have been waiting for the government's help to tide over this difficulty. But the stimulus package of the government as announced has nothing much for the food processing industry to rejoice about (Baisya, 2020b).

There are large industries which operate on a contract manufacturing system. Even some of the big-volume brands like Parle G are produced on contact manufacturing plants. These companies will face heightened pressure to maintain control over new safety and quality standards. Some of these initiatives will be influenced by regulatory bodies, while others will be influenced by customer demand. However, it is imperative for processors to thoroughly assess these criteria and implement measures to substantiate their claims, thereby persuading consumers that they are setting new benchmarks and implementing them with the utmost dedication to distinguish their product from competitors. This approach can facilitate accelerated growth and the recapture of lost market share. It has to be seen how smaller players will gear up to these new challenges to ensure their growth and survival. The food businesses will not be as usual any longer in the post-pandemic period (Baisya, 2020c).

Impact on the Food and Beverage Industry

During the pandemic, food and beverage manufacturers have encountered a substantial decrease in consumption as well as supply-chain-related issues. Consumers indulged in panic buying to overstock due to fear of scarcity in addition to supply chain derailment.

The supply of raw materials, food ingredients and other input materials to the manufacturing sites has also been seriously affected, which in turn has hampered production, forcing processors to discontinue manufacturing operations. Besides, the availability of manpower at the time of social distancing has been yet another major constraint. A study conducted by French trade group ANIA indicates that food and beverage manufacturers have suffered a 22 per cent loss in sales revenue globally as a consequence of all these factors (Batch Master ERP, 2020). In India, a tropical country, 45 per cent of the beverage sales take place during the peak summer months. Unfortunately, the entire summer season was lost due to the pandemic, leading to a significant revenue decline of over 50 per cent in this industry.

The domestic consumption of these products has reduced drastically for the reason that consumers have become sceptical about the consumption of these discretionary food products. Besides, there is an unusual concern and awareness of health and hygiene, which has impacted some of the product categories. In-home consumption was facilitated through e-commerce retail stores like Bigbasket and Grofers, which kept the supply line open, although they have limited reach. But out-of-home consumption, which traditionally generates a higher margin, came to a standstill.

Post-Lockdown Scenario

The lockdown has been gradually relaxed and withdrawn in phases. The objective is to start economic activities slowly and gradually. Railways and airlines have resumed services, but occupancy has been very low. Industries have been preparing for the resumption of production. Comparatively, the food industry has suffered losses to a lesser extent than other categories of industries. However, that is valid only for primary and basic foods. As such, there was a significant loss of revenue for processed food and food service industries largely due to the disruption in the production and distribution of goods and services.

On average, the projected sales for the last month of the financial year 2020–2021, March, are approximated to be 20 per cent of the year-end sales in the final month of that year. However, the lack of operational channel partners and restricted stock movement prevented the realisation of these sales. During the year end, businesses normally announce many discounts and promotional schemes to push stock in the trade. The same is the case during the festival season. The festival season sales also plummeted due to poor consumer demand. In the MSME sector, many small processors have already closed down permanently, and many others are struggling for survival. Those who are supported by large processors will have a comparatively higher level of sustainability (Baisya, 2020a).

Industry Learnt New Lessons from the Pandemic

The year of the pandemic has imparted valuable lessons to the food processing industry, altering perceptions regarding their products and services. These insights should be taken into consideration when deciding the future direction of the business categories that they own. During lockdown periods, food products have been classified as essential items in numerous countries, resulting in the continuous operation of food stores while adhering to specific criteria. In the days of disruption, the old ball games do not work, and new rules and practices take precedence over the established understanding of consumers.

Despite the development of vaccines and a decline in the number of new cases and deaths, the pandemic is still ongoing in India. Furthermore, it is possible for other countries to encounter comparable circumstances to those currently unfolding in the UK and other countries in Europe and the USA. Thus, the food processing industry has to focus on future strategies and draw up plans for managing the business for performance. As consumer perception has changed about processed food, their consumption and purchase behaviour will also change, thus dictating product formulation, quality, standards of operating practices as well as the gross margin of the products that processors will sell.

For consumers, the pandemic seems to have strengthened their concerns about product safety as well as employees' health. According to a study carried out by Mckinsey, 20–25 per cent consumers in developed markets research food brands and products prior to making purchasing decisions. Key considerations are product safety and healthiness, the hygiene of the packaging and the well-being of the employees. However, in emerging markets such as India, South Korea and China, these figures exceed 40 per cent, 35 per cent and 45 per cent respectively, indicating that concerns in emerging markets are much greater for similar criteria. It is quite significant that in India 40 per cent of consumers' buying decisions are now based on new criteria and considerations where hygienic packaging, employee welfare and health stand as the top-most important criteria (McKinsey & Company, 2021).

New Food Safety Standards Post-Pandemic and Compliance With New Standards

The food safety standards will also undergo changes keeping in mind the new perception of consumers with regard to quality, safety and employee welfare criteria. This itself will pose serious challenges to many processors and more so to the MSME sector, which has limited resources and a low degree of technology adoption, impeding the necessary adaptations to the evolving situation.

108   *Warehousing and Distribution Management*

Product quality and safety will also dictate the product composition and formulations. Many large companies are also reviewing their product compositions in the light of new expectations of consumers and also based on new knowledge on the subject and latest scientific literatures. Several major corporations are currently reassessing the content of their products in response to evolving consumer expectations and the newest scientific research in the field. That itself is a challenge which is unique to the food processing industry.

In the United States, specific social issues have emerged. According to a survey by the US Centers for Disease Control and Prevention, a certain ethnic group working in the meat industry accounted for 87 per cent of the confirmed Covid cases at meat processing plants between April and May during the pandemic (Dyal, 2020).

In view of these findings and as a result of the pandemic-induced scrutiny on the social belief and practices of companies, it is now generally believed that the food processing industry is unlikely to maintain the pre-pandemic operational status quo. It appears that food processing enterprises will need to adopt varying pricing structures, product standards, and potentially even discontinue specific items in order to progress. Some of these changes are likely to be driven by government agencies and regulators seeking to limit the spread of contagious diseases. For example, the German Federal Government announced a ban on contract and temporary workers at meat processing plants from January 2021. This will compel meat processors in Germany to directly hire all their staff and workers, resulting in significantly higher costs. Consequently, the pricing of the product will be adjusted accordingly, potentially affecting the business volume. This ban has come into force based on the suggestion by the European Federation of Food Agriculture and Tourism Trade Unions. In the Netherlands also a similar move is on the cards, where trade unions are demanding direct employment of workers engaged in food processing (Overton, 2020).

In order to comply with stricter regulations, firms and brands seeking growth must distinguish themselves in a favourable manner based on these social variables in order to increase their market share. Large companies and MNCs are evaluating these new pandemic-related parameters. Some companies are also seen taking proactive actions, such as fitting hospital-grade air filter in the ventilator and air handling unit, voluntarily reducing the working hours in a shift and implementing social distancing convention for workers.

The impact of all these will be that the companies will inevitably face increased operating costs, squeezed margins and unused capacity for an indefinite period, in addition to the possibility of labour shortages as migrant workers stay in their home countries due to travel limitations. Technology adoption in the processed food industry has long lagged behind, but other consumer goods sectors have already adopted advanced technologies such as robotic automation. Nevertheless, these modifications may potentially incite a shift in the food processing business. However, this is unlikely to occur in the near future because of the substantial investment and requirement of highly skilled labour. Besides, it will also lead to a decrease in employment.

Agriculture Sector Delivered Higher GVA

The gross value added (GVA) performance of the agriculture, forestry and fishing sector in the first quarter of the financial years 2019–2020 and 2020–2021 has exhibited growth. This is the only sector that has shown growth during the pandemic, as can be seen from the data in Table 4.2:

The share of total GVA of agricultural sector has experienced a rise in the first quarter of 2020–2021, escalating from 13.3 per cent to 17.8 per cent. However, it is important to consider this in light of the fact that all other sectors have shown a decline in growth. The Indian economy has greatly benefitted from the agriculture, forestry and fishing sector's impressive growth rate of 3.4 per cent. Thanks to our farmers who really delivered. But in spite of this, the food processing industry has not

Table 4.2 Sectoral GVA for Quarter 1 (April–June) of FY 2019–20 and 2020–21 at 2011–12 Prices

	2019–20 (INR billion)	*2019–20*	*2020–21 (INR billion)*	*2020–21*	
GVA at basic prices	Quarter 1	Share of total GVA (%)	Quarter 1	Share of total GVA (%)	% Growth
	4398.43	13.3	4546.58	17.8	3.4 %

Source: Ministry of Statistics and Program Implementation, Government of India.

performed well in the domestic market and also in the export of processed foods. All categories of processed food have registered a significant decline (Taneja and Zaidi, 2020).

According to the available data, India exported Basmati rice worth USD 3.88 billion and buffalo meat worth USD 3.01 billion during FY 2020 until February 2020. Additionally, non-Basmati rice worth USD 1.84 billion was exported during the same period. In FY 2021 until October 2020, Basmati rice exports were reported at USD 2.43 billion, non-Basmati rice worth USD 2.33 billion and buffalo meat worth USD 2.71 billion. Furthermore, other processed foods worth USD 2.71 billion were exported during FY 2020. Indian agricultural, horticultural and processed foods are exported to more than 100 countries and regions, including the Middle East, South East Asia, SAARC countries, the EU and the US. During the pandemic, the export performance has in fact declined in spite of the fact that in terms of GVA the sector showed a real-term growth of 3.4 per cent (Baisya, 2020e).

The Ministry of Commerce and Industry, Government of India, implemented the Agricultural Export Policy in 2018. The main goal of this policy is to increase the income of farmers by 2022 by doubling the country's agricultural exports. Additionally, the policy aims to connect Indian farmers and their agricultural products to the global value chain. The government focused on the export of agricultural products in order to develop a policy aimed at achieving a USD 60 billion export objective by 2022. Keeping that in view, the government also introduced a new set of farm bills that is currently being opposed by the farmers. The readers can easily see the gap between the actual performances in the export of agricultural products, which is hovering at USD 29 billion. In FY 2020, until January 2020 exports of agricultural and processed food products were reported to be worth USD 28.94 billion, which is only the halfway mark of the projected figure of the government for FY 2022. This is obviously not achievable.

We are the leading global producer of agricultural commodities such as pulses, milk, and buffalo meat. However, we are unable to effectively compete in the market. Despite the imposition of high customs duties, imported pulses such as chickpeas and kidney beans can still compete with local producers in terms of price. This highlights the need for continued protection of indigenous farmers, as imported products have the potential to readily enter and compete in Indian markets. Furthermore, this applies to countries such as Vietnam that have a Free Trade Agreement (FTA) with us. We lack competitiveness in milk and meat exports compared to Australia and New Zealand. It is imperative to enhance the export competitiveness of all these products. Our farmers have demonstrated exceptional diligence, even during the epidemic, surpassing other industries, which have experienced a consistent fall. However, their income level is not increasing in terms of purchasing power. Given the inability of farmers to obtain a greater price in the international market, the sole means of augmenting income is by enhancing productivity. Increasing pricing in the domestic market would render the processing business uncompetitive and impede its growth. Enhanced agricultural management techniques are required for our growth.

110 *Warehousing and Distribution Management*

Way to Recovery Needs New Strategic Direction

All major categories of the processed food industry have suffered significant losses and decline in performance during the Corona pandemic due to a decline in demand and disruption in the supply chain. However, all disruptions and challenges also bring new opportunities along with it. Once the dust settles, the processors will find it imperative to innovate and change with time to remain relevant. New strategies for survival and also to regain the lost opportunities should include the following:

- Review the existing product portfolio and rationalise the products and SKUs
- Revisit the current sourcing strategies and evaluate alternative suppliers in view of new criteria of sourcing requirement
- Evaluate alternative distribution routes, channels and strategies
- Explore and optimise e-commerce and distribution network
- Introduce organisation-wide cost management initiatives to reduce cost of operation
- Revisit pricing and promotional strategies
- Implement strategies for regaining lost customers
- Assess the existing supply chain agility and how to make it more resilient
- Review the crisis management system and emergency response plans

Customers may have transitioned to substitute items or even migrated to other companies. It is possible that some of the competitors may have even altered their dietary habits. Some may have transitioned to consuming natural and organic foods instead of processed goods. Hence, challenges hold great importance. In difficult times like this, businesses need both innovation and financial resources to regain lost ground, which most of our MSME players don't have. There are a large number of MSMEs in the food processing sector that have closed their shutter. The majority of them will be unable to commence anew. Small vendors, such as roadside restaurants and dhabas, have also ceased operations. The food retailers and neighbourhood stores have permanently closed down, and their owners returned to their home state not to come back again. They, therefore, will take a longer time to get back to their pre-pandemic positions. The worst sufferers from the pandemic would be the MSME sector across categories of food industries. Those who have survived will take a long time to get to the pre-pandemic level. Industries that are dependent on the international market will take still longer.

Chapter Summary

Warehousing is a very critical function to be managed effectively, which will determine the productivity and cost efficiency of the entire supply chain. Warehouse is required to be located in a strategic location from the consideration of providing ideal level of customer service at least cost, which is a prerequisite for survival in a dynamic market environment. Warehousing, therefore, plays a key role in distribution management, and efficiency of distribution management will determine the success of the business itself. Distribution management is an area therefore demands the attention of the top senior-level management team and key decisions are taken at the highest level of the corporation. The decisions related to distribution strategy and performance criteria are taken by senior management team in the business. The chapter deals with the functions and activities undertaken in the warehouse as well as types of warehouses and which type suits for what kind and size of business. Warehouse design and construction for efficient warehouse management, warehouse cost, activities, warehouse

Warehousing and Distribution Management 111

location decision criteria which were discussed with examples. This chapter also discussed strategies and planning of taking warehousing decisions as well as warehouse management systems and warehouse operation. WMS implementation strategies and advantages as well as challenges were discussed in detail. Warehouse performance metrics and factors influencing the performance of warehouse are also discussed in detail. Criticality of warehouse management and their implication on distribution performance has been discussed. Distribution challenges and complexity were discussed particularly in the Indian market environment Finally, a case of FMCG product distribution was discussed to explain the typical complexity and challenges and how those are tackled by the marketers of FMCG products. Also, distribution management task, scope, organisation, channel management and channel partners role, distribution cost, performance criteria and what it takes for efficient distribution management were discussed in this chapter. The Corona pandemic disrupted the supply chain, impacting businesses. This was discussed with particular reference to the agriculture and food processing industries in the MSME sector in India and tracing the possible recovery in terms of recreating the lost demand in domestic and international markets.

Discussion Questions

1. Discuss the various functions of warehousing. What are the key indicators of efficient warehousing management?
2. What are the different types of warehousing that industry uses and for which conditions those are preferred?
3. Discuss the key design criteria for layout of a warehouse for efficient operation. What constitutes warehousing cost?
4. What are the key activities being performed in a warehouse and factors influencing effectiveness of warehouse performance?
5. Discuss the advantages of implementing WMS and when WMS can be advantageous.
6. Discuss the key performance matrix of a typical warehouse, and also discuss the productivity improvement tools.
7. Define distribution objective and scope. What are the various distribution channels available for FMCG products? How are channel partners selected?
8. Discuss the channel distribution strategy for a new product to be introduced under consumer durable category. Also design a distribution organisation for this product.
9. Discuss distribution policy and key performance indicators of effectiveness of distribution system. What are the critical success factors?
10. How distribution cost is calculated? What factors impact the distribution network design?
11. What were the impact and key challenges of supply chain management during the pandemic for food and agricultural products in India?
12. Discuss some remedial measures that are needed to be implemented by industries to gradually recover from the impact due to disruption in Supply Chain.
13. What were the specific challenges of MSME sector during pandemic and why they were arisen?

References

Baisya, R. K. (2015a, January) "Challenges in Logistics Management – I: Complexity of Covering BOP Market", *Processed Food Industry*, 18(3), 9–11.

Baisya, R. K. (2015b, February) "Challenges in Logistics Management – II: Choosing the Right Distribution Mix and Building", *Efficient Distribution System*, 18(4), 10–12.

112 *Warehousing and Distribution Management*

Baisya, R. K. (2020a) "Festival Season Did Not Push Performance of Processor and Small Food Vendors", *Processed Food Industry,* 24(1), 8–10.

Baisya, R. K. (2020b) "Impact of Lockdown so far in Processing Industry", *Processed Food Industry,* 23(8), 8–10.

Baisya, R. K. (2020c) "Lower Consumer Demand Result in Declined in Production Consumption of Process Food", *Processed Food Industry,* 23(3), 8–10.

Baisya, R. K. (2020d) "New Ways to Manage Food Supply Chain in Pandemic", *Processed Food Industry,* 23(10), 8–10.

Baisya, R. K. (2020e) "Poor Supply Chain Management Responsible for Food Industry not been Globally Competitive", *Processed Food Industry,* 23(2), 10–12.

Baisya, R. K. (2021) "Impact of COVID-19 on Future Direction of Process Food Industry", *Processed Food Industry*, 24(3), 8–10.

Batch Master ERP. (2020, December 30) *Impact of COVID-19 on the Process Manufacturing Industry.* Available at: https://www.manufacturingtomorrow.com/article/2020/06/readers-choice-2020-impact-of-covid-19-on-the-process-manufacturing-industry-2020/15487 (accessed on 7 February 2021).

Bhalla, V., Bhattacharya, A., Singhi, A., & Verma, S. (2007) *Creating Distribution Advantage in India.* Boston Consulting Group Publications.

Dyal, J. (2020, May 8) COVID-19 Among Workers in Meat and Poultry Processing Facilities — 19 States, *Morbidity and Mortality Weekly Report (MMWR,* Weekly/May 8, 2020/) 69(18), 551–561.

Hammond, A. L., Kramer, W. J., Katz, R., Tran, J. T., & Walker, C. (2008) *The Next 4 Billion-Market Size and Business Strategy at the Base of the Pyramid.* Washington, DC: World Resource Institute and International Finance Corporation.

Huhmann, S. (2004) "Tapping India's Rural Market", *Journal of Student Research*, 92–99.

McKinsey & Company. (2021, February 3) Covid-18: Briefing note # 41. Available at: https://www.mckinsey.com/business-functions/risk/our-insights/covid-19-implications-for-business (accessed on 6 >February 2021).

Mossman, F. W., & Norton, N. (1965) *Logistics of Distribution System.* Boston: Allyn and Bacon, p. 3.

Overton, A. (2020, November 12) *COVID-19 could be an Ingredient for Change for Food Processing Industry.* Available at: https://www.newfoodmagazine.com/article/125728/food-processing-industry/ (accessed on 8 February 2021).

Shukla, S., & Bairiganjan, S. (2011) *The Base of Pyramid Distribution Challenge.* Chennai: IFMR Research, Centre for Development Finance.

Taneja, G., & Zaidi, A. (2020) *Managing the Impact of COVID-19 on India's Supply Chains – Now, Next and Beyond*, Available at: https://assets.ey.com/content/dam/ey-sites/ey-com/en_in/topics/government-and-public-sector/2020/09/managing-the-impact-of-covid-19-on-india-supply-chains.pdf (accessed on 7 February 2021).

Bibliography

Eisenhart, T. (1990, January) "Drawing a Map to Better Sales", *Business Marketing*, pp. 59–61.

Maher, P. (1984, December) "National Account Marketing: An Essential Strategy, or Prima Donna Selling?", *Business Marketing*, pp. 34–45.

McDonald, M., & Rogers, B. (1995) *Key Account Management.* London: Butterworth-Heinemann.

Millman, T. (1996) "Global Key Account Management and System Selling", *International Business Review*, 5(6), 631–645.

Millman, T., & Wilson, K. (1995) "From Key Account Selling to Key Account Management", *Journal of Marketing Practice*, 1(1), 9–21.

Millman, T., & Wilson, K. (2001) "Structuring and Positioning Global Account Management Programmes: A Typology", *Journal of Selling and Major Account Management*, 4(1), 11–38.

Moss, C. D. (1979) "Industrial Salesman as a Source of Marketing Intelligence", *European Journal of Marketing*, 13, 3.

Tally, W. J. (1961, January 25) "How to Design Sales Territories", *Journal of Marketing*, 3.

5 Managing Inventory for Satisfying Customer Demand

Learning Objective

Section I: Inventory Management for Servicing Customer Requirement

- Understand why businesses need inventory and how it impacts business performance
- Identify types and classification of inventories, inventory cycle
- Explain inventory cost, control and management
- Understand replenishment of inventory, economic ordering quantity, business response to excess stock as well as to stock-out situations
- Recognise the impact of trade discounts and trade promotions on cycle inventory

Section II: Dealing with Demand Uncertainty in Supply Chain

- Describe different measures of product availability and key concern to manage them.
- Appreciate the role of safety stock in terms of managing the supply chain performance.
- Identify the various factors that influence the required level of safety inventory.
- Detect the ways and means of reducing the levels of safety stock without compromising product availability.
- Understand the impact of uncertainties in supply chain and estimating safety stock.

SECTION I: INVENTORY MANAGEMENT FOR SERVICING CUSTOMER REQUIREMENT

Introduction

The inventory management policy of any organisation has to be designed to hold minimum inventory at all stock points, including stocks of input materials and finished stocks in manufacturing locations, intermediate stock points, and warehouses as well as trade stock of distributors and retailers to ensure servicing customer demands on real-time basis, which would mean that there is no stock-out situation so that sales is not lost as well as there is no extra stock increasing the working capital requirement in the business. Inventory has to therefore be linked with sales order processing. And sales order processing has to be linked with production planning and procurement. The problem starts when the sales order does not match the real-term consumer offtake as determined by the sales happening from the front-end retailers in any business. Retailers are selling directly to the end customers and that is exactly the measure of the term sales. Corporations many times lose out on that focus for not knowing the exact sales to the end consumers. The longer the channel length is, the higher will be the trade inventory or even total

DOI: 10.4324/9781003469063-5

114 *Managing Inventory for Satisfying Customer Demand*

inventory in the system. The trade channel, therefore, has to be efficient and short to make the task of inventory management more controllable.

All organisations have an inventory policy determined on the basis of several criteria, which include service frequency, consumer demand, the cost of the product(s), replenishment time, industry and trade practices, commercial terms to be implanted and enforced, consumer offtake data as revealed from the company's own sales report as well retail audit data which companies subscribe from A.C. Nielsen, seasonality of demand, company's own marketing and promotional policy including activities during a particular period which can spur the demand, production and procurement lead time, manufacturing plant capacity etc. In spite of the best intention, inventory level is always seen to be a matter of great concern for all companies.

The production plant has to run as per its optimal capacity; otherwise, manpower and other overheads will not be fully utilised. The manufacturing plant capacity also has to be aligned with the demand forecast. If the capacity utilisation of the plant becomes an issue, the cost of production will go up because under-utilisation of the capacity will lead to underabsorption of the overhead expenditure, which will impact both SCM performance and productivity. Managing inventory, therefore, is very critical to the management of the SCM performance as it has to optimise several factors both controllable and un-controllable. For efficient and effective inventory management requires not only the reliable and past historical data of the business but also the experience of the operations manager who will be entrusted for delivering the key objectives and goals of SCM performance. Inventory management also requires close coordination between departments in the business including production, distribution, warehousing and sales department within the business and customers who need to be serviced effectively, outside the business. It is, therefore, a very challenging task.

Inventory Management

Inventory is constituted by the stock levels of raw, packaging material and other input material such as standard spares and also the finished goods as well as work in progress carried in the business to service the demand in the market. Most often than not, the inventory in business is disproportionately higher than the required or optimal level resulting in very high working capital locked up in business impacting performance of the organisation itself. Managing inventory effectively to avoid a high level of stock of input material and finished goods is, therefore, the key to improve business profitability. Most of the time, management is not well informed about the inventory it is carrying, leading to not only a high level of stock tied up in the system costing not only a huge sum of money but also often facing write off, wastage and obsolescence and expiry or even redundant stock particularly when a model and or design of a product is changed or when a product formulation is changed and earlier product is substituted by a new product.

The inventory, therefore, is material that the firm obtains in advance of need, holds until it is needed, and then uses, consumes, incorporates into a product, sells, or otherwise disposes of it. A business inventory is temporary in nature. In that respect inventories are stock of any kind like fuel and lubricants, spare parts and semi-processed materials to be stored for future use mainly in the process of production, or it can be known as the ideal resource of any kind having some economic value.

In the supply chain, one of the key variables which has to be managed is inventory. The inventory includes a vast spectrum of materials that is being transferred, stored, consumed, produced, packaged, or sold in one way or another during a firm's normal course of business. The planning, storing, moving and accounting for inventory is the basis for all logistics. Inventory

Managing Inventory for Satisfying Customer Demand 115

has a financial value, which for accounting purposes is considered a floating asset. However, it may be very difficult to convert physical inventory into liquid assets, hence the inventory is a very risky investment. The problem of liquidating excess inventory normally results from the very basic reasons of over-estimating the current demand. The demand can be wrongly estimated but sometimes businesses deliberately target higher level of market share to be achieved and plan the production and sales to achieve the higher level of performance, but in reality they might even fail to achieve the target resulting in stock pile up and loss of profitability. It has been seen that sometimes it becomes an unmanageable proportion.

All businesses want to improve the performance of their operations over the previous year. As such it can be noticed that at year-end sales figures are abnormally high. In order to show the year-end closing performance of the business better, businesses often overtrade and invoice more stock than the requirement of the market in the last quarter of the financial year and more so in the last month of the year closing. For example, businesses are seen to invoice large stocks to their distributors before the close of the year on credit basis. As this is not aligned with the customer requirement, the distributor will not pay for the stock and he has agreed only to take a book entry with a clear understanding that company will take that excess stock back after the close of the year. The last day of the year will always be seen for all companies to sell very large stock to clear the inventory as the company's account will show better result with lower stock. For this purpose, companies even resort to extra promotional drives to liquidate the stock by giving discounts. The excess stock is then often brought back to company's warehouse or stock point. This is what we can call pseudo sales and helps only dressing the books of accounts. Such practice only can create distortion in the level of inventory. While year-end inventory will be lower than actual, soon it will show higher value because of stock return.

If sales can be achieved with minimal or no inventory that would be the ideal. Most businesses do not have any idea of how much inventory the business is carrying at any given point in time and as such management sometimes wakes up with a shock when they have come to learn about huge stock that they are carrying in inventory in factory, warehouse and also in trade channel. The retail industry normally takes physical inventory at regular intervals to manage the stock better just because the entire profit of the operation normally depends on the efficient management of store inventory. In spite of using ERP packages for managing the store operations, the stock discrepancy still happens because of pilferage that is happening within the retail stores which often go undetected in spite of having CCTV monitoring system in place. The book inventory and physical inventory often don't match. The organised retailers take about 1–1.5% of the stock, which can disappear from the system as acceptable due to pilferage, and there is a constant surveillance and monitoring of stock movement to control the pilferage. Anything in terms of reduction of losses due to pilferage can be considered as an incremental profit straight sitting at the bottom line of the profit and loss statement. From all these considerations and issues managing inventory assumes additional importance.

Inventory Management Goal

Inventories represent the largest single investment in assets as current assets for many manufacturers, wholesalers and retailers. Inventory investment represents over 20% of the total assets of manufacturers and more than 50% of the total assets of wholesalers and retailers. Thus, one goal in operations is to keep the level of inventory in the supply chain as low as possible and free up funds for other productive purposes.

Holding the inventories is connected with significant costs. Despite all the efforts and technological innovations, inventories are often still the asset with lowest return in the company.

116   *Managing Inventory for Satisfying Customer Demand*

Arguably, majority of companies hold 25–40% more inventories than actually needed. Unreasonably high inventory levels lower the company's profit and return on assets. The stated goal or objective therefore is to reduce or minimise the level of the inventory without any loss of sales. For some sales like seasonal products, food products etc., loss of sales would mean permanent loss and that cannot be retrieved. Moreover, in such situation your customers will also shift to competition resulting in losing a customer for non-performance and non-delivery, which itself is a big loss to the company. It takes a long time and effort to create a customer and therefore losing a customer will always be considered as a big loss for the business. It takes six times more effort to create a new customer and by switching to competition if your customer is satisfied bringing him back will be all the more difficult. The goal of the inventory management thus is to manage inventory without facing stock-out situation but also not to overstock.

Why Do We Need Inventory?

Ideally, inventories should be as low as possible or if we can manage just-in-time inventory, it is excellent as in that case we can eliminate the inventory altogether. Although that will be an ideal situation, it cannot be possible to manage under all situations and, therefore, in business we invariably need to have inventories of all kinds. There are several reasons for having inventories and these include the following:

- **Improve customer service**: Ready in stock can make faster delivery for any customer orders. Delivering immediately on receipt of customer order or reducing the lead time of customer servicing helps in improvement in customer service and hence also the satisfaction. In FMCG, retailing is normally done with ready stock so that orders from the retailers are executed immediately and this also eliminates the possibility of the retailers changing their minds later on and cancelling orders.
- **Provides immediacy in product availability:** Having inventory means product is always or even immediately available.
- **Encourages production, purchase and transportation economies:** Inventory policy and holding also trigger other associated activities like transportation, procurement and production.
- **Allows for long production runs:** Higher inventory would mean larger production capacity utilisation.
- **Takes advantage of price-quantity discounts**: Buying a larger quantity of input materials can help in getting quantity discount.
- **Allows for transport economies from larger shipment sizes**: A larger volume shipment can be more cost-effective in terms of transportation cost.
- **Act as a hedge against price changes:** The higher level of inventory would also mean a hedge against any fluctuation or increase in price of the input and thus saves on any eventual input cost increase.
- **Allows purchasing to take place under most favourable price terms:** If inventory of finished goods is adequate, businesses can buy input material at the most attractive price and also can avoid purchasing under pressure arising out of reaching zero inventory situation.
- **Protects against uncertainties in demand and lead times:** With adequate inventory level, businesses are protected from any uncertainties in demand and lead time of delivery.
- **Provides a measure of safety to keep operations running when demand levels and lead times cannot be known for sure:** Inventory also provides adequate safety stock in uncertain situation in the market.
- **Act as a hedge against contingencies and buffers against unusual events like strikes, fires and other disruptions in supply line:** Inventory also acts as buffer stock in terms of

calamity, disaster as well as other types of disruptions in production and operations such as riots, fires, strikes or even any other socio-political upheaval and uncertainties.

- **Buffers against such events of disruptions in supply:** If the critical material suppliers are either facing difficult situation or acting tough because of monopoly of supplier, a comfortable level of inventory can provide sufficient breathing time to face such situations and still can continue the supply line.

Inventory Impacts Business Performance

Inventory blocks capital in the form of working assets. It is, therefore, a cost to the business and hence impacts performance of the business. The best way to run business is without having any inventory and if it is possible if business can run as 'made to order' basis or as JIT inventory to be delivered which has been produced against a confirmed customer order. In some business categories in B2B model, this even may be possible. However, it is almost impossible to operate with zero inventory unless businesses are willing to forego the sales and lose customers under certain situations. Businesses can decide to trade-off between the cost of holding buffer stock to address certain situations and not servicing or accepting customer orders beyond a cut-off date keeping the bottom-line performance of the business as a sole criterion for decision. It is also possible to manage with very low to almost zero-level inventory for short-supply items. Normally short supply items are overstocked by the customers and, therefore, possibility of losing a customer for non-delivery is very low. Such items are also normally monopoly products and thus in those situations one can take policy decisions of either 'made to order' or as 'just-in-time' inventory.

But it may be impossible to manage in the FMCG category without having any inventory. Depending on the type of distribution channel chosen for distribution as well as redistribution of products and also with width and depth of the distribution, the level and quantum of stock in inventory will depend. And that will block a large resource in working capital. Efficient management of working capital thus holds the key to reducing the negative impact of inventory holding cost on business. Inventory utilises capital resources that might be possible to put into better use in the business. It also diverts management's attention away from careful planning and control of supply and distribution channel.

In many European countries, which are small having only a couple of million in population and customer base is small, customers are serviced through the organised large-format retail outlets and also cash and carry wholesale format. These stores can be directly connected to the company's distribution systems, and daily production programme can be linked with the daily sales from these stores which can be replenished in the next working day. In this situation procurement programme is also linked with the production plans of the day and vendors are contracted to make the input material to be made available well in time for the day's production to start. This JIT line can be managed in an environment where information of the customer requirement is made available on real-time basis to be synchronised with daily production, procurement and customer services and associated logistics issues. But in a complex diverse market like India or in other Asian countries having a JIT production line is almost impossible to practice. We have discussed this complexity in the earlier chapter (Chapter 4).

Types of Inventories

There are many types of inventories. The form of inventories depends upon the type of concern or business. All types of inventories do not require the same treatment and therefore policy with regard to each may also differ. Inventory can be classified based on business requirement for better control and management for least cost of holding the inventory and better supply chain

118 *Managing Inventory for Satisfying Customer Demand*

performance. Broadly, one approach to classifying types of inventories could be based on the type of use of the item(s) to be stored or stocked. Based on the type of use the classification can be as follows:

- **Raw material inventories:** These are raw materials and other supplies, parts and components, which enter into the product during the production process and generally form part of the product.
- **Packaging material inventories:** This can include all types of packing material required to be used in the manufacture or production of an item such as primary packaging, secondary packaging, tertiary packaging as well as shipping cartons.
- **Work-in-process (WIP) inventories:** These are semi-finished, work-in-progress and partly finished products formed at the various stages of production.
- **Spare part inventories:** Maintenance, repairs and operating supplies which are consumed during the production process and generally do not form part of the product itself are referred to as spare part inventories.
- **Finished goods inventories:** These are complete finished products ready for sales. In a manufacturing unit, they are the final output of the production process. Finished goods are intended as ready for sales. The finished goods itself can be further classified as follows:
  - **Movement inventories**: Includes inventory for items that are held due to a process delay while some inventory is moved from one location to another.
  - **Lot size inventories**: Inventory that results whenever quantity price discounts, shipping costs, set-up costs, or similar considerations that make it more economical to offer inventory in one economic lot
  - **Anticipation inventories:** These are stock or inventories built in excess anticipating sudden levels of demand and kept on hand to deal with uncertainty in customer demand. Fluctuations in buying activity or seasonal demand or even demand arising out of unusual activities in the market can lead to complexity in inventory management and be managed under demand uncertainties.
  - **Fluctuation inventories:** It is an inventory system in which the balance in the inventory account is adjusted for the units sold each time a sale is made.
  - **Physical inventories:** It is a manual count of the on-hand inventory. Physical inventory thus would mean the actual count on a given date or at the end of a period.
  - **Transit Inventory:** These are inventory of items between two stock points or point of use.

Alternative Approach for Classification of Inventories

Inventory classification can have several approaches, and these approaches will depend on the company's primary accounting and recording approach so that data can be captured accordingly from the corresponding location where physical inventories are lying and in what form and for what period that will facilitate the accounting and recording process and system software that are being used by the company. Corporations can even have their own approaches to facilitate accounting and stock management easier for them. There are many such approaches but, broadly, we can have the following approaches for classifications:

By the position in company's production/operation process: This would facilitate in locating the inventory in relation to production and operation processes of the company and can include the raw materials, packaging materials, works-in-process and finished goods as well

Managing Inventory for Satisfying Customer Demand   119

as goods purchased for resale and advance payments to suppliers (suppliers holding inventory on business owners' cost). This approach has been discussed in the preceding section.

By the financial accounting rules: This approach deals with and facilitates accurate accounting of the inventories under specific class. This will facilitate the management to take action on those class where inventory level is higher than projected or anticipated.

- **Cycle stock** – These are inventories for satisfying usual (predicted) demand between replenishments (receiving new ordered quantities)
- **In-transit inventories/pipeline stock** – These are items that are en-route from one location to another. They may be considered part of cycle stock even if they are not available for sale or shipment until after they arrive at the destination.
- **Safety or buffer stock** – It is held in excess of cycle stock because of uncertainty in demand or lead time. The amount depends on the extent of demand fluctuation, replenishment lead time and planned availability level for customers. This makes the majority of inventory in the typical logistic system
- **Speculative stock** – It is held for some reasons other than satisfying current demand such as getting quantity discounts, forecasted purchase price increase or materials shortage, and protecting against strikes/natural disasters. Production economies may also lead to the manufacture of products at times other than when they are in demand.
- **Seasonal stock** – It is a form of speculative stock that involves accumulation of inventory before a seasonal period begins like festival season or say harvesting period in agriculture.
- **Near-expiry stock** – It is the stock that is nearing expiry and therefore to be sold on priority basis through special promotion or even price reduction and, if necessary, directly to the end consumers by-passing the channel partners. Near-expiry stock can be sold by heavily discounting the price or even can be donated for a cause. Pharmaceutical and Food manufacturers are often seen to donate the near-expiry stock to NGOs, who in turn redistribute to the needy and poor for immediate consumption and use which helps them to create goodwill as well as a positive image for the company.
- **Expired stock**: The expired stock sometimes is possible to be reprocessed to make it good for sale again. Sometimes and for some categories of products, a small quantity of expired stock is added to a fresh batch of production without compromising the quality of the final products. Every organisation has their unique method and policy that they follow to deal with such inventory permitted under law instead of just throwing it out as useless stock. However, under normal circumstances, expired stock needs to be written off impacting the financial performance of the company. Sometimes, the out-of-warranty or expired stock requires special treatment for disposal as waste, which is an additional cost for the business. This is true for stock which is hazardous in nature and therefore cannot be directly disposed of without special treatment of processing.
- **Dead stock**: These are the items for which no demand has been registered for some specified period of time (obsolete products, demand season ended, fashion changed rendering existing stock out of fashion and so on). Dead stock needs special disposal plan and depending on the products sometimes are sold as scrap or waste. When the design of a model of a product changed in the marketplace, the inventory related to that older model is normally a dead stock. Such things happen in business although companies make transition plan from one model to a newer model to minimise such dead stock. But even the best plan for such transition will also leave behind some dead stock to be dealt with in the best possible manner. If nothing else, dead stock can be sold as scrap material.

120 *Managing Inventory for Satisfying Customer Demand*

It can be mentioned here that all companies have their own methods of dealing with dead stock, out-of-warranty stock as well as scrap or waste disposal, which are approved and accepted as standard norms of accounting practices.

Inventory has a significant impact on the material flow time meaning the time that elapses between the point at which material enters the supply chain as input material to the point at which it exits at the time of delivery to the customers, in the supply chain. In the supply chain, sales throughput will normally dictate the inventory level. For example, sales throughput S, material flow time T and Inventory I can be correlated by Little's law as follows:

$$I = ST - \qquad (5.1)$$

If an organised retail outlet like Flipkart or Walmart holds 150,000 units in inventory and sells 1500 units every day, little's law tells us that the average unit will spend $150000/1500 = 100$ days in inventory. If, however, flow time is reduced, the inventory holding will also reduce. For example, if flow time is reduced to say 50 days from 100 days while sales throughput is still constant, the inventory holding will reduce to 75,000 units. This is valid only when inventory and sales throughput have consistent units.

Example

Reckitt Benckiser has very fast-moving products in their portfolio like Dettol antiseptic liquid, Harpic toilet cleaners and Mortein household insecticide. It also has slow-moving products like Brasso and Silvo metal polishers. Dettol and Harpic require fast response time and the sales happen more or less in predicted lines as per budgeted sales forecast. For fast-moving regular selling high-volume products inventory is maintained at all stock points and in company-operated and managed warehouses. Whereas for slow-moving products which sell in select locations like Brasso and Silvo, the inventory level is low. Sometimes these products are produced once or twice a year to be sold throughout the year, which is possible if the product has a very long shelf life like that mentioned in this example. However, for low shelf life, low demand products better policy is to produce only against confirmed customer orders.

Amazon sells a wide variety of books. Most authors and publishers prefer to keep the book stocked on Amazon. Some books are in high demand, whereas others are not and therefore slow moving. Best-selling books are kept in all regional stock points and warehouses so that they are closer to the customer locations and the response time to service the order will be low. But for slow-moving books, the inventory is not kept and on receipt of the customer order books are procured from the publisher and distributors to execute the order on receipt of the customer order.

These days some of the best-known publishers take very small print runs. And even books that are marketed or launched globally are printed on demand and sold.

From these examples, you can understand that both inventory levels and locations have a direct relationship with the product demand and material flow time.

Components of Inventory Decisions

For creating the most efficient and responsive supply chain operations, managers must take decisions related to major inventory types.

Cycle Inventory

Cycle inventory is in fact the average inventory used to satisfy the demand between receipts of supplier shipments. As such the size of the cycle inventory is a result of the production, transportation or purchase of material in large lots. Businesses normally produce or purchase in large lots to benefit from the economies of scale in the production, procurement and also in the transportation process. But with increase in lot size, holding cost also increases. Supply chain managers have to therefore balance or optimise these two apparently opposing impacts from a careful cost-benefit analysis. The basic trade off manager will face is the cost of holding larger lots of inventory when cycle inventory is high against cost of ordering more frequently when cycle inventory is low.

Safety Inventory

Safety inventory is held to cater to the excess demand than what has been anticipated. It helps if demand is more than expectation and thus acts as buffer against any uncertain situation. Prediction often is not correct and if reasonably reliable futuristic prediction is possible, we don't need to have safety stock. In that environment cycle inventory would be enough. Companies normally keep safety stock only to satisfy an unexpectedly high demand. But it is not easy to determine how much safety stock is enough to be considered safe. If there are past records of unusual seasonal demand, then one can go by past experience to avoid losing sales when all of a sudden demand spurts or increases, which would otherwise mean that determining the safety inventory involves making a trade-off between the costs of having too much inventory against the cost of losing sales for not having enough inventory.

Seasonal Inventory

Some products are highly seasonal such as soft drinks and ice cream. For these products in a tropical country like India, demand significantly increases during summer months. Also, during the festival season like Diwali in India and Christmas in Western countries or even during Eid in Muslim countries, there is sudden increase in demand. There are two ways companies can manage this situation of significant higher demand during a season. One is to produce a higher amount in lean season and sell the inventory during peak season. Alternatively, create capacity of the production plant to take care of incremental demand during the season. In the first option, there will be some incremental cost of holding stock piled up during the lean season. And in the second option, there will be incremental capital cost to be incurred for setting up larger production plants. Other options could be to source from third parties during peak season. If the stock is built up during the lean season, it is likely to get aged when it is offered for sale during peak season and for some products like say food products consumers don't like to buy old stock. However, for a consumer durable category, building stock for sale during lean season is an acceptable practice. Still, there are products for which input material is available only during certain period of the year to be sold throughout the year. For example, marine products, a particular type of fish is caught during the season but the fish is sold throughout the year, all over the world. The fish is processed and frozen during the season to meet the demand during the whole year till such time next catching season arrives. Such practices are true for many other product categories as well.

Level of Product Availability

A high level of product availability ensures high level of responsiveness, but it also increases the cost of holding a higher level of inventory. The level of product availability is actually the fraction of the demand that can be served from the inventory of the product. Although low level of product availability lowers inventory holding costs, it also increases the fraction of customers who are not serviced on time. The trade-off for determining the level of product availability,

122   *Managing Inventory for Satisfying Customer Demand*

therefore, is the cost of inventory to increase the product availability and the loss from not serving the customers on time.

Inventory Cost Management

Inventory is the single-largest cost that businesses incur in terms of working asset. Inventory therefore needs to turn around as fast as possible and we thus consider sales to working asset ratio as an important parameter to be monitored. We also need to ensure that the inventory which has entered the system first has to also exit first, following first-in first-out (FIFO) principle. Most companies don't have any idea about how much money is locked up in various kinds of inventory at various locations. It gets revealed only when physical stock audit is done. To manage the inventory more effectively corporations have to know the location-wise inventory and also the type of inventory which constitutes the inventory holding cost.

Inventory costs are traditionally categorised into four basic cost groups:

- **Purchase cost:** For items that are purchased from outside the firms, this is usually the unit price that the firm pays to its vendor. As an item moves through the logistics system of the firms, its purchase cost in the inventory analysis should reflect its fully landed cost, which would mean the cost to acquire and to move the item to that point in the system from where it will be used.
- **Ordering cost:** In addition to the per unit purchase cost, there is usually an additional cost which is incurred whenever we order, record and or replenish the inventory. If we produce items internally, then there will be an organisation set-up cost. This happens because we have to shut down the manufacturing line and change over and reconfigure the line to make a specific item. This is the cost involved with processing the order, involving paying the bill, auditing and so forth.
- **Holding cost:** The cost that accrues due to the actual holding of the inventory over a period of time. Many different kinds of costs can be considered as holding cost. The key characteristics of holding cost vary with the amount of inventory being held and the time that the inventory is held.

  The holding cost can also be classified as follows: The holding cost can also be classified as follows: Storage cost or cost of space, damaged spoiled goods cost and handling labour and insurance cost.

- **Storage cost:** When demand arises which cannot be satisfied from available inventory an inventory shortage occurs.

  Purchase, ordering and holding costs can be thought of as the cost of having inventories, while shortage cost results from not having inventory, or from not having enough inventory at the right place at the right time.

Inventory Control

Inventory control is the process of managing materials inventory of the right quality and quantity to be made available as and when required at least cost without facing any stock-out situation resulting in either loss of production or sales. The desired level of inventory can be neither high nor low because high level of inventory will lead to increase in carrying cost while low level of inventory will lead to increase in ordering cost.

The main criterion for managing inventory is deciding on inventory policy regarding the level of inventory to be maintained based on the classification and types of inventory, the buffer stock as well as reorder points and lead time and economic ordering quantity. Periodically inventory control policy is reviewed to see how the policy is working in terms of cost and availability in real life.

The primary objective of inventory control is to ensure smooth flow of stock in terms of supplying required quantity and quality of materials at minimal cost and investment locked up in inventory. The control processes must also take care of fluctuating demand and production providing adequate flexibility and minimising the associated risk and uncertainty as well as obsolescence.

Effective Inventory Management

Inventory management refers to the methods that are used for organising, holding and replenishment of stock. The main purpose of inventory management is to minimise differences between customer demand and availability of items. These differences are caused by three factors: customer demand fluctuations, supplier delivery time fluctuations and inventory control accuracy.

The main goal is to keep the inventories on an optimal level, without stock-outs and excesses. For this, two controversial but simultaneously mutually dependent tasks should be solved: to have enough inventories to fulfil orders from external and internal clients and to satisfy their requirements.

Order Fill Rate and Pack Fill Rate

Usually, customer service level is measured as availability or by order fill rate. Businesses normally keep track of order fill rate and pack fill rate by having a budgetary objective to achieve a target order and pack fill rate and every year trying to improve upon that target. Many have achieved above 99% of orders and pack fill rate target, and they have well-controlled inventory and demand management system in place.

By order fill rate, we mean that the customer order in terms of value and volume has been satisfied. When inventory of a particular item is not there, the order value still can be managed by replacing one type of stock with another if that is acceptable to the customers. Sometimes, customers are persuaded to take another product in place of the product that customer ordered and customer normally accepts such request to maintain the relationship with the business and even sometimes when the product offered in place of the product that customer ordered is a fast-moving product and is in demand.

But marketers and business objectives are to fill not only the order but also the pack. By pack fill rate we normally mean that customer order is fulfilled not only in terms of product types and categories as well as in terms of value of the order but also in terms of SKUs that customer ordered. And as said earlier businesses target to achieve above 90% or even 99% pack fill rate and to achieve that kind of perfection both demand forecast as well as production planning and control needs to be managed well, and there has to be enough flexibility built into the process to achieve that targeted pack fill rate. Businesses who have not achieved such high order fill and pack fill rate try to improve upon these criteria and budget that target to be achieved every year as an improvement target.

To minimise inventory-carrying costs, trade-off between cost of capital tied up and business profitability has to be achieved following economic ordering quantities and timing. This would mean having accurate, complete and timely inventory transactions record and avoiding differences between accounting and real inventory levels. Two tools commonly employed to ensure

124 *Managing Inventory for Satisfying Customer Demand*

inventory accuracy and control are ABC analysis and cycle counting. Inventory management includes all activities of planning, forecasting and replenishment.

For effective inventory management, other techniques and tools that can be employed are as follows:

Cross-docking. This involves unloading goods arriving from a supplier and immediately loading these goods onto outbound trucks bound for various retailer locations. This eliminates storage at the retailer's inbound warehouse, cuts the lead time, and has been used very successfully by Walmart and Xerox, among others.

Delayed differentiation. This involves adding differentiating features to standard products late in the process. For example, Benetton decided to make all of their wool sweaters in undyed yarn and then dye the sweaters when they had more accurate demand data which arrived as the season neared. Another term for delayed differentiation is postponement.

Direct shipping. This allows a firm to ship directly to customers rather than through retailers. This approach eliminates steps in the supply chain and reduces lead time as well as reduce pipeline inventory. Reducing one or more steps in the supply chain is known as disintermediation. Companies such as Dell use this approach.

Inventory Transaction

Inventories normally move positions and or locations to be used for various purposes. The transactions of inventories can therefore happen for various reasons. When transactions of inventories take place, there will be legal transfer of ownership of the inventories in case of sales. But transaction of inventories can also take place internally from one section to another and thereby control mechanism as well as authority and responsibility can also shift. Some of the routine transactions of inventories that take place within as well as outside the business may include the following:

- Normal stock receipt – from previously issued purchase orders and transfers
- Unexpected stock receipts – the stuff that just shows up on receiving stock
- Requisitions – a request for material to be consumed within company
- Emergency requisitions – unplanned and unscheduled and sudden demand of stocks
- Sales – the stocks that are sold to the customers as per order

Transactions of various types can arise out of numerous reasons like a sales orders to be delivered to the client, orders to be picked up, cash sales from stock point and warehouse, direct shipment to end customers, transfer to other warehouses or facilities when required, stock return, returning the material to suppliers for say non-conformance to standards, scrapping and writing – off stocks.

Stock-keeping Unit

The inventory control is made by a stock-keeping unit. SKU is an individual product that differs from other products in some ways and inventories are kept SKU-wise. The difference could be in size, colour, brand, model, package function or some other relevant characteristic such as flavour, fragrance, or combination of these. Each SKU has its own unique identification code (product code) in inventory accounting system, and it is counted and stored separately from other items.

Much of inventory control is directed at controlling each SKU in inventory. Although daily operations of inventories may require SKU level control, strategic planning of inventory levels can be accomplished by substantially aggregating products into broad groups by some characteristic– product groups. The basic approach is when managing the inventory investment of all SKUs collectively is the issue.

As the number of SKUs increases in a business, the complexity of inventory management also increases and as such businesses need to rationalise the SKUs based on their performance in terms of sales volume, customer segment that it served and importance of that segment in business as well as profit contribution it makes. Sometimes, small volume SKUs are also carried in business inventory in order to be a player in all sub-segments of the business category for other strategic reasons. The strategic reasons could be the need to be present in all sub-categories and sub-segments of the business to keep the leadership position in the category. For example, Reckitt Benckiser is a leader in the shoe care category and their brand is Cherry Blossom. There are many sub-categories in this shoe care range and that includes, wax, liquid, cream, cleaners, shoe shampoo, chalk for canvas shoes, handy shine etc. Some of these sub-categories have very small volume of business contributing small amount in sales and profit but to keep their leadership position in the market Reckitt has to keep inventory of all these products adding complexity to the system. But the fact remains that SKUs add to complexity in inventory management. If a corporation has a leadership position in certain types of product or product category and growing at a healthy rate, competition is normally seen to be making attempts to break that monopoly and to do that competition will constantly explore the possibility of finding a suitable entry point to carve out a niche for them from the leader. This niche will be some segment of the customers who would be looking for some differentiation or they even might be left uncovered and not serviced. To eliminate those possibilities of entry point, new SKUs are often introduced by the marketer just to cover all segments even if some segments are either small or not profitable. SKUs thus increase and so also the complexity in inventory management in particular and SCM in general.

Bullwhip Effect

Manufacturers would like to produce in large lot sizes because it is more cost-effective to do so. The problem, however, is that producing in large lots does not allow for flexibility in terms of product mix. It also adds to the inventory which business may not require immediately. The downside is that ordering/producing large lots can result in large inventories of products that are currently not in demand while being out of stock for items that are in demand.

Retailers find benefits in ordering large lots for benefits such as quantity discounts and advantages of many trade schemes and promotions. And it also provides enough safety stock. Distributors and wholesalers would like to stock more products which are fast moving and for which schemes and other promotions are being announced to meet the demand coming from the retailers they serve.

Ordering and producing in large lots can also increase the safety stock of suppliers and its corresponding carrying cost. It can also create what's called the bullwhip effect. Everyone linked in the supply chain will have a natural tendency to keep enough margin of safety stock when they place their demand. This has a multiplier effect on the whole chain impacting the performance. This effect is what we call the Bullwhip effect.

The bullwhip effect is the phenomenon of orders and inventories getting progressively larger (more variable) moving backwards through the supply chain. This is illustrated graphically in Figures 5.1–5.3.

126 *Managing Inventory for Satisfying Customer Demand*

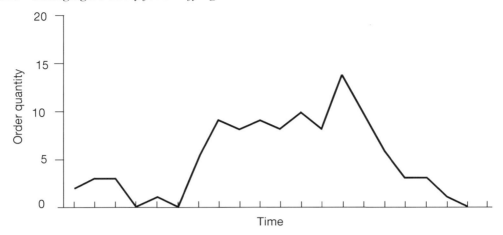

Figure 5.1 Wholesaler/Distributors' Orders to the Manufacturers

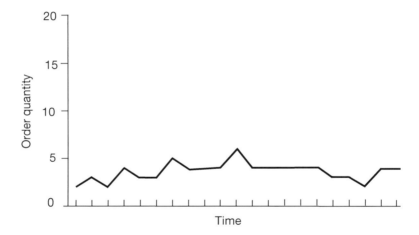

Figure 5.2 Consumer Offtake at Retail Sales Point

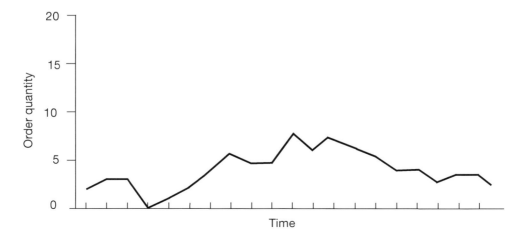

Figure 5.3 Manufacturers' Order to the Suppliers/Vendors

Causes That Lead to the Bullwhip Effect

There are many reasons that are responsible for the Bullwhip effect. Some of those reasons are discussed subsequently:

Demand forecasting: Many firms use the mini-max inventory policy. This means that when the inventory level falls to the reorder point (min), an order is placed to bring the level back to the max, or the order-up-to-level. As more data are observed, estimates of the mean and standard deviation of customer demand are updated. This leads to changes in the safety stock and order-up-to level and, hence, the order quantity. This leads to variability.

Lead time: As lead time increases, safety stocks are also increased, and order quantities are increased. This also leads to more variability.

Batch ordering. Many firms use batch ordering such as with a mini-max inventory policy. Their suppliers then see a large order followed by periods of no orders followed by another large order. This pattern is repeated such that suppliers see a highly variable pattern of orders.

Price fluctuation. If prices to retailers fluctuate, then they may try to stock up when prices are lower, again leading to variability.

Inflated orders. When retailers expect that a product will be in short supply, they will tend to inflate orders to ensure that they will have ample supply to meet customer demand when stocks are unlikely to be made available when they need. When the shortage period comes to an end, the retailer goes back to the smaller orders, thus causing more variability.

The Effect on Supply Chain Performance

To contain the impact of the bullwhip effect, there is a great deal of coordination required within the business between various departments. The lack of such coordination may lead to impact the performance of the business negatively. The consumer offtake or retail sales normally follows an established pattern. However, wholesalers' and distributors' orders come to manufacturers most of the time that do not reflect the real-term demand of the customers, and there are various reasons for that including retailers deciding to stock higher quantity when some offer or quantity discount is announced by the company or during festival season or even on hearing the news of possibility of short supply. Besides, for fast-moving items retailers always would like to stock higher quantity (Crowther, 1964).

Wholesalers on the other hand trade on heavy discount to liquidate the stock and for that reason they order higher quantity from the manufacturers. Wholesalers are having a tendency to rotate the stock faster even if it is necessary to sell at a low margin. Because by increasing the stock turnover ratio (STR) total profit will be higher. But this approach can lead to overstocking the market as consumer offtake in most of the cases follows a more or less uniform pattern. The result is the bullwhip effect. Wholesalers are also performing the role of the redistributors, where traditional channel partners cannot directly reach. Wholesalers also have the tendency to trade in other territories whenever an opportunity arises creating distortion of the sales figure. Manufacturers, therefore, orders the input materials from their vendors and suppliers, which varies widely, and vendors are not in a position to estimate the manufacturers' requirement and plan their production schedules to meet their clients' requirement. These variabilities are shown in Figures 5.1–5.3.

This distortion due to the impact of the bullwhip effect will result in the rise in various costs like manufacturing costs as company and its suppliers have to cater to the orders which are at variance with customer demand. This also increases the inventory costs because company as well as the trade channel partners have to keep a much higher level of the inventory in

128 *Managing Inventory for Satisfying Customer Demand*

comparison to the real-term customer demand. Because of the bullwhip effect, transportation requirements fluctuate significantly over time because higher quantity needs to be transported during the high-demand period raising transportation costs. The Bullwhip effect also increases the cost of handling for receiving the goods as well as for shipping the goods out. This also can result in occasional stock-out situations particularly with the retailers who did not order more and others have cornered the stocks by buying more than required which in turn results in loss of sales. It should be noted that company's real-term sales will be the quantity sold by the retailer to the ultimate consumer or consumer offtake. The fluctuation and all distortion of sales take place because of the bullwhip effect impacting not only the performance and profitability of the business but also creating confusion and misunderstanding in the whole supply chain.

Reducing Impact of Bullwhip Effect

Centralising demand information occurs when customer demand information is available to all members of the supply chain. This information can be used to better predict what products and volumes are needed and when they are needed such that manufacturers can better plan for production. However, even though centralising demand information can reduce the bullwhip effect by reducing uncertainty, it will not eliminate it totally. Therefore, other methods that are needed to cope with the bullwhip effect include the following:

Reducing variability. This can be accomplished by using a technique made popular by Walmart and then Home Depot called everyday low pricing (EDLP). EDLP eliminates promotions as well as the shifts in demand that accompany them. Large retail stores and wholesale stores run EDLP programme regularly on select stock to reduce the impact of the Bull Whip Effect.

Reducing lead time. Order times can be reduced by using EDI (electronic data interchange) with the partners in the supply chain. Access to the data base by the concerned people will reduce the lead time of ordering.

Strategic partnerships. The use of strategic partnerships can change how information is shared and how inventory is managed within the supply chain. These will be discussed later in greater detail.

Business Response to Stock-out

In spite of the best plan and best forecast, businesses can still face a stock-out situation for various reasons including disruption of regular production schedules and sudden spurt in unusual demand as well as disruption due to strikes, riots and other natural disasters. In that environment, there are standard responses that businesses can display. Some of these are as follows:

Backordering – The quantity requested by the customer is placed on a separate order called a backorder and the special order is filled as soon as the product is available from internal or external source. In some cases, the backorder is shipped directly from its original source to the customer to ensure that customer order is fulfilled in the shortest possible time.

Substitution – It occurs when a product acceptable to the customer is substituted for product that is not available. Sometimes customers are persuaded to accept alternative products or SKUs in place of what customer has ordered by offering special discounts to attract the customers so that customers still remain loyal to the product and company. If the substitution is done with a product or SKU which are in regular demand, customers will normally accept.

Lost sales – It occurs when an unsatisfied client annuls the order. This is common in retail situations as retailers will very willingly offer customers an alternative but equivalent product from competition and in that environment there will be a permanent loss of sales for the corporation. If a product not much in demand is substituted by another product, the loss of sales of that product is a permanent loss. Also if a customer switches over to the competition when there is stock-out situation there will be permanent loss of sales.

Replenishment of Inventory

The aim of inventory replenishment is to ensure that the level of each SKU is kept at a level, optimal for established customer service level (availability). Inventory replenishment is done after determining what is the demand and what is currently available for satisfying that demand and information regarding pending orders yet to be received. Based on these inputs you can work out what stock will need to be ordered and when will the orders to be released (reorder point, ROP)

There are various approaches followed to determine what needs to be ordered, how much to be ordered and when. These are as follows:

Periodic or fixed interval review system: The periodic review system is very widely practised in industry by taking the inventory details once in a fixed predetermined time interval to decide the ordering quantity, This time interval for review is determined based on the company's past practice as well as experience and lead time for ordering of long delivery items.

Reorder point system: The point triggers when reordering has to be done taking the information related to stock level as well as other input regarding any delay in receiving stock than normal lead time as well if there is any excess consumption arising out of unusual demand. At this point, procurement is initiated. The recorder point is actually average daily consumption multiplied by lead time of procurement plus the safety stock (Figure 5.4).

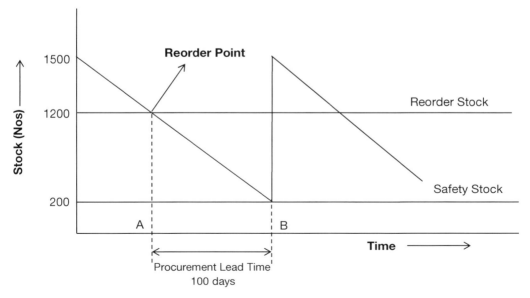

Note: A- ROP triggered & Procurement initiated.
B- Material received.

Figure 5.4 Reorder Point for Inventory

130 *Managing Inventory for Satisfying Customer Demand*

Time-based order point system: TPOP is a computerised management tool that plans inventory needs in priority sequenced, time-phased manner to meet customers and forecast demand as it occurs. This technique is at the heart of MRP and DRP systems used for the control of manufacturing and distribution channel inventories. The main advantage is that inventory actions are triggered by matching supply with anticipated demand as it occurs in time. At the point where demand exceeds the supply, the system will alert the inventory planner to order the item according to predetermined lot size and to have it available at the anticipated date on which stock-out will occur. In addition, each time TPOP is generated, the system will re-sequence demand and supply relationships and suggest a new set of required order actions for the order planner

The information or inventory management system must generate data regarding order level, average inventory level, lead time of ordering, demand during lead time and safety stock. The average inventory level is max level + min level/2 or ½ of the replenishment order. As SKU stock is a sum of cycle and safety stock, the average inventory is ½ replenishment order + safety stock. Normal practice in industry is, however, periodic or fixed interval review system. Order cycle time is actually the ratio of estimated total annual demand to average ordering quantity.

Inventory Position

The replenishment decision is made when an inventory position of item reaches reorder point. The replenishment decision model includes the following components:

- **On-hand inventory**: This refers to the quantity that inventory system shows as being physically in stock. This value should never be negative. This is the starting point for the replenishment calculation
- **Available inventory**: It is found by subtracting from on-hand inventory all order demand quantities, whether allocated or unallocated. The balance remaining is the quantity available to immediately satisfy new customer demands. This value can be negative, if open customer orders exceed the on-hand inventory
- **On-order inventory**: It is the replenishment stock that has been ordered but has not yet been received. Although the inventory position calculation considers on-order inventory as if it were on hand, this stock should not be allocated to open customer orders or existing backorders within the replenishment lead time.
- **Inventory position**: It is the value that is determined for a given item by subtracting the inventory requirements generated by open customer and inter-branch transfer orders, allocated (committed) and backorders from the total on-hand stock and expected on-order inventory.

Average Inventory

It is the average quantity or value of the whole stock or quantity. If the SKU is in the warehouse at the maximum level having value of USD 5000 and at minimum level valued at USD 2000. The difference between these two levels (5000–2000) or USD 3000 is the order quantity resulting in cycle inventory of USD 1500. At the beginning of the cycle stock level is at max. Customers deplete inventory when it reaches its minimum level.

Average inventory is therefore = max level + min level/2 or ½ of the replenishment order.

As SKU stock is a sum of cycle and safety stock, the average inventory is: ½ replenishment order + safety stock.

Order Cycle Time

Interval between Orders

Order cycle time is the time period between placing one order and the next order or the time period between two successive orders.

T = Q/D, where T = Order Cycle Time, Q = Quantity and D = Assumed annual demand.

For example, If assumed annual demand is 5000 units and order quantity is 60 units then, Order Cycle Time T = 60/5000 = 0.012 years or 0.012 × 52 weeks or 0.012 × 365 days = 4 days.

Implications of Economic Ordering Quantity

Following are the implications of EOQ:

- A formula is used for calculating optimal production batches: as 'lot size' formula and S is set up cost and V is manufacturing cost.
- While EOQ may not apply to every inventory situation, most organisations will find it beneficial in at least some aspect of their operation. At any time if having repetitive purchasing or planning of an item, EOQ should be considered.
- Obvious applications for EOQ are purchase-to-stock distributors and make-to-stock manufacturers; however, make-to-order manufacturers should also consider EOQ when they have multiple orders or release dates for the same items and when planning components and sub-assemblies.
- Repetitive buy maintenance, repair and operating (MRO) inventory is also a good application for EOQ.

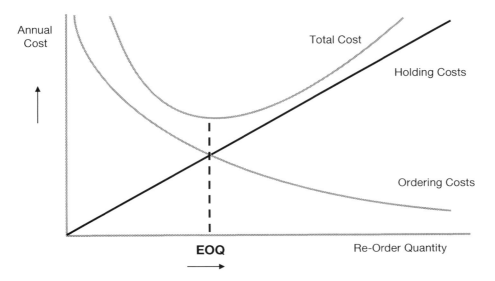

Figure 5.5 Economic Ordering Quantity

132   *Managing Inventory for Satisfying Customer Demand*

- Although EOQ is generally recommended in operations where demand is relatively steady, items with demand variability such as seasonality can still use the model by going to shorter time periods for the EOQ calculation.

In the economic ordering quantity (EOQ) model, it was assumed that there is no time lag between ordering and procurement of materials. Therefore, the reorder point for replenishing the stocks occurs at that level when the inventory level drops to zero and because of instant delivery by the suppliers, the stock level bounces back to the desired level.

In reality, however, there is always a lead time of ordering and the stock required during that period needs to be there in the inventory. In real-life situation, one never encounters a zero lead time. There is always a time lag from the date of placing an order for materials and the date on which materials are received and as a result reorder point is always higher than zero. If the firm places the order when the inventory reaches the reorder point, the new deliveries will arrive before the firm runs out of goods to sell. In the JIT line, which is not easy to practice receiving the stock when needed is possible. It will be always the endeavour of the procurement manager to reduce the lead time of ordering in an attempt to reduce the stock holding in the system and the associated reduction of working capital and saving the interest on the same for the business.

Materials Requirements Planning (MRP)

The objective of MRP is to prepare a procurement plan to meet the production target derived from the company's sales order processing. This, therefore, helps the business to optimise production, procurement and inventory for better performance.

- **Principle** – The materials requirement planning starts with sales order processing. The sales orders are generated by the company's sales system and each order generated by the salesman will be required to be serviced by a defined time limit which we normally call order delivery schedule. The purpose of MRP then would be to work backwards to generate the bill of material to deliver that order as per schedule and check the existing inventories to determine what needs to be ordered when based on their lead time of delivery and finally release the orders as per material requirement plan. This is a complex task and is most often managed by having enterprise resource planning software (ERP). If it is known what final product should be produced, it is also known how much materials and components are needed for manufacturing this product. Theoretically, there is no need for safety stock of materials, if the quantity of finished products and production schedule is known, then received inputs will be immediately used. But the reality is different from what could be theoretically possible simply because there is uncertainty and failure on the part of vendors to meet the commitment. These uncertainties can also occur if there is fluctuating demand in a dynamic and highly competitive business environment. Safety stock thus needs to be provided for considering these issues, but the quantity of safety stock is determined by businesses based on their own past experience. And as such one can find that some businesses are working with very low level of safety stock and some have relatively higher level of safety stock.
- The timing of incoming material flows according to production schedule is the basis of MRP. MRP links procurement operations with manufacturing or material management functions.

What MRP Indicates

The MRP indicates the following:

- The types of material and the quantity that has to be purchased from outside, taking into account current inventory levels
- The types of materials that need to be manufactured internally and in what quantity, taking into account current inventory levels
- At what time to place these orders, either by purchasing outside or for manufacturing inside

Components of MRP II

MRP II stands for manufacturing resource planning. Manufacturing Resource Planning (MRP II) is an integrated information system which subsequently came in business to be known as enterprise resource planning (ERP). Many ERP packages since then have been launched and all businesses are using this to optimally manage various business functions.

Master Production Schedule

It is the list of the products and services to be supplied within a specific period of time. This period must be sufficiently long to allow for the ordering and delivery of required sub-assemblies and parts, as well as to allow sufficient time for manufacturing the product in question. It may be made up of forecast demand and actual known demand. It also lists the required outputs for the system and when the goods and services are required through the use of due date.

Bill of Materials

It is a diagram, engineering drawing or a listing of all materials and materials at various levels. The product structure is often presented in a hierarchical form, where the end product would be at the highest level (level 0 or 1) and then components that go into making this product are at a lower level.

Inventory Status File

This refers to the complete record of the quantity of each material held in inventory. A detailed file would show transactions, receipts, disbursements, scrapped materials, planned orders, order releases, projections of delivery dates, quantities of each material to order, and when to place orders. Also, would be the lead times or the time required to produce a production lot in-house or receive a lot purchased from suppliers. To take into account the lead time, a requirement in one time period will necessitate the release of the order in some earlier period according to the established delay or lead time.

Output of MRP

It is a list of purchase requirements, which includes what needs to be purchased and when including the following:

- A manufacturing schedule, which will list what will be made and when it will be made
- The closing stock of parts, components and sub-assemblies after the master schedule has been completed

134   *Managing Inventory for Satisfying Customer Demand*

- The closing capacity available after the master schedule has been completed
- A list of anticipated shortfalls in production – these may be due to shortages of parts of capacity

The differences between order point system and MRP system are summarised in Table 5.1.

MIN–MAX Replenishment System

The most popular replenishment method and normally practised by the industry because it is easy to operate. It is a variant of reorder point (ROP) model with two differences.

1   If the SKU inventory level reaches the reorder point or below it, the variable size order is made to raise the inventory level to predetermined maximum level (which is EOQ + ROP).
2   If the inventory level of some SKU has dropped to reorder point or below it, the inventory levels purchased from the same supplier are reviewed, despite being above their reorder points. Besides ROP, each SKU has a predetermined minimal order quantity. Replenishment orders for SKUs which need replenishing in quantities above the minimal size (but have not reached ROP) are added to the order submitted to a given supplier. So, this approach enables joint ordering, therefore decreasing the number of submitted orders and increasing order sizes.

An example: Let us take an example to explain how this popular method works in industry by taking the data presented for two items in Table 5.2. A company manufacturing two products like say ash tray requiring two items (item 1 and item 2) to manufacture. If the stock, the data related to ROP and EOQ are as given in Table 5.2, we can work out the order size.

From the example presented in Table 5.2, we can see that the stock level of Item 1 has dropped to reorder point. Also, the level of Item 2, ordered from the same supplier as item 1, is reviewed. The difference between the max and current level of item 2 is (1800–1000) = 800

Table 5.1 Order Point System versus MRP System[1]

Criteria	Order point system	MRP system
Demand	Independent	Dependent
Ordering philosophy	Replenishment	Need based
Control principle	ABC grouping	All items are equally important
Forecasting	Based on demand	Based on master production schedule
Purpose	Satisfying customer needs	Satisfying production needs
Order size determination	Economic ordering quantity (EOQ)	Firm request for concrete items
Design pattern	Unvaried	Changing but predictable
Inventory types	Finished product, spare parts	Work in progress (WIP), raw material

Table 5.2 Principle of Min–Max Replenishment System[2]

	Item No 1 Mustard Oil (units)	Item No 2 Corn Oil (units)
Reorder Point (ROP)	200	400
Economic Ordering Quantity (EOQ)	1000	1400
Maximum Stock Level (ROP+EOQ)	1200	1800
Minimum Order Size (½ of EOQ)	500	700
Stock at the Moment	200	1000

Managing Inventory for Satisfying Customer Demand   135

units. As the difference 800 units exceeds the predetermined min order size for item 2 the order for this item is also placed in addition to order for item 1.

How Much Should Be Ordered?

Majority of inventory replenishment methods are the variations of following three theoretical basic models:

- Periodic review system or fixed interval system
- Reorder point (ROP) system
- Time-based order point (TPOP) system

Total Cost of Inventory

The objective of most companies is to buy every item at the lowest total cost per unit. The total cost is the sum of three elements:

1 **Material cost (landed cost)**: It is the purchase price of product plus freight and any other charges that are related to specific shipment, including taxes and transportation. Or manufacturing cost in production.
2 **Ordering cost**: It is the cost of issuing, receiving and paying on a vendor. These are costs associated with ordering frequency, not with quantity ordered.
3 **Inventory-carrying or holding cost**: It is the cost of maintaining inventory in warehouse before it is sold, transferred or otherwise used. These are costs associated with quantity ordered, not with ordering frequency.

Out-of-Stock Costs

It is an additional cost element related to inventories – cost incurred when an order is placed but cannot be filled from inventory from which the order is normally assigned. Finding these cost is quite complicated and inaccurate.

There are two kinds of out-of-stock costs:

1 **Lost sales cost** – when a customer is faced with an out-of-stock situation and chooses to withdraw request for product. This relates to cost of lost sales, which is equal to unearned profit from the sales which is lost plus possible negative impact on further sales as customer might even switch to competition or divide orders between suppliers.
2 **Back order cost** – when customer decides to wait in out-of-stock situation. The sale is not lost, only delayed, but it incurs backorder processing costs and additional transportation and handling costs (if backorder is processed and delivered as separate shipment).

Inventory-carrying Cost

Inventory is part of the working capital in the business and consists of raw material, packaging material and other input material, including spares and components, work-in-progress, as well as finished inventory. The following are its features:

- Cost associated with having inventory in hand
- The term 'inventory-carrying cost' may be used in two different contexts.

  - Determining firm's total logistics cost (TLC)
  - Calculating EOQ for SKU

136 *Managing Inventory for Satisfying Customer Demand*

Inventory is a significant part of the working capital of the company. Keeping excess inventory leads to loss in terms of interest cost and the capital blocked in inventory. As such total cost as well as location-wise and under-account head-wise inventory should be periodically reviewed to ensure that there is no unnecessary stock holding at any point. Excess inventory can also become a deterrent for the company to consider either introducing a new model or new design and or new formulation as the case may be. The inventory can also become obsolete and wasted. Some inventory of raw and packaging material and more particularly finished goods can become a waste after their prescribed expiry period. Organised retailers take inventory audit almost every month to see that the records in the books are correct and also if anything is becoming dead inventory soon. If they identify near-expiry stock or even dead stock, a special disposal and salvation plan is worked out to recover as possible from such situations. Inventory needs a very close scrutiny and valid periodical audit to ensure that inventory management practices are as planned in the budget document

Total Cost Approach

Capital cost is the major cost component of inventory holding. Capital cost is the opportunity cost of money tied in firm's inventory which may represent over 90% of total inventory-carrying cost in certain cases although the cost can be subjective depending on the interest rates used for calculating the opportunity cost. The interest rate can be based on:

- WACC (weighted average capital cost) – considered most objective for realistic cost overview
- Hurdle rate – minimal acceptable return on investment, accepted by the company
- The lowest bank loan interest rate (currently around 10–12% in India), which can be different in other countries
- Inventory service costs – which includes typically insurance and taxes on inventory
- Storage costs – part of warehousing costs depending on inventory level
- Inventory risk costs – obsolescence, damage, pilferage and relocation costs

Structure of Inventory-carrying Cost

The structure of inventory-carrying cost is as follows:

Capital cost: 82%
Inventory Serving cost: 0.75%
(Insurance 0.25% and taxes 0.5%)
Storage Cost: 3.25%
Inventory Risk Cost: 14.0%
Total: 100%

If total inventory-carrying cost is found, this can be divided by the average inventory investment or average stock value and can be expressed as a percentage of the average. This will help in determining how much it costs to maintain a unit worth of inventory in business which typically ranges from 18% to 28%. Inventory risk cost should be included while calculating EOQ.

If a company uses private or rented warehouse, mistakes in calculating storage costs are common in EOQ implementations. Generally, companies include all costs associated with the warehouse. This tends to include costs that are not directly affected by the inventory levels and does not compensate for storage characteristics. Carrying costs for the purpose of the EOQ

Managing Inventory for Satisfying Customer Demand 137

calculation should only include costs that are variable based upon inventory levels. For storage area, the proportionate share of depreciation and rent and communication costs need to be included whereas shipping, receiving and other working areas are not included.[3]

Demand Estimation

Reorder Point (ROP)

The Reorder Point is the level of inventory which triggers an action to replenish the particular stock of inventory item, and it is normally calculated from the demand forecast during the replenishment lead time plus safety stock. As such reorder point is a method to determine when to order for the particular material, but it does not address the issues related to how much to order and when to order.

Reorder point (R) = Normal consumption during lead time + Safety stock.

As such two factors that determine the appropriate order point are the delivery time stock which is the inventory needed during the lead time which is the difference between the order date and the receipt of the inventory ordered and safety stock which is the minimum level of inventory that is required to be held as a protection against shortages due to fluctuation in demand (Maxwell 1985).

Exercise 1: When Demand and Lead Time Are Constant or Fixed

Problem: An e-Paint Internet store is open 311 days per year. If annual demand is 10,000 gallons of Iron coat paint and the lead time to receive an order is 10 days, determine the recorder point (ROP) for paint.

Solution: In this problem both demand and lead time are constant and hence as per basic EOQ model with constant demand and constant lead time to receive an order is equal to the amount demanded during lead time.

Reorder Point = Normal consumption during lead time.

$$R = D * LT \qquad 5.2$$

where
D = demand rate per period (day or week) and
LT = lead time in days or weeks
Demand (D) = 10000 gallons/year
Store open 311 days/year
Daily demand = 10000/311 = 32.154 gallons/day
Lead time =LT = 10 days
$R = D*LT = (32.154)*(10) = 321.54$ gallons

Case Study: Vendor-managed Inventory at Tata Steel

Vendor-managed inventory (VMI) is one of the outcomes of integrated supply chain management approaches designed to improve the supply chain performance. This is one of the methods applied to reduce the impact of the bullwhip effect and help to achieve a better inventory accuracy. VMI is a means of optimising supply chain performance in which manufacturer is responsible for

138 *Managing Inventory for Satisfying Customer Demand*

maintaining the distributor's inventory levels. Manufacturers thus will have access to the distributors' inventory data and accordingly will raise the purchase orders. The objective and goal of the vendor-managed inventory is to streamline and optimise the supply chain operations for both the suppliers and the manufacturers. This would mean that vendors monitor the buyer's inventory level and replenish the stock as required, which would be equal to the sales performance of the distributors or it will be optimised keeping the manufacturer-marketer's sales objective taking the real-life inventory data into consideration. In this system, although manufacturer manages the distributor's inventory that would not mean that manufacturer will have the liberty to overstock the distributors because in that case the whole purpose of the optimisation will be lost. As such, a lean manufacturer will be able to make use of this concept to significantly improve their performance. The data related to physical inventory of the distributors actually helps the manufacturer to control the trade inventory without loss of sales or facing any stock-out situation. The success in supply chain management is drawn from the clearer understanding of the relationship between inventory cost and customer service levels. VMI in that perspective helps to reduce cost by reducing the inventory level without any negative impact on performance of the business. On the contrary, VMI in reality helps in increasing customer service frequency by delivering smaller quantities as required by the consumer demand. The distributors who are the first-level customers benefit from the lower cycle stocks and not just low end-of-the-month stock.

To achieve this objective, the focus should be to reduce or minimise the total supply chain cost which will help to achieve cost savings benefits for all the parties linked in the supply chain. Before implementing VMI on a full scale, one should first do it on a pilot scale which might involve select distributors, for select SKUs and a clear understanding of the relationships and responsibilities covering the Electronic Data Interchange (EDI) protocol standard to transmit information at the end of each working hours every day and a common understanding of the performance measures of the distributor's performance. The success of VMI will depend on EDI which provides vendors with essentially the same point of sales (POS) and inventory information retained by the consumer, which will enable improved forecasting because the vendors can observe demand for its product(s) over a wider range of customers and can incorporate the effects of sales promotion activities, competing products and also of seasonal variations in demand, if any. Many global businesses including Walmart and Proctor & Gamble have implemented VMI in their business and derived significant advantages and demonstrated improved performance. P&G implemented the project 'Golden Eye' to reduce the distributors' stock significantly to improve profit. We have discussed these earlier in this chapter.

Strategic Consulting Group (SSG) at Tata Steel uses analytical skills and cross-functional expertise from within Tata Steel and its suppliers involving their dedicated group of analysts from different streams. Each of those commodity analysts is attached to asset class of specific commodities, and they identify, evaluate and negotiate with suppliers and manage overall pricing issues along with the segment leader and commodity analyst and are responsible for meeting the objectives and are constantly looking for ways to reduce cost and formulate the sourcing strategy for the assigned commodities by working with the cross-functional teams called 'Commodity Competence Team' (CCT).

These analysts provide tools, resources and knowledge through techniques such as Benchmarking, QIPs and VMI, E-procurement and Knowledge Management. These tools contribute to optimising the overall costs, material flow and response time with respect to suppliers as well as customers. Tata Steel has steering committees, strategic sourcing team, commodity competence teams as well as strategic sourcing groups working together to reduce the number of discrete one-time purchase orders and include more products and suppliers in Annual Rate Contract (ARC).

Tata Steel's B-to-B procurement platform is one of the first among similar initiatives taken by the other large competing companies. The site offers web-based multi-directional flow of

Managing Inventory for Satisfying Customer Demand   139

transaction and business information between transaction participants. All cross-organisational elements of the inbound supply chain including enquiry and or RFQ details, order placements, delivery compliance monitoring, order amendments, material receipts and payment tracking are covered. Value-added services like negotiation chat room with bid revision tracking or reverse auction, transactional correspondence and e-mail notifications and acknowledgements are also offered, and site is constantly upgrading and revised with new releases.

Tata Steel is self-sufficient in iron ore, the key raw material for steel production, through its captive mines, which is a distinct advantage. It is 60% self-sufficient for coking coal and the rest is procured mostly through imports. However, for Corus (Tata Steel Europe Ltd) operations, the company needs to source raw materials through contracts with mining companies in UK and the Netherlands and is striving towards raw material security through joint ventures in Thailand, Australia, Mozambique, Ivory Coast in West Africa and also Oman and in addition has signed an agreement with Steel Authority of India to establish 50:50 joint venture coal mining company in India and has acquired 19.9% stake in New Millennium Capital Corporation, Canada, for iron ore mining, exploration of opportunities for Titanium Dioxide in Tamil Nadu, commissioning of a Ferro-chrome plant in South Africa and setting up of a deep sea port in Coastal Orissa to meet company's long-term growth objective. All these initiatives to have greater control over raw material resources and achieve its security across global operations. Procurement division of Tata Steel plays a critical role for business to make Tata Steel successful, profitable global organisation which is working under the overall guidelines for conformance to company's policies, its governance model and Tata Code of Conduct.

The Supply Chain Management Department (SMD) of Tata Steel is one of the core departments interfacing between the suppliers and the operations and therefore is a huge cost centre responsible for indenting of stock items that are ordered by all departments of Tata Steel. They follow strictly the quality objectives and parameters following procedures as laid down for material procurement for both consumption-based material and materials based on direct supplies. The first materials management system in Tata Steel was that of Burroughs and then came IBM in 1993, which took six years to mature and meet the requirement of company's supply chain management requirement and then came Enterprise solutions to integrate all the business functions comprising SCM, logistics, HRM, Marketing and Finance. In 2001 management implemented SAP in a record of nine months' time with the help of Price Water house Coopers.

Tata Steel was finding it difficult to manage the inventory which was rising impacting the bottom line. To reduce the inventory level, Tata Steel eventually came up with the idea of implementing VMI which was successfully implemented in retail as well as in the automotive sector. VMI, if not implemented properly, can have a negative impact on the whole system as well. This requires well-thought-out preparation in advance. The modification that Tata Steel made was segregating the materials into A, B, C, D classes of items for easy reference and close monitoring of the level of inventory. This classification was made on the basis of two identified criteria, namely, consumption quantity and Last Year Consumption Value (LYC Value).

ABC Classification

ABC class of items are actually regular moving items. And D class items are slow-moving items. ABC is again further subdivided on the basis of Last Year Consumption (LYC) value on the basis of the following:

Top 80% of LYC value = A class (high consumption value)
Next 15% of LYC value= B class (medium consumption value)
Next 5% of LYC value= C class (low consumption value)

140 *Managing Inventory for Satisfying Customer Demand*

High-cost and slow-moving items are those classified as D class items which are not stocked in large quantities. Based on this classification the inventory levels at Tata Steel were found to be:

Table 5.3 Class of Inventory at Tata Steel

Class Type	Total Value in INR	Total No of Items	% Shares in Value
A	76,792,478.7	180	0.3206
B	3,317,455.93	24	0.0138
C	317,833.81	15	0.0013
D	159,126,366.22	3821	0.6643
Grand Total	**239,554,134.66**	**4016**	**1.0000**

As can be seen, total inventory cost of these items at Tata Steel was valued at INR 2390 million (INR 2.39 billion), which was of course alarming with high amount blocked in D class items representing about 67% of the total inventory. This prompted Tata Steel to implement VMI, which was implemented in Tata Steel way back in the year 2002–2003, and VESUVIUS being one of the prominent vendors along with TATA REFRACTORIES were associated in implementing VMI. These two vendors represent about 50% of the total inventory in the system and were involved in implementation of VMI. Some of the vendors and their production data are given in Table 5.4.

Table 5.4 Refractories Purchase Records for 2009–2010

Vendor	Vendor's Name	Quantity in kg	Loc. Curr. Amount	% of Total Value-wise Buy
TC81	TATA Refractories Ltd	6,965,719.230	258,236,182.910	37.12
V216	Vesuvius Ltd	2,256,805.400	88,127,436.030	12.67
TF2F	TRL China Limited	2,495,144.800	70,810,110.500	10.18
A751	ACE Refractories Limited	1,226,606.800	57,550,881.210	8.27
O009	OCL India Limited	734,681.000	36,688,701.220	5.27
R50F	RHI Refractories Asia Ltd	483,335.300	31,478,567.880	4.53
O083	Orient Abrasives Ltd	859,268.200	20,354,446.830	2.93
S489	Singhbhum Refractory	1,162,032.970	16,875,752.760	2.43
M165	Maithan Ceramics Ltd	1265720.000	16,824,363.430	2.42
R48F	RHI Refractories	218,351.700	16,652,000.200	2.39
C92F	Calderys	168,110.400	14,714,737.180	2.12
GA21	Foseco India Ltd	152,195.000	12,971,292.830	1.86
M340	Murugappa Morgan Thermal	72,294.590	9,498,421.970	1.37
A02H	Aegis Business Ltd	194,688.000	7,669,605.320	1.1
N53F	Sojitz Chemical Corporation	58,549.000	6,421,295.240	0.92

Managing Inventory for Satisfying Customer Demand 141

VMI was implemented in Tata Steel before implementing ERP system like SAP. Post-implementation of SAP in the year 2005, the whole system of inventory management was further integrated. The values of VMI items as compared to the total consumption value were monitored and measured by SAP. It was also possible to compare plant-wise and storage location-wise inventories, and it also enabled Tata Steel to get a detailed analysis using various other measuring criteria. By implementing VMI in Tata Steel, the level of inventory holding at warehouses and inventory holding cost had come down from INR 2390 million to as low as INR 280 million.

Large MNCs like say HUL (Hindustan Unilever Ltd) or even large companies like say Reliance Industries derive great advantage from their strength of buying power and vendors are extending credit to them when company's own sales are all on cash. HUL, for example, manufactures almost all of its requirement through contract manufacturing route buying inputs from the suppliers and approved vendors extending credit. A company like HUL and Reliance can afford to get long supply line credit and because their own sales are in cash these companies have distinct advantage over the others in terms of inventory holding and inventory-carrying cost.

Source: The case is based on the data reported by Chakraborty and Swain (2011).

Case Questions:

1 On what factors will the success of implementation of VMI depend?
2 How did Tata Steel implement VMI in the company?
3 Discuss the approach of Tata Steel towards inventory analysis.
4 What was the outcome of the implementation of VMI at Tata Steel?

SECTION II: DEALING WITH DEMAND UNCERTAINTY IN SUPPLY CHAIN

Managing Uncertainty in Supply Chain

Due to dynamic nature of the business and changing environment demand fluctuates. Higher level of inventory increases cost of holding and other associated problems related to company's performance, but company also cannot afford to lose sales on account of non-availability of stock. Safety inventory therefore is carried in the system to satisfy demand that exceeds the demand forecast. The two factors that determine the appropriate order point are the **delivery time stock,** which is the inventory needed during the lead time, that is the difference between the order date and the receipt of the inventory ordered and the **safety stock** which is the minimum level of inventory that is held as a protection against shortages due to fluctuation in demand.

Reorder point ® = normal consumption during lead time + safety stock.

In the context of today's business environment, customers can go around and search across stores for a stock of an item that customers are looking for. If Amazon is out of stock of a book title, a customer can easily check if the same title is available on Flipkart or even other stores like barnesandnoble.com. Searching online is easy, and that makes a more valid case to ensure that the stock is available. For any supply chain, following questions are required to be considered when business is planning for safety stock: what is the appropriate or desired

142 *Managing Inventory for Satisfying Customer Demand*

level of product availability, how much safety stock is required for the desired level of product availability and what actions can be taken to reduce safety stock without compromising product availability level?

Measuring Product Availability

There are several ways to measure product availability. One of those measures is product fill rate, which means the fraction of the product demand that is satisfied from the product available in the inventory. It is the corporation's decision about the fill rate but in an intensely fought competitive environment, companies aim at a very high fill rate nearing 99%.

$$\text{Product Fill Rate} = \text{Product Demand/Product available in inventory} = 99/100 = 99\% \quad (5.3)$$

The other measure of product availability is order fill rate, which again is a fraction of the order received that is filled by the inventory of the product itself and that also measures the specific numbers of the orders. Besides, product fill rate and order fill rate companies also measure pack fill rate to ensure higher degree of customer satisfaction. In addition to these measures, product availability can also be determined by cycle service level which is the fraction of the replenishment cycles that end with all the customer demands being met. The replenishment cycle is the interval between two successive replenishment deliveries and therefore cycle service level (CSL) is the probability of not having a stock-out in a replacement cycle and is measured over a specific number of replenishment cycles.

Estimating Safety Stock

Safety stock is the average stock on hand when a replenishment order arrives. Therefore, for example, lead time of order is LT weeks for a product, say mobile phone, and mean weekly demand of the product is D.

Expected demand during the lead time is $= LT \times D$

Given that the distributor places the replenishment order when reorder point (ROP) of the product (mobile phones) is on hand, then

Safety Stock, $SS = ROP - (LT \times D)$

This we will work out as in the following example.

Example 5.1: Estimating Safety Stock from Replenishment Policy

Let us assume that a distributor of mobile phones has a weekly demand with a mean of 3000 and a standard deviation of 500. Let us also assume that the manufacturer takes about two weeks to fill the order (lead time of order). The distributor currently orders 12,000 mobile sets when inventory on hands drops to 7000.

As per the replenishment policy of the distributor,

- Average demand per week $= D = 3000$
- Standard deviation of weekly demand $= \alpha D = 500$

Managing Inventory for Satisfying Customer Demand 143

Average lead time for replenishment = LT = 2 weeks and ROP = 7000 and average lot size (ordering quantity) = 12000.

Safety Stock = SS = ROP-T × D = 7000−(2×3000) = 7000−6000 = 1000.

The distributor thus will carry 1000 safety stock as a safeguard against uncertainty in demand.

- The cycle Inventory = 12000/2 = 6000 and
- Average inventory = cycle inventory + safety stock = 6000 + 1000 = 7000.

The distributor thus carries on an average of 7000 mobile sets in stock.

Average flow time = Average inventory/average demand = 7000/3000 = 2.33 weeks, which means that each mobile set thus remains in the distributor's stock for 2.33 weeks.

Example 2: Estimating Safety Stock from Desired Cycle Service Level (CSL)

Cycle service level (CSL) is the probability of not getting into stock-out situation in a replenishment cycle. Thus, CSL = probability of demand during lead time should be less than or equal to ROP. And to evaluate this probability we need to determine the distribution of demand during the lead time which again follows a normal distribution with a mean of DT and a standard deviation of αT.

Taking the earlier case of mobile phone in a store with an average sales per week of 3000 and standard deviation of 500, lead time of ordering is 2 weeks. If the store reviews the replenishment policy continuously, then estimate the safety stock that the store should carry to achieve a cycle service level of 90%.

Here we have

- Demand per week = D = 3000
- Mean standard deviation = αT = 500
- CSL = 0.9
- Lead time = T = 2 weeks.

Because demand across time is independent, we can have

- DT = 2 × 3000 = 6000

$$\alpha T = \sqrt{T}\, \alpha T = \sqrt{2} \times 500 = 707$$

Thus, safety stock will work out as = NORMSINV (0.90) × 707 = 906.

(Note NORMSINV(P) returns the standardised Normal deviate z corresponding with one-tailed probability P, where P must be a value between 0 to 1. NORMSINV is the inverse function of the NORMSDIST function. NORMSINV (0.9) = 1.28155)

Therefore, to achieve the cycle inventory service level of 90% the safety stock is 906 mobile sets.

Businesses need to have a measure of product availability from the business performance criteria like service level or order fill or pack fill rate and using those criteria of measures companies will work out the safety stock in the business but most importantly it is critical to business to use available managerial levers to lower the safety stock without hurting product availability or losing out on sales and impacting customer service levels as per objective of the business.

144 *Managing Inventory for Satisfying Customer Demand*

Reorder Point (ROP)

Example 1: When the Demand Is Variable but Lead Time Constant

When there is variable demand and constant lead time, the inventory level might be depleted at a faster rate during lead time (Figure 5.6).

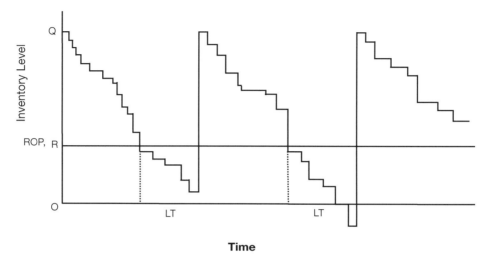

Figure 5.6 Reorder Point with Variable Demand

When demand is uncertain, a safety stock of inventory is frequently added to the expected demand during lead time (Figure 5.7).

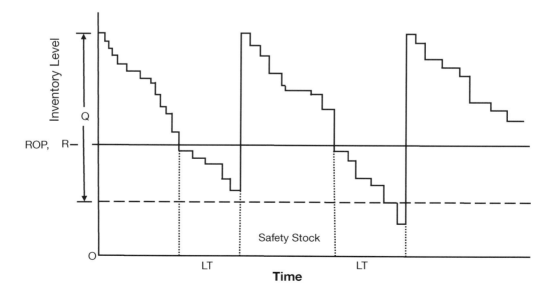

Figure 5.7 Reorder Point with Safety Stock

Service Level

Service level to be achieved provides an assurance to the customers regarding what will be the lead time to meet the demand of a customer from time of receiving the supply order to what level of accuracy. Following are its features.

- The probability that the inventory available during lead time will meet demand.
- Stock-out means an inventory shortage.
- A service level of 90% means there is 0.90 probability that demand will be met during the lead time and the probability that a stock-out will occur is 10% (Figure 5.8).

When there is variable demand and constant lead time, The Reorder Point (ROP)

$$R = \bar{d}\,LT + z\,\sigma_d \sqrt{LT} \qquad (5.6)$$

where
$\bar{d}$ = average daily demand
LT = lead time
σ_d = standard deviation of daily demand
Z = number of standard deviations corresponding to the service level probability
$z\,\sigma_d \sqrt{LT}$ = safety stock

The term $\sigma_d \sqrt{LT}$ in this formula for the Reorder Point (ROP) is the square root of the sum of the daily variances during lead time:

Variance = (daily variance) × (number of days of lead time) = $\sigma_{d^2} LT$
Standard deviation = $\sqrt{\sigma_{d^2} LT}$ = $\sigma_d \sqrt{LT}$

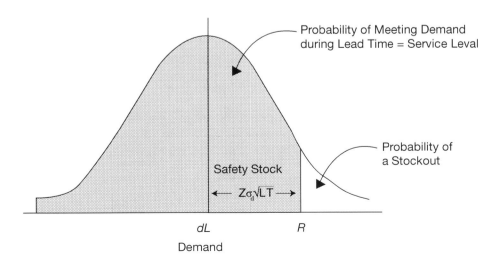

Figure 5.8 Service Level Determines the Safety Stock

146 *Managing Inventory for Satisfying Customer Demand*

Example 2

For the same e-Paint internet store, let us assume that daily demand for Ironcoat paint is normally distributed with an average daily demand of 30 gallons and a standard deviation of gallons of paint per day. The lead time for receiving a new order of paint is 10 days. Determine the Reorder Point (ROP) and safety stock if the store wants a service level of 95% with the probability of a stock-out equal to 5%

Solution

$$\bar{d} = \text{gallons per day}$$
$$LT = 10 \text{ days}$$
$$\sigma_d = 5 \text{ gallons per day}$$

For a 95% service level, Z= +1.65 (from table Area under the standardised normal curve)

$$\text{Safety stock} = z\,\sigma_d\sqrt{LT}$$
$$= (1.65)\,(5)\,(\sqrt{10}\,)$$
$$= 26.1 \text{ gallons}$$
$$R = \bar{d}\,LT + z\,\sigma_d\sqrt{LT}$$
$$= 30(10) + 26.1$$
$$= 326.1 \text{ gallons}$$

When there is constant demand and variable lead time, if only lead time is variable, then $\sigma_{dLT} = d\sigma_{LT}$

$$R = d\,\overline{LT} + zd\sigma_{LT} \qquad\qquad 5.7$$

where

d = Demand rate

$\overline{LT}$ = Average lead time

σ_{LT} = Standard deviation of lead time

Z = Number of standard deviations corresponding to the service level probability

Example 3

A motel uses approximately 600 bars of soap each day, and this tends to be fairly constant. Lead time for soap delivery is normally distributed with a mean of six days and a standard deviation of two days. A service level of 90% is desired.

1 Find the ROP.
2 How many days of supply are on hand at the ROP?

Solution

$$d = 600 \text{ bars per day}$$
$$SL = 90\%, \text{ so } z = 1.28 \text{ (from table area under the standardised normal curve)}$$
$$\overline{LT} = 6 \text{ days}$$
$$\sigma_{LT} = 2 \text{ days}$$

$$R = d\overline{LT} + zd\sigma_{LT}$$
$$= 600 \times (6) + 1.28 \times (600) \times (2)$$
$$= 5136 \text{ bars of soap}$$

No of days = R/d = 5136/600 = 8.56 days

ROP: Variable demand and variable lead time expression

If both demand and lead time are variable, then

$$\sigma_{dLT} = \sqrt{\overline{LT}\sigma^2_d + \overline{d}^2\sigma^2_{LT}}$$
$$R = \overline{d} \times \overline{LT} + z\sqrt{\overline{LT}\sigma^2_d + \overline{d}^2\sigma^2_{LT}}$$

where

$\overline{d}$ = Average demand rate
$\overline{LT}$ = Average lead time
σ_{LT} = Standard deviation of lead time
σ_d = Standard deviation of demand rate
z = Number of standard deviations corresponding to the service level probability

Example 4

The motel replaces broken glasses at a rate of 25 per day. In the past, this quantity has tended to vary normally and have a standard deviation of 3 glasses per day. Glasses are ordered from a Cleveland supplier. Lead time is normally distributed with an average of 10 days and a standard deviation of 2 days. What ROP should be used to achieve a service level of 95%?

Solution

$\overline{d}$ = 25 glasses per day
SL = 95%, so z = 1.65 (from table area under the standardised normal curve)
$\overline{LT}$ = 10 days
σ_{LT} = 2 days
σ_d = 3 glasses per day

$$R = \overline{d} \times \overline{LT} + z\sqrt{\overline{LT}\sigma^2_d + \overline{d}^2\sigma^2_{LT}}$$
$$= 25(10) = 1.65\sqrt{10(3)^2 + (25^2)(2^2)}$$
$$= 334 \text{ glasses}$$

Single-period Model

Sometimes referred to as the newsboy problem, single-period model is used to handle ordering of perishables (fresh fruits, vegetables, seafood, cut flowers) and items that have a limited useful life (newspapers, magazines, spare parts for specialised equipment). It focuses on two costs: shortage cost and excess cost.

148　*Managing Inventory for Satisfying Customer Demand*

As the product is perishable and has a very limited shelf life or useful life – if there is excess stock then businesses lose as they are perishable and therefore unsold stock is lost. Also, if there are shortage of stock, then the loss will be arising out of loss of sales, dissatisfied customer and customer moving to competitors.

Shortage cost may include a charge for loss of customer goodwill as well as the opportunity cost of lost sales. Generally, shortage cost is simply unrealised profit per unit.

C shortage (C_S) = Revenue per unit – Cost per unit

Excess cost pertains to items left over at the end of the period. In effect, excess cost is the difference between purchase cost and salvage value.

C excess (C_e) = Original cost per unit – Salvage value per unit

Continuous Stocking Levels

Demand from customers should not ideally exceed the stocking level of the inventory. As per the demand of the customers, inventory is constantly adjusted and replenished with fresh stocks to keep the stocking level at optimum. The following are the features:

- The stocking level equalises the cost weights.
- The service level is the probability that demand will not exceed the stocking level, and computation of the service level is the key to determining the optimal stocking level (S_o). Service level has to be determined from the experience to avoid excess stock and not losing the customer for shortage of stock, which will lead us to optimal stocking level which is a trade-off between the two.

Service level (SL) = $C_S /(C_S + C_e)$

where
C_S = shortage cost per unit
C_e = excess cost per unit

Example 5

Sweet cider is delivered weekly to Cindy's Bar. Demand varies uniformly between 300 litres and 500 litres per week. Cindy pays 20 cents per litre for the cider and charges 80 cents per litre for it. Unsold cider has no salvage value and cannot be carried over into the next week due to spoilage. Find the optimal stocking level and its stock-out risk for that quantity.

C_e = Cost per unit – Salvage per unit
= $ 0.20 – $0
= $ 0.20 per unit
C_S = Revenue per – Cost per unit
= $ 0.80 – $ 0.20
= $ 0.60 per unit

Managing Inventory for Satisfying Customer Demand   149

$$SL = C_S /(C_S + C_e) = 0.60/(0.60 + 0.20) = 0.75$$

Thus, the optimal stocking level must satisfy demand 75% of the time. For the uniform distribution, this will be at a point equal to the minimum demand plus 75% of the difference between maximum and minimum demands.

$$S_o = 300 + .75(500–300) = 450 \text{ litres}$$

The stock-out risk $= 1–0.75 = 0.25$

Impact of Uncertainties

Uncertainties in supply, process and demand are recognised to have a major impact on the manufacturing function. Uncertainty propagates throughout the network and leads to inefficient processing and non-value-adding activities. The uncertainty arising out of uncertain customer orders leads to the question: how much stock should the business carry and will the supplier deliver the requested stock on time and as per specifications? But those who can manage the uncertainty better delivers much superior performance.

Walmart Outperforms Its Competitors

The Walmart successfully managed the uncertainty problems. The following table shows the difference at various stages in the supply chain between Walmart and the other competitors.

Table 5.5 Comparison of Walmart and Its Competitors

Sr. No	Stage Chain In Supply	Walmart	Competitors
1.	Direct inventory supply from warehouse to retail Stores	85%	55–65%
2.	Shipping cost	3% of total Expenditure	5% of total Expenditure
3.	Replenishments Time	Maximum 2 Days	Maximum 5 Days

Source: Chandran (2003)

(P. Mohanchandra, Walmart supply chain management practice, Online research paper 2003)

Chapter Summary

This chapter has dealt with the core issues which influence the level of inventory to be kept at various stock points to cater to the real-term customer demand. Most of the businesses really don't have any idea about how much money and other resources are locked up in the inventory impacting their business performance. This chapter has discussed the methods and processes to bring efficiency to inventory management by elaborating and analysing the key issues and their consequences are very critically. It is better to run the business without any inventory following JIT principles or 'make to order' policy. But this may not be always possible and always businesses will end up holding some inventory at various locations. Inventory normally builds up in business often without the knowledge of the management, and it comes to the knowledge of the management when annual or periodic stock audit is conducted. In some businesses like retail operations including organised retail and online retail inventory management is the most critical operation and in fact the whole profit from the business hinges on the effectiveness of the inventory management practices. These issues were analysed and discussed in the chapter. In an integrated supply chain management, the entire planning for production and inventory including ordering of input materials like raw and packaging materials starts from the sales order received from the customer and optimised for resource management as well as for the better performance of company's operations. The issues concerning demand management and inventory management and control were discussed. The concept of cycle inventory and safety inventory were discussed with examples. Importance of efficient inventory management in terms of servicing customer orders and also avoiding stock-out situation was critically analysed taking many real-life business situation to understand how inventory can impact business performance. Inventory management goals, objectives, types of inventories, classification of inventory, inventory cost and management were also discussed with examples. Inventory control, transaction, rotation and stock-keeping units were explained. Bullwhip effect and reasons thereof and how it can be controlled were also discussed. The impact of excess inventory within business as well as in trade channels and how those could be managed for optimum performance was discussed. How to work out economic ordering quantity and making decisions regarding stock ordering and inventory levels of various SKUs for least cost satisfying the customer demand were also discussed. Material requirement planning as well as master production schedule were also discussed in this chapter. A case study on Tata Steel on Vendor-managed Inventory (VMI) was discussed.

In a dynamic business environment, demand fluctuates and businesses need to cater to the fluctuating demand. There are various reasons for demand uncertainty and this chapter discussed those reasons with examples and exercises as well as a case to drive the point. How safety stock is calculated to ensure product availability under uncertain conditions was discussed with examples. How global retailer Walmart manages to outperform its competitors in terms of managing the uncertainty in demand in dynamic and fluctuating business environment has been briefly discussed.

Discussion Questions

1 Why do we need inventory? What are the important goals and objectives of inventory management?
2 How does inventory impact business performance? Discuss the different approaches to classify the inventory. For efficient and responsive supply chain operations how should the inventory of various types to be analysed?
3 What constitutes inventory cost? Discuss the tools and techniques of effective inventory management.
4 What is bullwhip effect, and what causes the bullwhip effect? How does it impact the supply chain performance?
5 How businesses can reduce the impact of bullwhip effect? Discuss the possible response of the businesses to stock-out situations.
6 Discuss time-based order point system for inventory management. What is economic ordering quantity and how it is determined?
7 Discuss the core concept of MRP, and how it is differentiated from the order point system?
8 Discuss the min–max replenishment system of inventory management. How do you calculate the total cost of inventory?
9 What is VMI, and how VMI helps in managing the inventory better taking an example of Tata Steel.

Notes

1 Source: www.vkok.ee/logontrain/wp-content/uploads/2014/03/Riga-3-july-2014.pdf (accessed on 20 August 2019).
2 Data available at www.vkok.ee/logontrain/wp-content/uploads/2014/03/Riga-3-july-2014.pdf (accessed on 20 August 2019).
3 See: www.vkok.ee/logontrain/wp-content/uploads/2014/03/Riga-3-july-2014.pdf

References

Ballou, R. H. (2004) *Business Logistics/Supply Chain Management* (5th ed.). New Jersey: Pearson Education, p. 339.
Chakraborty, M., & Swain, S. C. (2011, January–June) "A Study of Vendor Managed Inventory with Reference to Tata Steel", *Anvesha*, 4(1), 12–21.
Crowther, J. E. (1964, March–April) "Rationale for Quantity Discounts", *Harvard Business Review*, pp. 121–127.
Maxwell, W. L., & Muckstadt, J. A. (1985) "Establishing Consistent and Realistic Reorder Intervals in Production – Distribution Systems", *Operations Research*, 33, 1316–1341.
Mohanchandra, P. (2003) "Wal-Mart Supply Chain Management Practice", *Online Research Paper 2003*.

Bibliography

Lee, H. L., & Billington, C. (1992, Spring) "Managing Supply Chain Inventories", *Sloan Management Review*, pp. 65–73.
Love, S. (1979) *Inventory Control*. New York: McGraw Hill Book Company.
Silver, E. A., Pyke, D., & Petersen, R. (1998) *Inventory Management and Production Planning and Scheduling*. New York: Wiley.
Vrat, P. (2014) *Materials Management: An Integrated Systems Approach*. New Delhi: Springer.
Zipkin, P. H. (2000) *Foundations of Inventory Management*. Boston, MA: Irwin McGraw-Hill.

6   Transportation

Learning Objective

Section I: Transportation in Integrated Supply Chain

1   Understand the role of transportation in supply chain and logistics management
2   Learn about the types and modes of transportation and decision criteria on selection of mode of transport system for business
3   Know about the global transportation network and challenges of ocean shipping
4   Appreciate the role of infrastructure in transportation and its impact on supply chain
5   Familiarise with the global shipping lines and alliances and competition
6   Recognise the key drivers of sustainable transportation in global trade

Section II: Packaging Issues in Transportation

1   Understand the role of packaging as an important marketing mix in trade and commerce
2   Appreciate the importance of packaging in transportation of goods
3   Know the different types of packaging like primary, secondary and tertiary packaging and their role
4   Address the packaging issues in transportation and get clarity about the role of packaging
5   Get acquainted with the packaging of hazardous goods and regulations
6   Understand the legal implications and requirement of packaging in trade.

SECTION I: TRANSPORTATION IN INTEGRATED SUPPLY CHAIN

Introduction

Transport sector is considered as the most vital sector of any economy. The goods and services move faster with well-developed road, port and rail infrastructure incurring lesser cost. If the roads are wide and good, suitable for movement of heavy transport vehicles, freight cost will come down making the economy more competitive. Transportation is, therefore, vital for growth and development of any economy and society. The supply chain performance of any corporation will be linked with the status of transport sector in that environment. One of the elements of cost of logistics operations is transport or shipping cost. There is therefore a need for businesses to study the transport systems, infrastructure as well regulation related to movement of company's goods and services from point of production to the point of consumption. Freight cost for both bringing input material to production site and taking the output material to the consumption point contributes a lot to the cost of the product. In a typical situation and market

DOI: 10.4324/9781003469063-6

Transportation 153

structure that prevails in India, which is highly complex, transportation cost is much higher in comparison to the developed countries of the world. Finding out better and more cost-effective options on mode of transport is a big challenge to the logistic manager. Managing transportation effectively helps businesses to have some competitive advantage over others. Manufacturing in-house against out-house options also hinges on savings that can be derived by such decisions on sourcing of products and services.

Role of Transportation

Transportation is the essential service and is the nerve centre of any economy. The economy will come to a grinding halt if transportation service is disrupted and no system can tolerate such situations. This can even create civil unrest if the essential goods and services are not reaching the locations in time where it is needed. In that sense transportation industry serves a very useful role in the economy. The products are produced and stored in one location but they are consumed in different locations. And invariably products are to be delivered in consuming centres and buyers are spread all over in a geographical area to be covered by a company. Transportation is thus a very important driver of the supply chain as hardly products are consumed where these are produced. There was a time when logistics was almost synonymous with transportation, but the transportation industry is really huge. India's logistics industry which is synonymous with transportation is worth about USD 160 billion growing at the compound annual growth rate (CAGR) of 10.5%, and with the implementation of GST, total logistics industry is likely to touch USD 215 billion by 2020 as per the Economic Survey of 2017–2018. The Indian logistics industry has grown at a compound annual growth rate of 7.8% during the past five years, and it provides employment to 22 million people. However, we have crossed that estimate. The revised estimate showed that the logistics sector in India was valued at USD 250 billion in 2021, with the market predicted to increase to an astounding USD 380 billion by 2025, at a healthy 10–12% year-on-year growth rate. India will also spend a whopping 1.7% of its GDP on transport infrastructure this year which is around twice the level in America and most European countries. In terms of global ranking of world bank's logistics performance Index India's rank has improved to 35th in 2016 from the earlier ranking of 54th in 2014 indicative of the fact that India has improved in terms of Global Logistics Performance Index. As per the latest, India has improved in the logistics ranking of the World Bank by jumping 6 places to Rank 38 out of 139 countries in the 7th edition of Logistics Performance Index (LPI, 2023; Transportation in India).

To a large extent, the logistics sector in India remains unorganised. The industry is facing challenges of high cost of logistics impacting its competitiveness in both domestic and international markets. Other factors responsible for higher costs of logistics are poor physical infrastructure, lack of use of technology for material handling, fragmented warehousing and lack of seamless movement of goods across modes. In order to develop this sector for integrated logistics management, it is important to focus on new technology, higher investment in the sector, skilling and removal of bottlenecks, improvement of intermodal transportation, automation, single window clearance and simplifying processes are the key imperatives.

Freight cost is a significant element of cost in the supply chain, and managing transportation effectively will be a key determinant of success criteria for the business. In a developing country like India, because of poor infrastructure, logistics cost is much higher. While in India logistics cost is about 15% of the selling price, in the USA it is about 8% and, hence, they are more competitive. Because of poor road conditions, it takes much longer for the truck to travel from one place to another for carrying the goods. The truck capacity is also lower because the roads are narrow in many places. Besides, we also use slow-moving vehicle and

154 *Transportation*

traditional transport system such as auto rickshaws, cycle rickshaws, bullock carts, horse or camel carts or even human being carrying stock as head load for last-mile connectivity. The last-mile connectivity adds not only cost but also complexity to the whole transport system. Before implementation of GST (Goods & Service Tax), there were checkpoints at the entry of every state which further delayed vehicle movement and added to both cost and complexity. The e-commerce players like e-retailers use courier service to deliver the packet to individual customers either sourcing it directly from the manufacturers-marketers or even sourcing it from company's strategic stock point where inventory of some of the high-demand product categories are always maintained. Because of the limitation of the reach of the courier service in a country like India as well as the complexity of tax compliance in addition to penetration of the internet, e-commerce services have not yet been able to reach their natural potential. Things, however, are now improving.

In global trade, freight is an important consideration of competitiveness. Some of the global companies like Walmart and IKEA's supply chain performance is dependent upon the logistics cost as these companies' source from low-cost countries and then sell their product throughout the world. Transportation is, therefore, an important element of consideration. The large-format stores and global supply chain network helped them to improve the cost-effectiveness. Their stocks are normally carried by large shipping lines. The shipper in this case is the company like Walmart itself as they are the party that requires movement of the product between sourcing point and delivery point of the supply chain and the carrier is the party that moves or transports the product and in this case that could be shipping lines like Maersk Lines or DSV.

The world's economic development is closely associated with the development of transport infrastructure. Transport logistics help sustain global economic growth and accelerate the globalisation of productive activities and markets. The continued growth of geographical infrastructure is critical for the persistence of transport logistics within global economy. International transport has evolved from its original relationships between ships, airport and other transport vehicles to physically making cargos between geographical points to match supply and demand requirement.

Functions of Transport

Transportation helps in the growth of the business in fast-moving consumer goods (FMCG) by quickly replenishing the goods at numerous stock points and retail outlets. An efficient transportation system is a prerequisite for delivering the growth target in a competitive business. Some products are consumed fast and if quickly replenished the incremental demand can be generated. For some product, the sale is lost permanently due to non-availability of stock. Thus, transportation helps in increasing the demand for the product as well.

Transport helps in creating both time and space utility by taking goods from production centres located even in remote locations where there is no local demand to places where demands exist, and also be moving goods and services faster from one location to another location. Transport helps the consumers to enjoy the quality goods produced in distant locations including overseas locations. Without efficient transport, this would not have been possible. Consumers need not have to consume only what is produced locally. Consumers get products produced and manufactured in distant locations as well. Transport makes that distance short.

If transport system is not efficient and effective, there will be scarcity of stocks in certain locations resulting in price rise. Transport thus helps in terms of stabilising the price of the goods. For essential goods, an efficient transport system is a must. Transport thus ensures even flow of commodities in the hands of consumers throughout the period of consumption.

Transport also provides competitive edge to the business by transporting large stocks at preferential rates to remain competitive in comparison to local suppliers of the similar or same product.

And lastly, transport increases the mobility of capital and labour from one location to another which is so vital for economic growth. Labours migrate from one location to another in search of jobs. Capital equipment are sourced and transported from various locations even from overseas for setting up large projects creating new opportunities. New projects would not have been possible to set up without having efficient transport system in place to take the goods to sell where customers exist. Or even to transport the plant and equipment to site for setting up the project.

Mode of Transportation and Criteria of Decision

Mode of transportation largely depends on whether it is a domestic cargo or international cargo. All international cargoes also involve transportation to the domestic area after cargo reaches the port of destination. In a typical supply chain, the following modes of transportation are used to ensure movement of goods from point of origin to point of consumption. They are also used in combination wherever required. For domestic cargo trucks and rails are most widely used mode of transportation.

- Rail
- Truck
- Air
- Water
- Pipelines
- Package carriers
- Intermodal

An international cargo is taken either by air or water (ocean). However, in Europe it is largely surface transport as small countries are all connected through excellent high-speed motor-able roads. Rail connectivity is also good. Broadly, the several modes of transport can be reclassified as follows:

1 Road transport
2 Water transport
3 Air transport

Road Transport

If we consider the typical transport system that still prevails in a country like India, we can have the following:

- **Pathways**
  Goods are also transported as headloads or on animal cart or even on animal backloads. In remote villages and forest areas including hilly areas this is still an important mode of transport where vehicle cannot reach. Goods reach in Gomukh from where holy Ganges emerged and Topovan which is about 18 km from Gongotri or similar such places in the Himalayan region goods are transported by human being in headloads or on animal back as road transport is possible only up to Gongotri. The goods reach such areas in animal transport mode. The animals like horse, pony, donkey, ass, buffaloes, camels, elephants, yak and sheep are used to transport goods in remote areas in hills, forests and deserts (The Economic Times 2017).

156 *Transportation*

- **Roadways**

  It is used for both vehicular and non-vehicular transport. Road transport is one of the most important modes of transport in commercial world. There is a significant improvement. Vehicular transport like cars, trucks, buses, lorries, auto-rickshaws, bullock carts, tongas, and hand carts etc.; non-vehicular transport like hamals; animals like camels, dogs, elephants, horses, mules etc. In developed countries like USA and EU, majority of the stock moves in heavy-duty fast-moving trucks, trailers and fast-moving transport vehicles. Because of excellent road network connecting most of the countries, road transport is a preferred mode of transport. Even in India large part of the stock is still moved by truckers. Roadways thus facilitate the movement of major portion of the goods. (Mover DB.com, 2016)

- **Tramways**

  Tramway is one of the cheaper, longer, quicker and safer modes of land transport, which is suitable only in large cities where it still exists. But in many cities, it has been phased out. It has many limitations as it is considered as slow-moving, limited area coverage, high cost as well as inflexible in nature and is hardly used for goods transport even in local areas.

- **Railways**

  Railway has been one of the most preferred modes of transport in many countries. It has helped in the growth of commercial and industrial development of various countries. Until the introduction of motor transport, railway had the monopoly as land transport. In India, it is the principal means of transport. It carries over 80% of goods traffic and over 70% of passenger traffic. It covers for more than 60,000 kilometres of distance in India. Railways include both passenger and goods train and is much cheaper and hence preferred for bulk goods carrier for essential goods.

Water Transport

Water transport is the cheapest and also oldest model of transport for large and bulky cargo. International cargo mostly moves by ship as ocean cargo. In Kerala a large part of the trade within the state is carried out by water transport. Boats carry stock through rivers and canals taking stock from one part to another part of the state selling the stock of goods en-route. This is cheap, environment-friendly and also economical. Accordingly, inland water transport can thus be divided into river transport and canal transport. River transport is suitable for small boats and steamers. It was highly developed in the pre-railway days. But with the development of railways, river transport was neglected and decayed gradually. Canals are the artificial waterways constructed for the purpose of navigation as well as irrigation. It is therefore limited to certain areas. A plan has been drawn up to develop some of these river transport for commercial movement of cargo. In northeastern areas again, the idea of water transport has been mooted and a plan has been drawn up for the purpose. Inland water transport has low maintenance cost but it is relatively slow in comparison to road and rail transport. In Kerala state in India trade is done through movement of goods in canals waterways connecting various parts of the state.

Ocean Transport

Ocean transport or shipping may be subdivided into various sub-categories based on their scope and services offered to the logistics operator

Transportation 157

- **Coastal Shipping**

Coastal shipping is a cheaper, speedy, flexible and economical form of transport for the movement of bulky and heavy cargoes. Usually, coastal shipping trade is reserved for the national shipping. In India also from 1951 and onwards the coastal shipping trade is extremely reserved for the national ships. Government has taken initiative to connect water ways through rivers which can reduce the cost of shipping. In places like say Kerala normal trade is also done carrying goods through canals and local rivers.

- **Overseas Shipping**

On the basis of their working, overseas shipping may be divided into the liner (those ships which follow defined routes with fixed places and fixed timetable), the tramps (those ships which have no set routes or fixed timetable) and the oil tanker (special sea carriers of crude oil in very large quantity). The liners may again be subdivided into passenger liners and the cargo liners. Major global carriers include Maersk Lines, DSV, American President Lines, Evergreen Group, Hanjin Shipping Company and so on. In India we have Shipping Corporation of India – a public sector acting as a major shipping line from India. The Great Eastern Shipping Company Limited is the India's largest private shipping company, which mainly transports liquid, gas and solid bulk products. In global trade, water transport is the most dominant mode of transport for all kinds of products and merchandise such as cars, food, grains and garments. Considering the quantities shipped and long distances involved, the recent trend is in the growth of the container shipment, which has led to the demand of much larger in size, faster and specialised vessels to improve the economy of the container transport.

Vessel used in ocean shipping, as mentioned earlier, will thus include the following:

- **Bulk Service:** It is engaged in the transfer of dry bulk commodities from rail or truck to deck.
- **Liner Service:** It is engaged in a service that operates within a schedule and has a fixed port rotation.
- **Tramp Service:** It is engaged in a service that operates where cargo has to be transported and does not follow any fixed schedule and port rotation.

Air Transport

It is the latest mode of transport of the twentieth century. The first air service started between London and Paris in 1919 and it became a regular mode of transport during the First World War (1914–1918), and thereafter it gradually increased and started giving competition to railways. Like railways, air transport also has two components, passenger and cargo, which are required to reach the destination urgently.

Air transport is considered for costly cargo like defence cargo and urgent cargo, which is required to reach the destination urgently. For example, during any disaster management situation or for a wartime situation, air cargo is preferred as cost is not that much of an important consideration during those situations.

Air freight is available to and from most countries including the developing world. Forty per cent of the world's manufactured product travel by air. Items that are high value or high in size

158 *Transportation*

tend to travel by air. Also, items that need to be moved in short notice need to travel by air and as such defence services and their logistics need to be transported by air.

Considerations for Selecting a Mode of Transport

There are many considerations to be taken into account for making decisions regarding which mode of transportation needs to be used in a particular case. These include the following:

- Transit time
- Cost
- Predictability
- Non-economic factors

The non-economic factors could be safety, reliability, past experience and even environmental and sustainability factors.

Package Carriers

Package carriers are actually transportation companies including FedEx, UPS, DHL, Blue Dart, Postal Service and many such courier companies, which take small parcels and courier packets for transporting all over the world. Given the small size of packages and multiple delivery points, consolidation of shipment is a key consideration in terms of increasing the utilisation and reducing the cost for package carriers. They make use of the trucks for local deliveries as well as for picking up of the packages. They also have collection points and delivery and pick-up boys to manage the huge task of collection and deliveries from multiple locations. Packages so collected are taken to large sorting centres from where the packages are delivered by road, rail and air as the case may be to various destinations. Key issues in this industry are location-specific challenges and capacity of delivery points and information flow for tracking the package en-route till delivered. This mode of transport is preferred for online businesses which handles customers in remote and multiple locations and as such with the growth of online businesses this industry has demonstrated significant growth.

Pipeline

Pipeline is normally used to transport water by municipal corporation or for crude petroleum oil or gas from port terminal to the refineries located in mainland. This requires dedicated pipeline installations involving huge capital investment. However, all refineries have their own network of pipelines to carry crude to the refineries. The pipelines are designed to utilise the full installed capacity. They also face security and pilferage issues and even disputes over the issue of laying pipelines which they need to resolve.

Intermodal

Intermodal transportation is when more than one mode of transport is used to carry the goods from point of origin to the point of consumption. A variety of intermodal transport is possible. For example, truck and rail. As container shipping volume increased in global trade, intermodal transport has also increased as containers are easy to transport from one mode to another and as such containerised freight often uses truck, water and rail combinations in global trade. Door-to-door deliverers of cargo in global trade will invariably use intermodal transport of water, rail

Transportation 159

and truck to make best use of the transport infrastructure available in a given situation. The key issue involved in intermodal transport is exchange of information flow to facilitate the shipment on real-time basis when goods are moving from one mode to another, as these transfers often result in delays in delivery and thus also the performance.

Major Mode of Transportation

Major modes of transportation are thus road, rail (surface transport) sea and air. Selection of mode depends on cost, urgency and destination, and also on the material to be transported. In global logistics most preferred transport is air and sea. However, sometimes special facility like cold chain or refrigerated containers are required for shipment of frozen goods like say frozen marine products that go from India to major European, Japanese as well US destinations. In domestic transport road is most preferred, next to road is railways.

In Europe, both road and railways as surface transport are most important because of most efficient surface transport network. European cargo movement is somewhat similar to domestic cargo movement in countries like USA and India. In domestic cargo surface transport is the major driver for delivery of the cargo. However, if waterways are available and efficient, that would be least cost transportation

Transportation Infrastructure

In any business, an important consideration is how to transport the goods and services required for bringing the input material into the production or manufacturing facilities and also for taking the finished goods to the consumption points where customers are located. The management and more particularly the logistics manager must familiarise himself with the typical issues that will determine the most optimum methods of shipping goods out from manufacturing locations as well as bringing goods into the manufacturing plants for processing. A lot of options need to be carefully evaluated before making such crucial decisions. Some companies manage task of transportations themselves using their own transport vehicle which is feasible if the organisation is relatively small and their customers are located close by. Some organisations manage the function themselves using transport services of third parties selected from a wide choice available. There are even organisations which have completely outsourced some of their distribution and freight forwarding activities. For example, Hero Honda has outsourced their distribution activities including international sales. Based on customer orders received, the products are picked up by third-party service providers from the factory gate premises. To take such important decisions, management needs to consider the following from strategic point of view:

- A firm's logistics platform is determined by a location's ease and convenience of market reach under favourable cost circumstances
- Public sector investment priorities, safety regulations, tax incentives and transport policies – each have major effects on the international logistics decision of the firm
- The logistics manager must learn about existing and planned infrastructures abroad and at home and factor them into the firm's strategy

Key Considerations on Decision on Type of Transport to Be Used

Cost of logistics is the primary consideration. The choice depends on the urgency of the customers and cost of transport. In India, Infrastructure is not yet fully developed and logistics cost is high. Transportation cost rises with high motor fuel price and state of transport infrastructure.

160 *Transportation*

In India global transportation takes place on a larger account and mostly by sea. Only small volume travels by air and also fresh and perishables go by air. The other key considerations are safety, reliability, experience and on-time delivery to destinations as well as service.

Factors Impacting Road Transport Cost

There are several factors that impact the road transport cost which is high in India when compared with that of developed countries. These factors include the following:

- Road condition and network
- Number of traffic signals and crossing on the road to cross
- Type of road and width of road
- Type of transport vehicles used for goods transport and their condition
- Loading capacity of transport vehicle used
- Regulation and Policy on surface transport
- Interstate controls and documentation
- Need for transhipment
- Loading/unloading facilities and mechanisation
- Monitoring and control system
- Arrangement of stock in transport vehicle
- Communication network
- Driver's personal efficiency and training
- Cost of motor fuel used (petrol, diesel, CNG)
- Last-mile connectivity

All these factors determine travel time and also travel cost. In India, from northeastern part to the south, time taken is more than the time taken for a cargo to move from Mumbai to European destinations.

Mode of Transportation – India

Domestic Cargo

This refers to all goods and merchandise required to be transported within the geographical territories of the country. The following are its features:

- Air cargo accounts for less than 1% of total cargo movement
- Railways contribute 35%
- Roads contribute 39%
- Sea contributes 24% (8000 KM of coastline)
- Surface transport (road and rail) takes care of the largest load
- Rail is cheaper and for certain categories of goods including bulk commodities, it is the best option.

International Transportation

However, for international cargo, port-to-port movement is all by sea. From destination port to customer location, cargo will follow domestic cargo movement facilities of that country

Transportation 161

again. International cargo, therefore, involves multiple agencies and channel partners. Communication and information flow is, therefore, very critical to the efficiency and cost of transport. Sometimes, it takes longer time for goods to reach the final consignee for delays in domestic movement and clearances than the time taken in the ocean freight for international cargo.

Hazards in Transportation

Transportation is associated with lot of hazard and risk, which needs to be managed well. Also, there are international regulations and safety standards to be complied with. There are reasons for such hazards. Some of those could be as follows:

- Air hazard is caused by variations and changes in temperature and pressure
- Sea hazards are due to water damage, corrosive atmosphere, wave impact and hostile storage conditions
- Road/rail hazards caused by shock, vibration, careless handling, impact breakage and trans-shipment
- Cargo overloading also is a cause of hazard in all forms of transport
- Hazardous chemicals and inflammable goods also increase hazards in transportation
- Security issues – increases with value of the consignment

Hazards and Risks

All kinds of hazards lead to risk, and to reduce hazard by taking adequate safety measures increase cost. Risk is also directly proportional to unknown travel conditions, particularly handling, transhipment and last-mile connectivity. Risk in business needs to be covered through adequate insurance against risk. And insurance will depend on risk assessment, which in turn will depend on the quality of cargo and cargo types, geographical location, mode of transport and delivery schedule. Risk is also associated with specific ocean route. There has to be a trade-off between all these risk variables and cost but nothing can be made absolutely risk free. To manage the hazard in transport, therefore, experience and gut feeling will come handy in taking such decisions. However, the most important factor, however, is the reputation of the ocean liners in terms of their past performance as well as dispute settlement mechanism in place.

What Is Risk?

Risk actually arises out of the unknown and is also directly proportional to the degree of the unknown. Nothing meaningful can be possible without taking some element of risk. A dictionary definition of risk is 'the possibility of loss or injury'. Risk involves the understanding of the potential problems that might occur and how they might impede the cargo and logistics movement. Risk management is like a form of insurance and, therefore, it is an investment. Risk utility or risk tolerance is the amount of satisfaction or pleasure received from a potential payoff. Utility rises at a decreasing rate for a person who is risk averse. Those who are risk-seeking have a higher tolerance for risk and their satisfaction increases when more payoff is at stake. The risk-neutral approach achieves a balance between risk and payoff

162 *Transportation*

State of Ocean Transport

International transport of cargo is highly competitive. Too many ships chasing same volume of cargo. Large vessel's introduction is replacing smaller cargo vessels. Very large mega ship requires huge volume of cargo to be economical. Slow and fluctuating growth of global trade triggered by occasional recession in many economies. Global ocean liners' losses are mounting – especially by operators in Asia – Europe sector and that includes many global ocean transporters and ocean liners. There are changing times requiring meticulous planning and execution.

Highly Fluctuating Business

The ocean transport industry is thus a highly fluctuating business. The importance of port and ranking of the ocean liners changes depending on cargo volume, and that results into fluctuating business for logistics companies. Constant change in ranking of port and shipping lines keeping the shipping lines on their toe to explore continuously the ways and means to remain competitive. That forces many acquisitions and global alliances. Cargo volume depends on global economic conditions and macroeconomic environment including socio-political and geo-political issues. Dependency on a few key customers make many shipping lines very vulnerable. Effective strategies and meticulous planning would be the key to grow and survive the turbulent and volatile as well as highly competitive environment. Ultimately those who can service better at lower cost will be able to run a sustainable business. Reducing cost which can impact service quality will not work. Shipping lines globally are working to eliminate non-value-adding activities and keeping critical functions in house and outsourcing the rest by identifying reliable partners through networking globally by forging strategic alignments and alliances to remain competitive.

Let us look at the top ten container carriers and how they have been performing over a period of time which can be seen from Tables 6.1–6.3.

It can be seen from these tables that the fortune as well as ranking of the global carriers and container ports are changing over the period of time. The reason being that global business is becoming more competitive. With trade shifting from one location of importance to another the services to those locations are also shifting, making difference to their ranking in global trade.

Table 6.1 Top Ten Container Carriers

Rank	1996	2010
1	APM-Maersk	APM-Maersk
2	Evergreen	MSC
3	Nedlloyd	CMA CGM
4	Sea-Land	APL
5	COSCO	Evergreen
6	Hanjin	Hipag-Lioyd
7	MSC	COSCO
8	NYK	CSAV
9	Mitsui	CSCL
10	Hyundai	Hanjin

Source: Packing and Labelling Dangerous Goods for Transport. Safety and Emergency Management, Thompson Rivers University 2016

Transportation 163

Table 6.2 Top Ten North American Ports

Rank	2000	2011
1	Long Beach	Los Angeles
2	Los Angeles	Long Beach
3	NY/New Jersey	NY/New Jersey
4	Charleston	Savannah
5	Oakland	Vancouver
6	Seattle	Oakland
7	Norfolk	Seattle
8	Houston	Virginia
9	Savannah	Houston
10	Tacoma	Manzanilo

Source: Packing and Labelling Dangerous Goods for Transport. Safety and Emergency Management, Thompson Rivers University 2016

Table 6.3 Top Ten Container Ports

Rank	1980	2011
1	NY/New Jersey	Shanghai
2	Rotterdam	Singapore
3	Hong Kong	Hong Kong
4	Kaohsiung	Shenzhen
5	Singapore	Busan
6	Hamburg	Ningbo
7	Oakland	Guangzhou
8	Seattle	Qingdao
9	Kobe	Dubai
10	Antwerp	Rotterdam

Source: Packing and Labelling Dangerous Goods for Transport. Safety and Emergency Management, Thompson Rivers University 2016

Large Shipping Lines and Global Alliance

Larger ships and larger air carriers are now introduced by the industry to become more cost competitive, which can carry huge volumes of cargo like mega-ships and aircraft carrier. But they come with the associated problems also. Big players are looking for cargo volume and smaller operators finding it difficult to sustain in such an environment. The issues these large ships are facing include the following:

1 **Megas (Express Three or Triple E)** – Their capacity is up to 18,000 + TEU now against 1000 TEU in 1970 and they have the advantage of lower operating costs. However, their problems include the following:

   - How will ships be filled? Getting that big a volume of cargo within the scheduled commitment will not be that easy.
   - Which ports will handle them? All ports are not even geared to handle such big or mega-ships.
   - These mega-ships also require huge investment which most of the operators are not in a position to mobilise on their own.

2 Besides, there are other operating bottlenecks.

164 *Transportation*

All mega express ships thus have their associated problems and challenges to be managed effectively. They are big and they also come with bigger problems. The large players are trying to corner the business by aligning themselves with other carriers and forming networks.

P3 Network-Global Politics

There are global politics to dominate the ocean transport industry resulting into formation of networks to get control over the cargo transport in global trade. There are alliances and networks amongst logistics operators to overcome the hurdles in global ocean transport. For example,

1 On June 18, 2013, Maersk Line, MSC Mediterranean Shipping Company S.A. and CMA CGM-West Trade announced their intention to establish a long-term operational vessel-sharing agreement on East-West trades called the P3 network.
2 On March 24, 2014, US Federal Maritime Commission (FMC) decided to allow P3 network agreement to become effective in the USA.
3 On June 24, 2014 (three months later), Chinese Ministry of Commerce announced that they did not approve the P3 network.

In spite of the fact that the Chinese Ministry of Commerce has not approved the P3 network, it is still a dominant network.

The P3 network consists of three largest container carriers such as Maersk, MSC, CMA CGM – the three largest carriers. They formed an alliance to control the market. They used big ships with hubs and ports with an objective to control the market share. Federal Maritime Commission (FMC, USA), EU and also China reviewed their agreement.

But P3 is still a dominant force and has the following market share in various regions:

1 44% Asia to Europe
2 24% in the Trans-Pacific
3 42% in the Trans-Atlantic Trade

The average vessel size of P3 vessel for Asia–Europe increased from 9300 TEU to 14,200 by end of 2015. Maersk's largest vessels surpass MSC and CMA CGM when all Megas are delivered. When vessel size increases, cost of operation reduces provided volume of cargo available. Smaller operators are facing challenge for survival. P3 network has forced other operators globally to rethink their strategies and there was a Domino Effect – because others have to follow for survival. The other alliances that came into existence are discussed further:

The G6 Alliance

The G6 Alliance members are consisting of:

*   APL
*   Hapag-Lloyd
*   Hyundai Merchant Marine
*   NYK Line
*   Mitsui (MOL)
*   Orient Overseas Container Line (OOCL)

It is a vessel-sharing agreement that allows container lines to achieve economies of scale.

The CKYH Alliance

The partners in this alliance are as follows:

- COSCO
- Hanjin
- K Line
- Yang Ming
- Evergreen

These alliances were created for survival in the competitive ocean cargo carrier industry, where big players have made deliberate attempts to corner the larger chunk of the business volume for their own survival. P3 Alliance has forced the formation of other alliances like G6 and CKYH for their survival. P3 took away larger chunk of the business because of their strength, resources and capabilities. Further realignment and takeover of the shipping lines are a distinct possibility. Such realignments are already happening. In 2016 Maersk acquired Hamburg Sud Lines. This is discussed further under the Maersk case study in this chapter.

New Global Alliances in Ocean Transport

New Ocean Alliance

- The new Ocean Alliance will consist of Evergreen Line, CMA CGM, Cosco Shipping and OOCL.
- There are two other alliances: 2M and the Alliance. While the Ocean Alliance will represent 37% of all the Asia-Europe trades' container capacity, 2M will represent 34%, and the Alliance 29%, making the Ocean Alliance the largest for Asian-European trade.
- The Ocean Alliance will deploy around 350 container vessels with an estimated total carrying capacity of 3.5 million TEUs and represent 38% of the entire global trade.
- There are going to be six services connected to Asia and Europe per week in total. The Ocean Alliance will call 18 ports directly in Asia and 13 ports directly in Europe.
- From this year on, the Ocean Alliance will also call ports directly in the Baltic Sea area. One of them is the Port of Gdansk in Poland, which will open up the possibility for the alliance to also extend the feeder network further in the Baltic Sea area.[1]

Shipping Route and Competition

The Panama Canal and Suez Canal are long-time rivals within the container shipping industry as both canals support the flow of global trade by shortening historical trade routes. Container ships have continued to grow in size and the canals noticed the need for expansion projects in order to keep pace with the industry. Next, we compare the two canals' history, expansion projects, individual market share and future. The original Suez Canal opened almost 150 years ago linking the Mediterranean Sea with the Red Sea. The canal took almost ten years to dredge and was opened for navigation in 1869. Vessels were then able to bypass the long route around the southern tip of Africa by transiting the 101-mile Egyptian waterway.

The Panama Canal expansion project started in 2007 and was completed in 2016. A new, third set of locks created an additional lane to accommodate larger container ships. After the completion of the project, the canal can now handle 13,000 TEU capacity vessels, more than two times its previous capacity.

166 *Transportation*

The Suez Canal Authority recognised it would need to compete with the expanding Panama Canal. Therefore, the canal authority announced its plan in August 2014 to deepen the canal and create a new 45-mile parallel lane to enable two-way traffic.

Previously, the Suez Canal only permitted one-way convoys which created delays for ships moving through the waterway. The expansion project shortened the transit time from 18 hours to 11 hours. The wait time to transit the canal also dropped from about 11 hours to around 3 hours.[2]

The Future of the Canals

At the conclusion of the Panama Canal expansion, ultra-large mega-ships (capacity of 14,501 TEU and higher) will not be able to transit the canal. Therefore, the Panama Canal Authority is contemplating yet another expansion project which would allow the canal to handle vessels as large as 20,000 TEUs.

Both the Panama Canal and the Suez Canal will likely continue expansion projects into the foreseeable future as mega-vessels continue to be introduced on carrier service strings. The anticipated construction of vessels with capacity of 20,000 TEUs will continue to affect the canals and industry as a whole.[3]

Not only will the canals be forced to accommodate the introduction of these ultra-large mega-ships, but they will also have a significant impact on infrastructure and terminal berthing around the world.

Suez and Panama Canals

Suez Canal connecting the Atlantic to the Indian Ocean and Panama Canal connecting the Pacific to the Atlantic Ocean have played an important role in global trade by reducing the distance for the cargo to travel. Their features have been discussed as follows:

1 The Suez route (Atlantic to Indian Ocean) is well-supplied with coaling stations, and so on., as there are plenty of islands and other points of call. The Panama route (Pacific and Atlantic Ocean) suffers for want of enough islands and halting stations as the Pacific is a dreary ocean with little commerce.
2 Coal is easily and cheaply available on the Suez route, especially as coal occurs in many of the areas served by the Suez route.
3 The Panama route serves regions which are deficient in coal. It has, however, a considerable amount of oil.
4 The Suez route serves some of the most thickly populated areas and carries, therefore, a much larger traffic than the Panama route which generally serves poor mountainous or desert regions like those on the east coast of North America or South America.
5 The Suez Canal is longer, has no locks and has cost less than the Panama Canal. It is not so deep, however, and the practice of tying up, so annoying in the case of the Suez, is not necessary in the case of the Panama Canal.
6 The Suez Canal dues are higher than those of the Panama Canal.

Other Important Ship Canals

Other important ship canals of the world are the Sault Sainte Marie Canal, (also called Soo Canal), the Manchester Ship Canal, the Kiel Canal, the North Sea Canal between Amsterdam and the North Sea, and the New Waterway between Rotterdam and the North Sea.

Current Issues

The current concerns are as follows:

1. Supply of ships and container space exceeds demand
2. Pricing and rates – flat and somewhat low
3. Unhealthy competition
4. Increased environmental and regulatory compliance
5. Shipping lines reporting losses

Shake Out Ahead

Many large shipping lines are incurring losses. For example, Hanjin's operating loss was USD 225 million in 2017. Mergers and Acquisitions are seen to be happening in this global logistics sector. Possibility exists for further realignment through acquisitions and mergers. CSAV/Hapag-Lloyd joining the P3 network.

The Next Few Years

As big ships are spread around globally, more rate volatility in more trade lanes is expected. Besides, scheduled/service vagaries and dropped weekly sailings and fewer carriers in global business are expected as a major shake-out, resulting in emergence of new business models, and realignment and diversification are a distinct possibility. Other signals that are emerging include the following:

1. Alliances, slot exchanges and vessel sharing – created and changed
2. Shipping routes – added and revised
3. Sailing schedules – made and reworked
4. 'Slow steaming' – ongoing practice
5. Irregular performance
6. Lack of service reliability
7. Potential changes as to ports to handle ships

These might result in supply chain management performance because of increased uncertainty for planning that will undermine inventory yield maximisation, resulting in more inventories and more capital tied up in the system.

Global Trends in Transportation and Logistics

A lot of things are happening in the logistics and transport Industry and the reasons are as follows:

- There are country-specific developments.
- Global market forces triggering changes.
- Every year logistics industry is facing new challenges.
- Changing regulatory and environmental requirements.
- Logistics is the new focus of global industry for competitiveness.
- Security concerns have increased.

168 *Transportation*

Bringing Production Location Closer to the End Customers

To reduce the cost of logistics, businesses and more particularly global businesses are seen to bring the production centres closer to the end users or customers, which has helped in reduction in both labour and transportation costs. This was necessary to offset the increased cost of labour as well as transportation and also due to increased competition. More and more European producers have realised that they can maintain the same level of cost and high quality of the product irrespective of the fact that they produce in their offshore manufacturing plants in Asian countries. Due to competitive pressure increasing amounts of production are being brought closer to the end user as a result of increased labour and transportation costs in Asia. More European producers realise that they can maintain the same low costs and high level of quality, regardless of whether their production plants are located offshore in Asia or even nearby countries in Europe, as bringing the production centres closer to the end users results in lesser transportations, shorter lead times and better planning of logistics flows in addition to making corrections much easier on the transportations and shipping plans as and when required. As a result, we can now see that some of the production plants are now seen to be shifting to East European locations from China and other destinations for the reason that market for the company's end product is closer and these European countries are now seen to be cost-effective when compared with their counterparts located far from the customer locations in other countries taking the increased logistics and transportation costs into consideration. The logistics thus are increasingly influencing such crucial and critical decisions related to global production and manufacturing locations.

Investments in Larger Vessels Created Overcapacity in Container Shipping

Large global shipping companies have invested in larger container vessels[4] in order to reduce operational costs to remain competitive. Larger vessels are expected to reduce the carrying costs of cargo per container unit. However, large shipping companies acquiring larger vessels have also created a situation of overcapacity. And capacity now is more than demand and that is expected to keep the freight rates low till the time the increased demand in terms of cargo volume can balance the overcapacity so created by the industry.

Sustainability and Compliance Becoming Important Issues in the Global Transport Industry

There is an increased global awareness of and concern about the environmental impact of the transportation sector and guidelines to be complied with. People, in general, are more aware and committed to taking care of it. As the transport industry is blamed for much of the emissions of carbon and nitrogen dioxide, and is, therefore, the key imperative for businesses to take care of the level of emissions and become responsible for such actions. In the global transport industry, there is a continued focus on sustainability and compliance, with regard to environmental issues and CSR. The more you are responsible for causing damage to environment more CSR you have. Also, the customers who are reputed and well-meaning companies will also distance themselves from you under public pressure, resulting in loss of business. In an environment where industries now are forced to take care of their own waste, players in the end-to-end logistics value chain are only interested in working with those companies which can offer sustainable transport solutions supported by good working conditions. This can be traced and also reflected by stricter compliance laws and regulations on a global level. Developed countries such as the USA, UK and Germany are working hard to prevent corruption through new laws that will be applicable globally.

Major Acquisitions in the Global Logistics Industry

Of late, we have been witnessing many large acquisitions in the logistics and transport industry. From a European perspective, the economic climate has not been very favourable in recent years, but the solution in Asia could be an acquisition. Other factors such as customer demand and better service at a lower cost to enable them to be competitive in the marketplace, logistics and transport industry are seeking the opportunities of acquisition to eliminate competition and become more cost-effective. We have seen this trend in North America and the trend is accelerating. The postal service in Japan is one example of a company that has made great investments in the industry. This is most likely a result of the prevailing low-interest rates, making the conditions right to expand into fast-growing regions. The Indian post and telegraph industry has been going through a transformation. Slovenian Postal Service seems to be the largest logistics company in the country although they still have to make the company profitable.

How Acquisition Helps Global Logistics Company

Acquiring a business has many advantages. Some of them are as follows:

- Helps getting critical mass and only after getting critical mass accelerated growth is possible.
- Increased market share
- Eliminates a potential competition
- Can eliminate your immediate competitor
- Financial leverage
- Can emerge as significant global player overnight
- Can draw on synergistic association
- Is a better way to enter a new geographical area

Many times acquisition is made just to destroy a formidable competition. However, acquisition also comes with its own challenges such as:

- Managing the merger of acquired entity post-acquisition
- Cultural diversity
- Value and ethics in two different entities in acquisition
- Integration challenges
- Human resource management issues – duplicate workforce and questions arising about which one to retain
- Sometimes companies acquired become more of a dominant force than the company which has acquired

Green Transport Solutions Preferred Over Air Freight

The Trans-Siberian Railway has recently been given a boost, as more players want to invest in eco-friendly transport solutions to and from Asia. This trend has shifted cargo from air freight to rail transport. For high-value goods, there is a significant increase in rail transport. Air freight is the fastest shipping method, no doubt about it, but looking at the entire logistics chain from Asia to Europe, the railway is extremely competitive – for both environmental and economic reasons. Global companies are increasingly concerned about protecting environment and are thus trying to reduce large parts of their transportation costs. As a consequence of environmental

170   Transportation

thinking, companies are reducing large parts of their transportation costs by choosing rail transport instead of air freight. This also helps to keep the planet less polluted.

Major Shift to Surface Transport

Rail transport is likely to get a significant boost as it does not add to traffic congestion on the road. Less pollution, cost-effective, its schedule does not get impacted and therefore normally runs on schedule. Road transport is also to get increasing support as it can provide end-to-end services and it is efficient. Also, a major mode of transport in any case now. Other reasons are as follows: faster movement, technology shift, fast-moving rail and road transport, and lesser cost. Air transport, as it is costly and has its associated constraints, will thus suffer for cargo movement. Air transport is increasingly becoming costlier with rise in aviation fuel cost. Bunker fuel is also coming under increasing regulatory pressure on environmental issues and as a result surface transport like rail and roads are becoming more preferred. In Europe, a large part of the cargo movement takes place by road and rail. This is a major shift that is now being witnessed.

Impact of Growing E-commerce on the Supply Chain

Consumers are increasingly buying goods and merchandise online instead of buying from physical bricks-and-mortar stores. This new trend in shopping has brought in the following challenges in supply chain:

- There is a growth in home deliveries commensurate with the growth of the e-commerce industry, which in turn increases the complexity and challenges of last-mile connectivity.
- For the postal services, the volume of letters is constantly falling, while the package deliveries are increasing.

The impact of these can be seen in a supply chain in the sense that logistics companies are required to optimise their supply chain and have to find out newer ways of providing last-mile delivery services. This would mean developing a cost-effective mode of transportation to private persons and individuals or to the nearest distribution points. This has helped growth in courier service business in India. This, in fact, is a new type of logistics chain than what we have been doing so far historically.

The fastest-growing segment in China and India is Internet shopping, which is pushing the logistics systems to cope with a booming number of deliveries to individual homes as well as offices. It is also being experienced that an increasing number of customers who have traditionally moved their production centres from their home countries, for example, Scandinavian countries to China are then importing back from China to their home markets. These companies have now started to sell even in China and Asia, which requires local SCM infrastructure.

These impacts require a change in the supply chain, and there could be several solutions for such a situation. Each solution has to be customer and situation specific, and no one solution can fit all.

This affects the supply chain, meaning that logistics companies need to optimise their supply chains and find new ways of providing last-mile delivery services, that is, transporting the goods to private persons or distribution points nearby.

This has helped growth in courier service business in India. This is a completely new type of logistics chain than what we have been doing historically so far.

These impacts require a change in the supply chain and there could be several solutions.

Increased Internet Shopping Changes the Supply Chain

The fastest-growing segment in China and India is online shopping, and this is pushing the logistics systems to cope with a booming number of deliveries to private homes and offices.

We also see an increasing number of customers who traditionally moved production from their home countries, for example, in Scandinavia, to China and then started to import from China to their home markets. These companies are now starting to sell within China and Asia as well which requires local SCM infrastructure.

The supply chain has to be changed and for that we have several solutions. The solutions are to be situation specific for such a situation. Each such solution has to be customer and situation specific.

New Geographies Will Provide the Economic Growth

So far, China has had a rapid economic growth and served as a growth engine for increasing global trade. But now we will be seeing the growth coming from other geographic regions including India. Africa is expected to become the next big market and that would mean a big challenge for the logistics operators, given the poor infrastructure, ageing road and seaports, and underdeveloped transportation systems. Exploiting this tremendous growth opportunity of the continent and figuring out how to overcome those challenges are of great interest for all players in the logistics chain. The African countries have to investigate how they can maintain the expected and potential growth to help the economy on a positive development track. If the African market opens up, then European logistics companies will have a distinctive advantage because of their geographical proximity. India is another country to watch, as it is also on a high growth trajectory. A lot of investment happening in logistics infrastructure in India. Road infrastructure and connectivity have also significantly improved in India offering new growth opportunities for logistics and transportation.

Increased Demand on Containerisation

Looking back at history, we can see that containerisation has been very crucial for the development of global trade as we have seen over the years for various reasons:

- Standardised containers made it possible to ship increasing volumes of goods around the globe in a cost-effective manner.
- The demand for containerised transports is thus constantly increasing because it helps in better space utilisation and better protection of the cargo.
- The future of the transport industry seems to be going in that direction for some inherent advantages.

Reasons for Containerisation

Global Shift in Trade Pattern

With manufacturing moving to new locations such as India and East European countries. Industries are adapting to containerisation. For example, the paper industry changes size of the paper to fit the container. There is a tug-of-war between containers and roll-on/roll-off (RORO). But containers are much more flexible and becoming cost-effective. gained ground from General cargo to break bulk. It is primarily from general cargo that containerised shipment has been

172 *Transportation*

and still gaining. It is believed that in ten years' time about 90% general cargo segment will be shipped in containers. There is further potential of containerisation of timber. Majority of cargo will now be moving in containers now instead of break bulk. Slovenia is an important port for timber trade. Almost certainly, the structural changes that container shipping is undergoing will provide large economies of scale and the demand and supply ratio will continue to put pressure on container freight rates. This will increase the attractiveness of container shipping (Levinson, 2006).

RORO and Break Bulk

Roll-on/Roll-off (RORO or **ro-ro**) ships are vessels designed to carry wheeled cargo, such as cars, trucks, semi-trailer trucks, trailers and railroad cars, which are driven on and off the ship on their own wheels or using a platform vehicle, such as a self-propelled modular transporter. This can be seen in all major ports around the world. Even in a small port in Slovenia at Luka Koper Port, this practice can be seen.

Break bulk cargoes are defined as general cargo or goods that do not fit in or utilise standard shipping containers or cargo bins. Cargo moved from one mode to another mode of transport when required.

CUSTOM BONDED WAREHOUSE

Customs-bonded Warehousing Solutions to Shorten Lead Times

A typical challenge for exporters in the Nordics is that some of their competing producers are located in China or Asia and the long lead time from the Nordics makes them less competitive.

Establishing customs-bonded warehousing solutions in, for example, Shanghai, Shenzhen and Hong Kong will cut lead times from order to delivery by more than two months.

Buyer's Consolidation Service and E-solutions to Keep Track of the Goods

Yet another Nordic importer buys vast amounts of small-quantity orders from a large number of suppliers – and has problems keeping track of shipments. Solution is the buyer's consolidation service, provided at the main ports of China, together with e-solutions to keep track of the goods. This can minimise administration and lower the costs for customer and can make their everyday operations more efficient.

Future of Green Carrier and the Logistics and Transport Market in China

As the environment is an important consideration, some customers on board train service from China to the Nordics. It would make a less impact on the environment – the cost is higher but saves on the transit time in addition to lowering the pollution. As the cost of pollution management will rise, the increased cost of rail transport for long distance will somewhat get compensated.

The Global Shipping Industry Will Face New Sulphur Regulations

The International Maritime Organisation (IMO) is on the cusp of implementing new sulphur regulations which will have a significant impact on the global shipping industry. On January 1, 2020, IMO will enforce a ban on ships using fuel that has a sulphur content of 0.5% and

Transportation 173

above. Ships will have the option to buy 'scrubbers' to reduce the emissions from the use of higher sulphur-containing fuel. But the incremental investment will be to the tune of 1 million to USD 10 million per ship and, therefore, it is not surprising that less than 3% of global ships have made this investment so far. The new regulations are part of the IMO's effort to reduce greenhouse gas emissions by 50% from the level of 2008 by 2050. IMO is determined to set a new global standard of shipping fuel with exception of the stricter sulphur limit of 0.1% of the existing Emissions Control Area (ECA) in North America, the Caribbean, the Baltic and the North Sea.

As the global shipping industry is not ready for this change in regulations that are forthcoming, they are under a very difficult, disruptive and turbulent transition since 2019. The implications of this are likely to go far beyond the shipping industry. With every passing month, the prices of a range of fuel including high and low sulphur-containing bunker fuel, diesel and jet fuel will become more volatile as the refiners and the fuel purchasers pursue a pricing advantage before the January 1, 2020, deadline. The ship owners are already sounding the alarm bell about the fuel scarcity and an estimated incremental USD 60 billion in fuel bills which is almost equal to the total fuel bill of the industry in the year 2016. Some of the largest crude oil tankers could foresee a 25% increase in shipping cost arising out of higher fuel cost itself. This has a cascading effect and prices of goods are getting impacted ever since the whole drama of new regulations got unfolded by the year 2020.[5] Despite the challenges brought about by the surge in low -sulphur fuel prices, several carriers have taken proactive measures to comply with the new regulations by installing scrubbers to remove sulphur in bunker fuel.[6]

Ocean Freight

Ocean freight or sea freight is normally the preferred mode of transportation in global trade for companies that need to ship large amounts of goods in one shipment and or when volume of cargo to be shipped is relatively large. While this is the longest mode of transportation, it is an ideal one for bulk shipment volume, which has to be transported across geographical regions at regular intervals such as minerals, oils and coal. It is a suitable option for products with long lead times, and for large volumes, it is an affordable and economical transportation solution. However, this mode of transportation tends to be quite slow and is subject to customs restrictions and can lead to product damage due to environmental hazards and movement if your goods aren't packaged properly. Ocean transport can also lead to multiple handling and transhipment. When transporting your products via ocean freight, it is crucial that you optimise your container load. Not only will you reduce your shipping expenses, but you will also reduce the potential for damage during transport. Non-optimised loads mean that you'll have unused space within the container, allowing your items enough room to shift and move up against each other during transport. For proper load optimisation, follow a few simple steps like:

- **Inspect the container first before loading**: It can happen that the container you are loading may have been used earlier for transporting goods which can be a source of contamination or even hazards for your goods. Your container needs to be inspected carefully before anything is loaded. Pay close attention to any contamination or residue on the floor, as these substances could cause a negative reaction to your cargo.
- **Load heavy materials first**: Large, heavy items should always be loaded first on the floor and against the container's front wall. Lighter items should be placed at the top. If your shipment is a part load you also need to check what other materials will be packed along with your goods and check compatibility with that to avoid facing problems later on. For example, food materials cannot be loaded with other materials like chemicals.
- **Distribute weight across the container for balancing**: If your container is loaded to maximum capacity, it is important that the weight is evenly distributed across the floor area.

174 *Transportation*

Before loading, it is important to plan ahead. There are advanced tools and software programs that use values such as package weight, dimension, volume and restrictions in order to help you reach an optimal container load. Your packaging should be able to withstand the shock and vibration and even scuffing during ocean freight.

Air Freight

Companies that work with short lead times and require their packages to be transported as quickly as possible often choose air freight. Also, for urgent cargo, defence cargo, emergency shipment of medicine and food during natural calamity as well as very costly cargo are normally transported by air. This is a relatively safe mode of transport, and it reduces supplier lead times while improving the overall service level. It can also take cargoes to difficult and easily accessible areas. However, only certain goods are suitable for air transport, and this expensive option often comes with airport taxes, custom and excise restrictions, and other regulatory requirements.

Hazards of Air Freight Transport

If you choose to transport via air freight, there are certain hazards for which you need to prepare by choosing the right packaging. High and low atmospheric pressures can have a dramatic effect on certain packages, and humidity changes can result in condensation or corrosion that could affect your product if not packaged properly. Shock occurs during transport and handling as a result of impacts on containers, racks, floors and other shipments. Proper cushioning within your package will reduce damage that results from shock, and most products will require some level of shock protection in order to prevent damage during transportation and handling.

In transport movement, your packages are liable to shift and move from their original place significantly during air transport. Acceleration and take-off to in-flight dropping and pitching in turbulent weather cause damage to your cargo, and as such your package needs to be able to withstand any unexpected pitching or jarring.

Road Transport

Almost all packaging will require road transport to a certain degree. Road transportation is cost-effective and ideal for transporting perishables for short distances. It is easy to monitor the location of your goods, but your packaging could be damaged by mishandling or careless driving. Or even multiple handling and transhipment and loading unloading shocks. If you are choosing road transport, it is important to prepare for potential delays, including traffic, truck breakdowns and bad weather.

When shipping your products via road transport, it is important that you choose the right packaging design. Appropriate cushioning can be designed for vibration protection if you consider that cushions should perform like springs. Depending on the thickness and load-bearing area of the cushion, it should be designed in a way that either does not get impacted by the input vibration or isolates the product from the vibration. The right design will make all the difference in how well the cushion can protect your product from damage due to vibration.

Rail Transport

Rail is a very important and cost-effective mode of transport and thus rail transportation is a great solution for domestic or intercontinental transport, especially for heavy cargoes. It is a fairly safe and reliable mode of transport that offers fast delivery at a cost-effective price point, and it is also more environmentally safe and friendly than air and road alternatives. Plus, rail freight doesn't add to traffic and roadway congestion like other modes of transportation.

Unfortunately, however, rail transport isn't a perfect mode of transport and also comes with its many disadvantages. All packaging solutions need to be prepared to protect against damage from shunting and vibration. The use of the right packaging system can reduce and absorb the negative effects that vibration can have on a product. The other disadvantages are that rail transport is only available on limited routes with inflexible timetables. It only can take goods to the closest railway stations and if you aren't located near a rail freight depot, you will also have to take care of the transport by road to deliver the goods to the cargo booking depot.

Case Study: Maersk Line

Maersk Line is the flagship company of A.P. Moller-Maersk Group, a diversified Danish Group and a global leader in the shipping industry. A.P. Moller-Maersk Group had a revenue of USD 60 billion in 2011, which grew to over USD 70 billion in 2016. This revenue is contributed by business divisions, including Maersk Line – USD 27 billion or 45%, oil and gas USD 12.6 billion or 21% and retail and banking USD 20.4 billion or 34% of the group's combined revenue. And in 2022 its revenue grew to USD 81 billion.

A.P. Moller-Maersk group employs 115,000 people worldwide out of which Maersk Lines employees are about 16,900 and have their presence in 167 countries. The founding family trusts control 58% of the total share capital and 76% of the voting rights. The company thus is family owned and controlled. Although this family is not known for their explicit commitment to environmental issues; however, reputation of company worldwide is extremely important for business and it is positive.

Maersk Line is the world's biggest container shipping company having 660 either owned or chartered vessels representing about 17% of the industry's operating fleet. Its vessel makes over 70,000 port calls per year. Maersk ships are eight years old on average, whereas competitors have 12–15 years old vessels.

Maersk Line has over 100,000 customers, and with most of these customers (50%) they have long-term contracts, with remaining 50% of the market being spot-price customers. About 25% of the customers are key customers like Walmart, Nike and Tesco, 15% are key freight forwarders and the remaining 60% are small customers and other freight forwarders. Maersk Line has 7600 seafarers and about 500 representative offices globally spread in over 167 countries.

Maersk's Business Strategy

Maersk has three fundamental challenges to differentiate itself from the rest of the industry. These are:

1 Unreliability
2 Complexity (hard to do business)
3 Environmental impact

Reliability

Maersk Line's goal is to become the industry leader and keep its leadership position. It is already the leader in on-time delivery up to 80% of the time, but the new goal is to improve upon further to help

176 *Transportation*

customers reduce their inventory level to reach 'just in case inventory'. Daily Maersk Asia–Europe route achieves 95% on-time goal requiring 70 new vessels. All service ports operate entirely as planned, and on other routes, they work with terminal partners to reduce time in port by 30% and have already achieved 10% reduction.

Simplicity

To reduce immense paperwork work Maersk Line has streamlined and digitised much of the paperwork. Implemented order and follow cargo online, simplified documentation process and implemented cargo tracking online and automatic notification to the customers updating the status through appropriate IT systems interface and improved customer service.

Environment Sustainable Strategy

Environment is a major concern in the global logistics industry. Ship exhaust emission from bunker fuel is considered a large source of greenhouse gas emissions, and this has become a major concern of the industry as clients are exerting pressure on the vessel operators. Earlier it was thought that climate change is occurring because of greenhouse gas emissions from human activity, but maritime shipping accounts for 3.3% of global emissions and bunker fuel releases 2000 times more sulphur than diesel fuel. A.P. Moller-Maersk Group has given considerable importance to the environmental impact and sustainability has become a key differentiator. The four key themes around this key strategic driver or key differentiator are:

- Environment and climate change
- Health and safety, which also includes piracy
- Social responsibility
- Responsible Business Practices (Similar To SOX, FCPA and Dodd-Frank): FCPA: Foreign Corrupt Practices Act. Dodd-Frank is a consumer Protection Act, Sarbanes Oxley Act.

This strategy will be executed through a number of initiatives including technology intervention, route optimisation, fleet type and sizes and market integration as shown in Figure 6.1.

The environmental goals of Maersk Lines are to become global leader in low-carbon shipping by having greater focus on environment and sustainability with an objective to lead the industry towards zero SOx emissions by reducing its impact on marine environment. Achieving these goals would meet the Group's environmental sustainability Initiative

Maersk Lines intend to differentiate from other competing global players on the following lines:

1 Focus on sustainability
2 Customer satisfaction and on-time delivery schedule
3 From order booking 24×7 online tracking of your consignment
4 Covers more destinations than others
5 More focus on key customers who are also long-term associates
6 Deliver incremental value over their competitor

Competitors like CMA CGM, and Hapag-Lloyd had CO2 calculators to measure the carbon footprint of shipment journey, but APL has been named sustainable shipping operator of the year for 2010. Maersk Lines is concerned and will not allow competition to score better in this score.

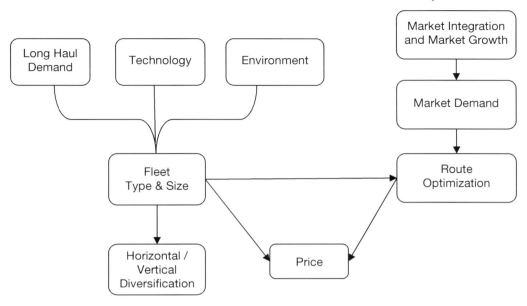

Figure 6.1 Business Strategy Initiatives of Maersk Line

Financial Performance

Due to difficult and volatile market conditions, the financial performance of Maersk Line has witnessed fluctuation during 2015 and 2016. The highlights of the financial performance of 2015 and 2016 are given next:

- **Maersk Line** made a profit of USD 1.3 billion (USD 2.3billion) and a ROCI of 6.5% (11.6%). The underlying profit declined to USD 1.3 billion (USD 2.2 billion) due to poor market conditions leading to significantly lower freight rates, in particular in the second half of the year, only partially offset by lower bunker prices, USD appreciation and cost efficiencies.
- Maersk Line placed three new building orders for a total of 27 vessels with a total capacity of 367,000 TEU. Further investments have been postponed due to the weak market conditions.
- During the first part of 2015, the implementation of the Vessel Sharing Agreement (VSA) with the Mediterranean Shipping Company (MSC) on the East-West network was completed successfully with the phase-in of 193 vessels.
- **Maersk Line** expected an underlying result significantly below last year (USD 1.3 billion) as a consequence of the significantly lower freight rates going into 2016 and the continued low growth with expected global demand for seaborne container transportation to increase by 1–3%.
- The underlying profit was USD 711 million (USD 3.1 billion), within the latest guidance, negatively impacted by a loss in Maersk Line.
- Lower container rates and weak market growth severely impacted earnings in Maersk Line during the year but with a positive underlying trend recognised through the fourth quarter.
- Stabilisation of oil prices in the second half of 2016 combined with cost and production efficiencies led to positive earnings growth in Maersk Oil.
- Maersk experienced a negative result due to impairments totalling USD 2.8 billion after tax primarily related to Maersk Drilling and Maersk Supply Service.

178 *Transportation*

- Free cash flow was negative USD 29 million (USD 1.6 billion excluding the sale of the Danske Bank shares).
- Cash flow from operating activities decreased to USD 4.3 billion (USD 8.0 billion), including a one-off dispute settlement in Maersk Oil.
- Gross cash flow used for capital expenditure was USD 5.0 billion (USD 7.2 billion) mainly related to the TCB acquisition and development of the Culzean and Johan Sverdrup oil fields.

Making Loss in a Decade

- The Board of Directors have proposed a dividend of DKK 150 per share approved at the Annual General Meeting on March 28, 2017.
- A P Moller unveiled one of the biggest losses in Danish corporate history as the conglomerate suffered from a weak container shipping industry and massive write-downs on its oil businesses last year.
- Shares in Maersk fell as much as 7% as it reported only its second annual loss in seven decades and halved its dividend to try to protect its investment-grade credit rating.
- Maersk recorded a net loss of USD 1.9 billion for 2016, compared with analysts' expectations of USD 960 million profit, as it booked impairments of USD 2.7 billion on its oil rig and supply services units.
- Maersk Line suffered a tough end to 2016, slipping to a loss in the fourth quarter and for the year as a whole in spite of a rebound in freight rates from record lows. It made a loss of USD 376 million in 2016 compared with a profit of USD 1.3 billion one year earlier.

Performance in 2017

- Due to gradual improvements in container, **Maersk Line** expects an improvement in excess of USD 1 billion in underlying profit compared to 2016 (loss of USD 384 million).
- Global demand for seaborne container transportation was expected to increase by 2–4%.
- Maersk Line reported a profit of USD 339 million after four consecutive lossmaking quarters, resulting in a ROCI of 6.7%.
- Market fundamentals continue to improve as demand outgrew nominal supply growth for the third consecutive quarter and further industry consolidation was announced.
- Revenue increased by 8.4% mainly driven by higher revenue in Maersk Line and Maersk Oil, partly offset by Maersk Drilling and APM Terminals.
- Profit declined to USD 264 million, negatively impacted by impairments amounting to USD 732 million in APM Terminals, Svitzer and Maersk Tankers.

The financial performance of Maersk Lines continued to be under pressure during later year also till 2020. The revenue increased during 2022 to over USD 81 billion. But the profit before tax was significantly down. Maersk Line acquired Hamburg Süd for EUR 3.7 billion (USD 4.4 billion) on a cash and debt-free basis through a syndicated loan facility. In 2022 Maersk Line reported loss at Profit after Tax level but never missed paying dividend to its shareholders.

Market Share Price Movement

It can be seen that the stock price of the Maersk Line has been fluctuating during 2016 and 2017. The company's performance was much better in earlier years during 2014 and 2015 but in 2016 company suffered a setback and incurred a loss but did not skip the dividend. The company expected a significant turnaround in the year 2017, and its new business strategy is expected to deliver better results.

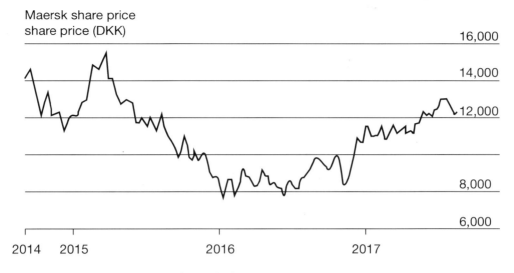

Figure 6.2 Share Price Movement of Maersk Lines

Source: https://investor.maersk.com/static files/maersk strategy and performance (accessed on 17th Nov 2018)

From the share price movement from 2015 to 2018 (Figure 6.2), it can be seen that share price was high at 15,000 DKK in 2015, and then due to recession, it started declining and came down to as low 8000 DKK in 2016 eroding almost 50% of the market value of the company and then started gradually going up again during 2017 showing a turnaround in the company's performance.

Financial results for the last 5 years

Table 6.4 Financial Performance of Maersk Lines[7]

Financial results for the last 5 years

Income Statement:	31/12/2022	31/12/2021	31/12/2020	31/12/2019	31/12/2018
	$ (Millions)	$ (Millions)	$ (Millions)	$ (Millions)	$ (Millions)
Revenue:	81,529.00	61,787.00	39,740.00	38,890.00	39,280.00
Operating Profit/(Loss):	30,728.00	19,188.00	3887.00	1496.00	221
Net Interest:	n/a	n/a	n/a	n/a	n/a
Profit Before Tax:	30,231.00	18,730.00	3307.00	967	−180
Profit after tax from continuing operations:	29,321.00	18,033.00	2900.00	509	−578
Discontinued Operations:					
Profit after tax from discontinuing operations:	n/a	n/a	n/a	n/a	n/a
Profit for the period:	n/a	n/a	n/a	n/a	n/a

180 *Transportation*

Financial results for the last 5 years

Income Statement:	31/12/2022	31/12/2021	31/12/2020	31/12/2019	31/12/2018
	$ (Millions)	$ (Millions)	$ (Millions)	$ (Millions)	$ (Millions)
Attributable to:					
Equity holders of parent company:	n/a	n/a	n/a	n/a	n/a
Minority Interests/Other Equity:	n/a	n/a	n/a	n/a	n/a
Total Dividend Paid:	c 623.00	c 3.85	c 55.00	c 22.00	c 23.00
Retained Profit/(Loss) for the Financial Year:	c n/a	c n/a	c n/a	c n/a	c n/a
Earnings per Share:					
Basic:	160.00¢	9.50¢	145.00¢	23.00¢	($30.00)
Diluted:	n/a	n/a	n/a	n/a	n/a
Adjusted:	160.00¢	9.50¢	145.00¢	23.00¢	($30.00)
Dividend per Share:	$0.00	$0.00	$0.00	$0.00	$0.00
Balance Sheet:	**31/12/2022**	**31/12/2021**	**31/12/2020**	**31/12/2019**	**31/12/2018**
	$ (Millions)	$ (Millions)	$ (Millions)	$ (Millions)	$ (Millions)
Assets:					
Non-current Assets:					
Property, Plant & Equipment:	39,161.00	37,209.00	34,804.00	35,976.00	31,107.00
Intangible Assets:	10,785.00	5769.00	5145.00	4219.00	4278.00
Investment Properties:	n/a	n/a	n/a	n/a	n/a
Investments:	n/a	n/a	n/a	n/a	n/a
Other Financial Assets:	n/a	n/a	n/a	n/a	n/a
Other Non-current Assets:	3671.00	3491.00	3432.00	3504.00	3261.00
	53,617.00	46,469.00	43,381.00	43,699.00	38,646.00
Current Assets:					
Inventories:	1604.00	1457.00	1049.00	1430.00	1073.00
Trade and Other Receivables:	n/a	n/a	n/a	n/a	n/a
Cash at Bank & In Hand:	10,057.00	11,832.00	5865.00	4768.00	2863.00
Current Asset Investments:	n/a	n/a	n/a	n/a	n/a
Other Current Assets:	28,402.00	12,513.00	5822.00	5502.00	14,040.00
	40,063.00	**25,802.00**	**12,736.00**	**11,700.00**	**17,976.00**
Other Assets:	n/a	n/a	n/a	n/a	n/a
Total Assets:	**93,680.00**	**72,271.00**	**56,117.00**	**55,399.00**	**56,622.00**
Liabilities:					
Current Liabilities:					
Borrowings:	3287.00	2867.00	758	721	1586.00
Other Current Liabilities:	10,034.00	9226.00	9296.00	9114.00	9813.00
	13,321.00	12,093.00	10,054.00	9835.00	11,399.00
Net Current Assets:	c 26,742.00	c 13,709.00	c 2682.00	c 1865.00	c 6577.00
Non-current Liabilities:					
Borrowings:	12,356.00	12,468.00	5868.00	7455.00	8036.00
Provisions:	n/a	n/a	n/a	n/a	n/a
Other Non-Current Liabilities:	2971.00	2122.00	9341.00	9272.00	3807.00
	15,327.00	14,590.00	15,209.00	16,727.00	11,843.00
Other Liabilities:	n/a	n/a	n/a	n/a	n/a
Total Liabilities:	28,648.00	26,683.00	25,263.00	26,562.00	23,242.00
Net Assets:	65,032.00	45,588.00	30,854.00	28,837.00	33,380.00

Maersk's Commitment to Environment and Sustainability

To outperform competition and retain the leadership position to remain as number one shipping company Maersk has a deep commitment to environment and sustainability issues in global ocean transport trade. Maersk purchases 25 Volvo e-trucks for climate-friendly container transports in Germany.

Figure 6.3 Sustainability Initiatives of Maersk Shipping Lines

Maersk, a leading innovator in integrated and sustainable logistics solutions, announces a new initiative to reduce GHG emissions in hinterland container transports by purchasing 25 state-of-the-art Volvo FH electric trucks in Germany. This strategic investment highlights the company's commitment to decarbonising global logistics and to becoming a net-zero company by 2040 across all business areas and all modes of transport.

Pioneering the first container vessel conversion to a methanol dual-fuel engine (As the first in the industry, Maersk will retrofit an existing vessel to a dual-fuel methanol powered vessel and thereby be able to sail on green methanol)

At Maersk, has set an ambitious net-zero emissions target for 2040 across the entire business and have taken a leading role in decarbonising logistics. Retrofitting of engines to run on methanol is an important lever in our strategy, and an agreement has therefore been signed with MAN Energy Solutions (MAN ES) to retrofit the engine.

In 2021, Maersk ordered the world's first methanol-enabled container vessel following a commitment to the principle of only ordering new-built vessels that can sail on green fuels.

	Environment		**Social**			**Governance**		
Commitments	**We will take leadership in the decarbonisation of logistics**		**We will ensure that our people thrive at work by providing a safe and inspiring workplace**			**We operate based on responsible business practices**		
	We will deliver on our customer commitment to decarbonise their supply chains in time and our societal commitment to act and have impact in this decade		We create an engaging environment for all colleagues	We facilitate diversity of thought	We ensure everyone gets home safe by preventing fatal and life-altering incidents	We live our Code of Conduct	We procure sustainably	We protect and treat data with respect
Strategic targets *All targets are for end of year*	**2040:** • Net zero across the business • 100% green solutions to customers	**2030:** • Aligned with the Science Based Targets initiative 15°C pathway • Industry-leading green customer offerings across the supply chain	**2025:** Top quartile score on engagement survey	**2025:** >40% women in management >30% diverse nationality of executes	**2023:** • 100% of High Potential Incidents trigger frontline Learning Teams • Global Leadership(Top 900) upskilled in Maersk safety and security principles	**2023:** 100% of employees trained in the Maersk Code of Conduct	**2024:** 100% of suppliers committed to the Supplier Code of Conduct	**2023:** 100% of employees trained on data ethics
Overview of all ESG categories	Climate change Environment and ecosystems(incl. ship recycling)		Employee relations and labour right-Safety & Security-Human Capital Sustainable and inclusive trade-Diversity, equity and inclusion-Human rights			Business ethics-Governance-Responsible tax Sustainable procurement-Data ethics-Citizenship		

Figure 6.4 Sustainability Initiatives by Maersk

Concurrently, we have explored the potential of retrofitting existing vessels with dual-fuel methanol engines. Having teamed up with MAN ES, we are now ready to demonstrate how retrofitting vessels with methanol dual-fuel capabilities can be done.

Maersk Is Sponsoring Corals' Plantation and Preservation[8]

In 2022, Maersk teams in the United Arab Emirates got together to sponsor a marine conservation programme with Freestyle Divers LLC to plant coral along the coast of Fujairah. Today, Amal (Arabic for 'hope'), Maersk coral structure, has become a habitat for seven different types of coral, which has attracted a variety of marine species to the area

Following the great outcome of sponsorship, Freestyle Divers is now embarking on a bigger plan to plant an area of 30 kilometres with the support of the sponsoring communities and organisations. For this purpose, James Campbell, Freestyle Divers Marine Biologist and Head of the Conservation Programme, will be training the certified diving colleagues in the United Arab Emirates to plant the coral themselves and support the propagation of this important species.

Decarbonising Logistics

Accelerating the net-zero targets Maersk is committed to its obligation – as an industry leader and with the resources available to it – to do all it can to get to net-zero operations as fast as possible and to help its customers decarbonise their global supply chains end-to-end. Decarbonisation is a core part of A.P. Moller-Maersk's overall business priorities and supported by a dedicated function that ensures collaboration across commercial, operational, technological and corporate entities.

Customer Engagement

Sustainability is an integral component of Maersk's offerings and can support you in discovering and implementing additional solutions to your customer business pains that go beyond moving goods from A to B. They can support you with the knowledge and means to effectively leverage sustainability in your customer relationship – enabling differentiation beyond price and activating the sustainability content with your customers. In collaboration, the Customer Sustainability Engagement team can help you to offer your customers the following.

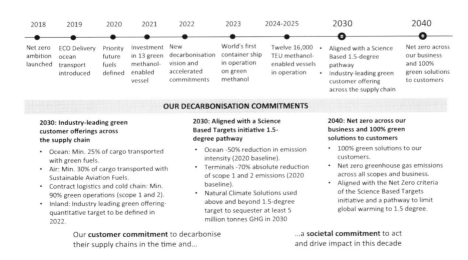

Figure 6.5 Decarbonisation Plan of Maersk Shipping Lines

184   *Transportation*

Partnership

It provides advice on how to handle and integrate sustainability in logistics through access to our sustainability experts. Maersk has supported hundreds of customers during the past ten years with advice, data and new solutions to reduce its CO_2 emissions and improve its sustainability performance.

It has access to Clean Cargo, the leading initiative to develop a more sustainable logistics industry. Clean Cargo can guide customers on how to handle sustainability in logistics and provide verified sustainability data and tools for benchmarking as well as innovation insights and inspiration on best practices in the industry.

Visibility

It provides detailed CO2 data and advanced CO2 dashboards to equip the customer with transparency in their supply chain and the possibility to identify how to reduce their CO2 emissions

It offers low carbon solutions based on analysis of the customer's supply chain such as mode shifts and most efficient services; it provides visibility and demonstrates leadership on other sustainability areas such as ship recycling, anti-corruption, human rights in the supply chain and more.

Cost Management

India's 'One Country, One Price' Fulfilment Solution Launched

This initiative has been launched with the aim of taking the complexities out of small and medium e-commerce businesses in India with truly integrated logistics and visibility.

India has vast e-commerce demand and potential, as well as an equally fragmented market and supply chain complexity, which are hurdles to many businesses' growth. The 'One Country, One Price' customer-led and network-empowered solution looks to disrupt the local marketplace and position Maersk as a single partner for e-commerce players in the nation encompassing platform integration, warehousing, country-wide distribution and returns, plus labelling and packing at a flat rate of INR 80 (USD 1) per order.

The fee applies for items weighing up to 500 grams. It will also support fulfilment for orders customers receive via other channels, such as digital marketplaces. Moreover, we will offer our customers rapid implementation (less than 3 weeks), making it possible to generate faster revenue and volume turnover.

With 700 million internet users in India, out of which 350 million use digital payments, the 2023 India E-economy Report states 220 million individuals in India did an online shopping transaction between May 2022 and May 2023. These staggering statistics prove the potential the e-commerce sector holds in India.

One Country, One Price and One Billing India Initiative

The prevalent fragmented logistics solutions are also responsible for fragmented billing. E-commerce businesses are charged differently and separately for each logistics service rendered, making for extremely complex billing. With the 'One Country, One Price' solution, Maersk are bringing all the services under a single charge, which will include 60 days of storage, delivery across India covering 18,000 zip codes in 48 hours, and 20% returns to origin (RTO) at no fixed monthly costs or no minimum orders.

Usually, when customers use external vendors, every order travels a different distance and therefore has a different cost for forward delivery. Tackling this challenge, given that they have a standard cost irrespective of the destination, cost becomes easy to reconcile.[9]

Maersk has launched new initiatives in many countries to tap opportunities by extending their services. For example, in India Maersk is now offering services to e-commerce businesses to reach out to millions of homes across India at a very reasonable cost. Maersk is making last-mile connectivity simpler and less costly by introducing logistics offering that streamlines all online deliveries and returns management. Also offering storage at any Maersk network warehouse along with services such as labelling, barcoding, packing and forward delivery – all with complete visibility at a low fixed cost per order. The package of composite offer includes storage for 60 days, delivery across India in 48 hours, return (RTO) up to 20% with no fixed monthly charges and no onboarding fee. In India this service is being provided by courier companies, and they have limitations of coverage which restricts the growth of e-commerce businesses. Now Maersk has recognised this opportunity and offering a comprehensive service with a commitment to reaching out places across India within 48 hours with warehousing facilities for handling small deliveries can make significant improvements in e-commerce delivery system. Maersk has announced this service for a minimum package size of 500 gm at INR 80, which is quite competitive and aimed at taking share of courier services in growing E-commerce opportunity.[10]

Business Development Strategy

Maersk has designed a comprehensive business development strategy to be ahead of competition in this highly competitive ocean transport industry in challenging times. In strategy, they have a three-pronged strategy engaging three separate teams, each focusing on specific tasks as discussed next:

Strategy Development Process

In strategy development, Maersk runs a company-wide annual strategy process in spring and translates that into a business plan in autumn. Outside of these processes, Maersk manage various strategic projects and conduct competitor analysis of their main competitors.

Strategic Intelligence

Strategic intelligence is tasked with monitoring and forecasting the global economy, container market fundamentals, and driving the company's future-proofing and strategy work. It engages with multiple senior stakeholders internally and supports Maersk's external communication and customer engagement.

In-house Consulting Service

Maersk Management Consulting (MMC) is the in-house management consultancy of Maersk with offices in Copenhagen and Singapore. They are a team of consultants with experience from top-tier external advisory firms, business development professionals, as well as top graduates.

186 *Transportation*

MMC offers a wide range of management consulting services to all business units and brands in Maersk, with a primary focus on strategy, organisation, and transformation and change management programmes. Through this in-house management consulting services, Maersk offers client-specific solutions for their valued clients who are channelling their ocean transport cargo in global trade preferentially through them.

Denmark's Maersk Changes Ownership Structure to Boost Finances

The foundation that controls the Danish oil and shipping group A.P. Moller-Maersk MAERSK. CO is to transfer its stake in the business to a new holding company to boost the group's financial flexibility.

A.P. Moller Foundation is controlled by the Maersk family but is obliged to use all dividends it receives from the shipping group for donations to benefit the public in countries across the Nordic region.

However, by moving the 41.51% shareholding and 51.09% of all A.P. Moller-Maersk voting rights into A.P. Moller Holding, it will be able to keep back funds as a cash reserve to be used by the shipping business.

'With the establishment of the holding company, the A.P. Moller Foundation wants to secure and strengthen its active ownership and provide financial flexibility and a financial buffer for the whole group', the foundation's chairman Ane Maersk Mc-Kinney Uggla said in a statement.

Sydbank shipping analyst Jacob Pedersen welcomed the move, saying that it will provide better control of cash flow to the foundation.

The group's 2012 dividend payout totalled 5.28 billion Danish crowns ($972 million).

A.P. Moller-Maersk owns Maersk Line, the world's largest container shipping company, but is also active in oil drilling and transportation and is behind three supermarket chains with a total of more than 1200 outlets in Denmark, Sweden, Germany and Poland.

A.P. Moller Foundation said that the new holding company will continue to observe the foundation trust deed by supporting cooperation between Denmark and the other Nordic countries, promoting Danish shipping and industry and supporting science and good causes.[11]

Maersk Acquires Hamburg Süd

The world's seventh-biggest container operator, Hamburg Süd, has been sold to Danish conglomerate A.P. Moeller-Maersk. The German shipper has been squeezed by massive overcapacity and falling cargo prices.

Maersk Line didn't disclose the purchase price of Hamburg Süd when it announced the takeover, saying it hoped to complete the deal by the end of 2017.

'The acquisition of Hamburg Süd is in line with our growth strategy and will increase the volumes of both Maersk Line and APM Terminals', Soren Skou, chief executive of Maersk Line and the Moeller-Maersk group said in a statement. The German shipping line and its Brazilian subsidiary Alianca were to continue as separate brands, he added.

Hamburg Süd is the world's seventh-largest container shipper, operating 130 container vessels and employing about 6000 people. It is owned by the German Oetker Group – a family-run conglomerate involved in shipping, banking, food and beverages.

According to data provider Alphaliner, Hamburg Süd accounts for 3% of global container capacity, with the ability to transport 600,000 containers. The value of its fleet is around $1.4 billion (1.31 billion euros), according to Vessels Value, another maritime data provider.

Transportation 187

Hamburg Süd, which traces its roots back more than 100 years, previously explored a merger with German peer Hapag-Lloyd but talks collapsed in 2013 over pricing and who would run the merged entity.

In November 2017, Germany's Oetker Group sold the liner shipping company Hamburg Süd to Maersk Line.

Maersk announced the acquisition[12] in December 2016, and it took the Danish shipping giant less than a year to secure all 23 regulatory clearances to complete the transaction.

Commenting on the sale at today's session titled Germany's New Dawn within Tradewinds Shipowners Forum, being held as part of the SMM trade fair programme, Alexander Oetker, Founder and CEO of AO Shipping, said the event was sad and also very emotional about losing control of the family-owned shipping company Hamburg Sud to A.P. Moeller of Maersk.

> _'To me, personally, it is a sad event as there was a lot of family history embedded into the company,'_ he said. We could not be the best owner for Hamburg Sud. (Sept 4, 2018)'.
>
> _'But of course, there is a rational question of whether we, as a family, as diverse and large as we are, can be the best owners of this particular vehicle, in the midst of a very strong consolidation process. And the answer, overtime, was that we couldn't'._
>
> _'As sad as I am on the one hand, on the other hand, I know that the new owners will preserve the continuation of the company's strategy and the people working in the company'._
>
> _'In shipping you have to be completely in, you cannot invest in it on the sidelines. We have other businesses that need capital, and we never want to take any debt, so there was just a rational point where we said that we should consider to sell'._

Describing the sale as _'absolutely tremendous'_, Oetker said that _'there couldn't have been a better buyer out there'_.

Maersk's acquisition of the German liner has paved the way for the creation of the world's largest containership fleet of 773 vessels, including owned and chartered ships.

Namely, Maersk Line's fleet of 668 vessels, with an average age of nine years, was enlarged by 105 ships from Hamburg Süd. The average age of the German carrier's fleet is six years.

The combined fleet has a capacity of 4,156,500 TEU, according to Alpha liner's figures.

Maersk Line acquired Hamburg Süd for EUR 3.7 billion (USD 4.4 billion) on a cash and debt-free basis through a syndicated loan facility.

Crippling Overcapacity

If the deal is approved by regulators in a number of countries, Maersk's share of the global market[13] will grow from currently 15.7% to 18.6%. Moreover, it will rejuvenate the Danish group's own fleet and help it boost its presence in global trade with Latin America.

'Hamburg Süd's strong presence in North-South trades makes it attractive to Maersk', said Lars Jensen, chief executive of Copenhagen-based Sea Intelligence Consulting. 'Maersk sees growth in refrigerated cargo like meat products from Brazil and Argentina and bananas from Ecuador, and teaming up with Hamburg Süd will give it a bigger footprint in that part of the world'.

While Maersk has bought or chartered vessels from distressed peers, its last full-scale acquisition was in 2005 when it bought P&O Nedlloyd.

188   *Transportation*

The takeover comes during one of the most challenging times for the industry,[14] with freight rates well below sustainable levels over the past two years. Container ships that transport 95% of the world's manufactured products are caught in one of the deepest ever downcycles, marked by anaemic global trade and a glut of tonnage in the water.

Those conditions have kicked off an unprecedented wave of consolidation, with many of the 20 biggest operators either joining alliances or merging to weather the crisis.

Last year, for example, France's CMA CGM – the third-biggest player – bought Singapore's Neptune Orient Lines for $2.4 billion, and Japan's three largest shipping companies said in October they would merge their container operations.[15]

Hanjin – South Korea's largest shipping company and once the world's seventh-biggest – filed for bankruptcy protection in August. This has left Hamburg Süd and Israel's Zim Integrated Shipping Services the only two shipping lines without a partner.

Case Questions:

1   Discuss the ownership and capital structure of the company. How has the owner's family A.P. Moller been able to keep control of the business?
2   What are the various business verticals the company has and what is their contribution in terms of revenue and profit.
3   What are the key competitive advantages of the Maersk Line? And what they are doing to keep the leadership on those differentiators
4   Explain the reasons of reason of sudden drop in profit in 2016.
5   What is projected performance for 2017, and how did they perform in those years and beyond?
6   Who are the key competitors of Maersk Line, and from what considerations have you identified them as Maersk Line competitors?
7   Examine the impact of the acquisitions that Maersk Lines did on their business in terms of performance of the corporation
8   Discuss what advantages Maersk derived by acquiring Humburg Sud.
9   How is Maersk shipping line keeping its leadership positions secured in the global ocean shipping industry?
10   Discuss Maersk's Environmental Protection strategy and Business Development Strategy and their effectiveness in current challenging environment in global shipping industry
11   Discuss the strategic initiatives that Maersk has undertaken in the e-commerce space in India in recent times.

Section II: Packaging Issues in Transportation

Introduction

Consumers first get exposed to the packaging before getting to know about the product. The way product is packaged therefore helps to create the first impression about the product kept inside. Depending on the product category as well the distance it has to travel and type of transportation to be used at various levels till it reaches its destination, packaging design as well as types of packaging to be used are decided. There are many products where multiple packaging system like primary, secondary and tertiary packaging is used to ensure the product's security and integrity till it is consumed. Tertiary packaging is normally the shipping cartons which also has to comply with the various requirements of size and shape as well as configuration. In addition, there is also a concern about cost and impact on the environment. While packaging has many other functions and roles to play for success of the product, transport packaging has the primary role to ensure the integrity of the products packed throughout its journey. Transport packaging is designed to protect goods that are in transit, especially products that are shipped by truck or train or ship or combination of all. In global trade, the product will invariably have to go through multiple types of transport and many transhipments. However, the supply chain often includes other modes of transportation as well. Therefore, transport packaging needs to be designed for both the local conditions and the export conditions if the goods are sent from one country to another. Any international cargo travels through both international cargo route and the domestic cargo route both within the country and the destination country till the goods reach the end customer. Some of these travel and transport infrastructure conditions are not really known to both senders and cargo operators. Packaging system design and the type of packaging material used have to withstand these unknown travel conditions and keep the product quality and integrity intact throughout its journey till the product is consumed by the end consumers. Packaging therefore has a very distinct role to play.

Importance of Packaging in Transportation

The goods and merchandise need to be packed well to sustain the vagaries of transportation. In global transport sellers always will not be aware of the physical transport infrastructure that are available for transporting goods to the ultimate customers and consumers but sellers have to ensure that the product is safe and fit for consumption or use as the case may be till it is consumed by the end customer. Transportation, therefore, is a very important parameter to be designed and developed by manufacturers and marketers. In some countries including India and Africa, the secondary and tertiary transport conditions to reach the product and merchandise to the ultimate destination from the port is so difficult and involves multiple agencies and people the task of packaging design and type to be very judiciously selected so that it preserves the integrity of the product and ensures delivery of performance at reasonable, affordable and competitive costs failing which even the best products in the world will be useless if you can't get them where they need to be at competitive price and in that respect from making transportation possible to protecting your goods during transit, logistics packaging is a vital part of the supply chain delivery process.

Sending something out for delivery, or supplying to retailers, involves far more than simply putting the goods into a shipping carton and or box. If enough thought and care are not taken in designing the packaging system it can prove to be a disaster.

International Packaging Issues

For international cargo movement, packaging is most important to secure the cargo from damages during transit and also for retaining the quality and integrity of the cargo intact. This can be done by strictly following the regulations according to the cargo types and mode of transport. The following points are to be noted:

- Packaging is instrumental in getting the merchandise to the destination in a safe, presentable condition.
- Because of the added stress of international shipping, packaging that is adequate for domestic shipping may be inadequate for international shipping.
- Packaging considerations that should be taken into account are environmental conditions and weight.

190   *Transportation*

- One solution to the packaging problem has been the development of intermodal containers.
- Cost attention must be paid to international packaging.

Reckitt & Colman introduced Mortein, a popular household insecticide brand and a new product in the market but did not carry out the transportation trial thinking that they have a wealth of experience in consumer product marketing globally. But when the product reached down south in Tamil Nadu for launch at many distribution points, it was found on the day before the product launch that the products reached distributor's warehouse all broken inside, which was a shock to everyone after making all preparations for the product launch. This was a huge cost forcing the company to postpone the launch date by about a month. This delay also had several associated problems that the company faced such as cancelling the release of media launch and advertisement which had an impact on the business. Every product thus has to go through marketed transportation test before clearing the primary packaging as well as secondary and transport packaging design and quality agreed and implemented.

Functions of Packaging

Without adequate packaging, transportation is thus just not possible. The right ***transport packaging*** makes it possible for you to get your products out into the world. In the case of smaller products, packaging allows you to deliver large quantities in a convenient and cost-effective way. There are many other functions that packaging serves.

Packaging Protects Goods

This is the primary function of the packaging as it has to keep and preserve the integrity, quality, taste, flavour, colour, texture etc. intact during the useful life of the product till the product is declared unfit for consumption and or use. Goods that are damaged upon arrival can cause major problems as explained earlier with an example. Not only do you lose the cost of the original item and shipping it in the first place, you may also have to send replacements at additional cost. Besides, there can be even claims from the buyers for non-performance of the contract and in addition such failure also brings in disrepute to the manufacturer of the product, which even can cause permanent loss of business. Several cases and compensation related to packaging failure have come to our knowledge. For inflammable products like say aerosol, defective packaging can even cause costly accidents during use. It is therefore the responsibility of the business to ensure safe and secured packaging at an affordable cost. Broken or marked items can upset customers and retailers, souring relationships and giving your company a bad reputation. ***Logistics packaging thus*** keeps all your items safe, so they arrive at their destination in perfect condition.

Packaging Provides Information about the Product

Packaging carries information regarding the product related to its contents, ingredients used, type of use or how it has to be used, special declaration for safe use etc. including the statutory information like name and address of the manufacturer, country of origin, date of production and date of expiry as the case may be, licence no, weight or volume, special declaration on promotion and scheme etc. There can be a lot of important information that distributors need to know about your product. Your *transport packaging* is the perfect place to display this information.

For example, transport packaging also carries identification mark. A lot of different things can be printed on your boxes. It could be something simple, like which way up the packages need to stored, stacked and kept, or that the contents are fragile and require handling with care. You can also specify more detailed handling instructions, such as a particular temperature range your products need to be stored at or any other special storing conditions.

Facilitating Storage and Warehousing

Transport packaging system needs to be designed to facilitate the storage requirement so that space utilisation is maximum both in warehouse and in container shipping. Odd-size packaging configuration has to be avoided. It will make handling the kinds of products easy to store. No matter what shape, or how fragile the products are, right packaging allows them to be stacked, placed onto pallets, or otherwise arranged for convenience.

Packaging Is Indicative of Quality of the Product Packed

For consumer products and, more importantly, for FMCG products, packaging is extremely important, and it serves also for promotion of your product. A good attractive and convenient packaging indicates that the product packed are of good quality and thus influences the customer to buy and try the product. It thus helps in selling and promoting the products. If you choose retail-ready packaging, your products can be displayed on the shelves in their own custom display. By choosing the appropriate packaging system featuring your brand colours, product details and other relevant sales information, you increase your chances of catching the eye of your target market. Getting the right packaging makes a big difference to your products. If you want logistics packaging that keeps your product safe, displays key information and assists with storage. Attractive packaging gets the attention of the buyers leading to trials, and if they like some of them may even become your permanent customers.

Ensure the Right Transport Packaging Solution

When shipping your products for distribution, your transport packaging solution and design is key decision that you should take with all seriousness. Transport packaging works to protect goods while they are in transit, and because most shipments are subject to more than one mode of transportation throughout their journey, packaging needs to be designed to stand up to both local and export conditions. Let us discuss the four major modes of transportation and the challenges of the packaging system and the solution needed.

Packaging and Safety Regulations for Hazardous Goods

Hazardous and dangerous goods require special packaging as per regulation. In global trade they also need special labelling following the regulation of International Maritime Institution (IMI). Depending on the product and their conditions, they are classified under various categories as given in Annexure 6.1. Dangerous and hazardous goods such as crude oil or gas require bulk transport and normally do not carry any other types of goods. The packaging, labelling and transportation of these types of goods need to follow the prescribed standards to be acceptable to the transporters and freight forwarders as well as carriers. (Thompson Rivers University, 2016)

Annexure 6.4

Table 6.5 Classification of Dangerous Goods

Class	Division	Characteristics
1 Explosives (Sections 2.9–2.12)	1.1	A substance or article with a mass explosion hazard
	1.2	A substance with a projection hazard but not a mass explosion hazard
	1.3	A substance or article which has a fire hazard and either a minor blast hazard or a minor projection hazard, or both, but does not have a mass explosion hazard
	1.4	A substance or article which presents no significant hazard beyond the package in the event of ignition or initiation during transport
	1.5	A very insensitive substance with a mass explosion hazard
	1.6	Extremely insensitive article with no mass explosion hazard
2 Gases (Sections 2.13–2.17)	2.1	A flammable gas which is easily ignited and burns
	2.2	A non-flammable, non-toxic, non-corrosive gas
	2.3	A toxic gas
3 Flammable Liquids (Sections 2.18–2.22)	None	A flammable liquid with a closed-cup flash point less than or equal to 60.0°C
4 Flammable Solids (Sections 2.20–2.22)	4.1	A flammable solid which is readily combustible and may cause fire through friction or from heat retained from manufacturing
	4.2	A spontaneously combustible substance that ignites when exposed to air
	4.3	A water-reactive substance which emits flammable gas when it comes into contact with water
5 Oxidising Substances, Organic Peroxides (Sections 2.37–2.39)	5.1	An oxidising substance which may yield oxygen and contribute to the combustion of other material
	5.2	An organic peroxide which releases oxygen readily and may be liable to explosive decomposition, or sensitive to heat, shock, or friction
6 Toxic and Infectious Substances (Sections 2.26–2.36)	6.1	A toxic substance that is liable to cause harm to human health
	6.2	An infectious substance
7 Radioactive Materials (Sections 2.37–2.39)	None	Radioactive materials as defined in the Packaging and Transport of Nuclear Substance Regulations
8 Corrosive Substances (Sections 2.40–2.42)	None	Solids or liquids such as acids or alkali materials that cause destruction of the skin or corrode metals

Class	Division	Characteristics
9 Miscellaneous Products, Substances, or Organisms	None	A regulated substance that cannot be assigned to any other class. It includes genetically modified organisms (GMOs), marine pollutants, and substances transported at elevated temperatures

Source: Thomson Rivers University. 2016. *Packing and Labelling Dangerous Goods for Transport.* Kamloops: Safety & Emergency Management, Thomson Rivers University.

Table 6.6 Packing Groups for Hazardous Items

Packing Group	Level of Hazard
I	Very hazardous substance
II	Hazardous substance
III	Moderately hazardous substance

Also, some dangerous goods from each group are assigned packing classes. These classes are determined by physical and chemical testing described in Part 2 of the TDGR. Table 6.5 briefly outlines the packing classes used by Transport Canada to classify materials.

Packaging Regulations

As per TDGR, shipping of some dangerous goods above certain specified quantities is prohibited in the absence of a developed Emergency Response Assistance Plan (ERAP). Consultation with the TDG Handbook will help determine if shipments fall under or are in excess of the value published in column 7 of Schedule 1. If an ERAP is required, consultation with TRU's OSEM is required.

Means of transport determine the packaging that is required for shipment to be in compliance with TDGR. Packages shipped exclusively via terrestrial means must meet the packaging instructions as stated in the TDG Clear Language Regulation and Transport Canada's Standard: 'Small containers for Transport of Dangerous Goods, Classes 3, 4, 5, 6.1, 8, and 9'.

If transporting by air, the packaging must meet International Air Transport Association (IATA) requirements which can be purchased from IATA. OSEM can also be contacted to obtain the correct information.

If transporting via marine means, if solely domestic, the TDGR are adequate guidance for shipping and receiving dangerous goods. On the other hand, if the package it to be shipped internationally, the International Maritime Dangerous Goods (IMDG) code must also followed.

Importantly, the OSEM at TRU can always be contacted to aid in obtaining the required information, depending on the shipping circumstances and concerns (Thompson Rivers University, 2016).

Case Study: Container Corporation of India Ltd (CONCOR)

Container Corporation of India Ltd. is a Navratna (nine Jewel) Public Sector Undertaking under the Ministry of Railways, Govt of India. Incorporated in March 1988 CONCOR commenced operations in November 1989 taking over an existing network of seven inland container depots (ICD) from Indian Railways.

194 *Transportation*

Four decades ago, the importing and exporting of goods were really a difficult and cumbersome task. Truck or lorry had to carry stock from factory gate to the port and unload it into a warehouse from where goods were loaded into the cargo ship piece by piece. Malcolm McLeans, a transport entrepreneur, developed the modern intermodal shipping container, which revolutionised transport and international trade in the second half of the twentieth century. His idea of containerisation changed the cargo transport by standardising the dimensions of the container to hold the cargo has changed the industry dramatically. Containerisation has also improved the productivity and cost. In future international cargo will be only in containers.

From its humble beginning, it is now an undisputed market leader having the largest network of 7 ICDs and 81 terminals in India. In addition to providing inland transport by rail for containers, it has also expanded to cover management of ports, air cargo complexes and establishing cold chain. It has played the key role of promoting containerisation of cargo movement in India by virtue of its modern rail wagon fleet, customer-friendly commercial practices and extensively used information technology. The company developed multimodal logistics support for India's International and Domestic containerisation and trade. Though rail is the mainstay of CONCOR's transportation plan, road services and also provided to cater to the need of door-to-door services, whether in the International or Domestic business.

CONCOR achieved the highest-ever throughput of 3.83 million TEUs and 43.5 million tonnes of containerised cargo by rail in FY 2018–2019. With 7 ICDs to 83 Terminal to date, CONCOR is diversifying into other logistics businesses like distribution logistics, coastal shipping and cargo handling at airports. With an objective of creating higher customer value, CONCOR has decided not to increase the tariff up to March 31, 2020, and by starting vertical integration in logistics by providing warehousing and first-mile/last-mile transportation to their customers.

Main Functions of CONCOR

CONCOR's core business is characterised by three distinct activities, that of a carrier, a terminal operator and a warehouse operator.

Carrier

Rail is the mainstay of CONCOR's transportation plans and strategy. Majority of CONCOR terminals are rail-linked, with rail as the main carrier for haulage.

Terminal and CFS Operator

CONCOR started operations in November 1989 with seven Inland Container Depots (ICDs). They have since extended the network to a total of 81 terminals, of which 18 are export-import container depots and 13 are exclusive domestic container depots and as many as 50 terminals perform the combined role of domestic as well as international terminals.

Warehouse Operator

CONCOR offers a comprehensive warehouse service for their customers in international trade. For example, transit warehousing for import and export cargo CONCOR provides bonded warehousing, enabling importers to store cargo and take partial deliveries, thereby deferring duty payment. Warehousing service is also provided for Less than Container Load (LCL) consolidation and reworking of LCL cargo at nominated hubs as well as Air cargo clearance using bonded trucking.

The total warehousing space available for CONCOR's Exim business is presently approximately 150,000 sqm. with facilities for handling bonded cargo, multi-stacking, consolidation of LCL cargo, air cargo handling etc. besides conventional transit warehousing. CONCOR also provides value-added services like palletisation/fumigation of cargo, repacking/strapping of cargo etc. at all its terminals.

The global trend is that 70–80% of containerised cargo moves directly between the hinterland customers and the seaports in containers. Of the total containers handled at Indian Ports, CONCOR at present moves 30%. There is therefore intrinsic potential for further growth in CONCOR business apart from the push given by increase in foreign trade. In the decades of its existence, the throughput growth of the company's Exim business has been almost 20% per annum.

CONCOR Containers

Concor has a wide range of containers for its containerised cargo movement and service. Although there are some differences in the dimensions between containers produced by various manufacturers broadly Concor has the following:

Conventional Dry Cargo Containers

20/40 ft Conventional End Open Containers: These are usually built to ISO standards and are used for the movement of conventional dry cargo. For domestic movement, CONCOR has inducted a fleet of approx. 12,000 such 20 ft containers either under direct ownership or on lease for internal movements within the country.

20/40 ft High Cube containers: These containers offer the added advantage of extra volumetric capacity due to their additional height and are especially useful for movement of light but bulky cargo.

20 ft Side Access Containers: These containers are used exclusively for domestic traffic movements within the country. They offer the advantage of having doors on the side panels, and this makes it convenient for use in locations where chassis stuffing operations have to be used. CONCOR has currently about 3300 such self-owned domestic side access containers in its fleet.

22 ft/High Cube Domestic Containers: These containers have also been exclusively introduced by CONCOR for the purpose of carrying cargo that requires greater volumetric capacity or container length. CONCOR has currently about 2000 such as company-owned domestic 22 ft containers in its fleet.

Specialty Containers

20 ft/40 ft/40 ft High Cube Refrigerated Containers: These are containers that can be used for the movement of refrigerated/perishable cargo where controlled temperature is a requirement. Special facilities such as the availability of plug points, portable clip-on generators for trailer movements, power packs for train movements etc. are required for moving cargo in these containers. It must, therefore, be ascertained whether such facilities are available at the handling terminals before planning such movements.

20 ft/40 ft Collapsible Flat Rack and Platform Containers: These containers are especially useful for carrying over-dimensional cargo or fully packed machines, equipment etc. Since most of the movement of containers on CONCOR's network is through rail, special permission must be obtained for movement of over-dimensional consignments to ensure that these do not infringe upon the standard moving dimensions of the Indian rail network.

20 ft/40 ft Open-top Containers: These containers are used mostly for cargo that needs to be handled with cranes and cannot be easily loaded from the front doors of the containers. Open tops can also be used for carrying over-dimensional cargo of certain types. Such containers have also been inducted for domestic service and can be supplied on demand if such cargo is offered. CONCOR has currently about 100 such self-owned domestic open-top containers in its fleet.

196 *Transportation*

20 ft Tank Containers: These containers are specially designed for the movement of liquid cargo of different types. Such containers have also been inducted for domestic service and can be supplied on demand if such cargo is offered. CONCOR has currently about 300 such self-owned tank containers in its fleet.

At the end of the financial year 2018–2019, the company had a fleet of around 26,000 containers for domestic business 82,342 own rakes, 82 RSTs and 16 gantry cranes.

Terminal Network in India

CONCOR has nationwide network of terminals to provide service to any part of the country for both domestic and international cargo movement. At present the company has the following terminals spread over various regions.

Northern Region: Babarpur (Panipat), Ballabhgarh, Dct/Okhla, Dhappar, Ghari-Harsaru, Gotan, ICD DDL (Ludhiana), ICD Moradabad, ICD Tughlakabad (Delhi), Jaipur, Jodhpur, Kharia Khangar, Moga, Panipat, Phillaur, Rewari, Sonepat

Western Region: CFs Dronagiri – Concor-DRT (Navi Mumbai), CFs Mulund (West)-Exports (Mumbai), DCT Turbhe (Navi Mumbai), ICD Chinchwad (Pune), ICD MIRAJ, ICD New Mulund (Mumbai), ICD Pithampur (INDORE), ICD Ratlam, J.N. Port, Mumbai Port Trust

Eastern Region: Balasore, Concor Terminal KoPT Coal Dock Road, Durgapur, Fatuha, Haldia, ICD Amingaon, Kolkata Port, Raxaul, Shalimar Terminal, Tata Nagar Terminal

Southern Region: Container Freight Station Milavittan (Tuticorin), Container Freight Station Tondiarpet, Domestic Container Terminal Salem Market, HAL/CONCOR/MSIL/JWG, Inland Container Depot Kudalnagar (Madurai), Inland Container Depot Whitefield, Inland Container Depot, Irugur, Inland Container Depot, Tirupur, Port Side Container Terminal Harbour of Chennai, Port Side Container Terminal, Vallarpadam, Rail Side Container Terminal, Cochin

Central Region: Bhusawal, Daulatabad (Aurangabad), Inland Container Depot, Nagpur, Mandideep Container Terminal, Raipur

South Central Region: DCT Guntur, ICD Desur (Belgaum), ICD Visakhapatnam, Inland Container Depot, Sanathnagar (Hyderabad)

North Western Region: CFS Gandhidham, ICD Sabarmati (Ahmedabad), ICD-Ankleshwar, ICD-Khodiyar (Ahmedabad), Mundra, Pipavav, RCT Vadodara

North Central Region: Agra, Dadri, Kanpur, Madhosingh (Mirzapur), Malanpur (Gwalior), Rawtha Road – Kota (RDT)

Hub and Spoke Services of CONCOR

One of the areas in which CONCOR faces competition in the transportation of goods is from truck operators offering transportation by road. Competition with such operators is primarily on the basis of price and dependability. The objective of Hub and Spoke transportation is to provide seamless door-to-door service.

The company believes that it competes favourably with road transportation on the basis of price on movement of heavier cargoes over longer distances, although the truck operators may offer, among other things, greater flexibility with respect to the timing of shipments. Volvo trucks, with vastly reduced transit times as compared to conventional trucks, are challenging the rail transit times of CONCOR and are set to heighten competition.

In the domestic arena as well, hub and spoke movements allow for better utilisation of transport potential and allow for long lead services to be generated on the basis of short lead traffic collections using road and rail shuttle services. This service can be especially useful for big corporates for whom production centres are concentrated in a single location, but distribution needs are from the whole country. CONCOR has already successfully moved white cement as a commodity using this experiment, whereby the product has been distributed over various locations after being picked up from a single production centre.

Integrated Freight Terminals

As part of the overall strategy for expansion of business and movement towards the provision of complete logistics services, the company is considering the option of moving into operating large railway goods shed hubs. This will mean managing integrated freight terminals. To achieve this, CONCOR in the long-term plans to set up district parks, freight centres, trade development centres etc. at some of its terminals. The focus of providing such services will be on the backward and forward integration of various value-added services with the core business of transport logistics, in which the company already has an established foothold.

Coastal Shipping

As part of its overall strategy of expansion and entry into areas of business that would complement its position as a multi-model logistics service provider, coastal shipping is an area of business the company is examining for making an entry. CONCOR's interface with coastal shipping can be easily established by undertaking all port operations for coastal vessels or only taking up the rail interface for such vessels at port terminals and providing hinterland connectivity. For getting into Coastal shipping the company is open to pick up equity stake in sea-going vessels and identify a strategic partner with adequate experience and resources.

Cold Chains and Reefers

A key business area with high potential for growth is the provision of cold chains. This involves providing transportation to perishable products from source to end user, while maintaining a certain temperature along the route. Today 85% of the cold storages are in the private sector and not a single complete cold chain solution provider is available in the market. Absence of reefer container linkages and high and increasing power costs are proving to be major impediments. CONCOR is already providing basic rail-based reefer services between Delhi and Mumbai, and could get into providing cold chains by making a few arrangements that would expand its market presence. These would mainly include the following:

- Tie up with an international major, preferably with developing country experience with both technology and equity commitment for bringing in the basic equipment.
- Organise terminal-to-factory transport, refrigerated warehouses –where needed – and delivery, while maintaining both temperature-controlled environments and transit commitments.
- Identify viable corridors for specific products. This will require tying up with producers and consumers independently or tie up with a food-processing major to distribute its products. Return trips wherever possible make cold chain operations more profitable and viable and as such desirable. Otherwise, the operation sometimes leads to break-even or even loss.

Total Logistic Service Providers

CONCOR offers most comprehensive logistics service under one roof. The infrastructure that they have built over time make them a dominant player in Indian logistics service.

Logistics signifies the integration of two or more activities for the purpose of planning, implementing and controlling efficient flow of raw materials, in-process inventory and finished goods from point of origin to point of consumption. Transportation is often the single-largest cost in the logistics process. Logistics is a source of value addition. By streamlining transport, storage and handling operations, by reducing inventories (and the corresponding financial and storage costs) and by making the most cost-efficient use of available assets, logistics reduces the overall cost of the delivered goods while increasing their time and space utilities (delivering in right time and at right place).

198 *Transportation*

Handling Hazardous Cargo

Transportation of hazardous cargo in containers by rail are subject to the statutory provisions of the IRCA Red Tariff. Railways have also accorded provisional permission for carriage of dangerous/hazardous/offensive goods, which fall under the International Maritime Dangerous Goods (IMDG) Code in containers, subject to their packing and stuffing being as per specifications of the IMDG Code.

The following is the procedure that shall be followed by CONCOR in booking of hazardous cargo in containers:

1 When a container is laden with a commodity classified as hazardous in IRCA Red Tariff or IMDG Code, CONCOR shall accept it for rail booking only on a pink forwarding note, and collect the prescribed additional surcharges.
2 There should be no restriction in acceptance of containers laden with commodities not classified as hazardous both as per IMDG Code and in IRCA Red Tariff.
3 In case, lines offer containers, containing some commodities with apparent dangerous/hazardous characteristics and if such commodities do not find any reference in either IRCA Red Tariff or IRCA Goods Tariff or IMDG Code, then such containers will be accepted for booking by rail after taking a specific undertaking from the shipping line that the cargo loaded in the containers is not hazardous.

Information Systems

A primary component of CONCOR's overall business strategy has been the development of an advanced information system. A container and cargo logistics information system went online at Company's Inland Container Depot at Tughlakabad in 1994, and most other facilities have been equipped with computer systems to monitor traffic movement and maintain inventory records.

CONCOR is using various online applications like Export/Import Terminal Management System (ETMS), Domestic Terminal Management System (DTMS), Oracle Financials-ERP, HR-Payroll system etc., which are based on centralised architecture deployed through Citrix environment and running over VSAT-based hybrid network.

CONCOR has been certified to ISO/IEC 27001 2005 standard for establishing and maintaining Information Security Management System (ISMS) for its IT functionality.

CONCOR has been awarded for its project titled 'Web-based Integrated Container/Terminal Management System', which has been adjudged by AFACT (Asia Pacific Council for Trade Facilitation and Electronic Business) as winner for e-ASIA 2009 award for the category 'Electronic Business in Public Sector'.

Source: CONCOR[16] and company annual reports (various).

Company Performance

CONCOR has delivered an improved performance during 2018–19 in which it gained market share and moved on the path of long-term sustainable growth. During the year it has handled 3.83 million TEUs and transported 43.50 million tonnes of cargo volume by rail which is an increase of 8.42% and 8.83% respectively over the previous year. There was 8.11% and 10.23% growth in the physical volumes of both EXIM and domestic segments respectively. The gross turnover also has increased by 11.71% to INR`72.160 billion and the net profit for the year was INR 12.15 billion showing a healthy growth of 16.37% over the previous year. The net worth of the company , thus, has increased from INR 93.74 billion to INR 103.68 billion during this period.

Case Discussion Questions

1 What are the main functions of CONCOR?
2 Discuss the comprehensive service that CONCOR offers for its customer

3 What are the different types of containers that CONCOR has?
4 What information system does CONCOR have for better online customer service?
5 Discuss the service that CONCOR offers for hazardous cargo as well as reefer cargo.
6 Why is cargo movement globally now containerised?
7 What business development strategy is the public sector like CONCOR adopting?
8 Discuss the typical advantages and disadvantages a PSU like CONCOR has.

Chapter Summary

This chapter deals with the most important function in logistics and integrated supply chain management which is transportation. Transportation is the most vital sector of any nation's economy. The growth and performance of any economy are reflected in the status of its transport industry. Goods and services need to be carried from the point of production to the point of consumption by several modes of transport system. If the transport system collapses whole economy with collapse. On the other hand, an efficient transport system can help making an economy vibrant. There are multiple modes of transport vehicles and systems that are used in industry to manage supply chain and operations including logistics, which are discussed in this chapter. Different modes of transportation used in both domestic and international cargo handling were discussed with their relative advantages and disadvantages and also the costs thereof. The latest trends in global ship or ocean transport citing competitive issues were taken up for discussion giving examples of a couple of global ocean lines. Recent collaboration and acquisition of very large vessels to be more economic and cost-effective were also discussed. Global ocean liner strategy and performance to be sustainable shipping lines of preference was also discussed. Within large countries like India and the USA as well as in regions like the EU, most of the stocks and goods are moved on surface; the issues concerning those and competition between rail and road transport were discussed in detail. Maersk Line, the largest shipping company and CONCOR largest domestic container transport in public sector in India cases were discussed in terms of their growth and development strategy to emerge as a sustainable transport company to stay ahead of competition. The challenges of new regulations and also environmental stipulations impacting the cargo movement were also discussed in this chapter, including recent trends in transportation in global trade. In global trade more and more collaboration and collective bargaining to get critical mass and bargaining power to retain the customer accounts are widely being witnessed. These recent alliances in global transportation were discussed. Finally, key concerns in energy sectors relating to cost, environment, ecosystem and sustainability issues were discussed, including how the logistics industry around the world is addressing those issues for their own survival and growth.

Discussion Questions

1 Why surface transport is going to rise in preference to air transport?
2 Discuss the reasons why containerisation is going to rise and 90% of break bulk cargo will be containerised.
3 What are the reasons for alliance and joint ventures in international cargo movement?
4 What kind of changes will be triggered by increased environmental and regulatory factors? And how those will be tackled?
5 Discuss if high-speed trains can make any difference to international cargo transport.
6 Discuss how custom bonded warehouse helps in cost reduction in international logistics.
7 Write a short note on New Ocean Alliance.
8 What are the various modes of transportation available for international cargo movement and what are the key considerations for taking decision on mode of transport?

200 Transportation

9 Discuss the transportation system for movement of cargo in EU countries. Compare the efficiency of various modes of transports for their functional efficiency
10 Discuss the container shipment scenario after large vessels have come into the market. What were the typical problems faced by large container liners?
11 What are the various joint ventures that were formed to leverage the collective strength in international cargo movement business? Discuss their relative strength and current scenario.
12 How have Suez Canal and Panama Canal changed the dynamics of global ocean transport? Discuss their relative importance.
13 Discuss the function and importance of packaging in transportation.
14 What are the various roles of packaging in trade and commerce of goods?
15 How does packaging add value in the business?
16 Discuss the packaging issues and regulations for transporting hazardous goods in global trade.
17 Discuss the classification of hazardous cargo in international trade and how those need to be packaged for shipping.
18 Discuss the information and their relevance that need to be provided on the package for transportation of goods.
19 Packaging configuration issues in container loading for optimum space utilisation.
20 Packaging is indicative of the product quality. Discuss.

Notes

1 See: https://greencarrier.com/new-ocean-alliance-will-be-the-largest-for-asian-european-trade
2 See: http://blogascentgI.com/the-panama-canal-vs-the-suez-canal, accessed on 16 April 2019
3 See: https://blog.ascentgl.com/the-panama-canal-vs-the-suez-canal
4 See: https://blog.greencarrier.com/5-trends-pointing-towards-more-containerisation/
5 See: US Energy Information Administration and A T Kearney Analysis based on data from US Energy Information Administration, www.energyfromshale.org 2011)
6 maritimefairtrade.org, March 29, 2023
7 Source: www.hl.co.uk/shares/shares-search-results/a/ap-moller-maersk-as-a-dkk1000/financial-statements-and-reports)
8 See: https://youtu.be/ll7oGRLj4JM
9 See: www.maersk.com/imea-one-country-one-price
10 See: solutions@maersk.com
11 See:www.hl.co.uk/shares/shares-search-results/a/ap-moller-maersk-as-a-dkk1000/financial-statements-and-reports
www.dw.com/en/oetker-group-sells-shipping-business-to-maersk/a-36600635
www.offshore-energy.biz/alexander-oetker-we-could-not-be-the-best-owners-for-hamburg-sud/
12 www.offshore-energy.biz/alexander-oetker-we-could-not-be-the-best-owners-for-hamburg-sud/
13 See: www.dw.com/en/weak-trade-oil-price-cut-into-maersks-profits/a-19037360
14 See: www.dw.com/en/hanjin-bankruptcy-sparks-global-shipping-crisis/a-19523407
15 See: www.dw.com/en/japan-shippers-merge-container-businesses/a-36206764
16 https://concorindia.co.in

References

The Economic Times. (2017) *India's Transport Infra Growth to Gain Pace over 5 Years: Report*. Available at: https://economictimes.indiatimes.com/news/economy/infrastructure/indias-transport-infra-growth-togain-pace-over-5-years-report/articleshow/57652534.cms?from=mdr (accessed on 2 June 2019).
Levinson, M. (2006) *The Box: How the Shipping Container Made the World Smaller and the World Economy Bigger*. Princeton, NJ: Princeton University Press.
Thomson Rivers University. (2016) *Packing and Labelling Dangerous Goods for Transport-Safety & Emergency Management*. Kamloops, Canada: Thomson Rivers University.

Top Ten International Container Shipping Companies. (2016) *Mover DB.com*. https://moverdb.com/shipping companies

Transportation in India. *World Bank Group-web*. worldbank.org/archive/website

Trans-Siberian Railway. (2019) www.transsiberianexpress.net

Bibliography

Ballou, R. H. (1999) *Business Logistics Management*. Upper Saddle River, NJ: Prentice Hall.

Eno Transportation Foundation. (1988) *Transportation in America 1998*. Washington, DC: Eno Transportation Foundation.

Hammond, J. H., & Morrison, J. E. P. (1988) *Note on the US Transportation Industry Harvard Business School Note 688080*. Boston, MA: Harvard Business School.

Robenson, J. F., & Copacino, W. C. (1994) *The Logistics Handbook*. New York: The Free Press.

Tyworth, J. E., Cavinato, J. L., & Langley Jr., C. J. (1991) *Traffic Management: Planning Operations, and Control*. Prospect Height, IL: Waveland.

7 Total Logistics Cost Management for Competitive Advantage

Learning Objectives

1 Define total cost in logistics
2 Explain total logistics cost and their components
3 Realise implications of each cost element on the total logistics cost
4 Manage each such element of the total logistics cost for better performance
5 Derive competitive advantage in business by containing the total logistics cost
6 Understand benchmarking parameters and practices to improve SCM performance

Introduction

Logistics cost is quite significant in impacting business performance in any country. In under-developed as well as in developing country, logistics costs as percentage of total cost of goods and service are much higher than that in developed countries, where logistics infrastructure are well developed. Analysis of the total cost offers insight and key to managing the logistics function for optimum performance. Management should strive to reduce the total cost of logistics by carefully analysing each cost component to understand the opportunity available to better manage that cost element to reduce the total cost. Logistics must be viewed as an integrated system in a business to be managed better. The need to view the logistics function as an integrated system is paramount because reduction in one cost element may even give rise to or lead to increase in the cost of other components. Therefore, understanding inter-relationships among various cost elements in order to take an integrated view to manage the total cost will be useful. Effective management and real cost savings can be accomplished only by viewing logistics as an integrated system and minimising its total cost keeping the firm's customer service objectives in focus. Businesses are exploring ways and means to reduce the logistics cost to become more competitive. With rising fuel costs total logistics cost also has been increasing. Besides, there are regulations relating to sustainability and environment forcing logistics companies to strategise to contain the freight and other related costs. Businesses are also evaluating the various options on sourcing the products from logistics cost and convenience point of view. Logistics cost management has thus assumed increased significance in business.

Organisations Are Huge Cost Centres

Businesses are normally managed to create wealth for the shareholders. Although businesses are managed as profit centres or SBUs, everything we do inside the business is all costs. Organisations are therefore huge cost centres. Profit actually lies outside the business. And profit comes by transacting your cost with a margin of profit. Today's customers are very discerning, and

DOI: 10.4324/9781003469063-7

they are not willing to pay for organisational inefficiencies. Cost management, therefore, is very important for business. Managing costs better will ensure higher profit and more competition. Excess cost is like excess fat; once you acquire it becomes very difficult to lose it. Better way to manage cost is not to allow increase in cost in the first place. Added cost is very difficult to shed. Non-value-adding costs are required to be eliminated. As once a cost is added into the system it is difficult to shed, it is better that we start allocation of resources including human resources less than desirable so that only after experiencing the performance we can decide if extra resources are required to be added or not. Cost management objective is to eliminate avoidable and non-value-adding costs. Logistics costs provide opportunities for cost reduction.

The Law of Lowest Total Cost

The law states: 'The total cost of producing and delivering product is usually larger than the sum of the lowest functional costs of each element in the supply chain'.

Individual functions or interconnected or interrelated functions and activities will incur a cost to perform, but when a series of such activities are to be performed the experience will be that total cost to produce end result is always higher than the individual cost of each element for the reason that there is always an additional cost of integration of activities. The focus, therefore, should be on the total cost management.

Logistics Cost – Brief History

Since 1974, The Davis Logistics Cost and Service Database contains logistics costs (transportation, warehousing, customer service, administration and inventory-carrying cost) and service performance level for many industries/groups. This database can serve as guidelines to see how such costs vary in a typical organisation set-up. This database offers standard guidelines, but it will vary from country to country as well as company to company in a given country. The database also helps in budgetary process for resource allocations and also for improvement budget and target.

Elements of Logistics Cost

The various components of logistics costs can be classified as given next:

- Transportation costs
- Warehousing costs
- Order processing costs
- Inventory-carrying costs
- Information and communication costs
- Administrative costs
- Customer servicing cost

Logistics Cost Accounting System

Nothing is possible to improve if it is not measured. Measuring the existing logistics cost incurred by the business is, therefore, the primary task. The more details of the logistics costs of each element are available, better it will be to manage those. It is the managerial task to decide in what format and in what details these costs are to be recorded for study to find out where

204 *Total Logistics Cost Management*

improvement is possible. There are two major cost elements, namely fixed cost and variable cost, as well as the process cost which impacts product cost and pricing,

Broadly there are two approaches followed in the business to determine the logistics cost. They are:

- The financial accounting system
- The managerial accounting system

Every company should have their total logistics cost budget to control the cost. For initiating any improvement on logistics cost budget, organisations have to generate management reporting system. Businesses normally generate both financial accounting statement and management accounting statement.

Financial Accounting

Financial accounting system provides reports such as balance sheet, income statements such as profit and loss statement and cash flow statements, which are required by outside parties like investors and stockholders as well as statutory authorities under law. But this system may fail to meet the needs of manager of the organisation. To manage the company's performance, the managerial accounting system serves the purpose better. For all companies, the monthly review and other periodical review are conducted by generating various kinds of reports to serve the internal needs of the company for managing its resources and profits better.

In this system, the logistics cost is often merged with other operating costs of the business and often loses focus as logistics cost elements are not differentiated and isolated to draw managerial attention to understand the reason why this system may fail to meet the needs of managers of the organisation.

Management Accounting

The logistics accounting system is a type of managerial accounting system which addresses the typical parameters and more particularly various cost parameters of logistics activities within the company, comparing those with the budgeted numbers as well as determining the variance against last year's actual costs incurred giving reason thereof. In addition, periodically these figures also compared with the industry standards as well as with the best practices and best performers in the same category of the business. It can help managers to plan, implement and control logistics system. Logistics accounting information is useful for budgeting which is an important part of the logistics planning process. It also helps in allocation of resources for implementing the plans. Logistics accounting statements are not standardised like financial accounting statements because the integrated information needs of one manager often differ from those of another. Logistics accounting system generally allows the user to analyse decisions, based on logistical costing.

Managerial accounting system can be prepared for the logistics manager's needs and focus, depending on which additional element specific cost data can be generated to give focused attention to specific problem areas to rectify or improve the scenario from the current level. It can help managers to plan, implement and control logistics system. Logistics accounting information is useful for budgeting which is an important part of the logistics planning process.

Logistics Cost Management Models

There are various approaches employed for management of logistics cost. They are:

- Activity-based costing (ABC)
- Total cost of ownership
- Supply chain costing
- Total cost of relationship
- Total cost/value analysis
- Cost-to-serve method

Logistics Is Omnipresent

Across functions in a business logistics is playing a role and therefore it is omnipresent. Improving logistics functions can help improve business performance in multiple ways. Logistics function is there not only in sales, marketing, customer service as well as in manufacturing, procurement and production but also in research and development and finance and administration as shown in Figure 7.1.

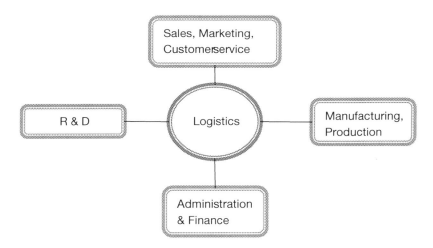

Figure 7.1 Logistics Is Omnipresent and Encompasses All Functions in Business

Logistics Improves Business Performance

Logistics cost in many ways impact performance and therefore ROI. The impact of logistics costs can get reflected in many ways in different business functions and processes as can be seen from Figure 9.2. For example, better logistics management can impact the quality of customer service and hence customer satisfaction positively, which can help in increased sales and revenue. Improved logistics performance can help reduce the inventory holding and thereby reduce the working capital requirement in the business. Logistics management can also reduce debtors and stock return as well as stock expiry. The collective impact of all these is higher profit for the business and higher return on investment as depicted in Figure 7.2.

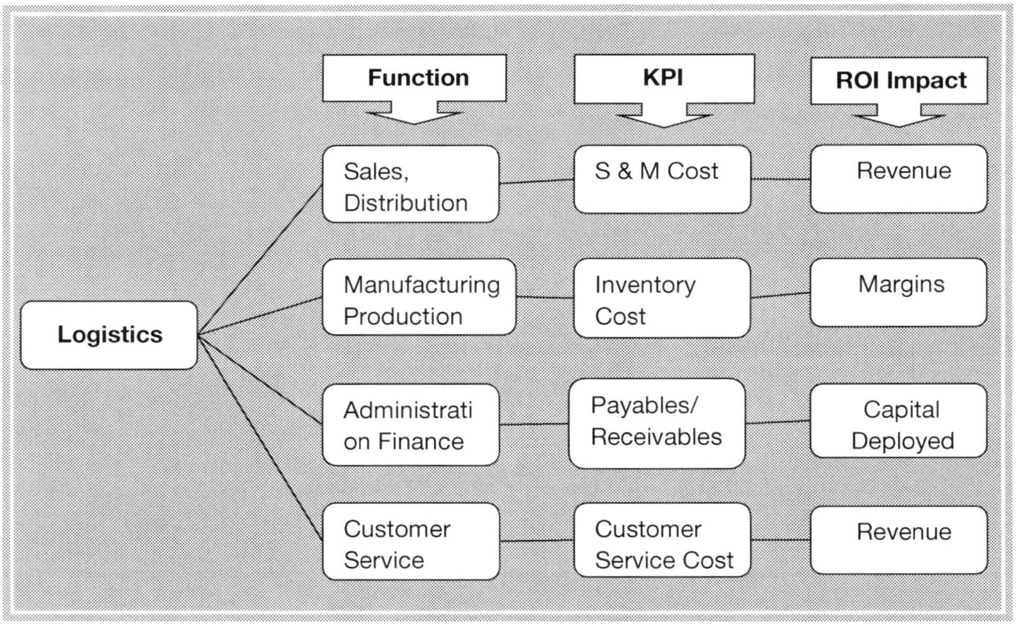

206 *Total Logistics Cost Management*

Figure 7.2 How Logistics Cost Impacts ROI

Difficulty in Estimating Logistics Cost

Problems with traditional cost accounting as related to logistics (Christopher, 1998) are as follows:

- The true costs of servicing different customer types, channels and market segments are poorly understood.
- Costs are captured at too high a level of aggregation.
- Costing is functionally oriented at the expense of output.
- The emphasis on full cost allocation to products ignores customer costs.

As a result, either customer is loaded with full cost (unjustifiably) or not apportioned the cost specific to customer (under recovery).

Traditional costing methods have many inherent disadvantages such as:

- Assumes all cost is volume-related
- Departmental focus, not process focus
- Focus on costs incurred, not cause of costs

Logistics costs can be better represented from the perspective of engineered costs and discretionary costs as has been shown in Figure 7.2. This way logistics cost management programme can be better managed.

Analysis of Logistics Cost

Broadly logistics costs should be analysed from the point of view of their input-output relationship in the sense that what amount of input delivers what output in the business in relation to delivering business objective. Some of the logistics costs incurred in the business can be considered engineered costs, but some costs incurred in managing logistics can also be discretionary cost. Hence, it is better to represent the logistics cost separately as engineered cost and discretionary cost. This discretionary cost can be assessed if these are really needed or serving the purpose. ABC costing is often helpful to find such issues if those are really helping the business. This can be explained by taking an example of quality cost which has really three different costs, namely, prevention cost, appraisal cost and internal and external failure cost. And prevention of failures often takes care of the cost of delivering the improved or better quality for the customers. Representing the logistics costs in its proper perspective is therefore important in order to better manage and control the logistics cost in business better.

Activity-Based Costing

Activity-based costing (ABC) represents a radical departure from the traditional cost accounting systems. The ABC methodology, rather than allocating costs to individual units, identifies the activities that consume resources, matching costs to the level of such activities.

The key aspect of this methodology is the development of models that represent a logical and quantifiable relationship between the utilisation of resources, the performance of activities, and the products or services that they provide. With these models, one can simultaneously mirror the flow of orders and products along the logistic chain, capturing the costs at a level of desegregation that enables the analysis of profit by type of client, market segment and distribution channel. This application of ABC costing to a logistic operator illustrates the main difficulties and benefits of this approach. ABC approach helps business to understand if there is any redundant or non-value-adding activities that are undertaken in the end-to-end logistics value chain so that those can be removed to get significant improvement in the logistics cost and performance.

When ABC Method Is More Useful

Large diversified global corporations should undertake ABC costing methods and cost audits. In general, companies having

- High overheads
- Product diversity or multiple products in the portfolio
- Customer diversity
- Service diversity
- Multiple location integrated logistics cost

They are better placed to undertake ABC method.

Let us examine in detail the components of various items constituting logistics cost.

Total Logistics Cost

Logistics costs for the average company as given in the Davis database is 9.34% of sales and USD 69.74 per hundred weights shipped. Logistics cost increased by 11% from 2013 to 214. Transportation cost is driving the increase. Transportation cost is again driven by fuel or energy cost. Good rail, road infrastructure and energy-efficient high-speed transport carrier can help logistics cost for handling domestic cargo. Companies with higher product values continue to have lower logistics costs. Smaller companies continue to have higher logistics costs. Service performance

208   *Total Logistics Cost Management*

Table 7.1 Logistics Cost Break-up

Items	% of Sales	S/C WT
Transportation	4.43	USD 36.42
Warehousing	1.99	USD 16.16
Customer Service	0.41	USD 1.92
Administration	0.30	USD 1.15
Inventory Carrying	2.22	USD 14.09
Total Logistics Cost	9.34	USD 69.74

Source: The Establish Davis Logistics Cost and Service Database (2014)

levels have improved since 2014. The Establish Davis Logistics Cost and Service Database is an ongoing annual survey that manufacturers, distributors and retailers participate to receive indicators of logistics cost elements.

Poor logistics performance will reduce the company's profitability by locking up increased amount of capital in working capital management which is basically the difference between current assets and current liabilities. The current asset would include the stock levels coverage for raw material, packaging material, finished goods, inventories in transit and work-in-progress. Poor logistics management performance will eventually raise the level of stocks in the system.

Total Cost Approach in Logistics

In competitive marketplace businesses are constantly striving to deliver higher value to their identified and target customers in relation to their immediate competition. This is tantamount to the fact that businesses are trying to make customers happy by improving service delivery. Customer has many alternatives and options to choose from and losing a customer thus is suicidal for many businesses. It takes time and resources to create a new customer and therefore it makes immense sense for businesses to try and retain an existing customer by constantly improving service level. Businesses exist because of customer and, therefore, customer service level and quality cannot be undermined or compromised even if it has to be met at a higher cost. As customer is the king, at whatever cost, the customer must be satisfied. Thus, the importance of customer service assumes additional significance in business.

A dissatisfied customer can easily spread negative image of the company when a satisfied customer can help create new customers by spreading positive word-of-mouth publicity. For example, if a customer has received goods which have been damaged in transit and which he is unable to return or if the goods are of very poor quality, he is likely to remain a one-time customer. He may further even publicise his adverse opinion to his colleagues, friends and others and caution them to be careful while purchasing goods from this particular manufacturer. On the other hand, a satisfied customer would recommend a particular product and a manufacturer and even give unsolicited testimonial to prospective customers. Thus, it has become important to keep the customer satisfied through good customer service, which requires an up-to-date logistics system. To make customers happy and to improve the customer's service level constantly logistic management performance has a great role to play. This would entail investment into the company's logistics system. But logistics system may require huge investments and at times may become a large portion of the total cost incurred by the company. The capital costs of logistics are quite significant if businesses want to improve on logistics performance and cost.

Total Logistics Cost Management 209

Holistic View of Total Logistic Cost

It is imperative that a holistic view is essential to reduce the logistics cost, and such total cost analysis is the key to managing the logistics function. The management has to strive for reduction of TLC rather than the cost of each activity, which would mean that the logistics function should be viewed as an integrated system rather than the individual system because sometimes reduction of cost of one activity may even give rise to the increase in cost of other logistics activity. As such effective management and real cost savings can only be accomplished by taking an integrated view covering all sub-elements and components of logistics cost as mentioned earlier, with an objective that customer service level will never be compromised.

The TLC will thus depend on the customer service levels that the marketers would like to maintain and that can include various costs discussed here.

Inventory Cost

All businesses are required to carry a certain level of inventory of input materials such as raw and packaging material, standard spares etc. as well as of finished goods and work in progress to manage the business by ensuring regular production or manufacturing operations of the corporation as well as for servicing the customers' orders and requirements. The level of inventory to be maintained depends on many factors, including lead time of ordering, for receiving the input materials, mode of transport, the number of warehouses planned, the levels of inventory to be maintained to ensure a certain level of service and safety stock. The inventory costs are the cost of the money locked up in the cost of goods, insurance, occupation of space, pilferages, losses, damages etc., as well as the maintenance of inventory. Inventory costs are directly affected by such factors as the mode of transport, number of warehouses planned and the levels of inventory maintained to ensure a certain level of service. These costs are increased by the cost of the obsolescence of a product over a period of time, especially when the company makes rapid changes in product models or when products are perishable. As and when a new product is introduced or an existing model is replaced by a new model some stocks of both input material and finished good become redundant and obsolete in spite of having the best plan for the transition. This obsolete inventory also adds up to the total inventory cost not only for the cost of material but also for the space this inventory occupies. When the manufacturer is unable to produce goods because of lack of raw materials or is unable to supply goods because of inadequate finished products stock, he loses particular sales. Therefore, it is necessary to examine both low and high inventory issues in relation to their impact in the business.

Warehousing Cost

Goods have to be stored for some time after production, however small that time interval may be. This is done either at the production centres, in the marketing area, or somewhere in between or at all three locations. Warehousing of raw materials as well as other input materials are kept closer to the manufacturing locations, whereas the finished goods warehouses are strategically located closer to the customer locations. The warehousing of raw materials either steps up the cost of their supply or of the cost of distribution of finished products. As a manufacturer wishes to approach the objective of zero stock-out of the finished products or zero loss of production, adequate warehousing capacity becomes essential, and this pushes the firm in higher fixed and operating costs of warehousing. Also, to improve customer service to certain levels, it becomes

210 *Total Logistics Cost Management*

necessary to increase the number of warehouses. Accordingly, the company management has to arrive at the optimum number of warehouses which is consistent with the minimum total cost of distribution, taking into account the effect on the other elements of cost in the total logistical system.

Production and Supply Cost

Production costs per unit of production tend to decrease with an increase in the volume of production with higher capacity utilisation. Also, these costs vary between various production points. If a manufacturer has several manufacturing plants producing the same product, company has to make a decision to vary the supplies or production from certain plants based on both cost of production in that particular plant as well as the customer demand that is planned to be satisfied from the goods produced from that plant. This move of shifting production from one plant to another taken for these considerations which inevitably affects the cost of production itself as well as the cost of transit times, warehouse and inventory costs. The decision related to produce 'in-house' versus 'out-house' is taken from the considerations of cost, quality and flexibility to manage today's dynamic business environment.

Channel Distribution Costs

Various alternatives for distribution are available to a manufacturer or marketer. The distribution channels are decided on various considerations including product types and distribution objectives and target markets and customers to be served which we have discussed in Chapter 3. Which channel to be opted for depends on numerous criteria including channel effectiveness and costs. This distribution may be through a sole selling agent at the national level, or through regional distributors or wholesale dealers, or by direct supplies to dealers and retailers and even to customers as in the case of e-retailers. Mail order sales or catalogue sales at different retail outlets of a manufacturer are direct sales to the customer, which automatically involve decisions on the establishment of stockists and storage points in strategic locations or warehouses. In the traditional marketing concept, the manufacturer is interested in scaling down the discount to the distributor to reduce the total cost. But if the distributor's discount is low, he may either not, perhaps because of his low-profit margin, distribute the goods in sufficient volume or not render satisfactory level of customer service. This may bring about a loss of present and future sales to the manufacturer. Similarly, changes in the distribution system may take place by alternative use of space, say, for inventory, marketing or production centre. This may also affect customer service in one way or the other. Therefore, a company has to carefully select channels of distribution since it affects decisions relating, ultimately, to customer service and satisfaction. Whatever channel of distribution company has decided to follow, there is a cost involved with it. The channel distribution cost typically includes the channel margin, freight, insurance and trade inventory holding cost as well as on frequency of servicing the channel partners and trade debtors. More frequent the service is less will be the trade inventory and less the trade inventory less will the debtors. In addition, the possibility of out-of-warrant or expiry stock and goods return will also come down.

Total Distribution Cost

Perhaps the most important research concerning logistics is going on in the area of design of efficient and cost-effective distribution systems. For this, an understanding of total distribution cost is essential, so that proper trade-offs can be applied as a basis for planning and reassessment of distribution systems. The urgency of dealing with transportation cost was highlighted by Thomas and Griffin (1996), who argued that since transportation cost accounts for more than half of the total logistics cost, more active research is needed in the area. To deal with distribution costs, measuring individual cost elements together with their impact on customer service encourages trade-offs that lead to a more effective and efficient distribution system.

Supply Chain and Logistics Cost

The efficiency of a supply chain can be assessed using the total logistics cost – a financial measure. It is necessary to assess the financial impact of broad-level strategies and practices that contribute to the flow of products in a supply chain. Since logistics cut across functional boundaries, care must be taken to assess the impact of actions to influence costs in one area in terms of their impact on costs associated with other areas (Cavinato, 1992). For example, a change in capacity has a major effect on cost associated with inventory and order processing.

Cost Associated with Assets and Return on Investment

Supply chain assets include accounts receivable, plant, property and equipment, and inventories. With increasing inflation and decreased liquidity, pressure is on firms to improve the productivity of capital – to make the assets sweat. In this regard, it is essential to determine how the cost associated with each asset, combined with its turnover, affects total cash flow time. One way to address this is by expressing it as an average day required to turn cash invested in assets employed into cash collected from a customer (Stewart, 1995). Thus, total cash flow time can be regarded as a metric to determine the productivity of assets in a supply chain. Once the total cash flow time is determined, this can be readily combined with profit to provide insight into the rate of return on investment (ROI). This determines the performance of top management in terms of earnings on the total capital invested in a business.

With customer service requirements constantly increasing, effective management of inventory in the supply chain is crucial (Slack et al., 1995). In a supply chain, the total cost associated with inventory can be broken down into the following (Slack et al., 1995; Lee and Billington, 1992; Levy, 1997): Opportunity cost, consisting of warehousing, capital and storage; cost associated with inventory at the incoming stock level and work in progress; service costs, consisting of cost associated with stock management and insurance; cost of finished goods including those in transit; risk costs, consisting of cost associated with pilferage, deterioration and damage; cost associated with scrap and rework; and cost associated with too little inventory accounting for lost sales/lost production (Lee and Billington, 1992; Levy, 1997; Slack et al., 1995).

Information Processing Cost

This includes costs such as those associated with order entry, order follow-up/updating, discounts and invoicing. On the basis of survey results from various industries, Stewart (1995) identified information processing cost as the largest contributor to total logistics cost. The role of information technology is shifting from a general passive management enabler through databases to a highly advanced process controller that can monitor activities and

212 Total Logistics Cost Management

decide upon an appropriate route for information. Modern information technology, through its power to provide timely, accurate and reliable information, has led to a greater integration of modern supply chains than possible by any other means (Naim, 1997; Benjamin and Wigand, 1995).

Communication and Data Processing Costs

An effective distribution system requires optimum management and control related to order processing, inventory control, accounts receivable, dispatches, communications etc. An increased number of distribution points would certainly improve customer service but would make processing of information more cumbersome and expensive. At the same time, if the time taken to process the information is decreased, it is likely to lead better customer service. A manufacturer has to decide about the speed and convenience with which information may be processed. One of the ways is the use of computers having advanced software. Communication and data processing have changed with technology and automation. A lot of improvement has been seen across manufacturing sectors to help reduce this cost. Many large global corporations have also outsourced these activities to provide much faster service and 24×7 communication and information to their customers. This is particularly necessary for global companies working in different time zones.

Administrative Costs

For providing efficient logistic service to improve customer satisfaction, the marketer not only needs adequate facilities and infrastructure and investment in technology and software as well as in material-handling equipment but to operate them trained manpower will also be required. To improve the efficiency of the whole system, there will be some administration expenses which are also part of the administration costs. Administration cost also includes documentation and record keeping costs.

Transportation Costs

The cost of transport varies generally with the speed with which goods are transported as well as with the mode of transportation and distance to be covered. Water transport is the cheapest, while air transport is the most expensive. Rail transport is cheaper than road transport, beyond a certain distance. Both rail and road transport stand somewhere in between water and air in terms of the cost of transport. Transport cost is a significant part of the total logistics cost. Businesses decide on the various modes of transportation based on the infrastructure available in a given geographical area. For international trade, bulk of the transportation takes place by ocean and in domestic trade bulk of the transportation takes place by road or rail. Certain categories of goods require special mode of transportation like refrigerated containers for frozen goods which are quite costly. The cost of transportation also will vary on the loading factor of the transport vehicle. Appropriate packaging design can help improve the loading factor of the product in a typical transport vehicle or container.

Material-handling Costs

A suitable material-handling system should be designed to reduce the cost of material handling to a minimum. Material-handling equipment is required both within production plant and inside the warehouse, and as such a significant cost will be involved in the investment on material-handling equipment but there will be savings on operation cost as well as on labour. Although one-time capital investment will be high, recurring cost will be less. This would require the consideration of several possible combinations of manual and mechanised handling of the goods and materials. But material-handling operations have an impact on other distribution aspects, such as the cost of packaging as well as damages and losses that result from material handling. The design of the material-handling system and the consideration of its cost also affect the selection of the mode of transport to be used and hence the cost of transport gets affected.

Packaging Costs

Decisions on packaging are affected by decisions on such factors as type of product, the mode of transport and type of material-handling equipment used. A total cost approach would make it necessary for us to select a packaging version, which takes into account other distribution factors as well. Thus, it would not be sufficient merely to reduce the cost of packaging to the minimum. Packaging has many functions including protection of integrity and quality of the product till it is consumed. Packaging can be of various types, including primary, secondary as well as tertiary or shipping cartons, and each has a specific role to play. Packaging has many functions in addition to its primary function to protect the product and integrity so that it can survive the hazards of transport, multiple handling and adverse storage conditions which are always not under control of the manufacturers-marketers. The other functions of packaging are:

- It provides all product information, identity of product with its distinctive characteristics as well as all statutory information, including messages like how the product has to be used and or consumed and how the product has to be stored till consumed.
- Packaging also serves as a primary advertisement for the product and its manufacturers and for that packaging also has a merchandising display value and so packaging needs to be made attractive to radiate the value of the product and its quality and cost also will be commensurate to those criteria.

Customer Service Costs

If the service level as well as service frequency increases customer satisfaction improves, but cost of service also increases. This needs to be viewed against reduction on trade inventory and a decision can be taken on the frequency of service. A company like HUL or P&G have significantly increased the service, thereby reducing the distributors and retailers inventory level making them happier as the channel partners investment on stock reduces and at the same time return on investment increases. If the manufacturer or supplier guarantees satisfaction with goods and agrees to give a refund on returned goods or exchange the returned goods, he must arrange for the movement of defective or returned goods from the customer (or retailer) back to the supply warehouse or manufacturing centre. For higher level of customer satisfaction if the marketers guarantee 100% return if not satisfied, there is a cost attached to this. Complaints of defects or of the deficiencies pointed out by the customer in the goods that are returned may therefore be utilised as management feedback to improve the quality of service. Incidentally, with such a guaranteed service the manufacturer, on a permanent basis, would win the customer's loyalty. Guaranteed customer service, therefore, involves certain costs to the organisation, but it also leads to

214   *Total Logistics Cost Management*

certain benefits in the long run. It increases the value of the company in the market. As servicing customer and ensuring satisfied customers are the primary task of a business for growth, survival and sustainability, there is always a cost attached to higher level of customer satisfaction. As we understand customer service is a process for providing competitive advantage and adding benefits to the supply chain in order to maximise the total value to the ultimate customer.

There can be three levels of products which marketers are trying to promote. The core benefit or service, which constitutes what the buyer is really buying. The tangible product, or the physical product or service itself and the augmented product, which includes benefits that are secondary to, but an integral enhancement to, the tangible product the customer is purchasing. Logistical customer service, installation warranties and after-sale service are examples of augmented product features.

Having the right product, at the right time, in the right quantity, without damage or loss, to the right customer is an underlying principle of logistics systems that recognises the importance of customer service.

Another aspect of customer service that deserves mention is the growing consumer awareness of the price/quality ratio and the special needs of today's consumers, who are time conscious and who demand flexibility.

Examples of Customer Service

Customer service can be improved by resorting to various kinds of extra services including supports and incentives that are not part of the marketer's obligation which can even include the following.

1 Revamping a billing procedure to accommodate a customer's request
2 Providing financial and credit terms
3 Guaranteeing delivery within specified time periods
4 Providing prompt and congenial sales representatives
5 Extending the option to sell on consignment
6 Providing material to aid in a customer's sales presentation
7 Installing the product
8 Maintaining satisfactory repair parts inventories

These are extended by the marketers to customers to make them loyal by helping the customers in turn to be more competitive in the market to earn better margin at the same time extending those to ultimate customers of the company.

Levels of Customer Service

In a competitive market environment, business has to deliver superior service to its target customers. To some extent, providing customer service is a legal requirement and contractual obligation in all sales agreements. But this level is the lowest level which can be considered as an activity or simple function. To be competitive in the marketplace, customer service has to graduate from a simple function to a level where it is ingrained in the company's mission and philosophy of existence and survival by focusing on higher level of customer service to retain customers to derive life-long value. This can be described as follows:

- **Customer service as an activity** – This level treats customer service as a particular task that a firm must accomplish to satisfy the customer's needs. Order processing, billing and invoicing, product returns and claims handling are all typical examples of this level of customer service. This is a basic level of customer service all manufacturer marketers have to perform and adhere to, failing which they cannot exist nor will have any reason to exist.
- **Customer service as performance measures** – This level emphasises customer service in terms of specific performance measures, such as the percentage of orders delivered on time and complete and the number of orders processed within acceptable time limits. At this level, manufacturers-marketers keep track of performance and also have a measurement of performance determined by occasional customer satisfaction surveys etc. and they try to improve upon those criteria to, improve the business performance itself.
- **Customer service as a philosophy** – This level elevates customer service to a firm-wide commitment to providing customer satisfaction through superior performance by delighting the customer at interface. They manage the business with an objective of providing customers always a higher level of performance and therefore they redefine the customer satisfaction criteria and levels and always strive to deliver those. In these types of corporations, customer service is managed as a philosophy.

Elements of Customer Service

Customer service has multifunctional interest for a company, but from the point of view of the logistics function, we can view customer service as having four traditional dimensions:

- **Time:** The time factor is usually order cycle time, particularly from the perspective of the seller looking at customer service. On the other hand, the buyer usually refers to the time dimension as the lead time, or replenishment time.
- **Dependability:** Dependability can be more important than lead time. The customer can minimise its inventory level if lead time is fixed.
- **Cost:** Providing service within a well-defined cost as percentage of sales.
- **Quality:** Delivering the quality of product and service every time as per agreed standards.

Cost Audit

Regular or periodic cost audit will reveal the following:

- Variance against company's own standard and budgeted cost heads
- Variance against last year's actual and also against budgeted is generated
- Variance against industry standard

Undertaking regular or even periodic cost audit can help organisations to perform better.

Benchmarking Logistics Cost and Performance

Organisations should periodically benchmark their logistics costs and performance to better manage and improve upon the cost and performance of select criteria, which will help them in terms of improving their performance:

216   *Total Logistics Cost Management*

- To identify opportunities and trend and cost and service performance drivers in their logistics cost.
- To know where to focus next to improve company's logistics network from the perspectives of cost and service
- Benchmark with best in competition as well as best in class to serve as objective

Case Study

Dry Ice Inc. is a manufacturer of air conditioners in the USA that has seen its demand grow significantly. Also, the demand is coming from various regions of the country. Nationwide demand will have significant cost on logistics. Company therefore is considering setting up production plants close to customer's centres in different regions in order to optimise on the logistics costs. They anticipate nationwide demand for the year 2001 to be 180,000 units in the South, 120,000 units in the Midwest, 110,000 units in the East and 100,000 units in the West. Managers at Dry Ice Inc. are designing the manufacturing network and have selected four potential plant manufacturing sites, which are – New York, Atlanta, Chicago and San Diego. From the consideration of capital cost in production, the capacity of the plants could be either 200,000 or 400,000 units. The annual fixed cost at the four locations is New York USD 6 million, Atlanta USD 5.5 million, Chicago USD 5.6 million and San Diego USD 6.1 million along with the cost of producing and shipping an air conditioner to each of the four markets.[1]

Case Questions:

1. Where should Dry Ice Inc. build its factories to cater to the increased demand of its air conditioners?
2. How large should the manufacturing plants should be in terms of capacity?
3. Discuss the key considerations for making these important decisions on investment.
4. Discuss the logistics costs with decentralised production system against one central location to cater to the demand from all regions.

Outsourcing Logistics Services

In recent years with increasing competition, specialisation in logistics function is growing. As a result, many companies choose to outsource their logistics requirements, accompanied by the rapid development of e-commerce, which has helped in acceleration of the logistics company's development. The rapid development of the logistics industry not only accelerated the delivery speed of goods and capital flow but also improved the economic growth rate. In order to maintain the rapid and healthy development of the logistics industry, many countries like say China introduced a number of incentive measures and policies. Like India, China's logistics industry also started relatively late. When compared to the American and European logistics industry, there is considerable room for development for China's as well as India's logistics industry. The technical level of the logistics industry is not high and the hardware is not good.

Reason Why Logistics Cost Management Programme Is Not Always Effective

Survey data indicate that domestic logistics company's profit margin is lower when compared with the international logistics company. Domestic logistics companies simply not only have higher logistics costs but are also seen to be much slower in implementing cost reduction programmes.

Another reason resulting in high logistics costs is that many logistics companies work in isolation and will not consider a company's supply chain operations analysis into account in order to provide an integrated service to improve the overall performance of the total supply chain. The services of logistics companies cannot be cost-effective by remaining in the middle of the supply chain cost control, including warehousing costs and shipping costs. Throughout the supply chain, logistics companies did not use the best way to arrange for the delivery process, which resulted in short positions departure, detour traffic, repeated situation, delivery and the resulting increase in cost. Supply chain is complex and logistics has many links in supply chain. Without seamless integration, it will not be easy to achieve the targeted cost reduction. Customer service level is also closely linked with the performance of logistics companies. Besides, logistics failure can even stop business in supply chain, leading to failure in meeting customer demand which even can result in loss of clients.

Difficulty is that many corporate managers cannot fully understand the importance and logistics cost control. It has not yet formed the concept of modern logistics. There is a lack of comprehensive understanding in this regard. Company executives did not pay sufficient attention to the concept of logistics cost control and failed to form awareness of modern logistics. But great opportunity exists for reducing the logistics cost without compromising the quality and service levels which can be key to providing the competitive advantage of business in a keenly contested global market.

Key Task to Improve Logistics Cost

To bring about improvement in logistics cost, businesses need to engage better trained and qualified personnel and not manage the logistics function in traditional mode of storage and transport. These managers not only need training but should have clear understanding of the business needs and implications of various cost parameters and industry standards. With a detailed analysis of the logistics cost performance data and focus on objective areas of improvement can be identified and implemented. In the context of logistics cost management, company's team members who are adapted to changed business needs and trained can better achieve supply chain logistics cost goal.

To achieve the company's supply chain logistics cost management objective, we need early training of the operators in all sectors, in order to maximise the use of company information in the supply chain software. Coordinating with network technology and supply chain logistics system between various departments of the company and between different companies would be necessary to put sales, customer service, and other aspects of production and order processing into right perspective and coordination. Companies need to change the previous mode of operation between departments and learn to view the supply chain as an integrated function. While team leaders play their exemplary role, active participation and cooperation in all aspects of the implementation, as long as all team members carry out their duties, and closely cooperate in order to implement the logistics cost control measures effectively.

The core concept of the formation of integrated supply chain cost control would mean that the logistics companies are required not only to implement cost control programme in the business of their own but also to help to control the external environment in relevant companies through cooperation to get advantage of collective gains. Logistics company itself has to determine systematically the total logistics costs as the key point to minimize that rather than achieving lowest cost in one component of the total cost for achieving the objective of company's

218 *Total Logistics Cost Management*

logistics management, and control over the supply chain. By forming the space and time effect, the goal of cost control is positioned as the lowest total cost of logistics, to maximise the value of logistics services. Logistics companies want to achieve the goal of cost control, balance the relationship between the cost of logistics and get maximum of logistics performance. It should be on the integration of the company's various logistics resources to choose the way the whole process of logistics costs in the supply chain from the point of control and manageability.

Depending on the logistics company's specific circumstances, the nature of the company and the scale of operations they will have different supply chain processes, and thus have different supply chain strategic objectives, using different costing methods.

Activity-based costing, as discussed earlier, can help in finding the avenues of cost control which facilitates more focused analysis of a company-wide cost control programme for better result and performance and hence should be implemented.

Logistics companies should reduce their own costs and should have close contact with all the companies in the supply chain, have partnership, mutual assistance, mutual benefit and reciprocity to benefit from each others knowledge and experience. It can also be an effective control and supervision of the entire total cost of logistics, covering the entire chain.

Case Study

Maruti Suzuki – How They Reduced Their Logistics Cost

In the early 2000s, Maruti Suzuki was the largest car manufacturer in India with over 50% market share. It relied on 400 major suppliers located across India, with some almost 2500 km distant from its main plant in Manesar, near New Delhi. Its total logistics costs were well above its wage bill (up to four times as high). It had to carry large buffer stocks and deal with substantial freight costs. In 2013 there was a turnaround and those costs were slashed by requiring almost all suppliers to build, warehouse or locate within a few hours' radius of the plant. Today approximately 80% of suppliers are located within 100 kms of the plant. Its buffer stocks are now down to zero, and it is running lean production processes. Maruti Suzuki is the leading automotive manufacturer in India and is an acknowledged industry category leader. Being a market leader with over 50% of passenger cars, Maruti Suzuki could command their approved vendors and suppliers to move closer to the factory location to be flexible and more responsive in terms of meeting the manufacturing schedule of the company. The number of vendors and suppliers was also rationalised based on their performance and ability. These vendors not only shifted their manufacturing location close to the factory of Maruti but also helped the company to reduce the inventory significantly. Company also implemented vendor-managed inventory (VMI) drastically reducing the input material inventory, making the company more competitive in the marketplace. Vendors and suppliers are dependent on the Maruti Suzuki for their survival and growth as most of those vendors are actually dedicated suppliers to Maruti Suzuki. Maruti has helped the well-performing vendors to deliver the expected return on their investment (ROI); many of those are quite big and are public companies. Because of the dependence, it was much easier for Maruti Suzuki to implement a drastic logistics cost reduction programme by leveraging their relationship and dependency of the vendors on the company for their survival and growth as well as performance.[2]

Case Questions:

1 What factors forced Maruti Suzuki to optimise logistics cost?
1 How did the company go about dealing with logistics cost reduction programme?
2 What factors helped the company to implement its decision and to what consequences?

Total Logistics Cost Management 219

3 What are the key challenges of implementing company-wide logistics cost management programme?
4 What did Maruti Suzuki achieve post-implementation of the project? Discuss the direct and indirect benefits Maruti Suzuki derived from this project.

Chapter Summary

The component of logistics and their influence on total logistics in global business environment has been discussed here and what are the implications and on what criteria those costs will depend and how they can be improved further were discussed. How some of these costs are better managed in a collaborative networked environment with direct real-time information exchange was also discussed. Different approaches to determining the logistics costs in a business and how customer service levels are costs are determined were also discussed. Large logistics businesses are increasingly seen to be outsourcing some of the key components and activities for managing end-to-end logistics for better performance were discussed with some case examples. Logistics management strategies in global trade and commerce and how companies are deriving competitive advantages by reducing cost of operations and unlocking incremental value have been discussed taking the case of a global logistics company. The logistics challenges in e-commerce trade and how large e-retailers like Amazon were addressing those challenges to create competitive advantages were also discussed. How international logistics management companies are developing relationships with other operators, both domestic and international players, to be more effective were discussed with cases. How better and effective logistics management can deliver competitive advantage to marketers was also discussed taking examples.

Discussion Questions

1 Explain the role of different cost approaches in logistics.
2 What are the different costs involved in logistics?
3 How is the total cost approach relevant in the case of global logistics cost management business?
4 Why is logistics cost management programme not always effective?
4 How can businesses organise themselves to benchmark their logistics cost performance?
5 How can an efficient SCM create shareholders' value?
6 How can effective logistics costs management improve ROI?

Notes

1 Source: www.chegg.com accessed on 4 September 2019
2 Source: www.ibef.org/download/Gujarat-March-2018.pdf (accessed on 4 September 2019)

References

Benjamin, R., & Wigand, R. (1995) "Electronic Markets and Virtual Value Chains on the Information Super High Way", *Sloan Management Review*, 36(2), 67–72.
Cavinato, Joseph L. (1992) "A Total Cost/Value Model for Supply Chain Competitiveness", *Journal of Business Logistics,* 13(2), 285–291.
Christopher, M. G. (1998) *Logistics and Supply Chain Management, Strategies for Reducing Cost and Improving Services.* London: Pitman Publishing.
The Davis Logistics Cost and Service Database. (2014) Available at https://www.establishinc.com/establish-davis-database (accessed on 22 August 2019).

220 *Total Logistics Cost Management*

Lee, H. L., & Billington, C. (1992) "Managing Supply Chain Inventory: Pitfalls and Opportunities", *Sloan Management Review*, 33(3), 65–73.

Levy, D. L. (1997) "Lean Production in an International Supply Chain", *Sloan Management Review*, 38(2), 94–102.

Naim, M. M. (1997, February) "The Book That Changed the World", *Manufacturing Engineer,* 76(1), 67–72.

Stewart, G. (1995) "Supply Chain Performance Benchmarking Study Reveals Keys to Supply Chain Excellence", *Logistics Information Management*, 8(2), 38–44.

Thomas, D. J., & Griffin, P. M. (1996) "Co-Ordinate Supply Chain Management", *European Journal of Operational Research*, 94(3), 1–15.

Bibliography

Rushton, A., Baker, P., & Croucher, P., eds. (1989) *The Handbook of Logistics and Distribution Management: Understanding the Supply Chain*. London: Kogan Page Publishers.

Stepien, M., Legowik-Swiacik, S., Skibinska, W., & Turek, I. (2016) "Identification and Measurement of Logistics Cost Parameters in the Company", *Science Direct-Transportation Research Procedia*, 16(2016), 490–497.

Toyli, J. (2008) "Logistics and Financial Performance: An Analysis of 424 Finish Small and Medium-Sized Enterprises", *International Journal of Physical Distribution and Logistics Management*, 38.

Xian-min, Z. O. U. (2005) "Management and Control of Logistics Coast in Enterprises", *Industrial Engineering Journal*, 4, 003.

8 Sustainable Transport Logistics and Supply Chain

Learning Objectives

1 Realise the importance of sustainability in supply chain
2 Identify challenges of sustainability issues in business and supply chain
3 Define the key dimensions of sustainability supply chain and their implications
4 Understand managing sustainability issues for better public image and performance of the business
5 How sustainability can improve competitiveness of the logistic industry
6 How global players are aligning with the demand of the clients to conform to sustainability standards

Introduction

Sustainability is a business issue affecting an organisation's supply chain or logistics network and is frequently quantified by comparison with SECH ratings. SECH ratings are defined as social, ethical, cultural and health footprints. Consumers have become more aware of the environmental impact of their purchases and companies' SECH ratings and, along with non-governmental organisations (NGOs), are setting the agenda for transitions to organically grown foods, anti-sweatshop labour codes and locally produced goods that support independent and small businesses. Because supply chains frequently account for over 75% of a company's carbon footprint, many organisations are exploring how they can reduce this and thus improve their SECH rating. For example, in July 2009 the US-based Walmart corporation announced its intentions to create a global sustainability index that would rate products according to the environmental and social impact made while the products were manufactured and distributed. The sustainability rating index is intended to create environmental accountability in Walmart's supply chain and provide the motivation and infrastructure for other retail industry companies to do the same (Walmart, 2013). More recently, the US Dodd-Frank Wall Street Reform and Consumer Protection Act signed into law by President Obama in July 2010 contained a supply chain sustainability provision in the form of the Conflict Minerals law. This law requires SEC-regulated companies to conduct third-party audits of the company supply chains; determine whether any tin, tantalum, tungsten or gold (together referred to as conflict minerals) is made of ore mined/sourced from the Democratic Republic of the Congo (DRC), and create a report (available to the general public and SEC) detailing the supply chain due diligence efforts undertaken and the results of the audit (Woody, 2012). Of course, the chain of suppliers/vendors to these reporting companies will be expected to provide appropriate supporting information. Due

DOI: 10.4324/9781003469063-8

222   *Sustainable Transport Logistics and Supply Chain*

to regulatory challenges as well as increased awareness of customers sustainability parameters are increasingly seen to be more important in terms of preserving the public image of
the large corporation. It is therefore very common for these companies to report on sustainability parameters in their annual report for information of their shareholders in particular
and general public in general.

Defining Sustainability

There is no universally accepted definition of sustainability, sustainable development or sustainable transport (Beatley, 1995).

Some of the popular definitions are as follows:

- Sustainable development 'meets the needs of the present without compromising the ability of
  future generations to meet their own needs' (Brundtland Commission, 1987).
- 'Sustainable development is the achievement of continued economic development without
  detriment to the environmental and natural resources' (Themes Sustainable Development,
  2004).
- 'The goal of sustainable transportation is to ensure that environment, social and economic considerations are factored into decisions affecting transportation activity' (MOST,
  1999).
- Sustainability is not about threat analysis; sustainability is about systems analysis. Specifically, it is about how environmental, economic and social systems interact to their mutual
  advantage or disadvantage at various space-based scales of operation (Transportation
  Research Board, 1997).
- Sustainability is 'the capacity for continuance into the long-term future'. Anything that can
  go on being done on an indefinite basis is sustainable. Anything that cannot go on being done
  indefinitely is unsustainable (Centre for Sustainability, 2004).

Transportation Impacts on Sustainability

Transportation facilities and activities have significant sustainability impacts, including those
listed next.

Table 8.1 Transportation Impacts on Sustainability

Economic	Social	Environmental
Traffic congestion	Inequity of impacts	Air and water pollution
Mobility barriers	Mobility disadvantaged	Habitat loss
Accident damages	Human health impacts	Hydrologic impact
Facility costs	Community interaction	DNPR
Consumer costs	Community liveability	
DNPR	Aesthetics	

Source: Developing Indicators for Comprehensive and sustainable Transport planning Todd Litman, Director Victoria
Transport policy Institute, 4 February 2011, p. 5.

Note: DNPR: Depletion of non-renewable resources

Simple Sustainability Indicators

To facilitate sustainable transportation analysis, some evaluations use a relatively simple set of indicators using relatively easily available data. The following are examples:

- Transportation fossil fuel consumption and CO2 emissions: less is better
- Vehicle pollution emissions: less is better
- Per capita motor vehicle mileage: less is better
- Mode split: higher transit ridership is better
- Traffic crash injuries and deaths: less is better
- Transport land consumption: less is better
- Roadway aesthetic conditions (people tend to be more inclined to care for environments that they consider beautiful and meaningful)

Sustainable Transport in Global Trade

Sustainable development should emerge in more regulation and control in global logistics. And we may need different ways of transporting and delivering goods and the current set of transport and logistics in many sectors is 'unsustainable' due to their energy consumption and resulting pollution. Transport logistics is evolving on a global scale. Global inter-shipping firms are working jointly to fast shipping alliances.

Economic Benefits of Sustainable Transportation

- **Attractive new business opportunity:** Sustainable transportation can open up other opportunities in business. For example, rail stations in London, Brussels, Philadelphia and Washington D.C. have all been renovated into vibrant commercial complexes with offices, restaurants and shops.
- **Help Generate Incremental sales:** Motor bike is a more fuel-efficient vehicle. In Toronto area itself, consumers spent over USD 56 million on bike accessories and repairs in 1991.[1]
- **Encourage local circulation of money:** To encourage public transport in Los Angeles, 80 cents of every USD 1.00 spent on public transport gets recirculated in the region, translating into USD 3.80 in goods and services. Conversely, 85 of every USD 1.00 spent on gas leaves the region.[2]
- **Promote other types cost-effective services:** When focus is on sustainability, other types of cost-effective services are introduced. For example, 'Cops on Bikes' programmes offer cost-effective police services for many areas, with lower cost and greater flexibility and faster service when compared with policing in automobiles.
- **Development of real estate around metro and rapid transit rails:** Real estate development takes place in high-value area in close vicinity of metro stations. For example, in Atlanta, USD 70 billion in apartments, offices and other developments and services have been built near the rapid transit rail lines. Around Washington D.C., 40% of new building space in the 1980s, worth USD 3 billion, were built within walking distance of a metro shop.[3] Similar developments have also been observed near metro and rapid metro in NCR regions and more particularly in Gurgaon, India.
- **Improves productivity:** Sustainable transport helps in increasing labour productivity. A study on the impact on worker productivity due to US government spending and its impact on worker productivity in a course of ten years estimated that USD 100 increase in public

224 *Sustainable Transport Logistics and Supply Chain*

transport spending of ten years would boost worker output to USD 521 billion, compared with USD 237 billion for the same spending on highways.

- **Reduction in transportation costs:** Sustainable transport can lead to reduction in costs. For example, as per business plan for a video conferencing network at the British Columbia (BC) Ministry of Transportation projects, an investment of USD 977,000 will recover USD 2,241,500 in travel costs over two years.
- **Helps growth in economic development:** Sustainable development is very much desirable. A study in Montgomery County found that if growth continued in the usual pattern, economic development would be stifled by traffic congestion. Whereas in contrast, if growth were focused preferentially in pedestrian and bike-friendly clusters along the expanded transit system, and commuter subsidies were revised to discourage car use, jobs and households could double in the County without any traffic congestion.
- **Reduces in infrastructure costs:** For building new urban expressways, the cost would be much higher. For example, of creating new expressways can be up to USD 100 million per mile, while rail and bike facilities cost can come down to an average of USD 15 million and USD 0.1 million, respectively.
- **Helps creating jobs:** Sustainable transportation offers job creation possibilities in services, high technology, construction, design, manufacturing, maintenance, education as well as in education and research.

Key Issues in Sustainable Transportation

- **Access, not mobility:** Movement in cities is not an end in itself. We move in order to gain access to people and things. But in car-oriented cities, activities tend to spread out. This forces people to travel further and further for the same level of accessibility as before. What we need is accessibility and not mobility.
- **Moving people, not cars:** We need to focus on moving people and goods rather than vehicles. In dense cities, public transport saves valuable space and energy compared to private transport and can make a healthy profit at the same time. But to achieve that cities need to nurture their public transport by giving them some priority on the road over cars. If public transport like buses always gets caught in traffic, then the vicious cycle begins, in the sense that people abandon public transport and shift to private vehicles, adding to the traffic jams.
- **Reclaim city space for walking and pedalled vehicles:** The healthiest and most sustainable modes of transport are walking and cycling. Even car drivers become pedestrians to complete a trip, and effective public transport depends on people being able to walk comfortably to stations and stops. But walking and cycling are vulnerable to the impacts of traffic. Many rapidly motorising Asian cities are quickly losing their walking spaces. In Bangkok, only 14% of all trips are on foot or bicycle compared to a whopping 45% in the enormous Tokyo metropolitan area. It requires planning by the city planners to create space for cyclists and pedestrians to walk or be cycle safe.

Sustainability Helps Business

A McKinsey report,[4] focusing on greenhouse gas emissions, reported, 'Almost forty percent of greenhouse gas abatement could be achieved at a negative marginal costs which means that investing in these options would generate positive cash flows and hence the economic returns over their life cycle'.

Walmart started its focus on sustainability as a defensive move, given the negative criticism they were receiving from environmental activists. The company, however, has seen many benefits to its bottom line after they had taken several such initiatives. For example, installing LSD lights had significantly reduced their energy bill (Walmart, 2013).

Starbucks (2013) is another example of a company that has focused on sustainability for significant business reasons. The company started its coffee and farmer equity initiative (C.A.F.E.), which evaluates the sustainable production of coffee along four dimensions: product quality, economic accountability, social responsibility and environmental leadership (Stewart, 1995).

S.C Johnson, a FMCG major in household goods, has reported that between 1990 and 1999 the company used eco-efficiency efforts to cut more than 410 million pounds of waste and saved USD 125 million.

Recycling boiler flue gas to recover carbon dioxide to used again in the product for carbonation as well as heat recovery from boiler flue gases is a common practice in carbonated soft beverages manufacturing plants like Coca-Cola.

Case Study: Volvo's Strategy for Sustainability

Corporate Overview

AB Volvo, at year-end 1998, is the largest industrial group in Scandinavia, with over 79,000 employees and 55 production plants in 26 countries. Sales in 1998 were SEK212,936 million (USD 25 billion). The Volvo Group's products include cars, large trucks, buses, aircraft engines, construction equipment, and drive systems for marine and industrial applications. About 88% of Volvo sales are outside Sweden, primarily in Western Europe and North America.

To students of management, Volvo gained recognition over 20 years ago for challenging the traditional approach to assembly-line production processes by designing production work around intact teams with 'whole tasks'. Volvo's innovative work redesign, which considered the 'social-system' in addition to the technical system, set the standard for creating self-managing work teams and improving 'Quality of Work life'.

In the past decade, this strength in high-performance work teams has been augmented by an impressive implementation of lean production methods such as JIT manufacturing, waste reduction, flexible manufacturing and concurrent engineering, to shorten time-to-market. Volvo now manufactures using a 'pull' production system produces cars to individual customer specifications and has inventory turns of about four hours in its car assembly plants.

To this powerful production capability and team synergy – driven by market demand, legislative requirements and a visionary strategy – Volvo has added a rigorous effort to reduce the negative environmental impact of its products. Based on a deep understanding of the entire life-cycle impacts of the automotive and transport industries, Volvo has integrated its value for 'Environmental Care' into design of products and services, production process design and management, product end-of-life handling, customer and employee education, supplier management, and new business services and products.

Volvo's strategy for sustainable development is an integral part of their wider competitive business strategy, and environment has been added as one of three core underlying values of the company.

There is alignment on environmental strategies and objectives, and their relevance to the business, from the board of directors to the shop floor.

By December 31, 1998, over 49,000 employees, suppliers and dealers will have been educated about the basic functioning of nature and conditions of life, the key environmental issues

226 *Sustainable Transport Logistics and Supply Chain*

facing our society today (e.g. climate change, ozone depletion, loss of biodiversity), the environmental aspects and impacts of energy and transportation, and the company's environmental objectives and programmes.

About 350 people from almost 60 European suppliers have received environmental education and clear performance expectations regarding establishment of an environmental management system, environmental impact improvements, data exchange for life-cycle assessments, 'black lists' and 'grey lists' of chemicals, optimised handling of waste and packaging, and materials recyclability.

Improvements have been made in production processes, where emissions (particularly from solvents) have been reduced substantially with the result that Volvo estimates its achieving savings of USD 2.50 per car directly to the bottom line simply from its improvements in waste sorting.

Volvo has implemented product design changes. For example:

1 Design changes focus on reduction of environmental impact 'in use' by providing: greater fuel efficiency; buses as alternative modes of transportation (one-third of the Volvo buses sold in Sweden in 1996 were designed to burn alternative fuels, and 21 natural gas buses were supplied to the UK in 1997); mobile data communication systems; and products with alternative fuels such as natural gas, biofuel, alcohol and electricity.
2 The degree of recycled materials in cars is increasing – with rising levels of economic viability. Today the average recycling percentage of cars is around 75%, and of heavy trucks over 90% (by weight higher than cars, given the higher metal content).

Volvo has developed a new company, 'Volvo Mobility Systems', to provide products and solutions for the design of safer and more environmentally benign transportation systems globally. For example, Volvo has partnered in developing a more sustainable transportation system based on bus systems which provide service and environmental impact equivalent to light rail systems – at a 1/100th of the cost.

Volvo's platform car S80 (May 1998) is the first car in the world with an 'Environmental Product Declaration' certified by a third party and based on life-cycle assessment.

Sustainable business practices are the foundation for the current and future successes in the era of new challenges arising out of increased concern for environmental as well as ecological issues. Any company planning to be a profitable company 50 years from now needs to be building sustainability into their strategic thinking. As such successful companies in the next millennium will be those that understand and practice sustainability.

Companies committed to integrating the sustainability agenda into their businesses tend to display the following: (Mapping the Journey, Case Studies in Strategy and Actions towards Sustainable Development, By Lorinda Rowledge, Russel R. Barton and Kevin S. Brady, Routledge, 2017)

- A clear and focused strategic perspective on how sustainability relates to the company, its value chains, markets, products and operations
- Management systems that enable the company to monitor and manage environmental and social issues and integrate them into core business decisions
- Stakeholder dialogue processes that ensure that internal and external concerns are heard and addressed effectively
- Product development processes that integrate triple-bottom-line thinking into the design process and account for impacts throughout the life cycle of the product
- Open, transparent, quantified and verified communication of the triple bottom-line performance, with growing numbers of companies signing up to the Global Reporting Initiative (GRI) following the reporting guidelines

- Innovative supply chain management approaches, where the environmental and social performance of a company's suppliers is seen as an important part of that company's overall performance
- A toolbox that includes life-cycle assessment, design for the environment and life-cycle costing methodologies that internalise what were previously external environmental costs
- And a range of tailored communications activities designed to carry the message through to key market actors, particularly consumers and customers (in terms of performance and quality messages) and financial markets
- Volvo added environment to its core values of quality and safety and views it as an integral part of company strategy for competitive advantage. Changes were targeted at three areas of highest leverage: (1) product design based on reducing environmental impact over the entire product life cycle; (2) business development – for example, market access in Asia and a new company 'Volvo Mobility Systems' aimed at providing products and solutions for the design of safer and more environmentally benign transportation systems; and (3) tough procurement standards for suppliers regarding environmental management and materials. All of this has been supported by clear messages from the boardroom to the shop floor regarding the business relevance of environmental issues, and by extensive education of engineers, employees, suppliers, customers and stakeholders and various measures of return on investment (ROI).

Sustainability as a Central Strategic Issue

Volvo's strategy for sustainability as a central issue covering the following:

- What critical insights can guide managers and governments as they make strategic decisions to position for the emerging economy?
- What will be the business context of the next decade?
- What innovations in business design and technology will redefine the future competitive landscape?
- What shifts in market demand will drive new requirements and expectations for winning customer loyalty?
- How can corporate policies and strategies be translated and implemented in multinational companies with very diverse product lines?
- What competences and practices from leading global companies and governments could inform our business strategies and practices?
- What is the key to achieving sustainable competitive advantage and value?
- By what measure should we determine success?

The principles of sustainability – perspectives and processes for redesigning our industrial system and practices and our social culture and metabolism (industrial throughput) to achieve sustainable development – offer critical insights for developing the answers to these strategic questions. The organisations in this book are using sustainability in forming strategic plans to:

- Position for the new economy
- Anticipate critical elements of the emerging business context
- Meet shifting customer requirements
- Build customer loyalty and brand introduction
- Stimulate innovations in business design and technology
- Develop new competences
- Achieve competitive advantage
- Increase value
- Redefine measures of corporate, community and national success

228 *Sustainable Transport Logistics and Supply Chain*

Key Drivers of Sustainability Strategies

Volvo's evolution towards sustainability has been influenced by a number of key market drivers: increasing customer demand, competitive pressures, stringent regulatory requirements and new business opportunities – additionally, Volvo's high-integrity, holistic, life-cycle approach to understanding customer requirement.

Market demand: Volvo is experiencing increasing market demand in certain segments in many countries. Industrial customers, fleet owners, leasing customers, 'authorities' and community sectors (e.g. city transport, airports) are intensifying their purchasing requirements, information requests and concerns about the environmental impact of their transportation choices. The ripple effect that is cascading through the supply chain, especially in northern Europe, is affecting Volvo. As any one corporation seeks to improve its environmental profile, it of course looks to lessen the negative impacts within its supply chain and transportation activities. So, for example, as Baxter Europe or Eastman Kodak communicated their environmental improvement expectations and goals to their transport company, ASG, this spurred ASG to be more selective in its choice of transport vehicles. Volvo's work in the development of fuel-efficient trucks, alternative fuels and other environmental performance attributes positioned it well for this business. There is growing demand for efficient and environmentally friendly transport solutions.

Legislative Pressures

The transport industry faces increasingly rigorous legislative standards regarding emissions (led by California's 2003 zero emissions law, and a plethora of European Union emissions standards for cars, trucks and buses, which will be introduced from 2000 onwards, recycling (e.g. Sweden's June 1996 legislation which established producer responsibility for scrap cars, mandating that, by 2002, 85% of the vehicle weight must be recovered for re-use, material recycling or energy recovery), waste handling, reduction of noise and traffic congestion, and packaging (e.g. the 1994 legislation in Sweden establishing producer liability for packaging requiring that manufacturers facilitate the sorting and re-use, recycling or energy recovery of all packaging made of glass, corrugated board, paper or cardboard, metal, and plastic). More stringent controls on diesel-powered buses and trucks are on the docket in the USA (1998), Japan (2000) and the EU (2001). Many of the regulations have parallels in other countries, and the overall expectation is that these provisions will continue to be tightened in the future. For example, in July 1999, the EU approved 'End-of-Life Vehicle' (ELV) legislation requiring take-back for new cars from 2001 and for all cars by 2006. By the later date, manufacturers must recycle or re-use 80% of vehicle weight (this legislation is awaiting ratification by the European Parliament). Volvo is working actively to promote harmonisation of regulations at an international level. (Overall, there has been exponential growth in the number of legislative restrictions on industry, and the expectation is that this trend will continue.) Legislative requirements related to environment facing the automotive and transport equipment industry are summarised next:

- California has the toughest emissions legislation, where the mandate for a 'zero emission vehicle' is expected to come into force in 2003. EU standards on car, truck and bus emissions tightened in 2000, 2005 and 2008.
- Greenhouse gas reduction goals in Europe require 25% reduction of 1995 levels of carbon dioxide emissions by 2008.
- Sweden legally requires producer liability for 'End-of-Life Vehicles' as of 1998, and at least 85% by weight of a vehicle will have to be recovered for re-use, recycling or energy recovery, increasing to 95% in 2015.

Sustainable Transport Logistics and Supply Chain   229

- The EU has approved a similar measure on end-of-life vehicles (awaiting ratification by the European Parliament), which will require manufacturers to take back new cars for recycling and re-use by 2001 and all cars by 2006.

Life-cycle Perspective

Another key driver of Volvo's journey towards sustainability stems from approaching strategy and decisions from its high-integrity, holistic, integrated life-cycle perspective, which stimulates powerful insights into customer requirements, generating and managing value, and reducing environmental impacts and effects. A holistic, life-cycle perspective based on facts and data has permeated Volvo's planning and decision-making at all levels within the organisation, from strategic planning efforts that examine Volvo's strategic positioning within the value chain to improvements in design and production to attain environmental efficiencies. Volvo managers have remarked that life-cycle thinking is a natural consequence of focusing on the environment, and that it has been dramatically reflected in priority-setting moving to a product (rather than production process) focus. Life-cycle analysis is now part of the basic public dialogue internally in Volvo, within its value stream and in Europe more generally.

Genuine Caring

Volvo managers are quick to point out that their interest in environment is not only externally driven. Since 1927, a deeply held concern for people has been a central underpinning of the Volvo company culture, so current efforts towards sustainability are not 'trendy', ancillary or superficial. Rather, it builds on a long-standing tradition in Volvo of commitment to supporting human safety in transport.

New Business

Volvo has identified its strategic strengths and capabilities within the context of more environmentally sustainable industrial practices. It is well positioned to take advantage of emerging business opportunities created by the need for more sustainable transport systems through their action programmes of supplying natural gas and biogas buses, providing integrated rapid transit system design services, addressing concern about pollution levels and emissions in emerging markets, assuring production facilities have strong environmental management systems, and providing transport and logistics information services. In some cases, these competences already existed; in others, Volvo is investing heavily in technology, process and human resource development to build them.

A major signal that a company is moving towards sustainable development is its willingness to fundamentally incorporate different products, services and business designs. The theoretical underpinning of this redesign is often a move towards dematerialisation. Industry, overall, is moving towards becoming solution suppliers rather than simply product suppliers. Volvo is actively working to be part of this. Although the company's primary focus is certainly still on production of transportation equipment, it is taking initial steps to lay the groundwork for an alternative business design as a provider of transportation system technology products and services, rather than simply manufacturing. A major success for Volvo in this area involves its collaboration with the city of Curitiba, Brazil, to develop an attractive, cost-effective, environmentally sensitive mass transport system. The system is based on buses and was implemented quickly at significantly lower costs than light rail alternatives. Based on value creation opportunities revealed by Volvo's experience in assisting Curitiba and other cities design transportation

230 *Sustainable Transport Logistics and Supply Chain*

systems, in 1998 Volvo established Volvo Mobility Systems (VMS) as a new company. The history behind the Executive Committee's deliberations in forming VMS, and its vision for the company, are described in Box 4. Volvo Mobility Systems is intended to 'Create value by providing efficient, clean, and safe mobility systems for goods and people to demanding customers, primarily in metropolitan areas'.

VMS guidelines are:

1 Work with and supply the development of environmentally sensitive mobility solutions.
2 Develop alternative power sources and fuels.
3 Develop sustainable transportation system.
4 Operate in the forefront of mobility systems, thus becoming known as credible partner.
5 Assist the development of intermodal transport system that managed the seamless transition between different modes of transport.
6 Leverage information technology to support transport.

Volvo's Curitiba Story

Volvo used innovative but simple technology to support the Brazilian city of Curitiba in creating a bus line that rivals the efficiency of light rail or subways, at a fraction of the construction cost and disturbance. Typically, a 12 m bus normally carries 1000 passengers per day. By incorporating double-articulated buses each with a capacity of 270, exclusive bus lanes, timed traffic signals for peak times, and tube stations for prepaid fares, these larger buses can each carry 4000 passengers per day along the main busway.

The 900 km network transports 23,000 passengers per peak hour, approximately the same number as on the Rio de Janeiro Metro. The double-articulated buses operate at 20 kmh, only 5–12 kmh slower than the New York City Subway. Although subways and light rail systems have a slight advantage if they have been previously established, Curitiba's transit system presents many advantages for cities that have not yet developed rail systems. The primary advantage is cost: Volvo's Curitiba system costs $200,000 per km, only.

This unsubsidised system carrying 800,000 passengers per day has been proven effective by those using it. Although Curitiba has the highest rate of car ownership in Brazil (one in three), it also has the highest rate of use of public transit: 75% of all commuters take the bus. In addition, 28% of car owners regularly take the bus. As a result, fuel consumption per capita is 30% less than in other Brazilian cities. Traffic has declined by 30% since 1974, while population has doubled.

Source: Rowledge et al. (2017). Included with permission from the publisher.

Case Questions:

1 What is Volvo's strategy for sustainability?
2 Discuss the key insights of sustainability as central strategic issues as pursued by Volvo.
3 What are key strategic drivers for evolving a sustainable development strategy?
4 Discuss the key economic benefits of sustainable transportation.
5 Discuss the life cycle analysis perspective of Volva's strategy involving in a public dialogue.
6 Discuss key lessons from Volvo's Curitiba story.
7 Discuss the new legislative pressures on vehicular emissions in Europe and US compelling industry to adjust to new standards.

Chapter Summary

Sustainable transportation is the new challenge to global logistics operators. Large global players are committed to environmental and sustainability concerns of the regulatory authorities due to public pressure. They are important customers to the logistics industry and bulk of the volume of the businesses are coming from those customers. Global ocean transport carriers as well as surface transport vehicles are trying to do everything possible to align with these requirements. This chapter covered these details with examples and cases. How these are being addressed in global transportation and logistics industry and their impact on economic development were also discussed. Finally, a Volvo case study on sustainable transport and technology development programmes within the company deriving the strategic direction for the business is discussed. There are new regulatory standards on vehicular emissions in the USA and also in many EU countries forcing global automobile manufacturers to design new vehicles to meet those standards and give necessary emphasis on sustainability concerns in the transportation industry and that also helps provide many economic benefits to the country as discussed in this chapter. The new regulations also insist upon recycling of over 90% of the old vehicle by weight on the concern of conservation of natural resources and also reducing the cost on waste management and disposal. These issues are discussed in detail in this chapter.

Discussion Questions

1 Why has sustainability become so critical in the logistics industry, and what are its key indicators?
2 How does transportation impact sustainability?
3 Why addressing sustainability issues helps businesses?
4 Discuss economic benefits of sustainable transportation.
5 How sustainability also improves the competitive advantage of the transport and logistics operators.
6 How transport and logistics industry are addressing these new challenges and trying to contain the cost escalations.

Notes

1 See: www.atkearney.com/documents/20152/434594/Shale%2BGas%2B-%2BThreat%2Bor%2BOppor tunity%2Bfor%2Bthe%2BGCC.PDF/de78698b-c701-e894-bf14-260a1fa52f72
2 Ibid.
3 Ibid.
4 See: www.mckinsey.com/business-functions/sustainability/our-insights/greenhouse-gas-abatement-cost-curves, accessed on 22 August 2019

References

Beatley, T. (1995) "Environmental Ethics and Planning Theory", *Journal of Planning Literature*, 4(1), 1–32.
Beyond the Green Corporation. (2007) *Bloomberg Businessweek*, January 29.
Naim, M. M. (1997, February) *The Book That Changed the World*. Manufacturing Engineer, pp. 67–72.
Revkin, A. C. (2007, April 1) "Poor Nations to Bear Brunt as World Warms", *New York Times*.

232 *Sustainable Transport Logistics and Supply Chain*

Rowledge, L., Barton, R., & Brady, K. (2017) *Mapping the Journey, Case Studies in Strategy and Actions Towards Sustainable Development*. London: Routledge.

Slack, N., Chambers, S., Harland, C., Harrison, A., & Johnston, R. (1995) *Supply Chain Operations Management*. London: Pitman Publishing.

Starbucks. (2013) *Starbucks Global Responsibility Report: Goals and Progress 2013*.

Stewart, G. (1995) "Supply Chain Performance Benchmarking Study Reveals Keys to Supply Chain Excellence", *Logistics Information Management*, 8(2), 38–44.

Story, L. (2007, August 2) "Lead Point Mattel to Recall 967000 Toys", *New York Times Report*.

Walmart. (2013) *Walmart 2013 Global Responsibility Report*. Available at https://cdn.corporate.walmart.com/39/97/81c4b26546b3913979b260ea0a74/updated-2013-global-responsibility-report_130113953638624649.pdf (accessed on 16 April 2019).

Woody, K. E. (2012) "Conflicts Minerals Legislation: The SECs New Role as Diplomatic and Humanitarian Watchdog", *Fordham Law Review*, 81(3), 1315–1351.

Bibliography

Rushton, A., Baker, P., & Croucher, P., eds. (1989) *The Handbook of Logistics and Distribution Management, The Chartered Institute of Logistics and Transport (UK)*. London: Kogan Page.

Stepien, M., Legowik-Swiacik, S., Skibinska, W., & Turek, I. (2016) "Identification and Measurement of Logistics Cost Parameters in the Company", *Science Direct-Transportation Research Procedia*, 16(2016), 490–497.

Toyli, J. (2008) "Logistics and Financial Performance: An Analysis of 424 Finish Small and Medium-Sized Enterprises", *International Journal of Physical Distribution and Logistics Management*, 38.

Xian-min, Z. O. U. (2005) "Management and Control of Logistics Coast in Enterprises", *Industrial Engineering Journal*, 4: 003.

9 Global Logistics Value Chain Management

Learning Objective

Integration of Global Value Chain Components

1 Define international logistics and key drivers of its evolution and tools that facilitated global logistics
2 Identify logistics value chain linkages and integration of value chain components
3 Recognise international logistics challenges and barriers to global logistics
4 Identify complexity in global logistics and source of competitive advantage
5 Classify features of International trade and impact of globalisation on international logistics
6 Know the global operating levels of logistics companies
7 Recognise security issues and environmental concerns in global logistics management

Introduction

By value it would normally mean a chain of activities that a firm operates in a specific industry to deliver valuable products or services for the market (first introduced by Michael Porter in 1985). Value is created by unlocking hidden value and also by removing non-value-adding activities from business processes. The value so created needs to be captured to be delivered for offering better cost-value-benefit to the customers to succeed in the marketplace. Value chain matrix will suggest the areas of improvement. In a competitive environment, businesses must have a better understanding of their consumers and also are required to deliver the customer requirements better in relation to their immediate competitors. Projecting and delivering superior values hold the key to success and for doing so businesses need to constantly upgrade the product and services to remain aligned with the technology. Speed of action and delivery as well as delivering the product where customer wants are also the key requirement for success. Business has to deliver its normal profits as returns to its shareholders. The normal profit will generate from pricing and costing of the product and services. But incremental profit for the business can only be generated by managing the business processes better. One way of improving the value or performance is to reduce cost or better cost management and by resorting to eliminating non-value-adding and redundant processes in the business. Other ways of reducing the costs by resorting to better working capital management such as reducing the average inventory holding or increasing the average settlement period of debtors and also the average settlement period of creditors.

Businesses have multiple objectives for their existence in addition to making profit for which any economic activities like business are undertaken first of all. Business also has to deliver growth by increasing market share and expanding geographical territory. Besides, businesses

DOI: 10.4324/9781003469063-9

234   *Global Logistics Value Chain Management*

also have to deliver their larger responsibility for the society by creating social value. Shareholder's value is normally measured by financial parameters like ROI, PAT, EVA etc., and those can be increased and managing logistics more effectively can also help in delivering incremental financial performance. The logistics cost can significantly impact ROI in any business. Although the significant cost of logistics is arising out of transportation function. Logistics competency is achieved by coordinating the various functions and logistics activities including network design, information, transportation, inventory, warehousing, material handling and packaging.

International Logistics

International logistics is the design and management of a system that controls the forward and reverse flow of materials, services, information into, through and out of international corporation and international geographic boundaries. This flow of goods and services happens through an international logistics channel. International logistics is a multidisciplinary function and covers a wide variety of disciplines and management functions.

Therefore, international logistic channel means the optimal routes created purposefully and in a systematic way, most often within the confines of the already existing international logistic networks (though in emergency logistics networks may be created individually, e.g. temporary landing sites or warehouses) to the recipient, along with accompanying information;

The physical network: It begins with the supplier and ends with the ultimate client and embraces all aspects related to product development, purchase, manufacturing, physical distribution, after-sales service and the circulation of information.

Key Drivers for Evolution of International Logistics

First: Global Sourcing of Components

In international logistic channels, the subjects are linked by the physical movement of goods and sending information. A good example may be the Singer sewing machine. The basic components of these machines are produced on three continents: the housing – in the USA, the drive shafts – in Italy, and the motors – in Brazil. The final product is assembled in Taiwan, while the customers are spread all over the world. The dispatch of supply, manufacturing and distribution-related functions between subjects located in various parts of the world is a huge challenge for logistics, which needs to unite and integrate the system.

Second: New Product Development – Global Expertise

International logistic channels are a network of companies established to develop a new product, exchange resources, gain advantages through its size, reduce costs, increase a competitive advantage etc. They could be either horizontal or vertical. The horizontal networks are established by manufacturers of similar or same goods. And the vertical networks are represented by a set of companies connected with one another in a 'supplier–receiver' relationship.

Third: Mining Companies Driving the Process

The subject structure of international logistic channels is created by mining companies, suppliers of materials and components, manufacturers, service providers, transport companies, warehouses and logistics centres, distributors and all the relationships between them.

Fourth: High Level of Customer Satisfaction

An international logistic channel is a quick, flexible and interconnected system driven by the mechanism of the customers' choice, aiming to achieve a high level of customer satisfaction, as well as, to gain the highest possible profit by the companies within this channel.

Fifth: High Degree of Process Orientation

Increased focus and process orientation for standardisation of business processes across countries in the network served as key drivers of global logistics operations. The international logistic channel can be described by means of the following characteristics: the process (the subject of the flow), the structure (the entity structure), and the objectives (the scope of action and the areas of cooperation of participating entities).

Sixth: Driven by Cost Quality Considerations

The range of international logistics channels consists of raw materials, auxiliary materials and cooperating elements, purchased on the supply market according to the need, passed on to the production process and finished products submitted for sale and delivered to the customer. The cost and quality consideration has driven the global logistics business.

Seventh: Channel Linked to Expertise in the Areas

Depending on the configuration of the international logistic channel, its links may consist of different kinds of mining, processing, service and trading companies. Their position within the channel results from the division of work in the next stages of production and sales of goods. Because of their role as senders and receivers of loads, as well as the accompanying information and finance streams, their basic role in the functioning of the international logistic channel is unquestionable.

Methods and Tools Facilitating International Logistics

Tools facilitating international logistics so that international logistics may function effectively and efficiently. If we effectively manage all participants and processes that constitute logistic channels, businesses can become more competitive and cost-effective.

Modern logistics management in reality is a decision-making process related to the synchronising of the physical, informational and financial supply and demand streams flowing between its participants so that they would gain competitive advantage and create added value with benefits for all its elements, customers and other stakeholders.

In supply international logistic chain management, many methods and devices are used, which have been and still are applied in effective economic systems management. To this group, we may include the following:

- **LM – Lean management**: This concept is about the elimination of all actions that do not create added value, that is such actions for which the customer would not pay. Or perceived value of the service will not improve.
- **AM – Agile management:** Agile management, in contrast to lean management, takes place under conditions of constant and unpredictable changes within the supply chain. Such cases

236 *Global Logistics Value Chain Management*

may be evoked by emergency situations (a temporarily organised supply chain in case of fires, floods, technical disasters etc.) or unplanned customer order.

- **ECR – Efficient consumer response** – It is a supply chain, including the Euro-logistic one, that is customer oriented. ECR is a modern strategy the foundation of which lies in the partnership of its participants – a synchronised supply management. It is a strategy to increase the level of services to consumers through close cooperation with retailers, wholesalers and distributors.

- **TQM – Total quality management** – The American Society for Quality has defined quality in the form of interdependent dimensions, as the characteristic features of a product or service that have impact on its ability to satisfy customer's specification as per contract every time at all interfaces.
- **BPR – Business process re-engineering** – BPR is the process of eliminating the non-value-adding and redundant services/activities from the end-to-end value chain.
- **TOC – Theory of constraints and queues** – Constraints in any business process limit or dictate the performance. TOC eliminates the constraints to improve performance. It has been observed that the .0.1% constraints can dictate 99.9% performance.
- **TBM – Time-based management** – Time-based management is an aspect of lean production. It is a general approach that recognises the importance of time and seeks to reduce the level of wasted time in the production processes of a business
- **JIT – Just-in-time** – In this, production lines up and delivers just when it is needed. It has driven global logistics business for improved performance and acted as a key driver. Sales order processing (SOP) and enterprise resource planning (ERP) helped logistics operators to perform better.
- **SCOR model – Supply Chain Operation Reference model** – In 1966, the SCC (Supply Chain Council), the organisation standardising supply support systems, published the Supply Chain Operation Reference (SCOR) model, which is used for description and comprehensive analysis of the supply chain. This model is continuously updated; the latest version of SCOR model bears number, was published in May 2008 and has been successfully applied in Euro logistics.
- **VMI – Vendor-managed Inventory** – Cost reduction, shortening the time of reaction to the customer's needs and the optimisation of inventory level in the supplier–customer relation are the main areas of interest and management in Euro-logistic channels.

Storage Facility

Storage facility generally refers to the stationery period involved with respect to merchandise because inventory is stored in the warehouse. The location decisions, addresses and how many distribution centres to have and where to locate them depend on various factors including cost, customer location and cluster of customers, availability of the infrastructure as well as service quality and frequency. The storage facilities abroad can differ in availability and quality, which need to be carefully assessed. The logistician should analyse international product sales and then rank order products according to warehousing needs. The storage facilities can be of various types and sizes depending on the purpose and quantity of the stock kept in those facilities. These facilities can be called logistics centres.

Logistics Centres (Nodal Points)

The function of logistics centres is to ensure the efficient movement of products within the region. Euro logistics has nodal points of nodal logistics network, which in practice,

Global Logistics Value Chain Management   237

depending on the time of formation, classification, purpose and strategy would be called the following:

- Storage building
- Storage centre
- Logistic services centre
- Distribution centre
- Logistics park
- Logistics hub

Decentralised Logistics System

When a firm serves many diverse international markets, total centralisation might leave the firm unresponsive to local adaptation needs. If each subsidiary is made a profit centre in itself, each one carries the full responsibility for its performance. Once products are within a specific market, increased input from local logistics operation should be expected and encouraged. When the market to be serviced is too wide and spread out centralised management of logistics will not be cost-effective and easy to control. The local logistics industry also performs and practices its own methods based on the available logistics infrastructure and business practices which a local logistics company can perform with much higher effectiveness. Decentralisation of logistics functions and system makes good sense in terms of managing global logistics value chain.

Outsourcing Logistics Services

The systematic outsourcing of logistics capabilities is the third option. Outsourcing logistics function is a very common practice in the industry. This saves a lot of resources and also reduces complexity. By collaborating with transportation firms, private warehouses or other specialists, corporate resources can be concentrated on the firm's core products and functions. For example, a company like Hero Moto Corp Ltd., formerly Hero Honda, is an Indian motorcycle and scooter manufacturer based in New Delhi, India. The company is the largest two-wheeler manufacturer in the world, and also in India, where it has a market share of about 46% in the two-wheeler category. The company has outsourced its logistics services to a third party who collects goods ex-factory and manages the transportation, distribution and delivery functions both for domestic and the international market. Operating at arm's length with third-party logistics company is advantageous in the sense that cost is less, there is flexibility and it prevents blocking of corporate resources.

Logistics and Environment

Since environmental laws and regulations differ across the globe, the firm's efforts need to be responsive to a wide variety of requirements. Reverse distribution systems are instrumental in ensuring that the firm not only delivers the product to the market but also can retrieve it from the market for subsequent recycling or disposal. Companies need to learn how to simultaneously achieve both environmental and economic goals.

Firm's Value Chain

The generic value chain of any firm is as shown in Figure 9.1 consisting of some primary functions of the business and supported by some support functions. The support functions help the business to perform its primary functions well.

The Value Chain

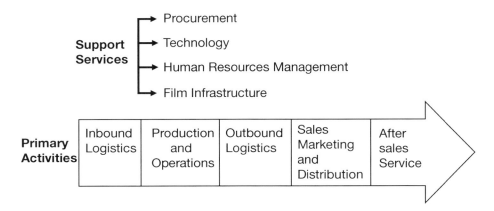

Figure 9.1 Firm's Value Chain
Source: Competitive Advantage, Michael E Porter, The Free Press (1985)

In firm's value chain, the company's activities are divided into technologically and economically distinct activities that the company performs in doing business. 'Value activities' are nine generic activities (split into two categories: primary and support) the value of which is the amount that buyers are willing to pay for a product or service. 'Primary activities' are those involved in the physical creation of the product or service. 'Support activities' provide the inputs and infrastructure that allow the primary activity to take place.

A company's value chain is a system of interdependent activities. A value chain for a company in a particular industry is embedded in a larger stream of activities that is called 'value system'. The various elements of the logistics value chain covering logistics and value-added services along the entire supply chain will include raw material procurement and inbound logistics, production and operations and outbound logistics and warehousing and distribution and return logistics to bring back the goods not needed or returned for any reasons.

Transforming the Value Chain

Businesses have both primary activities and support activities, and logistics is all pervasive. Value chain can be transformed by improving the business processes as well as using relevant and appropriate technology. For example, firm's administrative infrastructure can be improved by implementing office automation system. Similarly, the HRM function can be outsourced as well as can be improved by workforce planning system. Procurement function these days are remarkably improved and is technology driven. EDI can help improve procurement function and like that designing and technology can be transformed by use of CAD/CAM in the business. These are all support activities in the business.

Global Logistics Value Chain Management 239

In terms of primary activities, inbound logistics can be transformed by implementing automated warehousing whereas outbound logistics can be transformed by implementing WMS and automated shipment scheduling. Computerised ordering and ERP as well as CRM can significantly improve the value in the areas of sales, marketing and customer service. Even process changes can bring in significant improvement and transform the firm's value chain in the areas of sales, marketing and customer service. In the operations and manufacturing or production function infusion of technology such as computer-controlled and programmed machines, robotics and artificial intelligence can greatly transform and unlock hidden value in the business.

Linkages within Value Chain

The same function can be performed in different ways – for example, conformance to specifications can be achieved through high-quality purchase input, specifying close tolerances in manufacturing process or even 100% inspection of finished goods. Cost or performance of direct activities is improved by greater efforts in indirect activities, for example, better scheduling (an indirect activity) reduces sales force travel time or delivery vehicle time (direct activities) or better maintenance improves tolerances achieved by machines. Activities performed inside a firm reduce the need to demonstrate, explain or service a product in the field, for example, 100% inspection can substantially reduce service costs in the field but will significantly increase the inspection cost and time. An enterprise value chain is linked and interconnected with its supplier's value chain, channel and distribution partner's value chain as well buyer's value chain. Linkage among activities not only connects value activities inside a company but also creates interdependence between its value chain and those of its suppliers and channel partners. Businesses need to manage the buyer's and supplier's value chain effectively to create incremental value in the business.

Corporations which are operating on a global scale also need a global logistics management strategy from the considerations of business objectives and how those objectives would be measured from the perspectives of shareholders as well as customers to align the key organisational processes to achieve the stated goal. In that strategic roadmap organisation's logistics performance and cost indicators are also required to be analysed and measured. The key organisational processes have to be synchronised across all regional markets. The logistics function has to be managed to ensure the movement and distribution of products to ensure product availability in all markets at least cost of delivery. This has been shown schematically in Figure 9.2.

Businesses have to be managed for support functions to ensure performance of primary functions as indicated in the firm's value chain for optimum performance. Many businesses are focused on volume performance by preferentially focusing on the primary functions instead of the results in terms of incremental value created in the business. To help create value in the business, functional activities in the value chain need to be closely monitored for results and for that financial control, profit and cost control, and value-based management are required.

International Business

International trade is in reality an extension of domestic trade. International trade would thus mean the import and export activities carried out by any nation with another nation or by any company in one country with a company in another country. For example, Japan is a highly

240 *Global Logistics Value Chain Management*

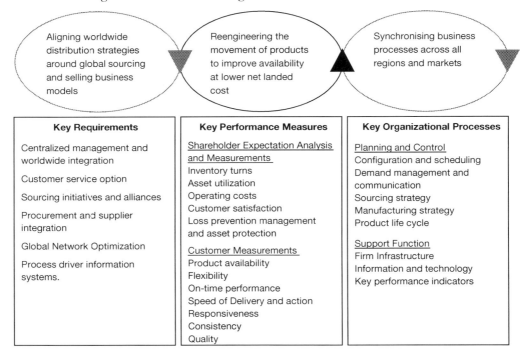

Figure 9.2 Global Logistics Strategy Drivers

industrialised country. The country exports high-quality machinery and imports agricultural products from Malaysia. Other examples of international trade are as follows:

- The exchange of services or goods between different countries.
- When the residents or businesses of two or more different countries do the transactions of sale and purchase of goods or services.

Features of International Trade

International trade is controlled and guided by various regulations which can be both country-specific as well as global trade practices and as per guidelines of World Trade Organization (WTO) signed by 164 countries. The World Trade Organization is an inter-governmental organisation created to regulate global trade between nations. The key features of international trade are as follows:

- **Involvement of different monetary units:** Each country has its own currency for domestic trade but for international trade only globally tradable and accepted currency are used, for example, USD and Euro.
- **Imposition of restrictions on import and export by various countries:** To protect the domestic manufacturers and trade, each country normally puts some restrictions on both imports into and exports out of the country.

Global Logistics Value Chain Management   241

- **Imposition of restrictions on release of foreign currencies:** Depending on the foreign exchange reserve of the country which has to be used for essential imports like oil or other essential goods, the foreign exchange is regulated in each country.
- **Existence of multiple regulations:** There exists both global and country-specific regulations that govern the global trade making it more complex for the operators.
- **Legal practices and rules in different countries:** Although there are regulations which govern international trade, legal framework of each country in global trade would be different and one has to familiarise with the local legal requirements, processes and practices for doing business in that country.

International Logistics Challenges

There are numerous challenges that global logistics players have to face to deliver performance. While effective logistic system is important for domestic operations, it is absolutely critical for global manufacturing and marketing. Domestic logistics focuses on performing value-added services in a relatively controlled environment. It is imperative that global logistics operations must accommodate all domestic requirements and also deal with growing uncertainties associated with distance, demand, diversity and documentation. In global trade the customers are demanding in terms of quality, lead time and order fulfilment criteria. The marketers need to have clear understanding of changing customer needs and expectations. The firms must be more and more flexible and proactive to anticipate and adapt to such changes. The quest for flexibility and reactivity affects the conception and the management of firms and more generally their logistic systems and contributes to the development of partnership relations, to the emergence of mergers or strategic alliances between companies. As a result, a firm can no longer be considered as an isolated entity but as a component of a wider supply chain network.

Operating challenges faced by global logistics systems vary significantly within operating regions. North American logistics vision is one of open geography with extensive demand for land-based transportation and limited need for cross-border documentation. European logistics views operations from a perspective characterised by relatively compact geography involving numerous political, cultural, regulatory and language barriers. Pacific Rim logistics has an island perspective that requires extensive water or air shipment to transcend vast distances. In the past, enterprises could survive and also could achieve substantial success with a unique north American, European or Pacific Rim logistics regional capability. This is still true for some firms. Those intending to grow regional capabilities are required to extend service zones. For global scale operations and economies, enterprises are developing global logistic expertise. Effective logistic system is important for domestic operations, but it is absolutely critical for global manufacturing and marketing. Domestic logistics focuses on performing value-added services in a relatively controlled environment.

Global logistics operations must accommodate all domestic requirements and also deal with growing uncertainties associated with distance, demand, diversity and documentation. Operating challenges faced by global logistics systems vary significantly within operating regions. North American logistics vision is one of open geography with extensive demand for land-based transportation and limited need for cross-border documentation. European logistics views operations from a perspective characterised by relatively compact geography involving numerous political, cultural, regulatory and language barriers. Firms intending to expand globally need to assess the barriers that they have to overcome.

Logistics principle is the same domestically and globally, operating environments are more complex and costly. Cost and complexity are represented by four Ds – distance (longer),

242 *Global Logistics Value Chain Management*

documents (extensive), diversity in culture (wide variation with cultural difference) and demand of customers (variable and fluctuating demand). Developing appropriate strategies and tactics to respond to these four Ds is a challenge for logistics management.

Barriers to Global Logistics

While many forces facilitate borderless operations, some significant barriers continue to impede global logistics. Every country is concerned about balance of trade, which has a reflection on the country's economy. Three significant barriers are as follows:

- Markets and competition
- Financial barriers and
- Distribution channels

Market and competition will cover entry restrictions, availability of information (market size, demographics, competition, infrastructure) and pricing. Competition law, transfer pricing, anti-dumping law. Entry restrictions limit market access by placing legal and physical barriers on import.

Protection of domestic industry by favourable tax structure and unfavourable import duty also acts as barriers in global trade. In addition, complex duty structure and compliance issues add to the barriers and challenges. Financial barriers normally result from forecasting and institutional infrastructures. Difficulty in forecasting in global environment considering customer trends, seasonality and competitive action. As such barriers to global trade can be broadly classified as trade barriers which are normally in terms of custom duties, and non-trade barriers which will be due to operational hurdles and other constraints which can be country-specific, including standards and specifications and other statutory requirements acting as hurdles in global trade.

In global environment custom laws, government policies and complexities compound the difficulty in forecasting. Facilitating intermediaries such as banks, insurance firms, legal counsellors and transport carriers. Logistics manager must allow for additional inventory, transportation lead time and financial resources to operate globally.

Distribution channel difference, infrastructure and trade agreements also act as barriers confronting global logistics manager. Difference in transportation and material-handling equipment, warehouse and port facilities and communication systems are such barriers.

Recently, efforts have been made to improve standardisation with respect to containerisation. However, major differences still exist with respect to transportation equipment, vehicle dimension, capacity, weight, rail gauge and so on. When infrastructure is not standardised, it is necessary for the products to be unloaded and reloaded into different vehicles or containers as they cross national boundaries, resulting in increased cost and time.

Impact of Globalisation on International Logistics

Globalisation brings homogenisation of consumer needs, liberalisation of trade and competitive advantages of operating in global markets. Companies are forced to think and act globally in order to survive in such a dynamic environment. All these elements have a deep impact on the development and positioning of companies in international marketplaces where competition is cruel.

Role of Global Logistics

Globalisation has helped in doing businesses beyond the national boundaries. Internet has made it easier, and world has become really a global village. Cargo movement is done physically using available options. Physical movement of cargo, intermediaries, freight forwarders and custom-house are indispensable. Knowledge, connectivity and documentation are crucial areas. Global operations of business increase complexity. Decrease in control over movement of goods is a challenge in global logistics operations.

Supply Chain and the Internet

Because of the Internet, firms are able to conduct many more global comparisons among suppliers and select from a wider variety of choices. When customer has the ability to access a company, they must be prepared for 24-hour order-taking and customer service. For all countries, but particularly in developing nations, the issue of universal access to the Internet is crucial.

Global Logistics Capabilities

Global logistics capabilities must include international transportation, cultural diversity, Multi-language capability and extended supply chain operations. Global operations increase logistics cost and complexity. As complexity and operational uncertainty increases in global logistics, control capability decreases. Control problems result from extensive use of intermediaries coupled with government intervention in customs requirement and trade restrictions and control.

Global Operating Levels of Logistics Companies

There are five levels of enterprise evolution from domestic logistics operation to becoming global logistics operator. These are:

* Level 1: Arm's length
* Level 2: Internal export
* Level 3: Internal operations
* Level 4: Insider business practices
* Level 5: Denationalised operations

Arm's Length

It is a preferred method of operation for players with limited international experience. Enterprise with limited international experience either sells or consigns its goods to the international specialist which accepts responsibility for ordering, providing international transportation, completing documentation as well as coordinating marketing, inventory management, invoicing and product support. The advantage is that it reduces risk substantially. However, the disadvantage is that it also reduces margins considerably. Also, loss of control in product and logistics operations.

Internal Export

When players develop the expertise to coordinate and manage international transportation and documentation, they graduate to this mode of operation. However, local agents or distributors are retained to provide marketing, inventory management, invoicing and

244　*Global Logistics Value Chain Management*

product support. The advantage is that margins are improved because of part control but full benefits are still not derived. And the disadvantage is that it reduces sensitivity to local requirements for not being involved in distribution and in sales, distribution and marketing for international market.

Internal Operations

At this level, companies would have local market presence in foreign countries, characterised by development of operations in the local or foreign country (local market presence). Internal operations include marketing, sales, production and distribution. Companies would engage parent company's people and follow parent company's practices and not engage local employees for better control and low-risk internal operations. The advantage is that it has a relatively lower level of risk, and there will be further increase in control and sensitivity. However, the disadvantage is that it still relies heavily on home country values, procedures and operations.

Insider Business Practices

This is a level up from the earlier level of operations in the sense that this further internalises international operations and follows local business practices by hiring host country management, marketing and sales organisations and even local business systems and practices, and, as it grows, a separate host country business philosophy emerges. The advantage is still a further increase in control and sensitivity at manageable risk. However, the disadvantage is that home country business practices and philosophy will still be dominant, and home country expectations and standards will still be applicable.

Denationalised Operations

This level operates and maintains foreign country operations and develops regional headquarters to oversee the coordination of operations in the area. Denationalised operations maintain foreign country operations and develop regionalised headquarters to oversee coordination of operations in the area. At this stage, enterprise is stateless in the sense that no specific home or parent country dominates policy. Local marketing and sales organisations supported by worldclass manufacturing and logistics operations. Also product sourcing and marketing decisions are made across a wide range of global alternatives. Systems and processes are designed to meet individual country requirement and aggregated to share knowledge and for financial reporting, acting as truly international or global company.

Global Operations Level

Most enterprises engaged in global logistics are operating at levels 2, 3 and 4. But truly international firms must focus on level 5 or denationalising operations. Enterprises at any of the other levels will retain a home country perspective. Denationalising operations require a significant level of management trust across countries and cultures, which can grow only when managers live and work in other cultures. A strong system approach and orientation is also a must. As the global operational levels progress, there is an increasing dependency on system and also on the process of integration.

Stages of Regional Integration

Four stages of economic integration are as follows:

- Free Trade Agreement
- Customs Union
- Common Market
- Economic Union

Free Trade Agreement

FTA normally is signed between friendly countries to facilitate trade which eliminates tariffs on trade between countries in a region. This helps when the participants in the free-trade area expect to gain by specialising in the production of goods and services in which it has comparative advantages and by importing such products and services from other countries in agreement in which it faces comparative disadvantages. In such a situation, trades among countries give them less expensive access to a number of goods. FTA as such may either stimulate or reduce international trade, and it can also reduce the access of the firms to more efficient producers or markets outside their region. FTA must ensure the complementarity. India has such FTA with countries in the Association of Southeast Asians Nations (ASEAN).

Customs Union

Customs union eliminates tariffs between member countries and establishes common external tariff structure towards other regions and non-member countries. Advantage of a customs union is that none of the member nations in the union can position themselves to gain a tariff advantage at the expense of other countries. Member countries are required to give some control over economic policies to the group.

Common Market

The tariff policy of common market is similar to that of the customs union. In addition, a common market allows factors of production such as labour and capital as well as goods and people to move freely between member countries as dictated by market conditions. This has a considerable impact on the local economy of the countries working as a common market as people move from relatively weaker economy country to stronger economy country.

Economic Union

This is the most advanced stage of development because it implies harmonisation of economic policies beyond a common market. Under this arrangement, member countries standardise the monetary and fiscal policies and although not essential but normally economic union likely to include common currency and harmonised tax structure. Here all goods and production factors can move freely according to market conditions and demands. and no major fluctuations in monetary exchange and interest rates will occur as we can see happening in the EU.

246 *Global Logistics Value Chain Management*

Complexity of Logistics Management

End-to-end logistics management covers delivering input material to the industry and then taking output to end consumers at the least cost. This would entail the following:

- Trade inventory – low
- Delivery time-fastest and timely
- Efficient system
- Failure rate – low
- Order fill rate and pack fill rate – accurate

Efficient service delivery at lower cost provides competitive advantage to business. Logistics cost in typical distribution of FMCG products in India would be anything up to 10–15% of end selling price including freight, insurance and warehousing but exclude channel margins. Managing it effectively obviously provides competitive advantage to the business in terms of distinctive cost advantage.

Entry of Global Retailers in Indian Market

Global retailers like Walmart, Tesco etc. have already entered the Indian market competing with local retailers like Big Bazar, More, Reliance etc. Global wholesalers (cash & carry format) like Booker, and Metro (Macro) also operating in the Indian market competing with local wholesalers like Reliance and Bharti Retail. Global online retailers like Amazon.com and e-bay also entered India and are competing with local e-retailers like Flipkart.com and SnapDeal.com. Overall retail market is about USD 300 billion growing at 6% every year. Together they only control about 4% of the total market. Rest is still covered in traditional mode of distribution

Retail density – 13 million retail outlets, 95% mom & pop stores. Organised retailing only 4–5%. Channel Intermediaries are large in numbers consisting of C&F agents, wholesalers, semi-wholesalers, consignment agents, super-stockists, distributors and retailers.

India has about 13 million retailers – 95% of those are small family-owned mom-pop stores. Even large global companies like P&G, Unilever, Nestle and Phillips which are operating in the Indian soil for over several decades can reach about 1 to 2 million retailers through their own network. Smaller players will not have the reach more than 0.5 million. The remaining market has to be covered through redistribution route. Traditional channel has limited reach. Innovation in channel management holds the key. Global logistics companies like DHL and FedEx are also operating in India competing with local players like GATI, Safe Express etc. and many more. 3P logistics providers offer only point-to-point service in B2B mode. The entire spectrum of the chain is never covered. Logistics industry has large, medium, small and tiny operators offering connectivity and control at various levels. Last-mile connectivity is always a challenge.

No single model will work for all markets. Some markets are reached through the wholesale route. Some markets are covered through organised retail route. Some markets are through dealer distribution network. Some markets are through super-stockists/consignment agents/C&F agents. No one model will work for all markets.

Logistics – A Source of Competitive Advantage

Procurement effectiveness of all these players is more or less the same. Success will depend on competitive advantage from efficient supply chain management – mainly logistics. Competitive advantage will have to be derived from the following:

- Time to deliver goods to the customer
- Reducing inventory in the system without losing out on delivery commitment
- Logistics cost which is the only source of competitive advantage is smart management of logistics

Supply chain delays and uncertainty are a major constraint to manufacturing growth and competitiveness. According to a World Bank report, halving the delays due to roadblocks, tolls and other stoppages could cut freight times by 20–30% and logistics costs by 30–40%. This alone can boost the manufacturing sectors by 3–4% of net sales. There are around 650 checkpoints at 29 state and 7 Union territory borders across India. Regulatory checks on the movement of goods across these borders raise truck transit times by as much as 25%.

Value Chain in Sales

Sales value chain will cover and include all processes from receiving the sales order to processing, executing as well as servicing the sales order. When customer places an order, it needs to be processed and executed as per customer's requirement as stipulated in the order. And post execution of the order customer has to be serviced as per commitment, which may include installation of the unit or equipment, demonstration and grievance redressal or attending to the complaints of the customer. Each stage of the processes starting from receiving the order to services has to conform to the contract and has to be competitive. The following parameters have to be continuously improved by benchmarking with the competition and industry practices:

- Sales order receiving
- Sales order processing
- Sales order executing
- Sales order servicing

As international trade continues to grow, imperatives on improving logistics would be as follows:

- Customers are more knowledgeable and demand higher quality, lower costs and better service.
- Competition is getting fiercer, and organisations must look at every opportunity to remain competitive.
- There is changing power in the supply chain. Very large retail chains demand customised logistics from their suppliers.
- Other changes in retail markets include the growth of 24-hour opening, home deliveries, out-of-town malls, retail parks, telephone and online shopping.
- Organisations are introducing new types of operation, such as JIT, flexible manufacturing, customised service, on-demand stock deliver and so on.
- Some organisations are turning from a product focus to a process focus. This encourages improvement to operations, including logistics.

248 *Global Logistics Value Chain Management*

- There have been considerable improvements in communication technologies.
- Organisations are increasing cooperation through alliances, partnerships, alliances, collaboration and other arrangements.
- Managers are recognising the strategic importance of the supply chain.
- Attitudes towards transport are changing because of increased congestion on roads, concerns about air quality and pollution, broader environmental issues and so on.

INTEGRATED SUPPLY CHAIN AND LOGISTICS VALUE CHAIN

Management Challenges for Integrated Supply Chain

Management challenges and complexities with respect to integrated supply chain will increase with the number of links within a business process, which can range from low to high (Ellram and Cooper, 1990; Houlihan, 1985), thus adding more management components or levels of each component can lead to an increase in the level of integration. Existing literature in BPR and SCM suggests various components requiring management attention. Lambert and Cooper (2000) have identified the following components:

- Planning and control
- Work structure
- Organisation structure
- Product flow facility structure
- Information flow facility structure
- Management methods
- Power and leadership structure
- Risk and reward structure
- Culture and attitude

But a more careful study needs to be done on previously identified supply chain business processes to understand what kind of relationship the components might have which are related to suppliers and customers.

However, a more careful examination of the existing literature leads to a more comprehensive understanding of what should be the key critical supply chain components, the 'branches' of the previous identified supply chain business processes, that is, what kind of relationship the components may have that are related to suppliers and customers.

Optimising the End-to-end Value Chain through an Integrated Solution

Well-managed supply chain processes are an important differentiator in the highly competitive environment of commoditised markets. Supply chain transparency is a key and companies are increasingly developing one-stop-shops for supply chain information and reporting.

Integrated performance management in supply chain and operations focuses on the following:

- A common understanding of supply chain objectives and disciplined target-setting
- Goal-oriented information on target achievements to all relevant stakeholders and the addressing of key messages to executives, managers and professionals
- Supply chain transparency by considering and aligning supply chain processes and technology with the organisational structure

- Aligned and agreed-upon supply chain metrics covering all perspectives in supply chain management and also process performance indicators to enable root cause analyses in the event of deviations
- Integrated technical solutions for the gathering of information and the distribution of reports covering the full cycle from planning to reporting to intervention
- A flexible enterprise data warehouse and the adaptability of metrics, reports and layouts

Multifaceted Analytical Functions

To understand the impact of issues arising out of say, the delivery failure or delay in servicing a customer order resulting in rescheduling or even in disputation in the total SCM function, supply chain performance management (SCPM) must have multifaceted analytical functionality. In such a situation, SCPM can help by comparing real-term demand, actual stock in transit, physical inventories in the system as well as consumption that can become a valuable input to materials management and planning. This would help the business to achieve an overall optimisation between logistics and transport cost, ensuring on-site inventories at the lowest level while ensuring the requirement of production and supply. To achieve this optimisation, every individual step has to be digitalised and added to the integrated software services of SCPM which would include the evaluation of the suppliers as well as carriers' delivery performance, analyses of inventory as well as of demand, transport costs, comparison on various targets against actual performance etc. to the level of relating to components or parts.

Integrated Logistics System

Integrated logistics system is an iterative process for developing the support strategy that optimises and leverages existing resources. An integrated system will help the businesses in the following ways:

- Integrated logistics system on strategic level is to minimise the logistics cost by concentration on core business processes and the transaction costs by getting the best relationship and cooperation between the parties involved.
- To reduce logistic costs, focus on core business processes is necessary. Core business of the company could be both primary and support. It is also required to eliminate non-value-adding processes to reduce logistic costs.

Integration of Logistics with the Organisation

Real-time customer demand can be met through the appropriate planning, control and implementation of the effective movement and storage information of goods and services from the point of origin to destination if logistics system is integrated with various functions within the organisation.

- Integrating logistics within an organisation has all the related activities working together as a single function.
- This is responsible for all storage and movement of materials throughout the organisation. It tackles problems from the viewpoint of the whole organisation and looks for the greatest overall benefit.

250 *Global Logistics Value Chain Management*

- In practice, it is difficult to integrate all the logistics within an organisation.
- The supply chain consists of many different activities, with different types of operation, using different systems and geographically dispersed.

Stages of Integration

The entire process of integration happens through stages of development of logistics function as part of the overall supply chain. There is increased consideration of how logistics will impact customer service, procurement and manufacturing to achieve productivity enhancements and cost reduction through competitive benchmarking and continuous improvement. This can be achieved through the following:

1 Separate logistics activities are not given much attention or considered important.
2 Recognising that the separate activities of logistics are important for the success of the organisation.
3 Making improvements in the separate functions, making sure that each is as efficient as possible.
4 *Internal integration* – Recognising the benefits of internal cooperation and combining the separate functions into one.
5 Developing a logistics strategy, to set the long-term direction of logistics.
6 *Benchmarking* – Comparing logistics' performance with other organisations, learning from their experiences, identifying areas that need improvement and finding ways of achieving this.
7 *Continuous Improvement* – Accepting that further changes are inevitable and always searching for better ways of organising logistics.

Benefits of Integration

The benefits of integration are as follows:

- **Genuine cooperation:** Between all parts of the supply chain, with shared information and resources.
- **Lower costs:** Due to balanced operations, lower stocks, less expediting, economies of scale, elimination of activities that waste time or do not add value.
- **Improved performance:** Due to more accurate forecasts, better planning, higher productivity of resources, rational priorities and so on.
- **Improved material flow:** With coordination giving faster and more reliable movements.
- **Better customer service:** With shorter lead times, faster deliveries and more customisation.
- **More flexibility:** With organisations reacting faster to changing conditions.
- **Standardised procedures:** Becoming routine and well-practised with less duplication of effort, information, planning and so on.
- **Reliable quality and fewer inspections:** With integrated quality management programmes.
- **Integration can be difficult and involve major changes:** There are, however, many benefits, and most companies have moved in the direction of internal integration.
- **Extending integration to more organisations in the supply chain:** There are several ways of organising this external integration, ranging from informal agreements to vertical integration. The most popular has some form of strategic alliance or partnership.
- First step is to achieve internal integration and then attempt external integration.

Logistics and Security

Logistics systems and modern transportation systems are often the targets of attacks. The need to institute new safeguards for international shipments will affect the ability of firm to efficiently plan their international shipment.

Logistics Security Issue

- Traditional security issues are follows:

  - Pilferage
  - Theft
  - Burglary
  - Cargo contents – tempering

- Since the terrorist attacks of September 2001, security has taken an increasingly significant role in the global supply chain.
- Manufacturing, transporting and delivering goods safely and securely are as important and as complex.
- Credential of participants in the supply chain need to be verified.
- Screening and validation of contents of the cargo being shipped.
- Advance notification of the contents to the destination country.
- Ensuring the security of cargo while in transit – use of locks and tamper-proof seals.
- Inspecting cargo on entry.
- Security of cargo is always a big challenge.
- In ocean cargo, nuclear bombs, radioactive material and explosive weapons or even terrorist operatives can be concealed in marine containers.
- The speed at which today's supply chain operates. It can be very difficult to reconcile with the security measures.
- Air transportation system has clearly been the mode of choice for terrorists, so air cargo is of special concern.
- Air cargo is vulnerable to a number of potential terrorist action – a bomb placed in cargo carried on a passenger plane could lead to a mass casualty event.
- A stowaway in a cargo freighter could hijack the place and use it as a weapon.

Supply Chain Security Initiatives in USA

Supply chains face a broad range of threats, ranging from physical threats to cyber security threats. The physical threats are perhaps the more blatant and obvious ones that can occur at various points along the supply chain. Think of terrorists disrupting a supply chain by attacking oil infrastructure. Supply chain terrorism is, in fact, a great concern for many countries. The supply chain security initiatives that are adopted in the USA are as follows.

- The Customs Trade Partnership against Terrorism (C-TPAT), a voluntary compliance programme for companies to improve the security of their corporate supply chains.
- The World Customs Organization (WCO) adopted the Framework of Standards to Secure and Facilitate Global Trade in 2005, which consists of supply chain security

252 *Global Logistics Value Chain Management*

standards for Customs administrations including Authorised Economic Operator (AEO) programmes.
- The Container Security Initiative (CSI), a programme led by US Customs and Border Protection in the Department of Homeland Security focused on screening containers at foreign ports.
- The Global Container Control Programme (CCP), a joint United Nations Office on Drugs and Crime (UNODC)/World Customs Organization (WCO) initiative working to establish effective container controls at select ports across the globe with the aim to prevent trafficking of drugs, chemicals and other contraband and to facilitate trade by strengthening cooperation between the customs, trade and enforcement communities.
- The Global Trade Exchange, a DHS data-mining programme designed to collect financial information about shipments, with the objective of determining safety of cargo shipments are safe.
- Efforts for countries around the world to implement and enforce the International Ship and Port Facility Security Code (ISPS Code), an agreement of 148 countries that are members of the International Maritime Organization (IMO).
- Pilot initiatives by companies in the private sector to track and monitor the integrity of cargo containers moving around the world using technologies such as RFID and GPS.
- The International Organization for Standardization have released a series of Standards for the establishment and management of supply chain security. ISO/PAS 28000 *Specification for Security Management Systems for the Supply Chain* offers public and private enterprise an international high-level management standard that enables organisations to utilise a globally consistent management approach to applying supply chain security initiatives.

Technology to Tackle Security

Creation of open smart manufacturing platform and network-based information technologies, blockchain technology, scanning etc. can help in tracking security concerns. The following are a few examples.

- A Boston-based company has developed a scanning technology that breaks down every item in a cargo container and provides the makeup of the cargo within – this tool could be a game changer.
- Cooperation among supply chain partners (including shippers, intermediaries, carriers, ports and government agencies) along with active data exchange, proper funding for security initiatives and effective technologies are all needed to secure the global supply chain.

Logistics Industry in India

A glimpse into various industrial sectors highlights the anticipated upsurge in trade and commerce and the consequent growth in the need for a strong logistics industry:

- Indian logistics sector is 13% of its GDP. This is both significant and inefficient.
- India's nominal GDP has grown from USD 3.17 trillion in 2021, USD 3.5 trillion in 2022 to currently to USD 3.75 trillion in 2023 at an annual growth rate of approximately 7%.
- India is currently the fifth-largest economy in the world.
- By 2030, India's crude steel production is expected to increase by a factor of 4.

Global Logistics Value Chain Management 253

- The demand for cement in the country is expected to double by 2030.
- Agricultural output, although reduced in size as a percentage of the economy, is expected to increase from 207 million metric tons (MMT) to 295 MMT by 2020.
- The Indian textiles industry is expected to triple from USD 78 billion currently to USD 220 billion by 2020.
- The share of organised retail is expected to increase from 15% currently to 25% by 2025.
- India's industrial energy consumption is expected to double by 2020. In this scenario, the country will need to mine 2 billion tonnes of coal by 2030 and transport 75% of mined coal. Further, around 30% of total transported coal will have to be imported through ports.
- Overall export-import (EXIM) cargo at Indian ports is increased to 1300 MMT in 2022 from 1208 MMT in 2018.
- Finished consumer goods, both imported and those produced in India, will have to be transported to the country's middle-class consumers, which, by 2030, are expected to increase fourfold from the current middle-class population of 160 million.
- Because of the constraints in the logistics infrastructure and more particularly in the road transport infrastructure, there is a negative impact on India's GDP growth (Table 9.1).
- A comparison of logistics performance index based on the data of 2014 between India, China and Germany has been shown in Figure 8.3 to indicate that India is well below in terms of global ranking.

Table 9.1 Comparison on Key Parameters: India versus Global

Logistics Efficiency Indicators	India	Global
Road Transportation		
Average truck speed (in kmph)	30–40	60–80 (China)
Four-lane road length (in km)	7000	34,000 (China)
National highway length (in km)	66,540	190,000
Average surface freight (in cents/km)	~7	3.7 (Japan)
Average distance travelled by a truck per day (in km)	200	400
Air Transportation		
Airport waiting time – Exports (in hours)	50	12
Airport waiting time – Imports (in hours)	182	24
Aviation turbine fuel as a % of operating cost	35–40%	20–25%
Ports & Sea Transportation		
Turnaround time at ports (in hours)	84	7
Annual container handling capacity	8.4 mm TEUs	60 mm TEUs
Containers handled per ship, per hour (maximum)	15	25–30
Throughout density (maximum)	45,000 TEUs/hectare	17,000–220,000 TEUs
Warehousing		
Average inventory days	33	24 (China)
Others		
3 PL share of logistics	9–10%	57% (USA)

254 *Global Logistics Value Chain Management*

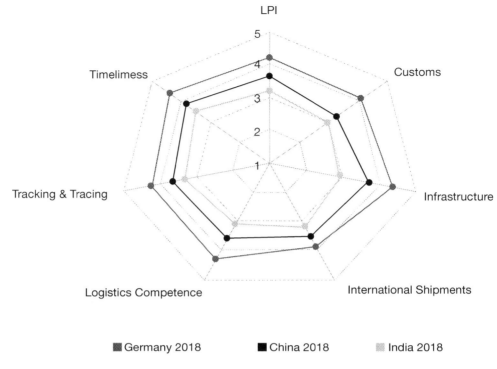

Figure 9.3 India against Global Indicators of Logistics Infrastructure

Table 9.2 Logistics Performance Index of India, China and Germany on Select Parameters[1]

Country Parameter	Germany 2018 Germany	China 2018 China	India 2018 India
LPI Rank	1	26	44
Customs	1	31	40
Infrastructure	1	20	52
International shipments	4	18	44
Logistics competence	1	27	42
Tracking & tracing	2	27	38
Timeliness	3	27	52

Case Study: Anand Milk Producers Union Limited (AMUL)

AMUL means priceless in Sanskrit 'Amoolya'. Brand name managed by an apex cooperative organisation – GCMMF (Gujarat Cooperative Milk Marketing Federation) producer of the World's biggest vegetarian cheese brand, world's largest pouched milk brand. AMUL, which is also the largest food brand in India, spurred the white revolution in India. It has accreditation with 9001 and HACCP certification by QAS, Australia.

The AMUL is a cooperative dairy founded in 1946 having annual revenue of INR 292.25 billion or USD 4.1 billion in 2017–2018. AMUL is the world's largest milk producer in the world. More

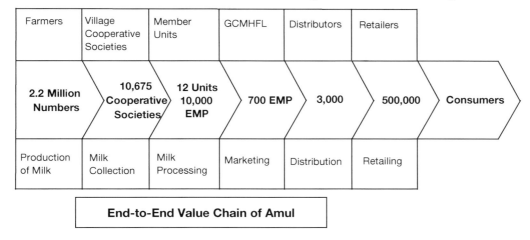

Figure 9.4 AMUL Value Chain

than 15 million milk producers pour their milk in 144,500 dairy cooperative societies across the country. One hundred and eighty-four district cooperative unions marketed by 22 state marketing federations and 18544 village societies. Total milk handling capacity of AMUL is 32 million litres per day. AMUL manufactures a wide range of milk, milk powder, health beverages, cheese, ghee, butter, ice cream and traditional Indian sweets and milk products as well as chocolates. It operates through 56 sales offices, having a dealers network of 10,000 and directly servicing one million retail outlets (Figure 9.4).

Logistics Challenge of AMUL

Procurement Logistics

- Handling of 32 million litres of milk per day
- From about 18,544 separate village cooperative societies
- Approximately 15 million milk-producing member
- 144,500 dairy cooperative societies across the country, 184 district cooperative unions marketed by 22 state marketing federation and 18,544 village societies

Logistics/Coordination

- Storing and transportation of the milk from collection centres to production centres and then to consumers
- Distributing milk and milk products through 10,000 distributors and more than 1 million retailers

Coordination between Participating Entities

The participating entities on the inbound side are as follows:

- Village Dairy Cooperative Society (VDCS)
- State Cooperative Milk Federation

256 *Global Logistics Value Chain Management*

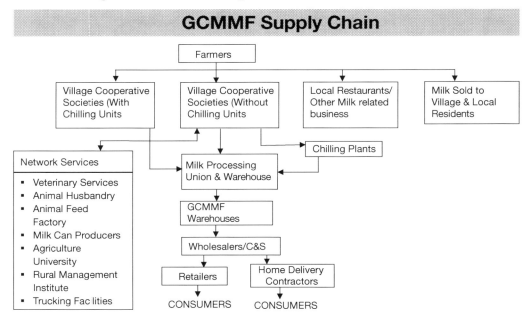

Figure 9.5 Supply Chain Network of AMUL

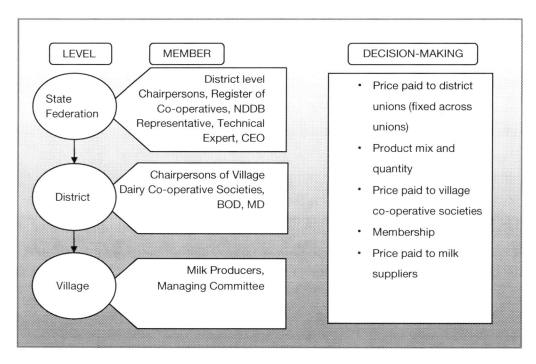

Figure 9.6 Decentralised Organisation Structure of AMUL at Different Levels

Main Function of VDCS

- Collection of surplus milk and payment based on quality and quantity
- Providing support services to the members
- Selling liquid milk for local consumers of the village
- Supplying milk to the District Milk Union

State Cooperative Milk Federation – Main Function

- Marketing of milk and milk products processed/manufactured by milk unions
- Establish a distribution network for marketing of milk and milk products
- Arranging transportation of milk and milk products from the milk unions to the market
- Creating and maintaining a brand for marketing of milk and milk products
- Providing support services to the milk unions and members like technical inputs, management support and advisory services
- Pooling surplus milk from the milk unions and supplying it to deficit milk unions
- Establish feeder-balancing dairy plants for processing the surplus milk of the milk unions
- Arranging for common purchase of raw materials used in manufacture/packaging of milk products
- Decide on the prices of milk and milk products to be paid to milk unions
- Decide on the products to be manufactured at milk unions and capacity required for the same
- Conduct long-term milk production, procurement and processing as well as marketing planning
- Arranging finance for the milk unions and providing them technical know-how
- Designing and providing training in cooperative development and technical and marketing functions
- Conflict resolution and keeping the entire structure intact

Upstream Procurement

- Activities at the village level comprise developing and servicing the DCSs.
- Increasing milk collection, procuring milk, and transporting it to the chilling and processing units twice a day.
- The DCSs provide the farmers with good quality animal feed, fodder and other services like veterinary first aid.
- On an average around a thousand farmers come to sell milk at their local cooperative milk collection centre.
- Each farmer has been given a plastic card for identification.
- At the milk collection counter, the farmer drops the card into a box and the identification number is transmitted to a personal computer attached to the machine.
- The milk is then weighed and the fat content of the milk is measured by an electronic fat testing machine.
- Both these details are recorded on the PC. The computer then calculates the amount due to farmer on the basis of the fat content.
- The value of the milk is then printed out on a slip and handed over to farmers who collect the payment at adjacent window. Now farmers get direct credit to their account and get paid for their milk supplies. Payment information comes on their mobile.

Cold Storage Network

- Chillers in proximity of villages
- Prompt transport to district facilities for further dispatch to consumers/processing units
- Chilled trucks to transport processed products
- Delivery to local chillers by insulated rail tankers and chilled trucks
- Refrigerators and freezers with retailers and departmental stores to retain freshness

258 *Global Logistics Value Chain Management*

Distribution Downstream

- GCMMF coordinated with various unions to get a regular supply of milk and dairy products.
- The processed milk and dairy products were procured from district dairy unions and distributed through third-party distributors.
- To ensure quality and timely deliveries, GCMMF and the district unions had several mechanisms in place.
- The unions monitored the supplies of milk and the distribution of finished products.

Complexity of Distribution Operation

- First leg: Manufacturing units to company depots using 9 and 18 MT trucks
- Frozen food – below 18°C, Dairy wet – 0–4°C
- Second leg: Depots to WDs, transport through insulated 3 and 5 MT TATA 407s
- Third leg: WDs to retailers, transport through rickshaws according to the beat plan

Technology to the Rescue

- Amul started implementation of ERP in phases.
- Automatic milk collection system units (AMCUS) at the village society were installed in the first phase to automate milk production logistics.
- AMCUS facilities to capture member information, milk fat content, volume collected and amount payable to each member electronically.

Automatic Milk Collection System

The benefits of the AMCUS system are as follows:

- Time reduction
- Reduction of pilferage
- Reduced human errors
- On the spot payments for farmers
- Wastage is reduced
- Transparency of operation
- Operational integration

Transformation

- Radical changes in business processes – eliminating middlemen.
- Improved delivery mechanisms and transparency of business operations.
- Due to this process, AMUL is able to collect 6 million litres of milk per day.
- Huge reduction in processing time for effecting payments to the farmers from a week to a couple of minutes.
- Processing of ten million payments daily, amounting to transactions worth USD 3.78 million in cash.
- Amul also connected its zonal offices, regional offices and member's dairies through VSATs.
- The customised ERP-EIAS has been implemented across the organisation integrating various operational departments.
- Amul is also using Geographic Information Systems (GIS) for business planning and optimisation of collection processes.
- Indian Institute of Management – Ahmedabad supplemented Amul's IT strategy by providing an application software – Dairy Information System Kiosk (DISK) to facilitate data analysis and decision support in improving milk collection.

Global Logistics Value Chain Management   259

- The kiosk would also contain an extensive database on the history of cattle owned by the farmers medical history of the cattle, reproductive cycle and history of diseases.
- Farmers can have access to information related to milk production, including best practices in breeding and rearing cattle.
- As a large amount of detailed history on milk production is available in the database, the system can be used to forecast milk collection and monitor the produce from individual sellers.
- Movement of 5000 trucks to 200 dairy processing plants twice a day in the most optimum manner.
- Practising just-in-time supply chain management with six-sigma accuracy.
- Online order placements of Amul's products on the web.
- Distributors can place their orders on the website.
- Amul exports products worth around USD 25 million to countries in West Asia, Africa and the USA.

Sources: Baisya, R.K., Amul Emerging as a Giant in Processed Food Industry. Processed Food Industry, Vol. 4 Issue 12, October 2001, pp 10–12.

Baisya, R.K., New Chapter to Begin with the Proposed Joint Ventures Between Dairy Co-operatives and MNCs. Processed Food Industry, Vol. 6 Issue 6, April 2003, pp 8–10.

Baisya, R.K., Interim Budget and Food Processing Industry. Processed Food Industry, Vol. 7 Issue 5, March 2004, pp 13–14.

Baisya, R.K., Amul will face Competition from other Milk Producing Countries, Processed Food Industry, Vol. 18, No 8, June 2015, pp 10–13.

2. Baisya, R.K., 'Amul vs Nandini' battle heats up in poll-bound Karnataka. *Processed Food Industry*, Volume 26, Number 7, May 2023, pp. 8–10.

Case Questions:

1 Discuss the complexity of the logistics task in the corporation.
2 How did management attempt to find unorthodox solutions to the problems?
3 What are the various operational constraints in managing the logistics task?
4 What are the key performance indicators which you find have improved?
5 What are failure risks that an organisation is taking and what are their consequences?
6 What are the possible improvement areas?
7 Discuss supply chain network of Amul.
8 How Amul is managing the decentralised organisational structure?

Chapter Summary

Value chain is another name for end-to-end supply chain. In global business environment, large companies manage their supply chain in a networked environment sourcing input material from many countries wherever they are available at best price and quality meeting required delivery schedule and producing or assembling it at yet another country capturing value at each stage of interface through effective logistics management were elaborately discussed. Key drivers as well as tools and methods that facilitate international logistics were discussed. Current scenario with respect to international trade and how companies are going for acquisitions to acquire critical mass and competitive edge in terms of managing international logistics challenges are also discussed. Several terminologies used in international logistics trade are defined with examples. Logistics management and cargo handling efficiency issues are also discussed. The value chain analyses and strategies for competitive advantage have been covered in detail.

260 *Global Logistics Value Chain Management*

Logistics industry in India and its status and ranking in the world logistics industry as well as logistics security issues are covered in this chapter as well as global operating levels of the logistics companies are discussed. The chapter also deals with the issues of managing the challenges of integrated supply chain and logistics management, including a discussion on stages of integration and benefits of integration.

The case of Anand Milk Producers Union Ltd (AMUL) has been discussed to explain how AMUL is addressing the very complex supply chain and logistics issues in the business and also how successfully they are able to integrate the functions.

Discussion Questions

1 Discuss the tools and processes that have facilitated international logistics.
2 Discuss the logistics value chain sources of competitive advantages
3 Discuss the key drivers of global logistics management strategy formulations.
4 Take five logistics companies and five manufacturing–marketing companies in India and Europe and determine their operating level giving reasons.
5 Discuss four stages of regional integration. Indicate tasks of logistics companies under those stages. Under which stage do Europe (Schengen countries) and India fall and why?
6 Discuss the challenges and barriers of global logistics operation.
7 What role can global logistics companies play, and what are the capabilities that they can display?
8 Discuss the benefits of supply chain integration.
9 How international logistics channel evolved over the decades of continued international trade? Discuss.

Note

1 Source: https://lpi.worldbank.org/

References

Ellram, L. M., & Cooper, M. C. (1990) "Supply Chain Management Partnership, and the Shipper-Third Party Relationship", *International Journal of Logistics Management*, 1(2), 1–10.
Houlihan, J. B. (1985) "International Supply Chain Management", *International Journal of Physical Distribution & Materials Management*, 15(1), 22–38.
Lambert, D. M., & Cooper, M. C. (2000) "Issues in Supply Chain Management", *Industrial Engineering Management*, 29, 65–83.
Porter, M. E. (1985) *Competitive Advantage*. New York: The Free Press.

Bibliography

Baufield, E. (1999) *Harnessing Value in Supply Chain: Strategic Sourcing in Action*. New York: Wiley.
Biullington, C., & Francois, J. (2008, January–February) "Procurement: The Missing Link in Innovation", *Supply Chain Management Review*, pp. 22–28.
Cachon, G. P., & Larivieve, M. A. (2001, March). "Turning the Supply Chain into a Revenue Chain", *Harvard Business Review*, pp. 20–21.
Cavimato, J. L., & Kauffman, R. (2000) *The Purchasing Handbook: A Guide for the Purchasing and Supply Chain Professional*. New York: McGraw Hill.
Coyle, J. J., Langley, C. J., Novade, R. A., & Gibson, B. (2016) "Supply Chain Management: A Logistics Perspective. Nelson Education: A Survey of SCM Professionals", *Journal of Business Logistics*, 28(1), 1–24.

Dekhne, A., Huang, X., & Sarkar, A. (2012, September–October) "Bridging the Procurement-Supply Chain Divide", *Supply Chain Management Review*, pp. 36–42.

Ferreira, J., & Prokopets, L. (2009, January–February) "Does Offshoring Still Makes Sense?", *Supply Chain Management Review*, pp. 20–27.

Goel, A., Moussavi, N., & Srivatsan, V. N. (2008, Winter) "Time to Rethink Offshoring?", *McKinsey on Business Technology*, pp. 14, 32–35.

Larsen, P. D., Poist, R. F., & Hallorsson, A. (2007) "Perspective on Logistics vs Supply Chain Management", *Journal of Business Logistics*, 28(1), 1–24.

Van Hock, R. I. (1998) "Measuring the Unmeasurable and Improving the Performance in the Supply Chain", *International Journal of Supply Chain Management*, 3(4).

10 Sourcing Decision in Global Supply Chain Management

Learning Objectives

1 Understand the importance of global sourcing in organisation performance of global corporations
2 Understand global sourcing challenges and strategies
3 Link global sourcing and supply chain sustainability
4 Identify global sourcing models and frameworks
5 Realise global trends in sourcing
6 Identify critical success factors in global sourcing and future factories
7 Role of contract manufacturers in global supply chain management

Introduction

Global sourcing refers to buying the raw materials, other input materials and or components that go into the manufacturing of a company's products from around the world, not just from the headquarters' country. For example, Starbucks buys its coffee from locations like Colombia and Guatemala. The advantages of global sourcing are quality and lower cost. From cost savings and increased flexibility to access new markets and suppliers, global sourcing can help companies optimise their supply chain and improve their bottom-line performance. This also offers scope of cost competitiveness in global market. Although at the same time global sourcing can increase the complexities to be managed for souring across countries and geographical regions working with different cross-cultural organisations as well as people. As such, considerable preparations as well-management control through appropriate processes and systems to be in place which is a prerequisite for effecting sourcing performance. To initiate global sourcing vendor analysis, vendor selection and vendor ranking for the components or ingredients or even raw materials and packaging materials have to be undertaken. Additionally, reliability tests as well as risk analysis as well as controllability and feasibility need to be undertaken. That itself is time taking and tedious process.

Global sourcing initiatives and programmes form an integral part of the strategic sourcing[1] plans and procurement[2] strategies of many multinational companies.[3] Global sourcing is often associated with a centralised procurement strategy for a multinational, wherein a central buying organisation seeks economies of scale[4] through corporate-wide standardisation and benchmarking.[5] As such global sourcing is proactively integrating and coordinating common items and materials, processes, designs, technologies and suppliers across worldwide purchasing, engineering and operating locations.

DOI: 10.4324/9781003469063-10

Sourcing Challenges and Strategies

Companies can source their products and services from their company-owned manufacturing plant. Companies also have the option to get the product manufactured by third parties through contract manufacturing route. Which option to be accepted will be governed by various factors. It can also be mixed sourcing in the sense that partly it will be sourced from contract manufacturers and part of the requirement is taken care of by the company's own manufacturing plant.

In the 1980s and 1990s companies were manufacturing the products themselves. When competitive pressure increased, companies started outsourcing to reduce cost as major sourcing strategies. We have seen many corporations closing down their production plants or even giving those plants on lease to contract manufacturers and focusing on the core functions of the business-like sales and marketing. Managing a product or manufacturing facility not only involves a lot of fixed capital but also requires working capital to run the day-to-day production operations. Additionally, there are numerous issues and challenges in terms of managing industrial workers. These challenges can be overcome through contract manufacturing route. In some cases, workers are even seen as highly volatile creating industrial relation issues to be tackled by the management. If there is proprietary technology to be safeguarded, it is better to have your own manufacturing plant. For capital goods and automobiles, most of the organisations and players opt for their own manufacturing plants. But if the same product has to be manufactured for global supply, companies will have the assembly line owned by themselves and the rest of the components are sourced from where it is cheapest and best in quality. For FMCG, it is now widely outsourced through contract manufacturing route. Global supply chain is highly complex and competitive, and components need to be sourced from global suppliers for specific markets.

Contract manufacturers play a vital role in the following:

- Reducing cost of production
- Reducing costs of distribution and logistics
- Providing much-needed flexibility in business
- Improves response time for variable customer needs
- Allows bigger players to focus on their core competency
- Providing competitive advantage to the business

Small but efficient contract manufacturers can be cost-effective for large companies and can provide support to the flexible market demand in a dynamic business environment. Small is therefore beautiful. Small but efficient contract manufacturers also play a vital role in logistics management.

Future Factories

There are two distinct possibilities that can emerge for global manufacturing and production operations. The future factories could be:

- Smaller
- More flexible
- Closer to the customers
- More cost-effective
- Will use latest technology
- Will be competitive

264　*Sourcing Decision in Global Supply Chain Management*

Or will it be large global-focused factories? It is the economy of scale against flexibility and productivity. Or both have to co-exist? Global players are getting products and services manufactured in low-cost countries like China and India. But there are other logistics cost that can force the global players to shift the production locations to even European locations. East European countries are seen to be cost-effective and closer to the market and therefore can emerge as preferred location for global production and supply requirements. The logistics cost of taking products and merchandise to European markets from China will be high and the inventory holding also will be high, making a valid case for production closer to the customer locations with more flexibility and higher productivity.

Four Levels of Global Sourcing

Depending on the current stage, and product complexities and coverage in the global market or even lack of it companies can be at one of these four levels in terms of global sourcing. Corporations generally grow from level 1 to level 4.

Level 1: Domestic purchases only.
Level 2: International purchases made on as-needed basis.
Level 3: Sourcing strategy that includes global purchasing.
Level 4: Centrally coordinated purchasing across global locations.

Global Sourcing Challenge and Sustainability of Supply Chain

In the past, there has been considerable concern for some time amongst many academics, businesses and government and non-governmental organisations about the so-called global sourcing and logistics 'carbon footprint' of supply chains; however, it is only recently that the debate has really taken off. There is now a growing realisation that in the not-too-distant future, organisations and even individuals will probably have to pay for the carbon impact of their activities. For the business sector, this penalty may take the form of taxes, levies or the capping of allowable emissions under carbon trading regimes. Potentially, these additional costs may bring the commercial viability of their operations into question. Hence, the argument is starting to be heard that companies should review their current carbon footprint and identify strategies for its reduction.

For any organisation it is not just the carbon impact of its in-house activities that needs to be understood but rather the total carbon effect of its wider supply chain. With the current trend to offshore sourcing continuing at a pace, the implications for total carbon impact are significant. Understanding the true carbon footprint of a supply chain for any product requires the ability to conduct a 'thorough life-cycle' analysis of the emissions generated from cradle to grave: what is the total environmental cost from raw material sourcing through manufacturing and distribution to consumption and disposal?

This new focus on carbon has served to bring the supply chain into greater prominence – in particular, the decisions that organisations are taking regarding manufacturing and sourcing locations. The significant trend to low-cost country sourcing over the last ten years or so has transformed the shape of many supply chains, particularly through the creation of longer and more transport-intensive pipelines. It can be argued that, as a result, in some cases, the true costs of global sourcing may be considerably more than companies realise. It is not only the logistics costs that must be borne by the company that have risen as a result of this trend but also the external costs in the form of an often-enlarged carbon footprint. Because transport represents such a large proportion of total worldwide greenhouse gas emissions – about 20% and growing – it is inevitable that supply chains will be under increasing scrutiny in the future. To put very simply, the search is on for ways to make supply chains less transport intensive.

Models and Frameworks for Sourcing

Meixell and Gargeya (2005) developed a comprehensive literature review on global supply chain design models. They summarise that models developed prior to 1990 focus on global plant location problems. Models developed in the 1990–1995 period continue the emphasis on the plant location issue and pay attention to transportation issue, infrastructure, lead time, currency fluctuation and supplier selection criteria.

Models developed in the 1996–2000 period consider price as a variable and reconsider the plant location issue. Models developed since 2000 take global sourcing as a part of global supply chain strategy and that global sourcing is linked with marketing. They conclude that global supply chain models need to address the composite supply chain design problem by extending models to include both internal manufacturing and external supplier locations. These can be summarised as follows:

- Global supply chain models need broader emphasis on multiple production and distribution tiers in the supply chain.
- Performance measures used in global supply chain models need to be broadened in definition to address alternative objectives.
- And finally more industry settings need to be investigated in the context of global supply design.

These authors have concluded that most of the models aim to solve a difficult problem related the globalisation. However, only a few of them address the practical global supply chain design problem in a more comprehensive manner. Jin (2004) tries to find the ideal point of postponement and speculation to minimise the cost/agility trade-off meaning a mixed sourcing strategy of global and domestic global sourcing. Vestring et al. (2005) proposed spreading foreign operation and outsourcing relationships over a broad, well-balanced mix of regions and countries to reduce risk and increase potential reward. For example, Hungary's labour cost is almost quadruple of China's, but it can be better for Western European companies looking to offshore skilled manufacturing from overall cost and performance point of view.

These models provide a comprehensive list of factors to consider when companies source their products or services globally and help us understand the concept of global sourcing. However, within the risk literature, some more comprehensive models dealing with the sourcing process can be found. Cousins et al. (2004) argue that the literature so far is weak when it comes to environmental supply chain initiatives in practice where risk identification needs to be more comprehensive to manage the risk arising out of environmental issues. Furthermore, no one has yet provided a more comprehensive approach to recognise and manage the risks involved in environment-related supplier initiatives. Therefore, the authors present a conceptual model for risk in environment-related supplier initiatives. In the model the types of exposure of environmental-related risks, how the types are perceived by the managers, and the strategic level of the purchasing function are linked to each other.

266 *Sourcing Decision in Global Supply Chain Management*

In global sourcing and logistics model, it is argued that the more advanced and strategic the purchasing function is, the more likely it is, that the company will undertake environment-related supplier initiatives.

Characteristics for Successful Global Sourcing

Based on a survey among companies using global sourcing, Trent and Monczka (2003) identify a number of critical success factors, which are summarised next:

- Personnel with required knowledge, skills and abilities
- Availability of required information
- Awareness of potential global suppliers
- Time for personnel to develop global strategies
- Availability of suppliers with global capabilities/suppliers interested in global contracts
- Ability to identify common requirements across buying units
- Operations and manufacturing support/internal customer buy-in
- Direct site visits to suppliers

Based on the same survey presented by Trent and Monczka (2003), and additional case studies on 15 companies, Trent and Monczka (2005) list the following sets of characteristics for companies with successful global sourcing:

- Commitment at an executive level to global sourcing
- Rigorous and well-defined processes
- Availability of needed resources
- Integration through information technology
- Supportive organisational design
- Structured approaches to communication

Global Sourcing and Logistics

Methodologies for Measuring Savings

The potential savings that can be accrued through global sourcing strategies will depend on various factors as discussed by Fagan (1991), which includes commitment of top management and total cost, not simply the direct cost. To derive the total advantage, the relationships with foreign suppliers should be developed on the basis of trust and respect. Monitoring and controlling through technology should also be used in addition to the ways of handling business risks. A contingency plan should be developed.

Global Sourcing Trends

Global sourcing is being practised in international trade for centuries, although the types of sourcing that we practice now are qualitatively different from the century-old practices for both technical and social reasons. Earlier, trade used to be mostly carried out on raw materials or final finished products and seldom in intermediate products such as components and services. Besides, unlike today, buyers–suppliers coordination and co-operations were not crucial, and all communications were limited to order processing.

Sourcing Decision in Global Supply Chain Management 267

In addition, we have plethora of rules, regulations, control and risks associated with the global trade.

A comprehensive global sourcing strategy will refer to the issues related to the following:

- Logistics to identify the production units and locations which will serve the particular identified market(s) and how input material and components will be supplied for manufacturing.
- The coordination and interfaces among manufacturing, R&D and marketing on a global basis.

The primary objective of global sourcing for the firm is to exploit both its own and suppliers' competitive advantages as well as comparative locational advantages of various countries in global competition. From the contractual point of view, the global sourcing of intermediate products of components and services takes place in two ways; these are as follows:

- From the parent or their foreign subsidiaries on intra 'firm basis', that is, insourcing.
- From independent suppliers on 'contractual' basis, that is, outsourcing.

Similarly, from a locational point of view, multinational firms can procure goods and services either (a) domestically (i.e. onshoring) or (b) from abroad (i.e. offshoring).

The new waves of global sourcing were observed during the last few decades. The first one was in the mid-1980s, which was focused primarily on global sourcing of manufacturing activities, and research work during that era was also focused on manufacturing firms. Kotabe and Omura (1989) did some study on global sourcing. During that period, large manufacturing firms set up their operation globally and started to use suppliers from many countries to exploit opportunities for best-in-class sourcing (Quinn and Hilmer, 1994). As a result, supply chain became more complex and global, with manufacturing firms sourcing from many suppliers in many countries for input materials, intermediates and also final product. We have discussed these taking cases earlier.

We witnessed in the early 1990s the second wave of global sourcing when firms started outsourcing IT services and companies abandoned in-house development of a new IS, and we have seen the emergence of specialist providers such as EDS and Accenture. Global sourcing is labour-intensive and involves standardised programming that can easily be sourced from countries like India. The rising commercial applications for a wide range of firm activities helped the introduction of ERP systems. All organisations were seen implementing ERP to optimise on the suppliers and vendors to make business operations more competitive.

The third wave was characterised by offshoring in the recent years since 2000. During this stage, we have witnessed the rise in business process outsourcing that extends beyond IT services and covers a wide range of other services relating to HRM, finance and account, sales and after-sales assistance provided by call centres. In this regard, India is still a primary source country for producing business process software by companies like Infosys, TCS and Wipro and many more. However, competition is also now seen from other countries for such services.

In this regard, it has been observed by many that the foreign business process suppliers may be moving up the knowledge chain more rapidly than expected by the sourcing firms. Such knowledge transfer could in the long run undermine sourcing firms' ability to differentiate themselves from their foreign suppliers, and these concerns have previously been raised by many authors (Bettis et al., 1992; Kotabe, 1998; Markides and Berg, 1988). Technology is therefore

268 *Sourcing Decision in Global Supply Chain Management*

Table 10.1 Recent Waves in Global Sourcing

Time Period	First Wave (Since 1980s)	Second Wave (Since Early 1990s)	Third Wave (Since Early 2000s)
Type of activity	Manufacturing	Information technology	Business processes
Suppliers	China, Central and Eastern Europe, Mexico and others	India, Ireland and others	India, Pakistan, South Africa and others
Type of firms	Manufacturing	Manufacturing, banks and others	Financial services, services more generally
Primary motives	Reduction in labour costs	Obtaining enough skilled programmers and cost reduction	Reduction in labour costs and round-the-clock service provision

Source: Kotabe and Murray (2018)

redefining business processes, which is increasingly being witnessed now in the Industry 4.0 environment. New technologies such as AI, blockchain technology, robotics and digitisation are redefining the supply chain and logistics management processes. The experience so far on these recent waves of global sourcing is summarised in Table 10.1.

Global Sourcing and Business Performance

It is widely suggested that global sourcing occurs in order to improve performance, particularly, cost-effectiveness (e.g. Trent and Monczka, 2003). Firms located in OECD countries often find that labour costs are excessive, compared to the value that is added to their products. While developing countries such as China lag behind in productivity, they compensate for this lower productivity by providing much lower hourly labour costs, sometimes even culminating in the de-automation of tasks when they are transferred to these locations. The same should be true in India as well. Labour productivity in India is also low. Indeed, in some cases, such as a range of bicycle components, the production cost differences are so large that it is not economically viable to use domestic sourcing, especially when the labour costs represent a substantial part of overall production costs.

At the other extreme, some global sourcing may be driven by knowledge concerns. Some inputs, such as aircraft parts and technical expertise, may be available only in other OECD countries, thus making global sourcing not a choice but an imperative. As for the sourcing of many raw materials, domestic sourcing is not an option since many raw materials are unavailable domestically. Besides, for certain intermediate products, many firms tend to source them from locations near the source of raw materials.

Another argument in favour of global sourcing is that it may allow a firm to produce closer to its customer markets, thereby increasing access to them. For instance, Japanese manufacturing firms have over time replicated supply chains in North America and Europe to operate closer to these markets. Production and sourcing experience in these regions has also allowed them to improve their product offerings. Another reason to opt for global sourcing is that demand from various regions can be pooled, thus achieving maximum scale and bargaining power through single sourcing from a foreign supplier.

However, there are disadvantages associated with global sourcing. A major problem is cultural differences between buyers and their foreign suppliers. Indeed, institutional and language problems may affect a relationship negatively while cultural misunderstandings and other communication problems can lead to quality problems, in addition to those caused by differences in technical standards or expectations. Another concern related to global sourcing is its long lead times and supply-chain uncertainty, and its feasibility is often determined by international trade rules (Swamidass and Kotabe, 1993). Finally, foreign suppliers may be able to integrate forward into the buyer's market by inventing around patents or ignoring them altogether.

This situation raises another layer of issues related to the long-term sustainability of firms' core competencies. There are two opposing views on the long-term implications of international sourcing. One school of thought argues that many successful companies have developed a dynamic organisational network through increasing cross-border joint ventures, subcontracting and licensing activities (Miles and Snow, 1986). This flexible network system, also known as supply-chain alliances, allows each participant to pursue its particular competence with each network participant complementing rather than competing against the other participants for the common goals. Such alliances are often formed by competing companies in pursuit of complementary abilities (e.g. new technologies or skills) from one another, thus helping the sourcing firm to acquire a competitive advantage by sourcing major components that involve high asset specificity from its alliance partners (Murray, 2001).

The other school of thought argues that while a firm may gain short-term advantages, there could also be negative long-term consequences. As the firm becomes more reliant on its independent suppliers, it may not be able to keep abreast of constantly evolving design and engineering technologies without engaging in those developmental activities (Kotabe, 1998). Consequently, the firm encounters the inherent difficulty in sustaining its long-term competitive advantages. In other words, over time a firm's technical expertise and capability surplus vis-à-vis its foreign suppliers may diminish to the point that its value added is limited, and it may become more like a trading company. An example of this is the development of Emerson Electronics which turned from an electronics producer into a trading company and then into nothing more than a brand that changed owners several times (see Kotabe, Mol, et al., 2008).

We summarise the advantages and disadvantages of global sourcing in Table 10 2.

Table 10.2 Advantages and Disadvantages of Global Sourcing

Advantages	Disadvantages
Increased size of potential supply base	Having to deal with foreign institutions such as legal differences
Lower production costs, especially for labour-intensive production and services	Having to deal with a foreign culture which could affect communication
Increased technical expertise, especially for high-tech products from specialised locations	Having to deal with a foreign language which could affect communication
More flexibility to switch between supply sources, whether internal or external	Need to pay import duties where applicable
Source closer to sales markets, experience in sourcing may be translated into sales	Increased transportation costs and supply chain uncertainty
Achieve scale economies through use of one global supply source	Forward integration by foreign suppliers, patent infractions possible
Source of intermediate products closer to source of raw materials	Quality problems
Raw materials only available from foreign sources	Negative effects on employee commitment and legitimacy at home base
Focus on core competencies	Reliance on independent suppliers, and decreased ability to keep abreast of emerging technical requirements

Source: Jean (2008, 266)

270 *Sourcing Decision in Global Supply Chain Management*

Degree of Outsourcing and Performance

A balance perspective can offer insights on the sourcing strategy–performance relationship. In proposing such a 'balance' perspective, Kotabe and Mol (2004, 2006) examined the relationship between the degree of a firm's outsourcing across all activities and its performance. Their underlying argument is that firms that outsource all of their activities run into a multitude of problems such as a lack of innovation and bargaining power, and an inability to be distinct in the eyes of the customer.

However, firms that only insource fail to use the powerful incentives supplied by markets, thus becoming bureaucratic and inefficient. Therefore, outsourcing some but not all activities provide the best solution overall, and there is an optimal degree of outsourcing. Deviations from that optimum are costly and the larger the deviations, the more severe the performance penalty will be. Hence, there is a negative curvilinear (inverted U-shaped) relationship between the degree of outsourcing and firm performance. Likewise, Leiblein et al. (2002) empirically found that deviations from the optimal form of sourcing, as dictated by transactional attributes associated with various contracting hazards, may have a detrimental effect on performance.

We believe a similar line of reasoning can apply to the degree of internationalisation of sourcing (i.e. onshoring and offshoring) and how IT affects performance. More specifically, there are advantages and disadvantages associated with global sourcing, as we highlighted earlier. As a firm does more offshoring, the disadvantages become larger to the point where they severely impede performance. However, if firms do not use offshoring at all, they cannot enjoy any of the advantages of offshoring such as having a wider supply base from which to choose. This line of reasoning is consistent with research in international business since it is, for instance, indirectly suggested by Dunning's (1993) treatment of international sourcing and neo-institutional economics traditions, particularly the transaction-costs framework (Williamson, 1985).

Williamson (1985) distinguished between production and transaction costs. The former refers to the costs of producing a good or service while transaction costs represent all the costs incurred as the product moves from one supply-chain partner to the next. On the one hand, when firms use offshoring by procuring from foreign suppliers, it may help reduce their production costs, while in some instances, a local supplier's production costs may be lower than those of foreign suppliers, this is often the exception rather than the rule. Transaction costs, on the other hand, tend to be higher for offshoring as there are many types of institutional, cultural and language barriers that must be overcome. Rangan (2000) discussed this situation in terms of the costs of 'search and evaluation'. Searching for supply sources abroad, whether internal or external sources, is somewhat more expensive than searching for local supply sources. Evaluating those foreign supply sources is much more expensive because the evaluation costs are strongly related to the familiarity that decision-makers have with the other party. Since firms are likely to be less familiar with foreign supply sources and decision-makers may not be able to draw on their networks in helping them evaluate these sources, this situation induces substantial evaluation costs. Rangan (2000) used this argument to explain why buying firms are much more likely to choose a domestic than a foreign supplier even when the physical distance between the buyer and each of these suppliers is the same.

We argue that offshoring is a 'balancing' act between production and transaction costs. Firms need to find the proper balance between domestic and foreign supply sources (i.e. using onshoring and offshoring) if they wish to locate on the top of the curve and obtain the highest possible performance. They can achieve this goal by using foreign sources for part but not all of their sourcing. Sourcing everything from abroad produces poor performance results because the disadvantages of offshoring, like the hollowing-out argument, become too large. Focusing all efforts on onshoring, however, is a serious form of myopia with equally disastrous effects on firm performance, primarily because the firm is not capitalising on important opportunities to improve competitiveness.

Some activities are best outsourced globally while others ought to be integrated (from a performance perspective). Optimal performance is reached when all activities are correctly outsourced and/or integrated. Deviations from the optimum are costly and in such a way that the farther from the optimum, the more costly these deviations become.

Key Issues in Global Sourcing

Despite the heightened publicity of global sourcing, many firms have been highly dissatisfied with their sourcing performance. The problem may be due to the fact that many researchers and practitioners have adopted a deterministic view in evaluating the global sourcing strategy–performance relationship, without exercising caution that such a view tends to over-generalise the sourcing benefits. Strategic-management scholars have conceptualised environment as one of the key constructs for understanding organisational behaviour and performance in that 'the appropriateness of different strategies depends on the competitive settings of businesses' (Prescott, 1986, 765). Thus, failure to include environmental factors in examining the sourcing strategy–performance relationship may neglect the effects of different environments on optimal sourcing strategies.

In the manufacturing context, Murray et al. (1995) concluded that the financial performance advantage of global insourcing over global outsourcing of non-standardised (i.e. major) components improved with increased product innovations, process innovations and asset specificity.

Technological Performance and Sourcing Decisions

Using foreign firms manufacturing in China as subjects of the study, Murray et al. (2005) found that global outsourcing of major components (in the form of strategic alliance-based sourcing) did not have an effect on market performance. Instead, product innovativeness and technological uncertainty moderated such a relationship. Specifically, at low levels of product innovativeness/technological uncertainty, the use of strategic alliance sourcing of major components by the sourcing firm is positively related to market performance. However, at higher levels of product innovativeness/technological uncertainty, the sourcing–performance relationships become negative.

Similarly, Leiblein et al. (2002) findings in the manufacturing context concur with the earlier conclusions. In refuting the popular arguments that insourcing or outsourcing will lead to superior technological performance, they found that sourcing strategy per se did not significantly affect technological performance. Instead, the sourcing strategy–performance relationship was driven by factors underlying sourcing strategy choice. They further cautioned against the universalistic normative implications for firms deciding on whether or not to insource or outsource their value-chain activities and stressed the value of contingency-based theoretical approaches.

Factors Influencing Outsourcing

The global sourcing of services did not take place until the second wave of global sourcing so the extant literature on global sourcing of services is limited when compared to that in global

272 *Sourcing Decision in Global Supply Chain Management*

sourcing of manufactured goods.[1] Consistent with previous studies of the global sourcing of manufactured goods, transaction-cost analysis (TCA) involving asset specificity, transaction frequency and business uncertainty offers a useful framework for studying the sourcing of services. Asset specificity refers to investments made in specific (non-marketable) resources. When these investments are made, a supplier and a buyer are 'locked into' the transaction because the assets are specialised to that transaction and have limited or no value outside that transaction (Williamson, 1985). Murray et al. (1995) found that, similar to components and finished goods sourcing, supplementary services were sourced globally by either insourcing or outsourcing.[2] In addition, the relationship between asset specificity and insourcing of supplementary services was moderated by the level of inseparability[3] and transaction frequency. Their empirical findings showed that firms tended to rely more on global insourcing for inseparable supplementary services with high asset specificity. Furthermore, the higher the asset specificity and the lower the transaction frequency of the supplementary services, the higher these firms would use global insourcing. Finally, insourcing and offshoring of supplementary services were negatively related to a service's market performance.

There is a range of contingency factors (i.e. capital intensity, degree of service inseparability, market uncertainty, transaction frequency) at the transaction, firm and context levels. These factors determine how much global outsourcing ought to take place from a performance perspective. To an extent, the contingency factors also explain how much global outsourcing actually takes place in practice. Fit is achieved when the actual global outsourcing level is in accordance with the level predicted, based on the contingency factors. If a company matches an outsourcing decision to the relevant contingency factors, the resulting strategic fit helps achieve superior performance.

It is important to note that these perspectives operate at three different levels: the transaction, the firm and the context. Taken together, they represent almost all the contingency factors that the academic literature has produced to date. Which of these perspectives matters most is, to an extent, determined by the empirical context in which outsourcing is investigated. Some of the perspectives have been more prominent than others in recent academic studies of outsourcing. Transaction-cost economics and the resource-based view may reflect their actual importance in practice, the scholarly knowledge production process or other factors. However, all of these perspectives have some bearing on global outsourcing. Global sourcing decisions are based on many complex and dynamic issues and require frequent review of cost, availability, flexibility and performance. In addition, there are numerous industry-specific issues. In this chapter two such industry sectors are covered from the perspective of global sourcing head.

Table 10.3 Perspectives on Global Outsourcing

	Firm Level	*Context Level*	*Transaction Level*
Past	Resource-based view	Social networks	
Present	Costly contracting Microeconomics core competences	Industrial organisation Institutional voids	Transaction-cost economics Agency
Future	Real options Relations and learning		

Source: Kotabe, Murray, et al. (2008)

Sourcing Decision in Global Supply Chain Management 273

Case Study A: Industry Sector: Retail

Global Sourcing Strategy: (Perspective of Global Sourcing Director)

Company A (a leading retail group in the UK) believe that it is a driver in leading change; its global sourcing strategy reflects this which is largely driven by its customers. Their sourcing portfolio is changing rapidly because the global marketplace has evolved so much over the past few years. However, in some product areas they are now sourcing more from Europe rather than the Far East because of emerging markets and changes in consumer behaviour. On the other hand, it is exploring new sources in the Far East where capabilities are stronger, that is, Vietnam, Madagascar and Shanghai. The sourcing strategy is determined by the product category for example quick response items are sourced primarily from Turkey, but new opportunities are arising from Bulgaria and Romania as they enter the EU. Other categories are sourced 95% from China. Some categories are planned to be sourced more from Britain to promote the local businesses.

Positive Factors

- Spreading risks – range of factories that can produce the same products at varying lead times and costs
- Increased number of options to source from
- Direct sourcing

Negative Factors

- Do not have a panoramic view of the supply base and have not always found the right supplier. Large number of suppliers.
- Large number of suppliers, hence, supply base is being consolidated.
- Maintaining control of factories.
- Communication with suppliers, lack of visibility. 'If you get it wrong direct sourcing could go very wrong'.

Main Mode of Transport

- Mainly sea freight, depending where products are procured from.
- Quick turnaround products are moved by road.
- Airfreight is used for strategic products only and this 0.1% of everything moved.

Key Priorities of Global Sourcing Strategy

- Reliability of product
- Shipment on time
- Right product
- Delivered on time

Supply Chain Risk Management Tools and Techniques

- Risk management is an integral part of the global sourcing decision-making.
- Supply management programme is a standard tool kit and enables decision-makers to identify how to best deal with the capabilities from the supply base and how to document performance.
- Key performance indicators enable Company A to analyse key suppliers' performance. The risk review is completed every three to six months and supplier scorecards are developed to assess the performance.

274 *Sourcing Decision in Global Supply Chain Management*

Major Risk Identified in Global Sourcing Decisions

- Factories are ethical and not breaking civil law.
- Communication with global supply base – do they truly understand company philosophy and product requirements.
- Missed opportunities which competitors can exploit.
- Lack of visibility.

Environment and Infrastructure Considerations

- Aim to reduce CO_2 emissions by 60% by 2010 Sponsoring sourcing locally and closer.
- Europe initiatives such as reducing the price of energy bulbs.
- Not enough choice for transportation, UK rail network is poor and unreliable.

Case Study B: Industry Sector: FMCG Food and Drink

Global Sourcing Strategy: (Perspective of Global Head of Procurement)

Company B is again a major FMCG Food and drink player based out of UK. The input was given by their global sourcing director. The sourcing strategy is based on balancing cost and customer service. The sourcing strategy is determined by types of products: bulky products (e.g. detergents and paper) are sourced locally to reduce logistics costs; small high-value products are produced in a few factories and then distributed around the world.

To make the sourcing decisions, the company looks at sales projections and service level requirements from different regions, then they look at local supply availability and import tariffs and duties, and finally at the capital costs involved. Find a balance between cost and service levels.

- A total of 90% of product comes from within the EU. In the future, Eastern Europe is more likely to develop.
- Contracts and supplier relationships vary in length. Tend to use short-term contracts (and relationships) for commodities and long-term for strategic supplies.

Positive Factors of Global Sourcing Strategy

To optimise total delivered cost (logistics and manufacturing).

Negative Factors of Global Sourcing Strategy

Difficult trade-off between cost and service.

Main Mode of Transport

- Road is the dominant source of transport (95%). Rail takes the rest.
- Rail is not used for delivery to customer because of long lead times and poor reliability.

Key Priorities of Global Sourcing Strategy

- Customer service
- Cost
- Quality

Sourcing Decision in Global Supply Chain Management 275

Supply Chain Risk Management Tools and Techniques

- There is a health and safety organisation focused on looking at risks at the plants.
- There is a business continuity plan for every plant, which the plant engineer is responsible for. This includes risks at suppliers.
- Business continuity planning and health and safety analysis are used to assess risks
- Generally, use dual sourcing or multiple sourcing to mitigate supply risks. For most products, they have several plants so can source from another one in case of a disruption

Major Risk Identified in Global Sourcing Decisions

Since most of the product comes from the EU. The company finds that there is not much risk of global sourcing.

Environment and Infrastructure Considerations

- Environmental issues are in line with the company's economic necessities, and the company aims to minimise transport as much as possible.
- The company looks for a high vehicle utilisation (90% +). The network is designed to minimise transport and achieve high utilisation.
- Life cycle analysis is conducted when designing new products. They try to design new products to have the minimum environmental impact.
- The company primarily use road, and road congestion is a big issue. Rail is not always appropriate, because rail is not as flexible as road, but also because it is not as reliable and not always more cost-effective. All of our plants have rail connections, but they are not fully utilised.

Source: Christopher, M., Fu Jia, Omera Khan, Carlos Mena, Palmer, A, 'Global Sourcing Logistics, Research Gate, June 2017[6]

Case Questions:

1 How and why do key priorities of global sourcing criteria in two different industry sectors differ?
2 Discuss the key drivers of outsourcing. What are the advantages and disadvantages of global outsourcing.
2 Discuss the positives and negatives of the global sourcing strategy.
3 What are the key motivations for global sourcing?
4 Discuss the risk involved in global sourcing as perceived by Company A and Company B.
5 How international logistics channel got evolved over the decades of continued international trade?
6 Discuss the recent trends in global outsourcing and the factors behind that.

Chapter Summary

When corporations expand their operations, sourcing of products and services across geographies becomes a key imperative for deriving competitive advantage. Effective sourcing strategies can provide cost competitiveness to corporations. However, global sourcing is an extremely complex in terms of locating ideal vendors across geographies and ensuring quality and timely deliveries to both manufacturing locations and customer locations operating in a cross-cultural environment remotely managing using communication technologies based on trust and reliability is the key requirement. These issues were discussed in this chapter.

276 *Sourcing Decision in Global Supply Chain Management*

However, organisations gradually upgrade themselves from initial stage of only sourcing to integrated procurement management. Key advantages and disadvantages of outsourcing and also the stages of evolution of global outsourcing have been discussed in brief. Global sourcing strategy and factors influencing global sourcing are discussed in detail in this chapter along with two cases from retail and FMCG sectors to show the key factors that these businesses need to consider in order to make global sourcing decisions. Also discussed are the recent trends in outsourcing.

Discussion Questions

1 Discuss key drivers of outsourcing and the advantages and disadvantages of global outsourcing.
2 Discuss the recent trends in global outsourcing and the factors behind that.
3 Discuss the concept of future factory and sourcing management in terms of technology development, global concerns with environment and sustainability as well as complexity and challenges of the global business environment.
4 Why global corporations are seen to be opting for outsourcing and even investing in contract manufacturers production facilities for quality and productivity?
5 Discuss the prospect of East European countries emerging as global supply source.

Notes

1 See: https://en.wikipedia.org/wiki/Strategic_sourcing
2 See: https://en.wikipedia.org/wiki/Procurement
3 See: https://en.wikipedia.org/wiki/Multinational_corporation
4 See: https://en.wikipedia.org/wiki/Economies_of_scale
5 See: https://en.wikipedia.org/wiki/Benchmarking
6 Available at www.researchgate.net/publication/308402707

References

Bettis, R., Bradley, S., & Hamal, G. (1992) "Outsourcing and Industrial Decline", *Academy of Management Executive*, 6(1), 7–16.
Cousins, P. D., Lamming, R. C., & Bowen, F. (2004) "The Role of Risk in Environment-Related Suppliers Initiatives", *International Journal of Operation & Production Management*, 24(6), 554–565.
Ellaram, L. M., & Cooper, M. C. (1990) "Supply Chain Management Partnership, and the Shipper-Third Party Relationship", *International Journal of Logistics Management*, 1(2), 1–10.
Fagan, M. L. (1991) "A Guide to Global Sourcing", *The Journal of Business Strategy*, 12(2), 21.
Jean, B. (2008) *Advantages and Disadvantages of Global Sourcing* (14 ed.). Bingley: Emerald Group Publishing.
Jin, B. (2004) "Achieving an Optimal Global Versus Domestic Sourcing Balance Under Demand Uncertainty", *International Journal of Operation & Production Management*, 24(12), 1292–1305.
Kotabe, M. (1998) "Efficiency vs. Effectiveness Orientation of Global Sourcing Strategy: A Comparison of US and Japanese Multinational Companies", *Academy of Management Executive*, 12(4), 107–119.
Kotabe, M., & Mol, M. J. (2004) "A New Perspective on Outsourcing and the Performance of the Firm, in: M. Trick (Ed) Global Corporate Evolution: Looking Inward or Looking Outward", *International Management Series*, 4, 331–340.
Kotabe, M., & Mol, M. J. (2006) "International Sourcing: Redressing the Balance", in: J. T. Mentzer, M. M. Myers & T. P. Stank (Eds.), *Handbook of Global Supply Chain Management*. London: Sage Publication, pp. 393–408.

Sourcing Decision in Global Supply Chain Management 277

Kotabe, M., Mol, M. J., & Ketkar, S. (2008) "An Evolutionary Stage Model of Outsourcing and Competence Destruction: A Comparison of the Consumer Electronics Industry", *Management International Review*, 48(1), 65–93.

Kotabe, M., & Murray, J. Y. (2018) "Global Sourcing Strategy: An Evolution in Global Production and Sourcing Rationalization", in: L. Leonidou, C. Katsikeas, S. Samiee, & B. Aykol (Eds.), *Advances in Global Marketing*. Cham, Switzerland: Springer, pp. 365–384.

Kotabe, M., Murray, J. Y., & Mol, M. J. (2008) "Global Sourcing Strategy and Performance: A 'Fit' Versus 'Balance' perspective", *Research in Global Strategic Management*, 14(5, June), 259–277.

Kotabe, M., & Omura, G. S. (1989) "Sourcing Strategies of European and Japanese Multinationals: A Comparison", *Journal of International Business Studies*, 20(1), 113–130.

Leiblein, M. J., Reuer, J. J., & Dalsace, F. (2002) "Do Make or Buy Decisions Matter? The Influence of Organizational Governance on Technological Performance", *Strategic Management Journal*, 23(9), 817–833.

Markides, C. C., & Berg, N. (1988) "Manufacturing Offshore Is Bad Business", *Harvard Business Review*, 66(5), 113–120.

Meixell, M. J., & Gargeya, V. B. (2005) "Global Supply Chain Design: A Literature Review and Critique", *Transportation Research Part E: Logistics and Transportation Review*, 41, 531–550.

Miles, R. E., & Snow, C. C. (1986) "Organizations: New Concepts for New Firms", *California Management Review*, 28(Spring), 62–73.

Murray, J. Y. (2001) "Strategic Alliance-Based Global Sourcing Strategy for Competitive Advantage: A Conceptual Framework and Research Propositions", *Journal of International Marketing*, 9(4), 30–58.

Murray, J. Y., Kotabe, M., & Wildt, A. R. (1995) "Strategic and Financial Implications of Global Sourcing Strategy: A Contingency Analysis", *Journal of International Business Studies*, 26(1), 181–202.

Murray, J. Y., Kotabe, M., & Zhou, J. N. (2005) "Strategic Alliance-Based Sourcing and Market Performance: Evidence from Foreign Firms Operating in China", *Journal of International Business Studies*, 36(2), 187–208.

Prescott, J. E. (1986) "Environments as Moderators of the Relationship Between Strategy and Performance", *Academy of Management Journal*, 29, 329–346.

Quinn, J. B., & Hilmer, F. G. (1994) "Strategic Sourcing", *Sloan Management Review*, 35(4), 43–55.

Rangan, S. (2000) "The Problem of Search and Deliberation in International Exchange: Micro Foundations to Some Macro Patterns", *Journal of International Business Studies*, 31(2), 205–222.

Swamidass, P. M., & Kotabe, M. (1993) "Component Sourcing Strategies of Multinational: An Empirical Study of European and Japanese Multinationals", *Journal of International Business Studies*, 24(1), 81–99.

Trent, R. J., & Monczka, R. M. (2003) "International Purchasing and Global Sourcing – What Are the Differences?", *Journal of Supply Chain Management*, 39(4), 26–37.

Trent, R. J., & Monczka, R. M. (2005) "Achieving Excellence in Global Sourcing", *MIT Sloan Management Review*, 47(1), 24.

Vestring, T., Rouse, T., & Reinert, M. (2005) "Hedge Your Off Shorting Bets", *MIT Sloan Management Review*, 46(3), 7–29.

Williamson, O. E. (1985) *The Economic Institutions of Capitalism*. New York: Free Press.

Bibliography

Baufield, E. (1999) *Harnessing Value in Supply Chain: Strategic Sourcing in Action*. New York: Wiley.

Biullington, C., & Francois, J. (2008, January–February) "Procurement: The Missing Link in Innovation", *Supply Chain Management Review*, pp. 22–28.

Cachon, G. P., & Larivieve, M. A. (2001, March) "Turning the Supply Chain into a Revenue Chain", *Harvard Business Review*, pp. 20–21.

Cavimato, J. L., & Kauffman, R. (2000) *The Purchasing Handbook: A Guide for the Purchasing and Supply Chain Professional*. New York: McGraw Hill.

Coyle, J. J., Langley, C. J., Novade, R. A., & Gibson, B. (2016) "Supply Chain Management: A Logistics Perspective. Nelson Education: A Survey of SCM Professionals", *Journal of Business Logistics*, 28(1), 1–24.

Dekhne, A., Huang, X., & Sarkar, A. (2012, September–October) "Bridging the Procurement-Supply Chain Divide", *Supply Chain Management Review*, pp. 36–42.

Ferreira, J., & Prokopets, L. (2009, January–February) "Does Offshoring Still Makes Sense?", *Supply Chain Management Review*, pp. 20–27.

Goel, A., Moussavi, N., & Srivatsan, V. N. (2008, Winter) "Time to Rethink Offshoring?", *McKinsey on Business Technology*, pp. 14, 32–35.

Larsen, P. D., Poist, R. F., & Hallorsson, A. (2007) "Perspective on Logistics vs Supply Chain Management", *Journal of Business Logistics*, 28(1), 1–24. https://harisportal.hanken.fi/en/publications/perspectives-on-logistics-vs-scm-a-survey-of-scm-professionals

Van Hock, R. I. (1998) "Measuring the Unmeasurable and Improving the Performance in the Supply Chain", *International Journal of Supply Chain Management*, 3(4).

11 Supply Chain Performance Management

Learning Objectives

1 Understand why achieving strategic fit of supply chain capabilities with business objective is critical to a company's overall success and how a company achieves strategic fit between its supply chain strategy and its competitive strategy
2 Getting insight into major challenges that need to be managed successfully for better performance
3 Realise key performance criteria of supply chain and how those have to be derived and measured within the system
4 Get clarity on how to start a company-wide performance management programme to succeed and create competitive advantage
5 To be exposed to a framework of performance management programme that can be applied in a given situation
6 Recognise supply chain maturity levels and models and their implications in business

Introduction

Supply chain management (SCM) has been a major component of competitive strategy to enhance organisational productivity and profitability. The literature on SCM that deals with strategies and technologies for effectively managing a supply chain is quite vast. In recent years, organisational performance measurement and metrics have received much attention from researchers and practitioners. The role of these measures and metrics in the success of an organisation cannot be overstated because they affect strategic, tactical and operational planning and control. Performance measurement and metrics have an important role to play in setting objectives, evaluating performance and determining future courses of actions of any organisation. There are frameworks to promote a better understanding of the importance of SCM performance measurement and metrics.

In ultimate analysis better supply chain management has to result in improved financial performance. The supply chain management objective primarily has to be achieving company's strategic business objective. Businesses achieve financial goals by pursuing a few key strategic drivers developed through careful analysis of the competitive environment and business opportunity and also key competitive advantage of the corporation itself. The strategic drivers of growth and performance of companies operating in a category will thus be different for different corporations. The methods of distributions and product pricing will also be different for companies operating in a typical business vertical derived from their target market and strategies to reach and service those identified market. Companies' supply chain thus has to be managed to

DOI: 10.4324/9781003469063-11

280 *Supply Chain Performance Management*

support the corporations' business strategy and, therefore, has to have an ideal fitment of supply chain strategy with the business strategy.

Achieving the strategic fitment of supply chain with the company's value chain, strategic goal and key drivers to achieve that goal is essential and will ensure the consistency between customer priorities that the competitive strategy of the corporation intends to satisfy and the supply chain capabilities that the supply chain strategy aims to build. To achieve that, different functions in the company must follow the appropriate and approved structure, processes as well as resources to be able to execute these strategies successfully. Also, the design of the overall supply chain and the role of each stage must be aligned to support the supply chain strategy. If this does not happen company may even fail either because of a lack of strategic fit or because its overall supply chain design, processes and resources do not provide the capabilities to support the desired strategic fit. Most importantly supply chain strategies and capabilities will be required to support the company's sales and marketing strategies.

For example, if company stands for immediate delivery on receipt of the order, supply chain has to ensure stock availability at all times at the stock delivery points and does not resort to delaying the delivery for achieving other objectives like economy in transport operations.

Another example that can be cited is of Dell. The competitive strategy of Dell computer is to provide a large number of options to the customer by providing customisable products with their unique customer-specific configuration at a reasonable and also competitive price. As their focus was on customisation, Dell's supply chain was designed to be responsive by ensuring that assembly units owned by Dell were not only strategically located but also flexible and capable to easily handle the variety of customer-specific product specifications. A facility focused on low cost and efficiency derived from producing large numbers of the same specification would not have been appropriate for Dell's business strategy.

Supply chain management performance then will be analysed if the business strategy has been supported well by the supply chain capabilities and strategies to deliver the corporation's business goals and objectives.

11.1 Supply Chain Management Performance Criteria

Several studies have indicated that there is a strong relationship between the largest number of supplier and customer integration to market share and profitability. This would mean that taking advantage of supplier capabilities and emphasising a long-term supply chain perspective in customer relationships can both be correlated with firm's performance in terms of growth and profit. The growth can be measured in terms of both business volume growth and increased market share. As logistics competency becomes a more critical factor in creating and maintaining competitive advantage, logistics measurement becomes increasingly important because the difference between profitable and unprofitable operations becomes narrower. Firm's logistics management needs to be integrated with the supply chain management in order to ensure improved customer service and satisfaction.

Power (2005) noted that firms engaging in comprehensive performance measurement realised improvements in overall productivity. According to experts, internal measures are generally collected and analysed by the firm generally and will include the following performance criteria:

1 Cost
2 Customer service
3 Productivity measures
4 Asset measurement
5 Quality

Supply Chain Performance Management 281

In addition to the internal performance criteria as mentioned earlier, there can even be company-specific additional criteria which are normally derived from the company's past performance indicators and typical issues and problems that company experiences in their supply chain. For example, vendor's performance and ratings can greatly influence supply chain performance of a corporation. Typically, it may be required to track and rate the performance of key vendors.

External performance measurement is examined through customer perception measures and benchmarking the 'best practice' as well as 'best in class' as mentioned next:

1 Customer perception measurement
2 Benchmarking with best practice

11.2 The Key Elements of Supply Chain Management

Supply chains comprise the flow of products, information and money. How they are managed greatly affects an organisation's competitiveness and profitability. Proper alignment with the business strategy is essential to ensure strong overall performance.

Supply chain performance management is a unified approach to improving the effectiveness and efficiency of all supply chain processes.

Key elements that need to be considered are as follows:

- Supply chain strategy
- Organisation
- Planning
- Management
- Control activities

The combination of these elements fills the gap between the business' decision-makers and IT systems for performance measurement with data structures and reporting tools.

In a nutshell, they are the bridge between strategic directives and successful execution by using available information to steer supply chains from an end-to-end perspective.

The foundation is aligned metrics that drive intended behaviour at the management and operational levels. Ultimately, this will create value for both shareholders and customers.

11.3 Supply Chain Performance Management as a Basis for Industry 4.0

Corporations are now looking at opportunity to improve their SCM performance which can only help them improve organisational performance. Industry 4.0 challenges forced organisations to implement digital transformation.

Traditionally, planning, procurement, logistics and transport management have been separate processes, whereas material planners determine how many parts are needed for production during the manufacturing process and order them while keeping an eye on safety stocks. Suppliers and transport service providers use their own systems. What is delivered when and in what quantity can usually be determined not until the goods are received. Integrated SCM can significantly impact organisational performance. Supply chain performance management (SCPM) can unleash untapped potential.

The elimination of information boundaries between individual departments (silos) can unleash a huge amount of untapped potential that companies want to exploit in the wake of increased costs and rising demand for flexibility.

282 *Supply Chain Performance Management*

When companies look beyond the horizon of their daily business operations and begin to think about Industry 4.0 and smart factory (or self-managed production), they soon realise that a stable supply chain and a reliable forecast of quantities and dates are prerequisites for Industry 4.0. With its wide range of functions, SCPM plays a key role by delivering the required information and data for an optimal production supply. Managing supply chain for better performance is a prerequisite to operate in Industry 4.0 environment when technologies including AI and robotics will redefine the way businesses are conducted and thus it will serve as a basis for entering the new era of Industry 4.0.

11.4 Digitalisation of Supply Chain Changing Today's Performance Management

Shortened product life cycle, product complexity, increased customer focus, increasing digitalisation and closer cooperation between partners in business are increasing the demand on performance management in supply chain. The main drivers behind these developments are customers' demands and new technology, which have already reshaped the traditional supply chain. The results are the customisation of products and services, real-time transparency, cost competition in global scale, and increased efforts in sustainability. Digital transformation in supply chain and big data in supply chain management are disrupting many large organisations. Sensors and other types of connected devices are increasingly deployed to track deliveries and also for monitoring assets. New technologies encourage process automation as well as precision in execution. With the help of analytics, some insight is derived from analyses of huge volume of data to achieve better management of conflicting supply chain objectives and trade-offs. As a result, access to analytical insights is now given to operations manager and supply chain executives and not kept limited to leaders in supply chain.

There are two sides to trade-offs. On the one hand, with the help of new technologies, companies can coordinate and manage their entire network better and more efficiently. Analysing value chain activities to identify performance deviations and irregularities has become easier and is based on more information than in the past.

On the other hand, real-life use cases and the increasing application of Industry 4.0 technologies are transforming supply chains across multiple industries towards digital supply networks. The technology is already there and has hit the ground. It affects all areas of the value chain, the established supply chain and operations processes, and the metrics a company utilises.

In summary, proven approaches to supply chain performance management need to be rethought to cope with increasing customer requirements, technological advancements and ongoing challenges in supply chain complexity as well as pressure to increase revenues and profit margins.

11.5 Current State of Supply Chain Performance Management

The purpose of a successful performance management approach is to give a complete and well-balanced view of all relevant supply chain information and underlying activities. Key performance indicators (KPIs) are intended to structure the desired information in different dimensions such as customer service, costs and assets. Ideally, KPIs are aligned across the reporting hierarchy levels and are available as required. Further supporting metrics allow deep dives into root causes to identify irregularities. However, for most companies the reality is different.

Many companies have implemented supply chain performance measurement systems solely focusing on a limited number of considerations. Most systems are isolated, static, and with

Supply Chain Performance Management 283

metrics that are backward looking and often not holistic. Root cause analyses are limited by data aggregation, with the loss of full details, or are simply not possible due to the lack of information. An end-to-end perspective has often not been considered, and an integrated performance measurement concept has not been implemented.

Supply chain leaders and businesses often face complex reporting landscapes with numerous options to measure and calculate performance. Different KPI definitions as well as specifics in the corporate structure and business processes make it hard to compare overall supply chain outcomes.

Among the reasons may be country-specific regulations or a unique business/supply chain steering logic. This complicates informed decision-making and in some cases results in significant costs to fulfil reporting requirements.

Balanced reporting ensures that trade-offs are transparent and properly managed. KPIs should cascade from strategy to tactics, and to the operational level. Successful organisations enable employees to understand the performance levers they influence and how they affect the overall performance.

Standardised processes and metrics are prerequisites for realising such advanced integration. These include the following:

- Planning details throughout the entire sales and operations planning process
- Customer service levels
- Accuracy of current inventories
- Transparency of supply chain costs

Leading performance management solutions utilise joint metrics to ensure the integration of all functions. For example, finished goods inventory is shared between production and sales. KPIs might be communicated to key supply chain partners using an overall perspective to optimise the end-to-end value chain and to manage trade-offs. Advanced solutions with dashboards exist that visualise a comprehensive suite of supply chain information at a single glance.

11.6 Implementing Robust Performance Management System

Many companies have already implemented a robust supply chain performance management and are steadily improving their capabilities. New technologies that drive supply chain digitalisation are being used increasingly and allow for ad hoc analyses and predictive analytics as well as improving report visualisation. However, the maturity of these supply chain performance management solutions varies. Leading companies differentiate in four areas.

1 Supply chain strategy

- Steering focus and related supply chain processes
- Characteristic measurements and metrics

2 End-to-end processes

- Integrated business planning and customer centricity
- Transparency on inventory and SCM costs

3 Organisational alignment

- Individual employees reacting are proactive to supply chain challenges
- Continuous improvement is encouraged

284 *Supply Chain Performance Management*

4 Integrated technology

- Single source of 'clean' supply chain and financial data
- Supply chain KPIs are calculated and distributed automatically

Key Differentiators in Implementation

1. Supply Chain Strategy Sets the Direction and Defines the Steering Focus

The foundation for performance management is a company's supply chain strategy with its unique value proposition to customers, the derived steering focus and related supply chain processes. Regardless of whether supply chains are response-oriented or configured for efficiency, the strategy defines what and where to measure. Companies that have mastered the challenge of measuring the right areas in their supply chain and that have the right metrics in place can say why those measurements and steering are important for the execution of strategy.

2. Supply Chain Management Processes Must Be Linked with Transparency of Inventories and Supply Chain Cost

Integrated business planning drives the alignment of all functions in business like sales, operations, and finance towards the highest level of performance. It is important that quality of information is not only coherent but also always up to date. End-to-end processes identified, harmonised for sustainability. An efficient customised ERP system which can act as the backbone of SCM processes to ensure that the performance of the process in execution is accurately measured.

Customer centricity is the key to delivering exceptional performance. KPIs such as perfect order rate, delivery reliability, or delivery capability would serve as appropriate metrics for measuring customer service. Different service levels and business-specific indicators are generally considered when overall supply chain performance is evaluated.

Accurate inventory levels of various items including details of batch inventories and critical material inventories are pivotal for taking meaningful decisions about supply and demand as also for working capital management. Seamlessly integrated inventory data will allow quick identification of any variances in stock level enabling detailed root cause analyses in material flow movements.

Supply chain cost might be aggregated, but it also should be made available at its cost component level. The focus however should be on production, warehousing, freight and inventories, as these are typically the largest cost components in supply chain. Leading companies utilise a total landed cost perspective and challenge their actual SCM cost. For example, logistics cost performance is agreed by sales, which is verified by operations who can object if agreed conditions and prerequisites are not met.

1. Organisational Alignment and Accountability for Metrics

Leading companies structure their organisation according to agreed customer service delivery. And to achieve that, objectives of supply chain organisation are clearly defined. By using an established set of SCM KPIs, individual employees are reacting proactively to supply chain challenges and risks. KPIs of supply chain and process indicators must have relevant performance attributes and that must be made available to the whole organisation.

Reasonable targets and established thresholds cover all dimensions of supply chain performance. Continuous improvement is encouraged by a performance evaluation process and recurring cross-functional and reliable feedback.

The ownership of performance management systems is typically with the CFO, who forms partnerships with other business functions such as sales and operations to achieve transparency of the company's performance.

2. Integrated Technology and Adaptive Reporting

Technology is a key enabler of world-class supply chain performance management. Successful companies operate an enterprise data warehouse that serves as single source of reliable real-time data for analyses. External data is collected as required and seamlessly integrated with in-house supply chain information.

Reporting can be described as a centralised data highway with a uniform reporting language which is integrated, cross-functional and adaptive. A supply chain dashboard application creates a single point of entry and provides an overview of the relevant supply chain metrics over multiple dimensions such as brands, products, locations, customers and segments.

A robust reporting governance process ensures continuous and automated monitoring. Supply chain KPIs are measured and distributed proactively to relevant stakeholders. Predictive algorithms are used for advanced business intelligence and to determine timely corrective actions along the end-to-end supply chain.

FURTHER DEVELOPMENT OF PERFORMANCE MANAGEMENT IN SCM

Many companies are evaluating the opportunities of new technologies offered by Industry 4.0 and are running pilot cases for applicability. Transparency and accuracy of information and the interoperability of machines and people are the key drivers that can take supply chains to their next level of performance.

As such one can say that supply chain performance management is gradually evolving, due to faster access to information and analyses that paves the ways for gaining deeper insights. Trends with significant impact on how supply chains are managed will now include the following:

- Ongoing digitalisation of supply chains and resulting exponential growth in data from connected devices, for example, fleet assets, containers, deliveries and in-use products
- A shift to real-time data enabled by sensors covering geographic locations and conditions such as temperature and pressure
- New ways of visualising SCM insights and increasing the use of predictive methods to forecast sales, evaluate maintenance requirements, or detect product quality issues early enough for a proactive mitigation management
- Easier linking of internal supply chain data with external data sources, for example, traffic and meteorological data for navigating trucks, the status of outsourced processes for enabling full supply chain transparency, or financial information about suppliers for improved supply chain risk management
- Improved analytics capabilities using cloud computing and in-memory data storage and analytics that allow for fast analyses and the processing of large volumes of data. To capitalise on trends and improved reporting possibilities, performance management frameworks and reporting systems should be periodically investigated and updated. As customer behaviour changes with the change in business environment and supply chain, it is essential to maintain the right focus on what and where to measure

286 *Supply Chain Performance Management*

TRENDS IN MANAGEMENT REPORTING ON SUPPLY CHAIN PERFORMANCE

In an information-enabled supply chain organization, more and more data are available. Deloitte predicts that reporting will advance towards finding the most relevant information in the data jungle by using web mining to quickly reach new events, predictive analytics with sound 'what if'? scenarios, and preselected content using artificial intelligence.

Manager's new working styles will shift reporting towards an always-on state with 24X7 availability. Reporting system prospectively provide a personalised view and enable target groups of one. When designing reports, neuroscience insights will be increasingly incorporated and design will be no longer based on matters of taste. Automation free up human time and robotics are being increasingly applied. Logistics companies around the world offer 24×7 real-time information about cargo movement. Well-performing corporations in a highly competitive environment as well as some MNCs review their SCM performance on identified and critical criteria at regular intervals and compare those with the budgeted and last year's actual to enable them to take corrective actions. Management reporting helps the business to compare its own performance also with the competition and industry standards to remain relevant as well as competitive to the category of industry that they represent.

Organisational boundaries are gradually being removed through flexible teams, communities and virtual organisations. This will affect the decision-making process that accelerates through collaboration, interactive, discussions in 'war rooms' and a shared performance culture.

SIGNALS FOR BUSINESSES TO IMPROVE SCM PERFORMANCE

Any time is right to initiate implementation of company-wide SCM performance management system to be more competitive and also more productive. However, there can be situations when company has to seriously consider improvement of their SCM performance.

Such indications are when customer expectations and new technologies are transforming supply chain management faster than ever. Signs of concern are sub-optimal overall supply chain performance, inefficient resource allocation, individual targets that are not aligned with strategic objectives, operational managers without clear accountability, or reporting analyses efforts that fail to highlight potential issues in a timely manner.

If one of these symptoms is present, it is time to rethink your company's performance management capabilities and the approach to measuring and managing supply chains.

Businesses have initiated strategies and supports for companies to drive large-scale transformation initiatives in their supply chains, help to institutionalise performance management, and enable the organisation to steer their value chain activities towards exceptional performance. With state-of-the-art supply chain performance management from strategy to processes to technology. Companies performance management should be covering a full range of services as a discipline and in managing value chains from an end-to-end perspective with an objective to increase the overall performance of the business in a highly competitive environment.

11.7 Performance Measurements and Metrics in SCM

Performance measurement can be initiated at strategic, operational as well as tactical levels in any organisation.

The metrics and measures can be discussed in the context of the supply chain activities and or processes such as plan, source, make or assemble, and delivery and customer service (Stewart, 1995; Gunasekaran et al., 2001).

Order Entry Method

This method determines the way and extent to which customer specifications are converted into information exchanged along the supply chain.

Order Lead Time

The total order cycle time, called order to delivery cycle time, refers to the time elapsed in between the receipt of customer order until the delivery of finished goods to the customer. The reduction in order cycle time leads to reduction in supply chain response time, and as such is an important performance measure and source of competitive advantage (Christopher, 1992) – it directly interacts with customer service in determining competitiveness.

The Customer Order Path

The path that an order traverses is another important measure whereby the time spent in different channels can be determined. By analysing the customer order path, non-value-adding activities can be identified so that suitable steps can be taken to eliminate them.

Evaluation of Supply Link

Traditionally supplier performance measures were based on price variation, rejects on receipt and on time delivery. For many years, the selection of suppliers and product choice were mainly based on price competition with less attention afforded to other criteria like quality and reliability. More recently, the whole approach to evaluating suppliers has undergone drastic change.

Evaluation of Suppliers

The evaluation of suppliers in the context of the supply chain (efficiency, flow, integration, responsiveness and customer satisfaction) involves measures important at the strategic, operational and tactical levels.

Strategic level measures include lead time against industry norms, quality level, cost-saving initiatives, and supplier pricing against market.

Operational level measures include ability in day-to-day technical representation, adherence to developed schedule, ability to avoid complaints and achievement of defect-free deliveries.

Tactical level measures include the efficiency of purchase order cycle time, booking in procedures, cash flow, quality assurance methodology and capacity flexibility.

Purchasing and supply management must analyse on a periodic basis their supplier abilities to meet the firm's long-term needs. The areas that need particular attention include the supplier's general growth plans, future design capability in relevant areas, role of purchasing and supply management in the supplier's strategic planning, potential for future production capacity and financial ability to support such growth (Fisher, 1997). Supply chain partnership is a collaborative relationship between a buyer and seller which recognises some degree of interdependence and cooperation on a specific project or for a specific purchase agreement (Ellram, 1991; van Hoek, 2001). Such a partnership emphasises direct, long-term association, encouraging mutual planning and problem-solving efforts (Maloni and Benton, 1997). Supplier partnerships have attracted the attention of practitioners and researchers (Macbeth and Ferguson, 1994; Ellram, 1991;

288 *Supply Chain Performance Management*

Graham et al., 1994). All have contended that partnership formation is vital in supply chain operations and as such for efficient and effective sourcing. Partnership maintenance is no less important. Performance evaluation of buyers or suppliers is simply not enough – relationships must be evaluated.

The parameters that need to be considered in the evaluation of partnerships are the ones that promote and strengthen them. For example, the level of assistance in mutual problem solving is indicative of the strength of supplier partnerships. Partnership evaluation based on such criteria will result in win–win partnerships leading to more efficient and more thoroughly integrated supply chains.

Performance Measures and Metrics at Production Level

Performance measures at production sites have major impact on product quality, cost and speed of delivery as well as delivery reliability and flexibility (Mapes et al., 1997; Slack et al., 1995) and thus constitute an important part of the supply chain, and therefore production function needs to be measured and continuously improved. Some measures of production levels are as follows:

After the order is planned and goods sourced, the next step is to make/assemble products. This is the activity carried out by organisations that own production sites, and their performance has a major impact on product cost, quality, speed of delivery and delivery reliability, and flexibility (Mapes et al., 1997; Slack et al., 1995). As it is quite an important part of the supply chain, production needs to be measured and continuously improved. Suitable metrics for the production levels are as follows:

Range of Products and Services

According to Mapes et al. (1997), a plant that manufactures a broad product range is likely to introduce new products more slowly than plants with a narrow product range. Plants that can manufacture a wide range of products are likely to perform less well in the areas of value added per employee, speed and delivery reliability. This clearly suggests that product range affects supply chain performance.

CAPACITY UTILISATION

The role played by capacity in determining the level of activities in a supply chain is quite important. According to Slack et al. (1995), of the many aspects of production performance, capacity utilisation directly affects the speed of response to customer demand through its impact on flexibility, lead time and deliverability.

Effectiveness of Scheduling Techniques

Scheduling refers to the time or date on or by which activities are to be undertaken. Such fixing determines the manner in which resources will flow in an operating system, the effectiveness of which has an important impact on production and thus supply chain performance. For example, scheduling techniques such as JIT, MRP and ERP have implications on purchasing, throughput time and batch size. In case of the supply chain, since scheduling depends heavily on customer demands and supplier performance, the scheduling tools should be viewed in that context (Little et al., 1995).

Supply Chain Performance Management 289

Evaluation of Delivery Link

The link in a supply chain that directly impacts customers is delivery. It is a primary determinant of customer satisfaction; hence, measuring and improving delivery is always desirable to increase competitiveness. Delivery by its very nature takes place in a dynamic and ever-changing environment, making the study and subsequent improvement of a distribution system difficult. It should be noted that it is not an easy matter to anticipate how changes to one of the major elements within a distribution structure will affect the system as a whole (Rushton and Oxley, 1989).

Measures for Delivery Performance Evaluation

According to Stewart (1995), an increase in delivery performance is possible through a reduction in lead time attributes. Another important aspect of delivery performance is on-time delivery. On-time delivery reflects whether perfect delivery has taken place or otherwise and is also a measure of customer service level. A similar concept, *on time order fill*, was used by Christopher (1992), describing it as a combination of delivery reliability and order completeness. Another aspect of delivery is the percentage of finished goods in transit, which if high signifies low inventory turns, leading to unnecessary increases in tied-up capital. Various factors that can influence delivery speed include vehicle speed, driver reliability, frequency of delivery and location of depots. An increase in efficiency in these areas can lead to a decrease in the inventory levels (Novich, 1990).

Number of Faultless Notes Invoiced

An invoice shows the delivery date, time and condition under which goods were received. By comparing these with the previously made agreement, it can be determined whether perfect delivery has taken place or not, and areas of discrepancy can be identified so that improvements can be made.

Flexibility of Delivery Systems to Meet Particular Customer Needs

This refers to flexibility in meeting a particular customer delivery requirement at an agreed place, agreed mode of delivery and with agreed-upon customised packaging. This type of flexibility can influence the decision of customers to place orders, and thus can be regarded as important in enchanting and retaining customers (Novich, 1990).

Of the factors by which supply chains compete, flexibility can be rightly regarded as a critical one. Being flexible means having the capability to provide products/services that meet the individual demands of customers in a dynamic market environment. Some flexibility measures include: (i) product development cycle time, (ii) machine/tool set up time, (iii) economies of scope (Christopher, 1992) – refers to the production of small quantities of wider range (e.g. JIT lot size) and (iv) number of Inventory turns.

Measuring Customer Service and Satisfaction

Measuring customer service is critical to the business survival and has, therefore, to be undertaken at regular interval and with utmost care. Without achieving customer satisfaction, the whole exercise of performance management in supply chain will become useless. In a modern supply chain, customers can reside next door or across the globe, and in either case they must

290 *Supply Chain Performance Management*

be well served for total satisfaction or even delight the customers. As such, Lee and Billington (1992) and van Hoek et al. (2001) emphasised that to assess supply chain performance, supply chain metrics must centre on customer satisfaction.

Customer Query Time

Customer query time relates to the time it takes for a firm to respond to a customer query with the required information. It is not unusual for a customer to enquire about the status of order, potential problems on stock availability, or delivery. A fast and accurate response to those requests is essential in keeping customers satisfied.

Post-transaction Measures of Customer Service

The function of a supply chain does not end when goods are provided to the customer. Post-transaction activities play an important role in customer service and provide valuable feedback that can be used to further improve supply chain performance.

Starting Performance Management Programme in the Organisation

The goal of this approach is to identify the necessary steps for a successful visibility programme that improves supply chain productivity, responsiveness and reliability. Companies must evolve through three levels of maturity when seeking operational improvement and financial value from visibility technology. In the first level (Shipment Tracking), the system provides shipment tracking to locate the product. This information improves customer satisfaction and helps internal operations planning. In the second level (Supply Chain Disruption Management), disruption management is notified proactively if shipments deviate from planned milestones and assists in problem resolution. This information improves the on-time delivery performance and lowers expediting costs. The greatest financial value comes in the third level (Supply Chain Improvement), when visibility information helps identify and eliminate root causes of delays. Effectiveness at this level has a positive impact on lead time, inventory investment and freight cost. The successful implementation of such a supply chain visibility technology requires five critical steps, described in the Roadmap for Supply Chain Visibility: First, it is important to devise a visibility strategy. Since visibility develops over time, the strategy should focus on the highest problem areas first and then expand from there. The creation of an 'as is' assessment of key metrics, targeted for improvement, is part of the strategy process. Key metrics should include both cross-functional and department-based metrics, such as cycle times, on-time delivery performance, or safety stock levels. The definition of the visibility strategy also includes the identification of responsibilities for the improvement of each metric and the establishment of a cross-functional team with an executive sponsor. Second, the company has to select a visibility technology that meets its requirements. There are different visibility technologies available. These can be classified into three categories: internally developed systems, systems provided by logistics providers and systems from commercial technology vendors. The most important aspect of a visibility project is the creation of a rollout plan, described in step three. The project team has to determine which areas of the supply chain to concentrate on first. This requires the identification of small, simple projects. Depending on the company, this can mean concentrating on certain regions, shipments for key customers, or certain product lines, perhaps those with the highest value or time sensitivity. Assessing the availability of quality status data is another consideration for determining the scope. Therefore, it is beneficial to start with the smallest data set possible that still drives value. Successful pilot programmes often focus on areas in which better visibility will lead to significant improvements in lead times and on-time delivery performance The fourth step deals with the improvement of disruption management. Many commercial visibility systems now include functionality to not only serve as a problem detector but also provide resolution insights and support. If necessary, these features help decide what actions should be taken if the actual status deviates from the planned status. As a result, resolution functionality can help enforce corporate policies for expediting, rerouting, reallocating inventory and so on. This has positive effects on customer service capabilities and delivery performance. Driving structural supply chain improvement, however, requires analytical discipline, as described in step five. Using visibility data to measure actual lead times across the supply chain network is one quick opportunity to update the inventory and customer service system with these times. Identifying bottlenecks and recurring points of variability, analysing their underlying causes, and taking corrective actions, on the other hand, helps companies achieve the highest value from visibility technology.

The conceptual background of the model describes the maturity of supply chain transparency with a special focus on the flow of goods. It therefore addresses the topics relevant for the organisation: first, the goal of this approach is to create transparency throughout the entire supply chain to increase customer satisfaction and improve the supply chain performance sustainably. Second, on-time delivery performance and lead time represent two very important parameters for measuring and improving supply chain performance. Third, the Roadmap to Supply Chain Visibility provides an appropriate project approach.

The Supply Chain Visibility Roadmap provides an appropriate project approach, especially by describing the necessary steps of defining a visibility strategy and creating the rollout plan. According to the Visibility Roadmap, the following elements are important when defining a strategy that aims to create transparency

- Focusing on the main problem areas first and then expanding from there
- Creating 'as is' assessment of key metrics, targeted for improvement
- Including both cross-functional and department-based metrics
- Establishing a cross-functional team with an executive sponsor when creating the rollout plan

It is recommended that we start with a small project to create a visible result and then extend to other areas of performance management in order of importance. Therefore, we need to start by doing the following:

- Determining which areas of the supply chain to concentrate on first
- Identifying small, simple projects
- Assessing the availability of quality status data

Starting with the smallest data set possible that still drives value the specific maturity models use different supply chain views to analyse the process performance of each viewpoint. This is especially important, since the SCM processes are cross-functional. The SCM Process Maturity Model uses the SCOR model as a conceptual basis to describe the process maturity of the supply chain activities plan, source, make and deliver.

The SCOR model is a management tool used to address, improve and communicate supply chain management decisions within a company and with suppliers and customers of a company. The model describes the business processes required to satisfy a customer's demands. The

292 *Supply Chain Performance Management*

SCOR model also represents the conceptual framework for measuring the SCM performance. However, this mainly represents the internal perspective on SCM performance. It is also important to consider other viewpoints, such as those presented in customer relationship management. For instance, assesses performance in terms of meeting the customers' expectations. According to the SCM definition, all SCM activities focus on the needs and expectations of customers. Therefore, the customer's viewpoint is indispensable to finding out about how SCM performance is perceived and how they measure their supplier's SCM performance.

Performance measurement systems represent an important viewpoint, since they determine the performance metrics to measure the enterprise's performance regarding processes, functions and employees. Some of the maturity models considered already emphasise the importance of direct process performance measures, such as delivery performance and lead times. This chapter aims to analyse the importance of performance measures and metrics in each of the four basic supply chain processes (plan, source, make and deliver).

The following four aspects are crucial for effective performance measurement and improvement:

- First, measurement goals must represent organisational goals. This allows measuring the achievement of those targets and evaluating the effectiveness of the strategy employed.
- Second, selected metrics should reflect a balance between financial and non-financial measures. Financial performance measurements are important for strategic decisions and external reporting, whereas non-financial measures support the day-to-day control of manufacturing and distribution operations.
- Third, metrics should be related to strategic, tactical and operational levels of decision-making and control. The decisions of top-level management are based on the strategic level and, thus, mainly on financial measures. The tactical-level measures deal with the allocation of resources and the achievement of the results specified at the strategic level. Operational-level measurements and metrics assess the results of the decisions of low-level managers in order to achieve tactical objectives.
- Finally, performance assessment can be better addressed by using a few performance measures that are critical to success and truly capture the essence of organisational performance.

Gunasekaran Patel and McGaughey (2004) reviewed the literature on SCM performance measurements and metrics in the context of the following activities/processes: (a) plan, (b) source, (c) make/assemble and (d) delivery/customer.

Planning Performance Evaluation Metrics

This section deals with financial and non-financial strategic-level performance measures. The importance of these parameters needs to be established by taking customer responses to determine the importance of performance measures from customers' perspectives which can be further categorised based on their importance such as highly important, moderately important and less important. The approach can be like the approach in the methodology used in ABC inventory (inventory item's annual cost is stated as a percentage of total inventory costs) to prioritise inventory management decisions (item cost percentages sorted in descending order and grouped into A – most important, B – moderate importance, and C – less important based on their contribution to total costs). However, it should be noted that categorising a measure as less important does not mean it is unimportant, but rather it seems less important compared to others in the measurement group taking customer service perspective in view. A similar approach could be

Supply Chain Performance Management 293

used by managers in setting priorities in the development of a measurement system for supply chain performance. A more rigorous study to validate the framework should employ a better data and more rigorous statistical techniques. The first set of measures can include four to five non-financial and three to four financial measures that pertain to planning, but more specifically to strategic planning.

This clearly indicates that customer satisfaction is of the utmost importance in increasing competitiveness. The measures considered within the moderately important category include three financial and three non-financial measures, which reflect the importance of a balance between financial and non-financial measures in strategic planning. Variances against budget represent the highest-rated financial metric, whereas order lead time represents the highest-rated non-financial metric. At the order planning level, the customer query time is highly important, whereas the product development cycle time is moderately important. Both metrics are related to meeting customer needs by performing in a timely fashion, which again emphasises the importance of customer service. At the bottom line, customer satisfaction and service are most important at the planning level.

Sourcing Performance Evaluation Metrics

The sourcing process includes purchasing and supplier management activities. The suppliers and vendors play a great role in terms of improving SCM performance of any organisation. Vendors need to be determined and selected following rigorous rating criteria. Most important criteria for sourcing performance can be delivery performance which is directly linked with production performance. The other criteria can be the lead time against the established industry norms, pricing, flexibility, quality and so on.

Production Performance Evaluation Metrics

In this section, supply chain production link metrics/measures are rated in importance. The performance measures for the production link can include percentage of defects (a measure of product quality), cost per operation hour, capacity utilisation, range of product and services, and utilisation of economic order quantity. Depending on the product category, the degree of importance of these production performance parameters could change. For example, percentage defects can emerge as the most important criterion than others. But two others, cost per operation hour and capacity utilisation, were also highly important. Percentage defects can directly impact customer satisfaction level. But the latter two are essentially measures of the efficiency with which resources are used in manufacturing or production plant (produce/assemble), and good performance in these two areas translates into lower cost per unit to manufacture products/ provide services. Efficiency of operations is important for all supply chain partners, if the elusive goal of supply chain optimisation is to be achieved. Note that the percentage importance of each of these three clearly sets them apart from the moderately important and less important measures.

The other measures can include a range of products and services. As noted in the literature, a broader range of products tends to result in fewer new products being introduced and a more narrow range is associated with greater product innovation. For this reason, the measure does seem worthy of the attention of managers, especially in making decisions about the breadth and depth of product lines. Economic ordering quantity (EOQ) could also be a measure but customer survey may not recognise that as an important measure as revealed in some surveys. It was the only measure rated less important. It may be that the participants, in assigning their ratings,

294 *Supply Chain Performance Management*

regarded the use of EOQ as a means to an end rather than an end in itself. In short, quality and efficiency seem to be more important considerations in evaluating production performance.

Delivery Performance Evaluation Metrics

After the orders are planned and goods sourced, produced and assembled, the remaining task is to deliver them to customer. There are criteria and measures that will determine the delivery performance and their degree of importance. Quality of delivered goods is first in importance, followed by on-time delivery of goods and flexibility of service systems to meet customer needs. These three measures are highly important. Note that there is very little difference in the rating of quality of delivered goods and on-time delivery of goods. Here again, these three are related to the perceived customer value of the product, the top-ranking strategic planning measure Providing the customer with a quality product in a timely fashion, and maintaining customer satisfaction with a service system designed to flexibly respond to customer needs are key in producing value for the customer.

The effectiveness of the enterprise distribution planning schedule, effectiveness of delivery invoice methods, number of faultless delivery notes invoiced, percentage of urgent deliveries and information richness in carrying out the delivery are moderately important. According to the rating of measures, while unquestionably important, these measures are not as important as the quality of the delivered product and on-time delivery. It would seem, at least on the surface, that on-time delivery would result from an effective enterprise distribution planning schedule, so it would probably be unwise to ignore the obvious importance of the enterprise distribution planning schedule – one is the means and the other is the end.

The customer responses tended to emphasise techniques like JIT and the application of automation alternatives to reduce costs. Trade-offs between centralisation of the distribution system and decentralisation of the system or even third-party logistics can become an important criterion.

Similarly, to the production performance metrics, there are three delivery performance metrics that are highly important. The first two measures, quality of delivered goods and on-time delivery of goods, have nearly the same rating. Flexibility of service systems to meet customer needs represents the third highly important metric. It is important to provide the customer with a quality product in a timely fashion, and maintaining customer satisfaction with a service system designed to flexibly respond to customer needs is key to producing value for the customer.

A framework to promote a better understanding of the importance of SCM performance measures and metrics that helps organisations in developing a performance measurement programme for SCM (Gunasekaran et al., 2004). The framework, presented in Figure 11.1, considers the four major supply chain activities (plan, source, make/assemble and deliver), as well as the three management levels (strategic, tactical and operational).

It seems that customer satisfaction is paramount in importance in increasing competitiveness, especially for the planning and delivery activities: each first-mentioned metric, at least on the tactical or strategic level, in some way deals with meeting the customers' needs. Companies can use this framework to identify the supply chain activity to be measured, the appropriate metric and the level of management to which the measure should be applied. However, not all supply chains are identical, and the company will certainly have individual performance measurement needs that reflect the unique operations of its business. In terms of the practical example, it is necessary to first devise a strategy and create a rollout plan to determine which areas of the supply chain to focus on. This allows for the selection of performance measures reflecting the operations of the respective supply chain areas.

Supply Chain Performance Management 295

A Framework for Performance Measurement in a Supply Chain

A framework for performance measures and metrics is presented in Table 11.1 considering the four major supply chain activities/processes (plan, source, make/assemble and deliver). These metrics were classified as strategic, tactical and operational to clarify the appropriate level of management authority and responsibility for performance. This framework is based in part on a theoretical framework discussed by Gunasekaran et al. (2001). Measures are grouped in cells at the intersection of the supply chain activity and planning level. For example, supplier delivery performance can be found at the intersection of the source activity and tactical planning level indicating that it pertains to sourcing activities (source) and the tactical planning level. Supplier delivery performance would thus be a measure useful in analysing the performance of mid-level managers as they undertake sourcing activities mid-level managers who are generally the ones

Table 11.1 Framework of Supply Chain Performance Matrix

Supply chain activity/process	*Strategic*	*Tactical*	*Operational*
Plan	Level of customer perceived value of product, variances against budget, order lead time, information processing cost, net profit versus productivity ratio, total cycle time, total cash flow time, product development cycle time	Customer query time, product development cycle time, accuracy of forecasting techniques, planning process cycle time, order entry methods, human resource productivity	Order entry methods, human resource productivity
Source	Technological capability of supply source, ability to develop alternative material and constant upgradation on cost and quality parameters	Supplier delivery performance supplier lead time against industry norm, supplier pricing against market, efficiency of purchase order cycle time, efficiency of cash flow method, supplier booking in procedures	Efficiency of purchase order cycle time, supplier pricing against market
Make/Assemble	Range of products and services. Manufacturing in-house versus out-house	Percentage of defects, cost per operation hour, capacity utilisation, utilisation of economic order quantity	Percentage of defects, cost per operation hour, human resource productivity index
Deliver	Flexibility of service system to meet customer needs, effectiveness of enterprise distribution planning schedule	Flexibility of service system to meet customer needs, effectiveness of enterprise distribution planning schedule, effectiveness of delivery invoice methods, percentage of finished goods in transit, delivery reliability performance	Quality of delivered goods, on-time delivery of goods, effectiveness of delivery invoice methods, number of faultless delivery notes invoiced, percentage of urgent deliveries, information richness in carrying out delivery, delivery reliability performance

296 *Supply Chain Performance Management*

responsible for tactical decisions. More detail could be added to fix personal responsibility for measures with individual managers, or management positions.

This framework should be regarded as a starting point for an assessment of the need for supply chain performance measurement. It is likewise important to understand that the rated importance of metrics in this framework is based on a relatively small sample, and thus, care should be taken in generalising results to all supply chains. The importance of individual metrics presented herein might not apply to all supply chains in all industries. Again, the framework is only a starting point. It is hoped that this framework will assist practitioners in their efforts to assess supply chain performance.

Maturity Models to Measure Supply Chain Performance

Essentially, maturity models are intended to describe the typical behaviour exhibited by a company at a number of levels of 'maturity'. This allows companies to codify what might be considered good practice (and, conversely, bad practice). In addition, there are some intermediate or transitional stages. The concept applies to a range of activities, including quality management, software development, supplier relationships and many more, both as a means of assessment and as part of a framework for improvement. One of the earliest maturity approaches was Crosby's Quality Management Maturity Grid (QMMG). For this reason, most of the following approaches have their roots in the field of quality management. The QMMG expects companies to evolve through five levels of maturity before ascending to quality management excellence, namely: uncertainty, awakening, enlightenment, wisdom and certainty.

At each level, the performance of a number of key activities is described. For this purpose, the approach provides a descriptive text for the characteristic traits of performance for each level. The Capability Maturity Model (CMM) for Software, developed by the Software Engineering Institute at Carnegie Mellon, is perhaps the best-known derivative from this line of work. 'The Capability Maturity Model for Software provides software organisations with guidance on how to gain control of their processes for developing and maintaining software and how to evolve towards a culture of software engineering and management excellence'. The CMM for software provides a framework consisting of five maturity levels that define the extent to which a specific process is defined, managed, measured, controlled and effective, which is widely accepted and implemented. The fundamental assumption of this approach is that quality can be cultivated through control. Therefore, companies at higher maturity levels are better managed, have less risk and are more likely to deliver a quality product that meets the budget and schedule. The software CMM inspired the development of other frameworks, such as the CMM for systems engineering (SE-CMM) and the CMM for integrated product and process development (IPD-CMM). The most recent attempt to consolidate the multiple models is the integrated CMM (CMM-I), which has motivated the development of similar frameworks in other disciplines.

During the various stages of development in terms of maturity models of SCM practices, the corporation progresses from some initial state to more advanced state. Some do it faster than others and with fewer detours, but fast or slow, every company that gets to world-class must evolve through these stages to get there. Therefore, no stages can be left out. In assessing performance or maturity level, a distinction is made between two types of models: On the one hand, there are models in which different activities may be scored at different levels. On the other hand, there are models in which maturity levels are 'inclusive', where a cumulative number of activities must all be performed. In practice, however, maturity models are not primarily used as absolute measures of performance but rather as part of an improvement process. In this regard, the purpose of using a maturity model is to identify a gap that can be closed by subsequent improvement actions.

Overview of SCM Maturity Models

Many of the aforementioned approaches and ideas of maturity have been adapted to supply chains and their management. To analyse the characteristics of maturity models in the field of SCM, Jording and Sucky (2016) developed a design-based characterisation of SCM maturity models. The goal of their work is to provide the reader with a purpose-driven design-based catalogue that serves as a guideline for a more efficient construction of maturity models.

The analysis of these models and their shortcomings reveal quality attributes of SCM maturity models, which then provide the basis of the purpose-driven catalogue. This catalogue specifies the essential building blocks of SCM maturity models.

A maturity model can be defined as a construction-based model, which consists of an anticipated, limited development path, separated into stages with defined characteristics and dimensions. It has one or more objectives related to the stage evaluation, gap identification and transformation. If a model of this kind focuses on intercorporate collaboration, customer focus, management of flow of goods and/or management of information flow, it is called a SCM maturity model. The examination of the numerous models identified in the literature review reveals that those models differ between the anticipated evolutionary content and the operationalisation of the stages.

SCM Process Maturity Model

The SCM Process Maturity Model shows the progression of activities towards effective SCM and process maturity based on five stages. Each of the stages contains characteristics associated with process maturity. These characteristics include predictability, capability, control, effectiveness and efficiency. Due to its process orientation and wide adoption by the supply chain academic and practitioner communities, the SCOR model serves as the basis to conceptualise the SCM Process Maturity Model. The five stages describe the process maturity of four areas: plan, source, make and deliver.

In Stage 1 (Ad hoc), the supply chain and its processes are unstructured without any process measures in place. Functional cooperation is low, and the process performance is unpredictable. As a result, customer satisfaction is low.

In Stage 2 (Defined), basic SCM processes are defined and documented, and process performance is more predictable. The improvement of functional cooperation requires considerable effort. Targets are defined but still missed most of the time. Customer satisfaction has therefore improved but remains low.

Stage 3 (Linked) represents the breakthrough, as broad SCM jobs and structures are put in place, and intracompany functions, vendors and customers are cooperating. Process performance is more predictable, and defined targets are often achieved. Increased customer satisfaction begins to show market improvement.

In Stage 4 (Integrated), organisational structures and jobs are based on SCM procedures, and traditional functions begin to disappear. Cooperation between the company, its vendors and suppliers takes place on a process level. Advanced collaboration with customers and suppliers helps process performance become highly predictable. Targets are reliably achieved, SCM costs are dramatically reduced and customer satisfaction becomes a competitive advantage.

298 *Supply Chain Performance Management*

In the fifth stage (Extended), individual companies are no longer just competing against each other but against entire supply chains. These supply chains represent a horizontal, customer-focused, collaborative culture that shares common processes and goals, as well as joint investments in improving the system. In order to investigate the relationship between SCM process maturity and overall SCM performance, the authors created a survey instrument.

Their investigation revealed significant relationships between SCM process maturity and overall SCM performance in the organisation. Performance measured by each area of the SCOR model is the measurement of performance most related to SCM process maturity. An explanation for this result is that the four areas of the SCOR model provide a clear process context. Delivery performance and order lead times are also significantly correlated with SCM process maturity.

To achieve the defined enterprise goals, a company needs to successfully manage the following seven supply chain views:

- **Supply chain management and logistics:** Functions, processes, activities and tasks related to the integration, collaboration and development of the suppliers
- **Production systems:** Functions, processes, activities and tasks regarding the transformation of the product or service
- **Inventory management:** Actions related to inventory management and control
- **Customer relationship management:** Actions regarding meeting the customer's needs
- **Human resource management:** Actions related to the enterprise's employees, their integration into the company and the work environment.
- **Information systems and technology management:** Actions linked to the development and implementation of information systems and the technology management process
- **Performance measurement systems:** To measure the enterprise's performance regarding processes, functions and employees

Table 11.2 Maturity Levels of the Supply Chain Maturity Model

Level	Level Name	Description
1	Undefined	Describes a competency area for which the enterprise has no documentation or standardisation. The processes are ad hoc, dependent on the person doing the activity and reactive to the environment.
2	Defined	Describes a competency area for which the enterprise has defined the process and procedures. The competency areas are isolated, and there is little forward effort to integrate the many processes.
3	Manageable	Describes a competency area for which the enterprise has defined established procedures that they measure and manage those measurements. Moreover, the enterprise has taken action to integrate and coordinate the internal processes and systems of the enterprise.
4	Collaborative	Describes a competency area for which the enterprise has established procedures to collaborate with suppliers and customers.
5	Leading	Describes a competency area for which the enterprise has established procedures to collaborate with suppliers and customers; it measures these practices and regularly obtains feedback to improve these practices.

Source: SCOR Model, Supply Chain Council, 7 October 2004

Supply Chain Performance Management 299

Discussion Questions

1 Why is performance management in supply chain so important, and how you will go about identifying performance management criteria?
2 Discuss a framework of performance measurement matrix.
3 How you will know at what level a business stands today and if there is a need to initiate performance management programme?
4 Discuss the SCM performance maturity models and stages of evolution.
5 What are the various tools and techniques of conducting performance management in supply chain?
6 Discuss the key performance measurement criteria of a supply chain and their implications in business.
7 Discuss a framework for measurement of a supply chain performance.
8 Discuss the supply Chain maturity model and describe competencies for achieving collaborative level.

Chapter Summary

This chapter deals with supply chain performance management and also measuring supply chain performance. The objective of integrated supply chain management practice is to improve the overall performance of the company. The chapter discusses in detail the performance criteria of a business and how those are identified and measured against stated objective as well as to deliver above-average industry-level performance. While performance measurement of supply chain can be initiated in a business any time, there are indications or signals for businesses to improve their supply chain performance for their own survival, those signals are discussed in the chapter. The performance criteria can include the general measurement criteria but the most important criteria that impact customer service and satisfaction have to be included. In this connection a broad framework of supply chain performance index was discussed in detail. Various tools and techniques used to measure supply chain performance were also discussed in detail. This chapter also discussed the maturity levels of supply chain management in organisation, which can be used by enterprises to understand their performance level and compare with their competitors in the industry. This will be a useful tool which will direct businesses regarding where they stand today in terms of supply chain management practices and what is the way forward for them. As supply chain management program directly impacts customer satisfaction level and index which is extremely important to deliver the organisations' overall performance including profitability and market share.

References

Christopher, M. (1992) *Logistics and Supply Chain Management*. London: Pitman Publishing.
Deloitte's Report, "Performance Management in Supply Chain and Operations – Steering Value Chain Activities Towards Exceptional Performance", The Report Is Available on https://docplayer. net/49296832-Performance-management-in-supply-chain-and-operations-steering-value-chain-activities-towards-exceptional-performance.html
Ellram, L. M. (1991) "A Managerial Guide for the Development and Implementation of Purchasing Partnership", *International Journal of Purchasing and Materials Management*, 27(3), 2–8.
Fisher, L. M. (1997) "What Is the Right Supply Chain for Your Product?", *Harvard Business Review*, 75(2), 105–116.
Graham, T. S., Dougherty, P. J., & Dudley, W. N. (1994) "The Long Term Strategic Impact of Purchasing Partnerships", *International Journal of Purchasing and Materials Management*, 30(4), 13–18.

300 *Supply Chain Performance Management*

Gunasekaran, A., Patel, C., & McGaughey, R. E. (2004) "A Framework for Supply Chain Performance Measurement", *International Journal of Production Economics*, 87(3), 333–347.

Gunasekaran, A., Patel, C., & Tirtiroglu, E. (2001) "Performance Measure and Metrics in a Supply Chain Environment", *International Journal of Operation & Production Management*, 21(1/2), 71–87.

Jording, T., & Sucky, E. (2016) "Improving the Development of Supply Chain Management Maturity Models by Analysing Design Characteristics", *Supply Chain Management Research*, 97–119.

Lee, H. L., & Billington, C. (1992) "Managing Supply Chain Inventory: Pitfalls and Opportunities", *Sloan Management Review*, 33(3), 65–73.

Little, D., Kenworthy, J., Jarvis, P., & Porter, K. (1995) "Scheduling Across the Supply Chain", *Logistics Information Management*, 8(1), 42–48.

Macbeth, D. K., & Ferguson, N. (1994) *Partnership Sourcing: An Integrated Supply Chain Management Approach*. London: Pitman Publishing.

Maloni, M. J., & Benton, W. C. (1997) "Supply Chain Partnerships: Opportunities for Operations Research", *European Journal of Operational Research*, 101, 419–429.

Mapes, J., New, C., & Szwejczewski, M. (1997) "Performance Trade-Offs in Manufacturing Plants", *International Journal of Operation & Production Management*, 17(10), 1020–1033.

Novich, N. (1990) "Distribution Strategy: Are You Thinking Small Enough?", *Sloan Management Review*, 31(1), 71–77.

Peter, G. (1999) "Benchmarking Supply Chain Operations", *Journal of Physical Distribution and Logistics Management*, 29(4).

Power, D. (2005) "Supply Chain Management Integration and Implementation: A Literature Review", *Supply Chain Management*, 10(4), 252–263.

Rushton, A., & Oxley, J. (1989) *Handbook of Logistics and Distribution Management*. London: Kogan Page Ltd.

Slack, N., Chambers, S., Harland, C., Harrison, A., & Johnston, R. (1995) *Supply Chain Operations Management*. London: Pitman Publishing.

Stewart, G. (1995) "Supply Chain Performance Benchmarking Study Reveals Keys to Supply Chain Excellence", *Logistics Information Management*, 8(2), 38–44.

van Hoek, R. I. (2001) "The Contribution of Performance Measurement to the Expansion of Third Party Logistics Alliances in the Supply Chain", *International Journal of Operations & Production Management*, 21(1/2), 15–29.

van Hoek, R. I., Harrison, A., & Christopher, M. (2001) "Measuring Agile Capabilities in the Supply Chain", *International Journal of Operations & Production Management*, 21(1/2), 126–147.

Bibliography

Bolstorff, P., & Rosenbaum, R. (2011) *Supply Chain Excellence: A Handbook for Dramatic Improvement Using the SCOR Model* (3rd ed.). New York: AMACOM.

Cryts, J., Derkach, A., Nyquist, S., Ostrowski, K., & Stephenson, J. (2007, December) *Reducing U.S. Greenhouse Gas Emissions: How Much at What Cost?* McKinsey & Company.

Ganga, G. M. D., & Carpinetti, L. C. R. (2011) "A Fuzzy Logic Approach to Supply Chain Performance Management", *International Journal of Production Economics*, 134 (1), 177–187.

Guide, V. D. R., Jr., & Van Wassenhove, L. N. (2009, January–February) "The Evolution of Closed Loop Supply Chains", *Operations Research*, 57, 10–18.

Lebas, M. J. (1995) "Performance Measurement and Performance Management", *International Journal of Production Economics*, 41(1–3), 23–35.

Lee, H. L. (2010, October) "Don't Tweak Your Supply Chain-Rethink It End to End", *Harvard Business Review*, pp. 61–69.

Lima-Junior, F. R., & Carpinetti, L. C. R. (2016) "Combining SCOR® Model and Fuzzy TOPSIS for Supplier Evaluation and Management", *International Journal of Production Economics*, 174, 128–141.

Logistics Performance Index (LPI) Report. (2016, March 20) "The Gap Persists", *Washington*. http://lpi.worldbank.org/international/global/2016 (accessed on 21 May 2018).

Mentzer, J. T., Keebler, J. S., Nix, N. W., Smith, C. D., & Zacharia, Z. G. (2001) "Defining Supply Chain Management", *Journal of Business Logistics*, 22(2), 1–25.

Min, H., & Zhou, G. (2002) "Supply Chain Modeling: Past, Present and Future", *Computers & Industrial Engineering*, 43(1–2), 231–249.

Neely, A., Bourne, M., & Kennerley, M. (2000) "Performance Measurement System Design: Developing and Testing a Process Based Approach", *International Journal of Operations & Production Management*, 20(10), 1119–1145.

Neto, M. S., & Pires, S. R. I. (2012) "Performance Measurement in Supply Chains: A Study in the Automotive Industry", *New Advances in Vehicular Technology and Automotive Engineering*, 19(4), 733–746.

Pierreval, H., Bruniaux, R., & Caux, C. (2007) "A Continuous Simulation Approach for Supply Chains in the Automotive Industry", *Simulation Modelling Practice and Theory*, 15(2), pp. 185–198.

Plambeck, E. (2007) "Wal-Mart's Sustainable Strategy", *Stanford Graduate School of Business Case OIT-71*.

Prokesh, S. (2010, October) "The Sustainable Supply Chain", *Harvard Business Review*, pp. 70–72.

Saad, M., & Patel, B. (2006) "An Investigation of Supply Chain Performance Measurement in the Indian Automotive Sector", *Benchmarking: An International Journal*, 13(1/2), 36–53.

Sako, M., & Helper, S. (1998) "The Information Requirements of Trust in Supplier Relations: Evidence from Japan, Europe and the United States", *Trust and Economic Learning*, pp. 23–47.

Supply Chain Council. (2012) *Supply Chain Operations Reference Model (SCOR)*. Available at www.supply-chain.org (accessed on 23 August 2019).

12 Benchmarking Supply Chain Performance

Learning Objectives

1 Understand importance and scope of supply chain benchmarking
2 Decide on supply chain performance metrics
3 Initiate benchmarking exercise within the company and standard benchmarking process
4 Understand the importance of identifying companies to be benchmarked
5 Gain clarity on some common misconception on benchmarking
6 Identifying benchmarking criteria in Supply Chain and also with whom to be benchmarked
7 Implementation of benchmarking process in the company and how to initiate performance improvement program based on the findings

Introduction

Supply chain management function covers a wide range of functions of the business. And becoming competitive in that area is a key imperative for all businesses which requires managing end-to-end supply chains for efficiency and effectiveness. The performance of supply chain depends on technology deployed and also processes followed and practised. One way of keeping a track if an organisation is competitive or not is to benchmark SCM performance periodically with identified competitors or industry leaders. Benchmarking criteria can be decided by the business based on the key differentiators that can make difference in performance. One such differentiator is, of course, the cost of production and another key differentiator is customer service level and customer satisfaction. If businesses can upgrade in these two parameters, then it can expect to deliver above-average performance. Benchmarking normally has to be done for those parameters which require further improvement. This section will deal with the issues concerning benchmarking criteria, and how to go about initiating supply chain performance benchmarking and what precautions are necessary to be taken to get a useful outcome. Benchmarking also can be done collectively forming a syndicate of a few progressive players in a business category to gain from each other's experience. However, benchmarking is not to be confused with typical syndicated survey that periodically some businesses participate in to find the larger issues and direction a business category players are likely to face in future.

What Is Benchmarking?

Benchmarking can somewhat philosophically be defined as follows (APQC, 1992):

> *Benchmarking is the practice of being humble enough to admit that someone else is better at something, and being wise enough to learn how to match them and even surpass them at it.*

DOI: 10.4324/9781003469063-12

Benchmarking Supply Chain Performance 303

This definition captures the essence of benchmarking, namely learning from others. The core of the current interpretation of benchmarking is:

- *Measurement* of own and the benchmarking partners' performance level, both for comparison and for registering improvements.
- *Comparison* of performance levels, processes, practices etc.
- *Learning* from the benchmarking partners to introduce improvements in your own organisation.
- *Improvement*, which is the ultimate objective of any benchmarking study.

The basic objective of using benchmarking supply chain is to increase the knowledge about the supply chain management process and to enable the industrial partners to learn from the best practice. This was done through identification and study of other enterprises in Europe and their processes.

To reach this objective, a process benchmarking study needs to be undertaken to compare the processes in this area within or even outside the country where business is located. The purpose was both to gain information that could lead to improvements in the areas of vendor management practices, supplier's efficiency etc., but most importantly to gain an understanding of best practice in this area.

The primary information from the benchmarking activity is flowcharts and process descriptions. It was more important to find 'best practices' than numerical performance data. The collection of data was done by visits to the benchmarking partners. To ensure consistent information from all the benchmarking visits, a questionnaire needs to be developed to be used during the interviews (Andersen and Randmael, 1997). The questionnaire should be so designed that it captures all information that needs to be understood related to supply chain management processes and practices.

Benchmarking Supply Chain Performance

Benchmarking of performance is required to be done to find if the company is competitive enough in a given market. After all, everything ultimately can be related to cost and businesses have to be cost competitive. Two companies with different cost structures cannot co-exist for a long time, higher-cost company has to close down sooner or later. Supply chain of a corporation can be considered the largest cost centre for the business and, therefore, it is imperative that SCM function is managed for delivering the company's performance objective. And performance objective, therefore, has to be competitive in order to survive in a keenly contested market. One way of knowing if a business is competitive enough is to conduct benchmarking periodically. Benchmarking is normally done against best in class as well as against best in the category. This would mean that benchmarking under a given set of parameters should be done against best performer in the same category of the business like an automobile manufacturer should benchmark against best-known performer in the automobile sector itself. Benchmarking also should be done against best in class. For example, same automobile manufacturer also should benchmark against say Unilever or P&G, who are known to have pioneered in their supply chain management practices (Stewart 1995).

Supply chain operations in a business should constantly be reviewed to identify areas of improvements possible. One method is to perform a series of benchmarking tests for parameters like price, quality, design, efficiency and cost-effectiveness.

In general, companies perform either benchmarking of results focusing on quantitative performance measures, and benchmarking of best practices focusing on how well processes are

304 *Benchmarking Supply Chain Performance*

executed by the competitor. The results of both these approaches of benchmarking are best used together. Benchmarking of results only provides a basis for ranking a company to understand where company stands but does not reveal how that performance has been achieved or what strategies are required to improve its performance. Successful supply chain benchmarking incorporates all of the elements in the global supply chain and focuses on product specifications, operational performance, management practices and software solutions (Peter, 1999). Supply chain benchmarking involves three major components – the supplier, the distributor and the interface of the two. However, primary focus of the business is to improve upon its customer satisfaction index and that should be the primary motivation for establishing a benchmarking programme.

How to Start

Companies benchmarking efforts has to help businesses to become cost competitive. The supply chain benchmarking can help them achieve this goal. It is therefore a good idea to use benchmarking exercise in conjunction with the companies' improvement initiatives. Benchmarking then offers a performance measurement tool that can measure companies' comparative operating performance, identify best practices and possible improvements, and determine how a business is performing against its potential. Benchmarks can also help businesses assess a variety of costs – the cost of goods, the cost of doing business (including inbound and outbound logistics), and opportunity costs.

But question normally will arise as to where companies should begin. Previously created benchmarking data – whether quantitative (performance-based) or qualitative (best practices) – can provide a good starting point. It always helps to engage consulting and research firms with experience to advise on how to organise or undertake competitive benchmarking projects. Companies can even first accomplish an internal benchmarking against their own standards of KPIs and then compare those with the identified competitors like best performer or leader in the category or even best in class.

Scope of Supply Chain Benchmarking

Supply chain performance and process benchmarking provide useful comparisons with other companies. In addition, it can also help organisations to identify areas of:

*   Performance improvements
*   Interdependencies and relationships between key performance indicators (KPIs)
*   Better business trade-offs
*   Opportunities for cross-industry best practices
*   Baseline information for goal setting, prioritisation, and ongoing performance measurements

Companies need adequate preparation to capture all data for a meaningful benchmarking exercise. The processes that need to be followed for an effective benchmarking can briefly be summarised as follows:

*   Determine the scope of the benchmarking exercise covering planning, procurement, manufacturing and logistics.
*   Decide on a set of KPIs under each identified areas for measurement and comparison.
*   Zero in on the companies to be benchmarked which can be immediate competitors, best in class and best performers in the category.

Benchmarking Supply Chain Performance 305

- Develop reporting templates and formats and frequency of measurement.
- Work out a plan of implementation and action.
- Identify resources required and data collection plan.
- Ensure agreements and involvement of stakeholders on its objective, process and benefits.
- Collect and validate the data.
- Analyse and interpret data collected.
- Compare with companies' own performance and identify the reasons thereof to plan for the future.

Supply Chain Performance Metrics for Benchmarking

Companies can use performance metrics to perform gap analyses and identify areas requiring improvement. Supply chain management KPIs should generally include the following:

- **Delivery performance metrics:** On-time delivery, performance to commitment, fill rates like stock fill rate, pack fill rate and order fill rate, and stock return rates.
- **Cycle-time metrics:** Promised lead time, actual lead time and supply chain cycle time.
- **Inventory and cash management metrics:** Inventory days of supply, days sales outstanding, days payables outstanding and cash-to-cash conversion.
- **Supply chain cost metrics:** Overall supply chain costs, order management costs, inventory-carrying costs, supply chain finance and planning costs, supply chain IT costs, procurement department staffing, and savings.

Specific benchmark data gained through these metrics are focused on the identification of key capabilities to enable an integrated demand-supply network (IDSN).

Supply Chain Benchmarks of Standard Processes

Another way to approach supply chain benchmarking is to look deeper into traditional supply chain processes.

Planning (demand management, materials planning and production scheduling). Many planning KPIs are available, but companies must determine the indicators that are truly important to their organisations' operational performance. Examples include cash-to-cash cycle time, inventory-carrying costs, days inventory outstanding, finished goods inventory turn rate, cost of goods sold as a percentage of revenue, forecast accuracy, number of full-time equivalents (FTEs) for the supply chain planning function per USD 1 billion in revenue, production schedule adherence, total expediting of costs to execute the production plan, value-added productivity per employee and return on assets.

Procurement (sourcing strategy development, supplier selection and contract management, order management, and supplier appraisal and development). Examples of KPIs benchmarked for procurement include total cost of the procurement cycle per purchase order or per USD 1000 in purchases, rate of annual raw material inventory turns, average supplier lead time in days, days payable, number of FTEs for the procurement cycle per USD 1 billion in purchases, and the percentage of purchases made via an electronic marketplace.

Manufacturing (production scheduling, production and performing maintenance). Common manufacturing KPIs include finished product first-pass yield (FPY), percentage of defective parts per million (DPMO), and scrap and rework costs as a percentage of sales and quantities shipped per employee. Other KPIs benchmarked for product manufacturing are manufacturing

306 *Benchmarking Supply Chain Performance*

cycle time, actual production rate as a percentage of maximum capable production rate, annual work-in-process (WIP) inventory turn rate, unplanned machine downtime as a percentage of scheduled run time, warranty costs (i.e. repair and replacement) as a percentage of sales, and labour turnover rate as a percentage of the workforce. Logistics (logistics strategy, planning for inbound material flow, warehousing, outbound transportation and managing returns and reverse logistics). Standard KPIs for product delivery include order fill rate, pick-to-ship cycle times for customer orders, total cost of outbound transportation process per USD 1000 in revenue, number of FTEs required to operate outbound transportation per USD 1 billion in revenue, the percentage of sales order line items not fulfilled due to stock-outs, the percentage of full-load trailer/container capacity used per shipment, and the percentage of orders expedited. Examples of KPIs for logistics/warehousing as a whole include total logistics costs as a percentage of revenue, freight costs as a percentage of revenue, the percentage of sales orders delivered on time, the number of FTEs for the logistics function per USD 1 billion in revenue, and the ratio of premium freight charges to total freight charges.

Importance of Identifying Right Companies to Be Benchmarked

Businesses formulate strategies to gain market share and deliver higher level of performance. Competitive business strategies are generally directed against identified competitors. No business considers all players in the category as its competitors. Benchmarking needs to be done only against identified competitors and best-in-class players.

The benchmarking team should also be clear about what it wants to learn before approaching a potential benchmarking peer group. Competitors will also expect learning from exchange of information related to specific KPIs. Both parties should understand and agree on the expected outcome and how the information will be gathered and analysed, who will have access to the data, and how the data will be used.

Best-in-class companies involve suppliers and customers in the sales and operations planning (S&OP) process and use customer feedback to ensure a more accurate match of demand and supply. These companies also collaborate with suppliers on inventory management levels and on invoice reconciliation to improve invoice and payment processes. Best-in-class companies offer good learning opportunities from their SCM practices to improve the customer satisfaction and reduce costs.

Improving Performance

The ultimate aim of benchmarking is to incorporate the best practices within the company to improve performance and to become more competitive in the marketplace. That is how company can ensure survival and growth. The analysis of the data collected to create meaningful and actionable process improvements plan holds the key. This needs a great care. The best practices can be captured from benchmarking exercise from various partners and then an agreed practice and process to be prepared for implementation considering the other constraints and limitations that a specific business can have. Experience from post-implementation of improved processes can help businesses to even improve further by resorting to eliminating the constraints and limitations. Thereby continuous improvement in business is possible through such kind of benchmarking and process mapping. Sometimes even some breakthrough improvement is also possible.

Different people will have different interpretations of the numbers, and there may be some organisational resistance to change. A structured approach should be used to coordinate the

Benchmarking Supply Chain Performance   307

action plan effort and ensure a meaningful outcome. The focus should be on relationships between the metrics rather than the comparison of individual KPIs to benchmark numbers (e.g. trade-offs between cost and service levels).

Some Common Misconception in Benchmarking

Participating in an industry survey covering a category of industry done on certain parameters is not benchmarking. This is too general and does not give any actionable standards of performance and they are too broad. For example, many companies participate in the syndicated research done by established market research agencies periodically. These should not be confused with benchmarking. These survey findings will be difficult to co-relate with customers of the company as they are too general and not specific to the corporation.

Businesses also should be careful about undertaking some action plan based on pre-existing benchmark. A narrow focus on cost parameters overlooking the customer service delivery and satisfaction will only serve as part of the story.

Benchmarking too many companies at the same time should be avoided as it will only complicate the whole exercise and diffuse the focus. The scope of benchmarking should be focused and limited to identified companies.

Not aligning the business goals with benchmarking criteria also will not be effective and meaningful. After all ultimate goal is to improve end-to-end performance of the business.

Not defining clear roles and responsibilities and the absence of an executive sponsor and a data coordinator can result in data access difficulties, defensiveness, blame and incorrect metrics. The effectiveness of benchmarking efforts is hampered when the details, costs and performance levels of all of the company's processes are not known.

Supply chains, which are a critical determinant of a company's competitiveness, are incredibly difficult to manage because they are cross-functional, covering enterprises from different geographic and political boundaries. To set appropriate goals and identify best practices, an individual company's supply chains should be understood and compared with those of industry peers and best-in-class organisations. Through this process, companies can gain greater understanding of the very latest systems and practices that are crucial for improving the management of their own supply chains.

Case Study

Supply Chain Performance Measurement of an Automotive Industry: Applicability of SCOR Model

SCOR model is proposed by Supply Chain Council for performance measurement is easy to understand, practical and suitable for the automotive sector

Introduction

Over the past ten years, the logistics sector in Morocco went through a strong growth which has been reflected in the improvement of the performance of the Logistics Performance Index (LPI), a ranking done annually by the World Bank. Morocco is currently at the 86th place worldwide in logistics performance after being at 94th in 2007. A national strategy has been implemented in Morocco to improve logistics performance and develop the competitiveness of Moroccan businesses. The automotive industry is a highly globalised sector, where there is competition from around the world. Faced with the increase in supply and the strong pressure on prices, reinforced by the power of

308   *Benchmarking Supply Chain Performance*

Asian groups (Toyota, Hyundai etc.) and the arrival of new players from emerging countries (Geely, Tata Group etc.), many companies seek to optimise their value chain in order to remain competitive. In the supply chain of the automotive industry, many factories are working together to manufacture a product (car, motor, truck etc).

Logistics can be considered a key competitive factor in the automotive industry due to the increasing number of variants and options of the model. With the growing importance of logistics, the evaluation of logistics effectiveness and efficiency is gaining increased attention. There are many continuous improvement tools such as total quality management, six sigma, continuous process improvement and others that are available for companies to improve their operations. However, none of these improvement programmes are dedicated to the logistics chain.

In order to improve business systems, the return on investment, to deal with competitiveness and optimise the efficiency of their supply chain, some global companies apply the SCOR model.

The Supply Chain Operations Reference (SCOR) Model

In SCOR model, the integrated processes of plan, source, make, deliver, return and enable from the supplier's supplier to the customer's customer represent supply chain management. Elements of business process engineering, metrics, benchmarking, leading practices and people skills into a single framework are combined with SCOR model. The model itself is structured around primary management processes. Using these process definition blocks, SCOR model can be used to model supply chains that are very simple or very complex using a common set of definitions in disparate industries. In fact, public and private organisations and companies around the world use the model as a basis for projects to improve the global supply chain.

Basic Approach to Determine Performance

The SCOR model has three levels of process detail. In practice, Level 1 describes the number of supply chains, how their performance is measured, and necessary competitive requirements. Level 2 presents the configuration of the planning and execution strategies in the material flow, involving standard categories such as 'make-to-stock', 'make-to-order' and 'engineer-to-order'. Level 3 considers the business processes and system functionality used to process sales orders, purchase orders, work orders, return authorisations, replenishment orders and forecasts. Level 4 process details are not contained in SCOR model but must be defined to implement improvements and manage processes. Advanced users of the framework have defined process detail as far as Level 5.

Organisations using the SCOR model performance metrics can compare their performance levels with other organisations in the supply chain using a benchmarking tool called SCOR mark. The SCOR mark database contains historical data from over 1000 companies and 2000 supply chains. The benchmarking process using the SCOR mark can be performed by the following steps: (1) defining the supply channels to be compared; (2) measuring the internal and external performances; (3) comparing the performance to relevant industrial companies; (4) establishing competitive demands; (5) calculating the opportunity value of improvement.

- 'Superior': is the performance (median value) on a specific indicator attained by 10% of the best classified SC's comparing to the total of the supply chains surveyed;
- 'Advantage': is the performance (median value) among the top ten companies and the median of all the supply chains considered;
- 'Parity': is the performance (median value) of all the supply chains considered.

The APICS an association, announced the launch of the SCOR model version 12.0. Developed by a panel of international supply chain experts, this latest version of SCOR model incorporates Omnichannel, metadata, blockchain and other emerging engines that supply chain professionals are using

Benchmarking Supply Chain Performance 309

today. SCOR model has been the global inter-sectorial standard for supply chain excellence over the last 20 years and, with this update, will continue to support ways to measure, improve and communicate the supply chain's business performance

APICS is the association for supply chain management and the leading provider of research, education and certification programmes that elevate supply chain excellence, innovation and resilience.

The company in this case is an international automotive company with more than 45 years of experience in the automotive sector, an annual turnover of approximately 3300 million Euro and 14,500 employees around the world. For evaluation purposes, a mixture of workshops across logistical functions and also based on interviews, documents made available and data analysis. The participants are dispersed across all levels of grading, from operative level up to logistics management of the different sites.

In the beginning, the first series of workshops were conducted with the aim of aligning the logistic objectives found in the literature with those used on the site. From these workshops the proposed performance indicators as per the model are aligned with those identified by the experts and proposed performance indicators with the ones identified in the experts' workshops. Performance indicators which were not named by the experts, but proposed in standard SCOR model, were highlighted and discussed in respect of their added value in a supplement meeting. The subsequent model was aligned in another round of workshops and additional interviews. After changing the detailed definition of the SCOR model and each measure (alignment with data sources, adding responsibilities), the system was implemented and data evaluation started, as well as a dashboard allowing performance indicator evaluation launched. Based on that, a quantitative evaluation of each metric was started, which also emphasised initial improvement potentials.

After having implemented the model and finalised its deployment, two brainstorming sessions were conducted to compare the different experiences with this project and to capitalise on it.

Brief Description of the Company

The company already presents at Tunisia, chose to develop in Morocco in order to accompany its client and to have a base of production of plastic systems able to deliver the manufacturers based in Spain. The production site Metal understands about ten presses to be followed from 150 to 800 tons and transforms approximately 10,000 tons of steel a year. It issues components for the body-in-white of the vehicles of a car maker. The plastic factory of production integrates approximately about 10 press 350 and 2700 tons and transforms approximately 3500 tons of plastic annually. It issues auto components and engines interior and external and engines for the two vehicles including components for the equipment suppliers also established associated with company.

Supply and Production Control

The trades of the supply model and production control are exerted in the factory where the role of the logistics consists in supplying the raw material, the components sub-contracted and the components necessary to the manufacturing of the components. The trades of handling interns (receipt, shipping, management of the warehouses . . .) are also part of this model.

Administration of the Sales

An administrator is in charge of the receipt of the customer orders, imputation of the prices, the establishment of the articles client whose finality is the satisfaction of the client in terms of quantity, quality and lead times. Shipping, receipt and transport: the trades of this model are exerted on upstream flows of supply raw material, components and sub-contracted components.

Shipping, receipt and transport: Currently, logistics is at the centre of all the activities of the company, divided into four business families that cover all logistics activities: from the supply of

310 *Benchmarking Supply Chain Performance*

raw material to the shipment of the final product. In addition, logistics is one of the services of the company that makes the most use of the computer tool: By following all the flows of the company, by anticipating these flows (forecasts, expression of needs etc.) and overflowing beyond from the company to suppliers and customers.

For the case it uses as management tools: (1) SAP where the information is centralised (Systems, Applications and Products, ERP), which integrates the different functions of the company (accounting, finance, production, supply, marketing, human resources, quality, maintenance etc.). (2) EDI: for the exchange of various documents internally and externally of the company, it is indeed commercial documents or transport such as invoices. The planning process within the company that was studied is managed by the planner who processes once a week his calculation of net need for finished products via SAP, checks the break dates of each part, and thanks to an Excel file it establishes the planning of all the week as well as the orders of manufacture of the parts to manufacture. These production orders are then issued to the production manager to be distributed to the production items, once the valid and closed planner has been completed and sent to the stock manager for the recorded-on SAP.

Establishing Performance Metrics

The benchmarking of the SCOR model is done by comparing the indicators of levels 1, 2 and 3; however, it is not necessary to apply the three performance levels in each axis. That is why it would be better to prioritise these axes in order to put the level indicators 1 for less important axes and up to level 3 for the most important. The prioritisation of performance axes depends on the company's type of business and its management. SCOR standard set the notations for prioritising strategic axes of the dashboard that will define for each one the objectives to be fixed during the benchmarking. Indeed, the notations S, A and P are used by the SCOR model to prioritise the axes, these are as follows:

S: Stands for Superior – corresponds to the 90th percentile: This means that it will line up with 10% of the best-performing companies.

A: Stands for Advantage – corresponds to the 70th percentile: The objective will be to reach the performance of 30% of the best companies.

P: Stands for Parity – corresponds to the 50th percentile: The objective is to exceed 50% of the best companies.

In order to evaluate the process performance, it will be very interesting to complete the indicators that were already in place by other indicators proposed by the SCOR model, which correspond to its strategic axes.

According to the baseline with which to compare, there are three types of benchmarking:

- Comparison on a historical basis: monitoring indicator development.
- Internal benchmarking: comparison between companies of the same group.
- External benchmarking: comparison is made by external organisations.

The SCOR model proposes external benchmarking because the more the reference database will be larger, the results will be significant. The objective here will be to line up with the best companies in the automotive sector based on logistics activities. After defining the indicators on the dashboard, the data were collected to calculate their values, which were considered depending on the importance as mentioned subsequently:

Reliability: basic information for these indicators was derived from the history of logistics rates and weekly reports.

Benchmarking Supply Chain Performance 311

Management of Assets: this data was collected from the Finance Department and management control. Most of them are confidential, so they will be expressed as a percentage.

- Logistics costs: this information was collected from the Accounts Department from history.
- Reactivity: this indicator corresponds to the lead time or the time required to complete an order.
- Flexibility: only the part of the supply was held in account for this axis because it is the most important component in terms of time.

The next step is the measurement of the performance indicators for the dashboard. Indeed, the formulas for calculating the different KPIs are presented next:

Equation

1. Service Rate (SR) $= \dfrac{Number\ of\ processed\ orders}{Number\ of\ total\ orders}$

2. Order Fulfilment rate = SR(Quantity by reference) × SR(deadline) × SR (accuracy of documents)

3. Fill rate $= \dfrac{Delivered\ volume}{Capacity\ of\ the\ truck}$

4. % of sales costs (COGS) = Sales – Profits – Administrative cost/sales.

5. Working Capital ratio $= \dfrac{Current\ assets}{Current\ liabilities} = \dfrac{Receivables}{Payables}$

6. Financial cycle delay = Delay of customer dept + number of days of stock – payables delay.

7. Payables delay $= \dfrac{Paybles \times 365}{Annual\ sales}$

8. Delay of customer debt $= \dfrac{Customer\ debt \times 365}{Annual\ sales}$

9. Number of days of available stock $= \dfrac{Stock\ value \times 365}{Annual\ sales}$

10. Forecast reliability rate $= \dfrac{\sum_{1}^{n} Abs\left(sales\ forecast(i) - sales(i)\right)}{\sum_{1}^{n} sales\ forecast(i)}$

11. Coverage rate $= \dfrac{\sum_{1}^{n} Warehouse\ stock(i) + Outstanding(i)}{week\ average\ forecast}$

12. Internal service rate $= \dfrac{\sum_{1}^{n} Abs\left(planned(i) - realized(i)\right)}{\sum_{1}^{n} planned(i)}$

13. Rate of stock variance $= \dfrac{\sum_{1}^{n} Abs\left(SAP\ stock(i)\quad physical\ stock(i)\right)}{\sum_{1}^{n} SAP\ stock(i)}$

312 Benchmarking Supply Chain Performance

14. Rotation of fixed assets in the supply chain $= \dfrac{Slaes}{Net\ fixed\ assets}$

15. Customer complain rate $= \dfrac{Number\ of\ written\ complaints}{Total\ number\ of\ affected\ deliveries}$

16. Service supplier rate $= \dfrac{Number\ of\ complete\ delivered\ orders\ on\ time}{Number\ of\ orders\ to\ be\ delivered\ by\ suppliers}$

17. Cost of an out of stock = total costs related to a cessation of customer activity

18. Number of days of available stock $= \dfrac{Total\ outstanding\ TTC \times number\ of\ days}{Total\ turn\ over\ for\ the\ period}$

19. Customer return rate $= \dfrac{Number\ of\ returned\ deliveries\ from\ customers}{Total\ number\ of\ deliveries}$

20. Supplier return rate $= \dfrac{Number\ of\ returned\ deliveries\ to\ suppliers}{Total\ number\ of\ deliveries}$

The established scorecard containing the benchmarking values provided by the SCOR standard as well as the improvement objectives for each metric are presented in Table 12.1.

Best Practices Proposed by the SCOR Model

As presented in the dashboard set out in Table 12.1, the difference between the current situation of the company and the value of benchmarking differs from one indicator to another. It is clear that better gap analysis implies good performance improvements. So, the first task to do is to know the root causes of these gaps and the processes involved. Regarding the processes mentioned earlier, the most performing companies have established certain practices that have reported to them tangible benefits. This is a kind of capitalisation of experience that the SCOR model offers through benchmarking. Table 12.1 lists best practices offered by SCOR Framework, taking into account the processes previously diagnosed and the anomalies observed.

The following figure shows the best practices according to their difficulty of implementation and the impact they will have on business processes. Priority actions for this project will obviously be those who have the greatest impact and the least difficulty.

Conclusion

Being part of a complex and highly competitive field, and in order to evaluate its position in the automotive industries, the company proposed to model its supply chain and to implement a Benchmarking to improve its performance. To meet this need, the SCOR model was opted as a diagnostic tool by the company. The first step was to model its supply chain, according to the SCOR model, this model aimed to standardise the structure of the process from the existing model. The next step is to develop the dashboard. Based on the results of this benchmarking, represent an opportunity for improvement for the company. A set of best practices were selected that can rectify the weaknesses detected at certain axes. To do this, an action plan was developed to implement these best practices. The key outcome of this performance measurement using SCOR model adapted to company needs will help the company for integration of proposals for improvements in future projects and Logistics Department of the annual performance of external benchmarking, in order to validate and renew the strategic direction of the company.

Benchmarking Supply Chain Performance 313

Table 12.1 The Best Practices Proposed by SCOR Model

Processes	Best Practices
P2 Supply planning	All Key Participants in the Supply Chain, Including Strategic Partners, Have Full Visibility of the Demand/Supply Plan VMI: Vendor-managed Inventory CPFR: Collaborative Planning, Forecasting and Replenishment
P2.1 Identify prioritise product requirements	The Demand Plan Is Updated Frequently to Reflect Actual Consumption or Customer Forecast Information Maximise Data Integrity and System Accuracy by Ensuring 99%+ Accuracy of BOM Configuration, Inventory Levels and Schedule Requirements
P2.4 Establish procurement plans	Digital Linkage (EDI, XML etc.) Is Used to Provide Real-Time Demand Information and Handle Routine Transactions Maintain Data and System Integrity by Ensuring Production Data, Inventory Levels and Schedule Requirements Are 99+% Accurate A Detailed Production Model That Synchronises PLAN and MAKE Activities in Real Time
EP.7 Manages Planning Configuration	ABC Classification
S1.1 to S2.1 Schedule Deliveries	Electronic Kanban Pull Signals Are Used to Notify Suppliers of the Need to Deliver Product

Case Questions:

1 What are the advantages and key features of the SCOR model of supply chain performance measurement?
2 Discuss how SCOR model can help businesses to improve Supply Chain Management performance.
3 Discuss the methodology adopted to implement the performance measurement system in the company.
4 How are the performance measurement criteria determined?
5 What are the key benefits of conducting and implementing such performance measurement model in the company in terms of its long-term objective delivery and strategic direction?

Chapter Summary

In this chapter benchmarking supply chain performance has been discussed in detail covering the purpose and objective of benchmarking, how to identify the companies to be benchmarked and what are the key performance criteria to be benchmarked. How the conclusions from the benchmarking exercise can be used to improve companies' performance has been covered in detail. Finally, some common misconceptions regarding benchmarking have also been discussed. SCOR model for supply chain performance for an automotive industry has been discussed. Benchmarking is periodically undertaken by the industry to understand the performance of the Supply chain based on identified parameters against the immediate competitors and also with the best in class for the processes. As such benchmarking can be undertaken for SCM processes, operations as well as for the performance. If benchmarking is not undertaken with the necessary precautions including the parameters need to be benchmarked, identifying the right candidate(s) to be benchmarked and without necessary preparation following the guidelines with process orientation and getting the right realistic figures as well as data to be

Table 12.2 The Scorecard Containing Performance Metrics Measured for the Company

Performance metrics	Criteria	Unit	Maximise/ Minimise	Frequency	Actual value	Benchmark class			The company objective	GAP
						S	A	P		
Service rate (SR)	Reliability	%	Max.	Week	92%	100%	90%	80%	S	8%
Order Fulfilment rate	Reliability	%	Max.	Week	77%	100%	90%	80%	A	13%
Fill rate	Reliability	%	Max.	Week	76%	96%	82%	75%	A	6%
% of sales costs (COGS)	Logistics costs	%	Min.	Month	5%	3%	8%	13%	S	−3%
Working capital ratio	Management of assets	Ratio	Min.	Month	2.2	1.2	1.5	2	A	−0.7
Financial cycle delay	Management of assets	Day	Min.	Annual	90	13	42	80	A	−48
Payables delay	Management of assets	Day	Min.	Annual	30	−	−	−	−	
Delay of customer debt	Management of assets	Day	Max.	Annual	45	−	−	−	−	
Number of days of available stock	Flexibility	Day	Min.	Annual	85	13	34	78	A	−55
Forecast reliability rate	Reliability	%	Max.	Annual	91%	100%	90%	80%	S	9%
Coverage rate	Flexibility	Ratio	Min.	Month	2.5	1	1.4	2	S	−1.5
Internal service rate	Reliability	%	Max.	Week	95%	100%	95%	90%	S	5%
The rate of stock variance	Flexibility	%	Max.	Week	88%	100%	95%	90%	S	12%
Rotation of fixed assets in the supply chain	Management of assets	−	−	Annual	C[b]					
Customers complaints rate	Flexibility	%	Min.	Week	6%	0%	2%	5%	A	4%
Service suppliers rate	Flexibility	%	Max.	Week	95%	100%	95%	90%	S	5%
Cost of an out of stock	Logistics costs	K€	Min.	Month	12	0	1	2	A	−12
Number of days of available stock	Logistics costs	Day	Min.	Month	15	3	5	7	A	−10
Customer return rate	Logistics costs	%	Min.	Week	2%	0%	0,5%	1%	S	−2%
Supplier return rate	Flexibility	%	Min.	Week	1%	0%	0,5%	1%	S	−1%

Source: The case is based on the data presented by Radouane LEMGHARI, Chafik OKAR & Driss SARSRI presented at MATEC conference held at Morocco (2018)

Benchmarking Supply Chain Performance 315

analysed to draw right conclusions and understand the key lessons for reason why, then whole exercise may not be very useful. Businesses would thus need experienced people and often external help of experts and consultants to complete a meaningful benchmarking exercise.

Discussion Questions

1 Discuss how benchmarking performance of supply chain can be helpful to improve the performance and also to get future strategic direction in the business.
2 How do you determine the benchmarking criteria as well as companies with whom a business needs to benchmark? Discuss the basic approach.
3 Discuss the relative advantages of business process benchmarking and benchmarking only the performance.
4 What are the common misconception about benchmarking and how to safeguard against common pitfalls.
5 Discuss how benchmarking helps businesses in terms of improving performance
6 We suggest that benchmarking has to be done with immediate competitor and also with best-in-class performer. Why? How frequently should benchmarking exercise be undertaken.

References

Andersen, B., & Randmael, S. (1997) "Questionnaire for the Benchmarking Visits", *SMARTMAN SME Document*. Trondheim, Norway.
APQC (1992) *American Productivity & Quality Centre: Basics of Benchmarking*. Houston, TX: APQC.
Peter, G. (1999) "Benchmarking Supply Chain Operations", *Journal of Physical Distribution and Logistics Management*, 29(4).
Pierreval, H., Bruniaux, R., & Caux, C. (2007) "A Continuous Simulation Approach for Supply Chains in the Automotive Industry", *Simulation Modelling Practice and Theory*, 15(2), 185–198.
Stewart, G. (1995) "Supply Chain Performance Benchmarking Study Reveals Keys to Supply Chain Excellence", *Logistics Information Management*, 8(2), 38–44.

Bibliography

Andersen, B., & Pettersen, P.-G. (1995) *The Benchmarking Handbook: Step-by-Step Instructions*. London: Chapman & Hall.
APQC (1993) *American Productivity & Quality Center: Basics of Benchmarking*. Houston, TX: APQC.
Beamon, B. M. (1999) "Measuring Supply Chain Performance", *International Journal of Operations & Production Management*, 19(3), 275–292.
Lima-Junior, F. R., & Carpenetti, L. C. R. (2016) "Combining SCOR Model and Fuzzy TOPSIS for Supplier Evaluation and Management", *International Journal of Production Economics*, 174, 128–141.
Neto, M. S., & Pires, S. R. I. (2012) "Performance Measurement in Supply Chains: A Study in the Automotive Industry", *New Advances in Vehicular Technology and Automotive Engineering*, 19(4), 733–746.
Pierreval, H., Bruniaux, R., & Caux, C. (2007) "A Continuous Simulation Approach for Supply Chain in the Automotive Industry", *Simulation Modelling Practice and Theory*, 15(2), 185–198.

Index

Note: Page numbers in *italics* indicate a figure and page numbers in **bold** indicate a table on the corresponding page.

activity-based costing (ABC) 207
administrative costs 212
advanced shipment notifications (ASNs) 84
aggregate forecasts 48
agro commodities in India, cost build-up and trade margins *33*
air freight hazards 174
air transport 157
automated material-handling equipment, integration with 83
available inventory 130

barcode 85
bar coding system 86
Bayesian decision theory 54
benchmarking: benefits 305; businesses 307; competitive business strategies 306; cycle-time metrics 305; definition 302; delivery performance metrics 305; inventory and cash management metrics 305; logistics 306; manufacturing 305; parameters 307; performance 306; planning 305; procurement 305; scope 304–305; supply chain cost metrics 305; supply chain performance 303–304; billing 84
break bulk 172
bullwhip effect 125–128; batch ordering 127; consumer offtake at retail sales point *126*; demand forecasting 127; effect on supply chain performance 127–128; inflated orders 127; lead time 127; manufacturers' orders to suppliers/vendors *126*; price fluctuation 127; reducing impact 128; wholesalers/distributors' orders to manufacturers *126*
business planning exercise 45
business process re-engineering (BPR) 10
business response to stock-out 128–129; back-ordering 128; lost sales 128–129; substitution 128

Capability Maturity Model (CMM) for Software 296
capital cost 136
carrying and forwarding (C&F) agents 92
carrying and selling (C&S) agents 92
case study: Anand Milk Union Limited (AMUL) 254–259; Apollo Pharmacy 67–71; complexity in logistics management in India 97–110; Container Corporation of India Ltd (CONCOR) 193–199; criticality of supply chain efficiency in agriculture sector 34–36; Dell's direct business model of virtual integration 40–41; Dry Ice Inc. 216; FMCG food and drink 274–275; KRKA's factory in Europe 78; Li & Fung 14–15; Maersk Line 175–179; Maruti Suzuki 218–219; Oriflame 97; P&G and its innovation success rate 37–40; Pepsi and Coke 51; Reckitt Benckiser 46–47; retail 273–274; SCOR Model as SCC for performance measurement 307–312; VMI at Tata Steel 137–141; Volvo's strategy for sustainability 225–230
channel distribution cost 210
CKYH alliance 165
communication and data: processing costs 212
competitive advantage 247
competitiveness 26–27; dependence *26*; logistics cost 26
Container Corporation of India Ltd (CONCOR) case study 193–199
containerisation: growing demand 171; reason 171–172; RORO and break bulk 172
Container Security Initiative 252
continuous stocking levels 148–149
cost associated with assets and ROI 211
cost audit 215
critical success factors (CSFs) 91
Crosby's Quality Management Maturity Grid (QMMG) 296
cross-docking 84

Index 317

cube utilisation and accessibility 79
customer service: costs 213–215; elements 215;
    examples 214; levels 89, 214–215
customer value 12–13
custom bonded warehouse: buyer's consolidation
    service 172; future of green carrier 172;
    solutions to shorten lead times 172
Customs Trade Partnership against Terrorism
    (C-TPAT) 251
cycle counting 84
cycle inventory 120–121

dangerous goods 193; classification **192–193**
decentralised logistics system 237
degree of sophistication in distribution 101
delivery time stock 141
Delphi method 54
demand estimation 137; ROP 137
demand forecasting 40, 52; Bayesian decision
    theory 54–55; consumer–user survey method
    53; Delphi method 54; exponential smoothing
    58–59; linear regression equation 59; MAPE
    method 57; methods 52; models types 53;
    moving average method 57–58; multiple
    regression 61; naive forecasting 56–57;
    panel of expert opinion 53–54; quantitative
    techniques 55–56; sales force composite 54;
    trend-corrected exponential smoothing 61–63
demand management 52, 64; definition 64;
    efficiency 65; estimating the total market
    demand 66–67; factors for accuracy 65
denationalized operations 244
digital transformation 281; direct 88; exclusive
    88; intensive 88; MLM production 88; online
    marketing 88–89; selective 88
distribution management: activities 90; challenges
    of BOP market *99*; channels 87; channel
    strategy 89; costs 95; definition and scope
    87; domestic cargo 155; efficiency 94;
    factors impacting network design 94–95; key
    challenges 95–96; methods 87–88; objective
    89–90; organization 90; physical 18; policies
    90–91; tasks 86; typical channel partners 92–94

e-commerce 9; impact on supply chain 170
economic ordering quantity (EOQ); implications
    131–132; model 132
efficient demand management 65–66
efficient logistics function management 17
electronic channels 93
electronic data interchange (EDI) systems 10
enterprise resource planning (ERP) system 10
exponential smoothing 58–59

financial accounting system 204
firm value chain 237–238

franchisees 93
future factories 263–264

G6 Alliance 164
Global Container Control Programme 252
global logistics: arm's length 243; barriers 242;
    capabilities 243; insider business practices 24;
    internal export 243–244; internal operations
    244; operations level 244; retailers in Indian
    market 246; role 243; strategy drivers *240*;
    supply chain and internet 243
global logistics industry: acquisition helps 169;
    major acquisitions 169
global sourcing 17; business performance
    268–269; characteristics 266; factors 271–272;
    issues 271; logistics 266; outsourcing and
    firm's performance 270–271; technological
    performance and decisions 271; trends 266–268
Global Trade Exchange 252
global transport industry sustainability and
    compliance 168
green transport solutions 169–170

hazardous goods packing groups 191
hazards and risks 161
highly fluctuating business 162–163

IKEA model 2
inbound logistics 17
information processing cost 211–212
Integrated CMM (CMM-I) 296
integrated logistics system: benefits 250;
    organization 249–250; stages 250
Integrated Product and Process Development
    (IPD-CMM) 296
integrated supply chain management challenges
    and complexities 248
intermodal transportation 158
international logistics 24–25
International Maritime Organisation (IMO) 172–173
international packaging issues 189–190
International Ship 252
international trade: agile management 235;
    business process re-engineering 236; challenges
    241–242; cost quality considerations 235;
    customer-oriented 236; customer satisfaction
    235; features 240–241; globalization, impact
    242; global sourcing of components 234; lean
    management 235; links 235; mining companies,
    logistic channels 234; new product development
    234; physical network 234; process orientation
    235; Supply Chain Operation Reference
    (SCOR) Model 236; theory of constraints and
    queues 236; time-based management (TBM)
    236; total quality management (TQM) 236;
    vendor managed inventory (VMI) 236

318 *Index*

international transportation 160–161
inventory cost management 122, 209; alternative approach for classification 118–120; bullwhip effect 125–128; components of inventory decisions 120–122; control on 122–123; effectiveness 123; goal 115–116; holding cost 122; impacts business performance 117; need 116–117; order fill rate and pack fill rate 123–124; ordering cost 122; purchase cost 122; stock keeping unit (SKU) 124–125; storage cost 122; transactions 124; types 117–118
inventory management policy 113
inventory position 130

large shipping lines and global alliances 163–165
Li & Fung business model: complexity in supply chain *15*; supply chain in competitive world 14–15
logistics 18; activities and goals 20–21; basic elements 19; centres, euro-logistics236; competitiveness 26–27; complexity of FMCG category *102*; core concept, definition and scope 18–19; environment, reverse distribution systems 237; industry in India 252–255; management, complexity 246; total cost approach 208–209
logistics cost 202–203; accounting system 203–204; analysis 2066–207; difficulty in estimating 206; discipline as 19–20; distribution and 9–10; elements 203; evolution 21–23; global trends 167–168; history 203; impact on ROI *206*; importance 17–18; importance in economy 25; improves business performance 205; inbound logistics 20; incremental value delivery 23–24; key tasks to improve 217–219; management models 205; omnipresent 205; operational objectives 20; outbound logistics 20; performance and 215–216; physical distribution 21; types 19–20
Logistics Cost and Service Database 203
logistics management function 5
long-term forecasts 50
lowest total cost law 203

Maersk Line: business strategy initiatives *177*; case study 175–179; share price movement *179*
management accounting 204
managing uncertainty in supply: chain 141–142; continuous stocking levels 148–149; estimating safety stock 142–143; measuring product availability 142; reorder point (ROP) 144; safety stock 146; service level 145–147; single period model 147–148
market potential 49
material-handling costs 212–213
material requirements planning (MRP) 81, 132–133; bill of materials 133; components

of MRP II 133; indications 133; inventory status file 133; master production schedule 133; order point system **134**; output 133–134; principle 132
materials management 10; function 4–5
mean absolute percentage error (MAPE) method 57
measuring customer service: customer query time 290; delivery performance evaluation metrics 294; planning performance evaluation metrics 292–293; post-transaction measures 290; production performance evaluation metrics 293–294; SCOR Model 291–292; sourcing performance evaluation metrics 293; starting performance management programme 290–292
medium-term forecasts 49–50
Megas (Express Three or Triple E) 163
methods of distribution 87–88
min–max replenishment system 134–139; demand estimation 137–139; inventory-carrying cost 135–136; out-of-stock costs 135; principle **134**; structure 136–137; total cost approach 136; total cost of inventory 135
modern transportation and logistics systems security issues 251
moving average method 57–58
multi-client warehousing 76
multifaceted analytical functions: supply chain performance management (SCPM) 249
multi-level marketing (MLM) 88

naive forecasting 56–57
new geographies 171

Ocean Alliance 165
ocean freight 173–174
ocean transport: coastal shipping 157; new global alliances 165; overseas shipping 157–158; state of 162; top 10 container carriers *162*; top 10 container ports *163*; top 10 North American ports *163*
on-hand inventory 130
online marketing 88–89
on-order inventory 130
order picking and assembly 80–81
organizations: huge cost centres 202–203
outbound logistics 17
outsourcing and procurement: key focus for cost competitiveness 23
outsourcing logistics services 216, 237

P3 Network: global politics 164
package carriers 158
packaging: costs 213; facilitates storage and warehousing 191; functions 190–191; indicative of quality 191; information about product 190–191; protects goods 190; regulations 193

Index 319

Panama Canal expansion 165–166
performance measurement in supply chain:
    framework 294–296; maturity models 296–297;
    performance matrix **295**
periodic review system 129
physical control and security elements 81
*Physical Distribution Management Logistics
    Problems of the Firm* 22
physical infrastructure 32–36; cold chain facilities 33;
    criticality of supply chain efficiency in agriculture
    sector 34–36; warehousing facilities 34
pick-to-carton 84
pipelines 158
Port Facility Security Code 252
private warehousing 75
procurement functions 2, 4
product availability 95; level 121–122
production and supply cost 210–216;
    administrative 212; audit 215; channel
    distribution 210; communication and data
    processing 212; cost associated with assets
    and ROI 211; customer service 213–215;
    information processing 211–212; logistics
    cost and performance, benchmarking
    215–216; packaging 213; supply chain and
    logistics 211; total distribution 210–211;
    transportation 212
production plant 114
Project Golden Eye 48
public warehousing 75
pull strategies 13
purchase function 2

quantitative forecasting techniques 55–56, 63

rail transport 174–175
regional integration: Association of Southeast
    Asian Nations (ASEAN) 245; common market
    245; customs union 245; economic union 245;
    free trade agreement (FTA) 245
reorder point (ROP) 137, 144; system 129
replenishment of inventory: average inventory
    130; economic ordering quantity (EOQ)
    model, implications 131–132; order cycle time
    131; periodic review system 129; position
    130; reorder point (ROP) system 129; time-
    phased order point (TPOP) systems 130;
    requirement 113
response time 95
retailers 93
reverse distribution systems 237; road transport
    155, 175; factors impacting cost 160; pathways
    155; railway 156; roadways 156; tramway 156
roll-on/roll-off (RORO) or ro-ro, ships 172

safety inventory 121
safety stock 142, 143
sales target 91

seasonal index: determining from historical sales
    data **51**
seasonal inventory 121
shipping route and competition 165–167; current
    concerns 167; future of canals 166; next few
    years 167; shake-out ahead 167
short-term forecasts 49
single period model 147–148
slotting 84
sourcing: models and frameworks 265–266;
    procurement 10
stock-keeping unit (SKU) 124–125
stock location: basic systems 80; central storage
    80; fixed 80; floating or random 80; point-of-use
    storage 80
storage facility 236
strategic triangle of 3C's 24
Suez Canal 165–166
super stockists 92
supply chain 16; complexity 3–4; cyber security
    threats 251; global sourcing challenge and
    sustainability 264–265; impact of growing
    e-commerce 170; linkages and stages *4*;
    logistics cost 211; technologies 252
supply chain forecasting 46–47; changing business
    environment 63; characteristic 47–48; demand
    52–63; demand management 64–66; factors
    influencing 48; levels 51; market potential 49;
    practice 63–64; seasonal variations 51–52;
    types 49–50; why 49
supply chain management (SCM); agriculture
    sector, efficiency 34–36; business functions
    8; business performance and 3–5; challenges
    5–6; cold chain facilities 33; complexity 4;
    creation era 10; digital transformation 281;
    estimating customer demand 44–45; evolution
    10–12; forecasting 46–67; globalization 11;
    hazardous and inflammable cargo, handling 6;
    IKEA model 2; importance 15–16; Industry
    4.0 and Smart Factory 282; innovations
    36–41; integration era 10–11; key elements
    281; Li & Fung, case study 14–15; linkages
    and stages *4*; logistics 17–41; maturity models
    296–299; measurement and metrics 279;
    objectives and challenges 12–13; performance
    criteria 280–281; physical infrastructure
    performance 32–33; procurement functions 2;
    purchase function 2; role 14–15; scope 8–10;
    security concerns 6; sourcing challenges and
    strategies 263; specialization era 11–12; trade-
    offs 282; transportation 6; unrealistic demand
    45–46; warehousing facilities 34–36
supply chain performance management (SCPM)
    249; accurate inventory levels 284; adaptive
    reporting 285; clear accountability for metrics
    284–285; continuous improvement 285;
    customer centricity 284; customer order path
    287; delivery performance evaluation 294;

320 *Index*

digital transformation 281; end-to-end processes 283; evaluation of supply link 287; flexibility in meeting 289; information transparency of machines 284; integrated technology 285; inter-operability of machines 285; invoice 289; key performance indicators (KPIs) 281–282; operational level measures 287; order entry method 287; order lead time 287; organizational alignment 283; partnership evaluation 288; performance measurements and metrics 286; performance measures at production sites 288; planning information 283; reporting 286; robust performance management system 283–284; scheduling techniques 288; shortened product life-cycle 282; signals for businesses 286; standardized processes and metrics 283; strategic-level measures 287; strategy 283; suppliers 287–288; supply chain cost 284; tactical level measures 287; trends 286
supply chain sustainability *see* sustainability
supply chain value 12
surface transport major shift 170
sustainability 221; definition 222; helps business 224–225; indicators 223; transportation impacts 222; Volvo's strategy 225–227
sustainable transportation: economic benefits 223–224; key issues 224

task interleaving 83
third-party logistics (TPL) 12
third-party warehousing 76
time-phased order point (TPOP) system 130
total distribution cost 210–211
total logistic cost: breakup **208**; holistic view 209; total logistics cost (TLC) 73, 207–208
total market demand 66; defining 66; division of total demand 66–67; forecast key drivers 67; sensitivity analyses 67
total quality management (TQM) 10
transportation 21–22; business logistics era 22–23; criteria of decision 155–157; functions 154–155; global trends 167–168; hazards 161; importance of packaging 189; infrastructure 159; major modes 159; mode 160; mode of transportation 155– 157; physical distribution era 21–22; physical supply and physical distribution era22; role

153–154; transportation deregulation era 22; transportation era 21
transportation costs 212
Transportation Journal 22
transport packaging solution 191; safety regulations for hazardous goods 191
Trans-Siberian Railway 169
trend-corrected exponential smoothing 61–63

uncertainties impact 149
United Nations Office on Drugs and Crime (UNODC) 252

value chain 15; businesses 239; CAD/CAM 238; corporations 239; cost or performance 239; CRM 239; electronic data interchange (EDI) systems 238; enterprise resource planning (ERP) system 239; HRM function 238; incremental profit 233; integrated performance management 248–249; key organizational processes 235; matrix 233; sales order 247; supply chain transparency 244; transformation 238–239; WMS 236
virgin polyester (PET) 5

Walmart outperforms: comparison **149**; competitors 149
warehouse layout design and activities performed *77*
warehouse management system (WMS) 81–82; advantages 82–85; enabler 81–82; implementing and setting up 83; necessary, when and why 82; new trends 85; productivity improvement tools 85–86; responsive development 84
warehouse performance metrics **85**
warehousing 73; activities 76–79; cost 76, 209–210; efficient management 74–75; factors influencing effectiveness 79–81; layout design criteria 76; primary function 74; purpose and scope 74; types 75–76
water transport 156
wave picking 83
wholesalers 93
World Customs Organization (WCO) 251–252

yard management 84

Printed in the United States
by Baker & Taylor Publisher Services